THE READING SPECIALIST

Also from Rita M. Bean

Best Practices of Literacy Leaders: Keys to School Improvement
Edited by Rita M. Bean and Allison Swan Dagen

The Reading Specialist

Leadership and Coaching
for the Classroom,
School, and Community

THIRD EDITION

RITA M. BEAN

THE GUILFORD PRESS
New York   London

© 2015 The Guilford Press
A Division of Guilford Publications, Inc.
370 Seventh Avenue, Suite 1200, New York, NY 10001
www.guilford.com

Printed in the United States of America

This book is printed on acid-free paper.

Last digit is print number: 9 8 7 6 5 4 3 2 1

Library of Congress Cataloging-in-Publication Data

Bean, Rita M.
 The reading specialist : leadership and coaching for the classroom, school, and
community / Rita M. Bean. — Third edition.
     pages cm
  Includes bibliographical references and index.
  ISBN 978-1-4625-2153-1 (paperback)
  ISBN 978-1-4625-2154-8 (cloth)
  1. Reading teachers—United States.   2. Reading—Remedial teaching—United
States. I. Title.
  LB2844.1.R4B43 2015
  428.4071′2—dc23
                                                                        2015001485

About the Author

Rita M. Bean, PhD, is Professor Emerita in the School of Education at the University of Pittsburgh, where she served as Director of the Reading Center for 25 years. Prior to joining the university, she taught at the elementary school level and also served as a reading supervisor for grades K–12. Dr. Bean has developed elementary and middle school reading curriculum materials and has published in many different journals and monographs on the topics of reading curriculum, assessment and instruction in reading, professional development, and the role of reading specialists and literacy coaches (K–12). She is a member of the Reading Hall of Fame and a former board member of the International Reading Association (IRA; now the International Literacy Association), and served as Chair of the IRA's Commission on the Role of the Reading Specialist. Dr. Bean received the University of Pittsburgh's Chancellor's Distinguished Teaching Award and the Distinguished Service Award for her community and outreach efforts in improving literacy.

Preface

The Reading Specialist is written for the many reading specialists, literacy coaches, and principals currently working in schools to improve the reading performance of individual students and the effectiveness of reading programs for all students. It is also written for those individuals who are enrolled in programs preparing them to become reading specialists or literacy coaches. In this third edition, I build on the framework established in the first and second editions—current research and knowledge in the field—to address important educational issues of the day.

The book identifies and describes the many roles that reading specialists at all levels (prekindergarten through grade 12) may be asked to fulfill. My goal in writing this book is to offer practical ideas for those working in the field, based on research and literature about the roles of reading specialists/coaches. I would like reading specialists to be able to take the book from their bookshelves as a quick resource to use when a question or issue arises. The book can also be used as a textbook for those enrolled in reading specialist or literacy coaching programs. Likewise, those involved in professional development programs designed to build leadership skills will find the book helpful, as will coaches involved in working with teachers, individually or in groups.

The book continues to focus on the many important responsibilities of reading specialists. The major changes or additions in the third edition include the following:

• *A new framework for describing the role of the reading specialist.* In Chapter 1, I introduce a new framework for thinking about the role of the reading specialist. In previous editions, leadership was considered to be a "separate" role, distinct from instruction and assessment. As a result of ongoing research about the ways that reading specialists and coaches function in schools, and related research about shared and teacher leadership in schools, I emphasize the importance of leadership across all roles and responsibilities of a reading specialist. Those responsible for supporting the work of teachers have leadership responsibilities, as do those who deliver instruction to students. When developing family or community involvement programs, leadership is necessary. Developing curriculum or facilitating school change requires the leadership of the reading specialist.

• *An emphasis on standards.* Given the adoption of the Common Core State Standards (CCSS) by most states, and the accompanying emphasis on rigorous, high-level standards preparing students to be college and career ready, I have included information about these standards and their influence on literacy instruction and assessment. I use examples throughout the book to discuss ways reading specialists can work with teachers to develop and implement instruction aligned with the demands of the CCSS. In Chapter 8, there is an extensive section in which I describe major recommendations of the CCSS and present a framework for developing a comprehensive literacy program.

• *A new format.* In this edition, I include key questions at the beginning of each chapter, followed by a short paragraph summarizing the contents of the chapter. At the end of each chapter, I suggest several resources for additional reading; each recommendation includes a brief summary of the content. Most often, I refer to those articles in the chapter, and follow-up reading can assist in developing a deeper understanding of the concepts presented. Instructors may wish to use the suggested readings for out-of-class assignments.

• *Response to intervention (RTI).* Given the impact of this federal initiative on the role of reading specialists, who have major responsibilities for helping teachers differentiate instruction for all students, in this edition there is more information about RTI, what it is, and what reading specialists can do to assist in the implementation of programs and procedures that help school personnel differentiate instruction for students. I also discuss in more depth how classroom data can be used for instructional decision making.

• *An emphasis on middle and high school literacy programs.* In this edition, there is even more emphasis on adolescent literacy and how reading specialists working at middle and high school levels can function effectively. In several chapters, there are specific sections that address adolescent literacy. Often these sections focus on supporting content-area teachers and disciplinary literacy. In Chapter 3, there is a description of the instructional role of the reading specialist at the middle and high school levels, and in Chapter 9 assessment at those levels is discussed. In Chapter 8, information about secondary-level reading programs is presented. Further, there are several vignettes that provide descriptive information about how reading specialists and literacy coaches function in their schools. In Chapter 3, Toni describes the instruction she provides at a middle school level; in Chapter 6, Wendy discusses her professional development efforts and the importance of building relationships with teachers, including content-area teachers.

• *Literacy coaching.* Current information about literacy coaching is included in the two chapters (Chapters 6 and 7) about coaching. I provide a framework for thinking about coaching and discuss important aspects of each of the elements of that framework. Ideas for "getting started" are described, as well as suggestions for coaching individual teachers. This edition also includes specific forms or tools that coaches can use as they visit classrooms.

There are some aspects of the first edition that remain, given positive feedback from readers:

• *"Think about This"*—a set of questions in each chapter to stimulate thinking about the various issues being discussed.

• *Reflections*—a set of questions at the conclusion of each chapter to provide opportunities for self-reflection or group discussion.

• *Follow-up activities*—suggested activities, listed at the end of each chapter, that can be used in a study group setting or in a course.

• *Ideas for course or workshop instructors.* There are activities in Appendix F for use with graduate students or with practitioners in professional development workshops. I hope those who use the text for teaching a course or a series of workshops will find this section to be helpful.

• *Vignettes.* Written by practicing reading specialists who represent the high caliber of exemplary reading specialists working in schools, the vignettes bring to life the excitement, passion, and commitment of these dedicated professionals. Throughout the book, I refer to these vignettes in sections titled "Voices from the Field," identifying specific ways that these professionals address the topic being discussed (e.g., Celia discusses how she and a teacher plan for modeling or classroom visits, after large-group professional development).

From the early days of my career, I have been interested and involved in areas of research and teaching that relate to the role of the reading specialist. This book is based on my own experiences as a reading specialist, struggling to meet the needs of students and teachers (K–12). In addition, it is based on my many interactions through the years with others who were faced with similar challenges. Many of the recommendations and ideas for working with others come from the interactions I have had with reading specialists and literacy coaches in the field.

As mentioned previously, I have had the opportunity to prepare reading specialists for many years. These potential reading specialists have taught me a great deal. They have shared their experiences in schools working with struggling readers and with teachers to improve the reading program. I have endeavored to make their voices heard in this book.

The field is a dynamic one; the work of reading specialists has never been more important, given the emphasis on literacy as a key to future success. It is my hope that this book will serve as a resource for reading specialists, enabling them to address questions or issues they face as they strive to improve student literacy learning by providing the leadership essential for developing effective literacy programs in schools.

Acknowledgments

I have been fortunate to work with colleagues in schools and universities across the country who are also committed to improving reading instruction for students in grades PreK–12. These colleagues have influenced my thinking about the role of the reading specialist and the literacy coach. They include many different faculty colleagues from institutions across the United States. I mention only a few here, recognizing that there are many more who have had profound effects on my work. Naomi Zigmond, a friend and colleague at the University of Pittsburgh, with whom I have conducted research for many years, has challenged my thinking and helped me to think more broadly about struggling readers and how to help them succeed. Likewise, I have been fortunate to work with and learn from Isabel Beck, who has conducted cutting-edge research on reading instruction. Members on the International Reading Association (IRA) committees on which I have served have influenced my thinking about the roles of the reading specialist: the IRA Commission established in the late 1990s, the IRA Standards 2010 Committee, and the committee appointed by IRA's Specialized Literacy Professionals Special Interest Group. During meetings, committee members raised important issues, alternative views, and ideas for how the role of the reading specialist/literacy coach might be defined and prepared.

As influential as faculty colleagues have been in shaping my thinking, students in the reading specialist certification program at the University of Pittsburgh whom I have had the pleasure of teaching, and the reading specialists and literacy coaches with whom I have worked, have had a profound effect on the contents of this book. I have learned much from these individuals, not only about what they do in order to be successful in their role, but also about the questions and concerns that they have about their positions and how to best serve the students, teachers, and administrators in their schools. Their passion for and commitment to their work has served as a source of inspiration for me.

I want to acknowledge the contributions of Celia Banks, Mark Beck, Katy Carroll, Karen DeNunzio, Wendy Salvatore, and Toni Saul for writing the vignettes in the book. Many thanks to Sandra Akers and Marsha Turner, former students in the reading specialist program at the University of Pittsburgh, for permitting me to include their work. Katie Regner, a former student and current reading specialist, provided useful information about her role and the importance of scheduling to address the needs of students and teachers.

Many thanks to my mentor, Robert Wilson, Professor Emeritus, University of Maryland, with whom I coauthored a text highlighting the importance of the leadership and resource role of reading specialists, *Effecting Change in School Reading Programs: The Resource Role* (Bean & Wilson, 1981). Certainly, we have learned a great deal about the leadership role since then, but many of the ideas in that text have withstood the test of time.

I thank my family for their support and encouragement. Thank you, Erin Eichelberger; Derek and Barbie Eichelberger; and Ethan, Ava, and Dylan (our grandchildren who are beginning their school journey). And finally, many thanks to Tony Eichelberger, my husband and best friend, for his encouragement, critical reading, and constant reminder that there is a need for the messages that this book conveys.

Contents

The Role of Reading Specialists and Literacy Coaches in Schools, Classrooms, and Communities

Key Questions

- How has the role of the reading specialist changed over the years?
- How have the results of national studies served to inform the role of the reading specialist?
- What educational and social factors are affecting the role of the reading specialist?

This introductory chapter, which provides an organizational framework for the other chapters, begins with a brief history of the reading specialist in schools, especially in regard to compensatory programs such as Chapter 1 or Title I. A discussion of what is known about the role of the reading specialist, based on research in the field, follows. I conclude by discussing factors that will affect the work of the reading specialist in the coming years.

Much has been learned about how to teach reading to all students, yet the evidence is clear: there are students in schools at all levels (preK–12) who are not learning to read or who are reading below grade-level expectations. Across the United States, legislators and policy makers, those in the business community, parents, and educators alike have been searching for ways to address this dilemma. The federal government has invested in large-scale programs such as Head Start, Reading First, the professional development initiative of No Child Left Behind (U.S. Department of Education, 2002a), Race to the Top (American Recovery and Reinvestment Act of 2009; Public Law No. 111-5, 2009), and other school improvement programs to support reading instruction. Recently, the federal government funded the Striving Readers program in which a state could apply for funding to develop a comprehensive literacy plan (birth–grade 12) to serve as a guide for the state in promoting literacy efforts at both state and district levels. The 2004 reauthorization of the Individuals with Disabilities Education Improvement Act (IDEIA) of 2004 (Public Law No. 108-446, 2004) promoted a response-to-intervention (RTI) model for identifying and instructing students who may be at risk for learning disabilities. RTI has great implications for reading specialists, as well as for general and special education teachers. It encourages schools to prevent academic failure by identifying students who are in need of supplementary or intensive instruction and then designing and implementing programs for those students. The goal of RTI is to provide instruction that might prevent students from being identified as needing special education services. These federal initiatives as well as others developed by states or local districts require that teachers have an in-depth understanding of how to teach reading. Furthermore, in order to reach the goals of these various initiatives, there is a need for reading specialists with dual roles: They must be able to teach struggling readers and provide support to classroom teachers so that all students are successful. The instructional role of the reading specialist is an important one given it increases the opportunity for students to receive appropriate and differentiated instruction. The leadership role, in which reading specialists work with classroom teachers, has been evolving, especially since the early 2000s, with many schools hiring literacy or reading coaches to work with teachers in the schools to improve classroom instruction. As cited in Hall (2004), "the concept of literacy coaching dates back to the 1920's—but they are increasingly in demand in 21st century schools" (p. 11).

Yet, the dual role of the reading specialist is not a new one. In 1981, Bean and Wilson, in their book *Effecting Change in School Reading Programs: The Resource Role*, wrote about the need for reading specialists to work as partners with teachers, parents, and administrators, and that "this partnership must be based on mutual trust and respect" (p. 7). In 1998, Snow, Burns, and Griffin reinforced this stance, stating, "every school should have access to specialists . . . reading specialists who have specialized training related to addressing reading difficulties and who can give guidance to classroom teachers" (p. 333). Moreover, the position statement of the International Literacy Association (formerly the International Reading Association) (IRA; 2000b) on the role of the reading specialist calls for such a dual role. It is this dual role that is addressed in this book. This role requires reading specialists to have expertise with reading assessment and instruction and to possess the leadership skills that enable them to work with other adults, such as classroom teachers, other professionals (e.g., speech teachers, special educators), and the community (e.g., parents, volunteers, universities, community agencies).

WHERE WE HAVE BEEN

The presence of specialists in schools dates back to the 1930s when they functioned essentially as supervisors who worked with teachers to improve the reading program. It was after World War II, in response to the raging criticism of the schools and their inability to teach children to read, that "remedial reading teachers" became fixtures in many schools, public and private, elementary through secondary. The primary responsibility of the specialist was to work with individuals or small groups of children who were experiencing difficulty in learning to read. Briggs and Coulter (1977) stated: "Like Topsy, these remedial reading services just 'growed,' aided and abetted by government at all levels and by private foundations quick to provide grants of funding for such programs" (p. 216). Even the IRA (1968), in their *Guidelines for Reading Specialists*, strongly supported the remedial role: Five of the six functions described for the "special teacher of reading" related directly to instructional responsibilities. However, there were those educators who began to see the difficulty of reading specialists serving only an instructional capacity. Stauffer (1967) described the remedial role as one of working in a "bottomless pit" and supported the idea of the reading specialist serving as a consultant.

Support for reading specialists serving in multiple roles continued throughout the next several decades. As mentioned previously, in 1981, Bean and Wilson wrote about the resource role of the reading specialist, emphasizing the importance of interpersonal, leadership, and communication skills for those in reading specialist positions. However, various factors helped to define the roles of reading specialists, including the source of funding that provided support for these specialized personnel, and, indeed, research that contributed to new ideas about reading instruction and assessment.

The Role of Reading Specialists in Compensatory Programs

Since 1965, a large percentage of reading specialists have been funded by Title I of the Elementary and Secondary Education Act (1965; Public Law No. 89-10). This large compensatory program, funded by the federal government, was developed to provide supplemental support to students who are economically deprived. In the initial conceptualization of this program, policies and procedures were developed to ensure that appropriate students were receiving support provided by these funds. Reading specialists who were funded by Title I were, therefore, required to work solely with eligible students and to purchase and use various resources and materials for those students only. Such policies led to what is commonly referred to as "pullout" programs; that is, large, separate, and distinct programs for designated students. By separating the Title I program from the "general" school program, it was easier for school personnel to maintain fiscal compliance. However, these programs generated many problems. Often, there was little congruence or alignment between the classroom program and the supplemental program, so students with reading difficulties who could least handle this lack of alignment, received two different programs, with no "bridges" connecting them. Some reading specialists were not knowledgeable about the instruction students were receiving in their classrooms (Allington, 1986; Slavin, 1987), nor did they share what they were doing with the classroom teachers! Moreover, when students who received Title I services returned to their classrooms, they were then asked to learn from materials that were too difficult for them or to use strategies or skills different from those they were learning in their pullout program. Another problem was that, too often, students in these supplemental programs spent their time doing workbook-type, skill-related activities. There was little opportunity to read nor was there much direct instruction (Allington & McGill-Franzen, 1989; Bean, Cooley, Eichelberger, Lazar, & Zigmond, 1991). And some classroom teachers seemed to think that the reading specialists had sole responsibility for teaching these students to read, even though the instruction provided by the specialists was identified as *supplemental*.

At the same time, teachers resented the "swinging-door" dimension of pullout programs; their instruction was interrupted by students coming into and going out of their classrooms. This feeling is illustrated in an article from a newsletter published by a teachers' organization:

> Over the past few months I've been noticing that my class has been quietly disappearing. They leave one by one, or in small groups. They come late due to dentist appointments and leave early for eye exams. They are being remediated, enriched, guided, weighed, and measured. They are leaving me to learn to speak English, pass the TELLS test, increase sight vocabulary, develop meaningful relationships, and to be PEP'd or BEEP'd.
>
> They slip in and out with such frequency that I rarely have my whole class together for any length of time on any given day.

I don't know when to schedule a test anymore. I've considered administering them during lunch when I'm on cafeteria duty—but then again the "packers" aren't sitting with the "buyers"—so we are still not all together.

One day I accidentally had the whole class in my room. As soon as I discovered it, I quickly gave them their language pretest and posttest! If it ever happens again, they're getting their final exam.

When the office calls for one of my students, I try to be fair about it. My policy is—if they can find them, they can have them. I find you can get one small advantage from all this coming and going, if you work it right. You seat your talkative kids in between the frequent remedials and half the time they'll be next to empty desks.

I am learning to deal with the disappearances. I teach in bits and pieces to parts of the whole. But you can help me out, if you will. If you even run into any of my meandering students, say "hi" for me—and take them over their time tables please. (Anonymous, 1986)

Another problem was the stigma associated with leaving the classroom; students were viewed by their peers as being dumb or different, creating a lack of self-esteem in these students. Also, Allington (1986) and others were concerned that pullout programs that provided minimal reading instruction (e.g., 35–40 minutes, several times a week) did not address the serious needs of students.

The results of large-scale evaluations of Chapter 1 or Title I were not always positive, although Borman and D'Agostine (2001), in their meta-analysis of Title I program effects, indicated that "there has been a positive trend for the educational effectiveness of Title I across the years of its operation" (p. 49). They contended that, without these services, students would have fallen further behind academically. The evaluation of Title I has been difficult because it is essentially a funding program, not one that requires specific instructional foci, and there are many variations in the ways that it is implemented in districts across this nation. At the same time, the great expectation for Title I—that it close the achievement gap between at-risk, poor students and their more advantaged peers—has not been met.

Many changes were recommended in the literature and in the new legislation of 1988. These changes included recommendations for additional collaboration with classroom teachers and special educators and more emphasis on programs in which reading specialists worked in the classrooms with teachers. These recommendations certainly influenced the role of reading specialists, making it essential that they be able to work well with other adults. Although this movement generated more interaction between teachers and reading specialists, it was not always a "marriage made in heaven"; both partners had to learn to work collaboratively in new and different ways (I address this further in Chapter 2).

Changes in Literacy Assessment and Instruction

In the early days of Title I programs, reading specialists carefully documented the reading achievement and reading expectancy of students who might be eligible for compensatory services. Reading expectancy was calculated in various ways, from obtaining the intelligence quotient of the students to administering a listening comprehension test. Teacher judgment, at times, was used. Only those students who were identified as "discrepant"—that is, their test performance revealed a gap between achievement and potential—were assigned to receive reading services. With growing recognition of (1) the limitations inherent in scores achieved on intelligence and standardized tests and (2) possible test bias in identifying students, the use of a discrepancy formula was eliminated and students were identified based on their actual reading achievement.

This criticism of standardized testing also led to the identification of new indicators of success for students and Title I programs, with a primary emphasis on how well students performed on "authentic" measures and indicators of success in the classroom such as grades in subject areas. Schools, therefore, found themselves in the position of creating their own measures, identifying what they wanted students to know and be able to do at various grade levels. And, often, reading specialists found themselves in the position of working with classroom teachers to develop such instruments.

Likewise, changes in reading instruction influenced the work of reading specialists. As mentioned previously, Allington and McGill-Franzen (1986; Bean et al., 1991), who studied Chapter 1 programs, found that reading specialists often spent their time using "skill-and-drill" methods. Students completed worksheets or participated in specialized programs that emphasized skill instruction. Students spent little time reading! Yet research evidence and theorists in the field were advocating the teaching of more explicit reading strategies and increased opportunities for students to engage actively in reading and writing tasks.

The changes described previously and the results of Title I evaluations led to a period in the 1990s when school districts eliminated or downsized the number of reading specialists in their schools. One reading specialist summarized the situation as follows:

> Our grant from Title I is substantial; yet rather than use the expertise of reading specialists in the district's reading program, the

number of specialists has dropped in the last several years from 14 to 4. Reading specialists have been assigned to classroom teaching positions or have not been replaced from attrition. Blame for dropping reading scores has been laid at the Title I door; reading specialists are an expensive liability. Reading specialists are being replaced with many, many inexpensive aides. (personal communication, May 1991)

Various programs and strategies were implemented to address the problems of struggling readers: increasing the competence of classroom teachers, reducing class size, using technology in the classrooms, adding after-school and summer programs, and employing volunteers and aides to work with students. All of these strategies, though they can be beneficial, did not seem to produce the desired results, however.

In 1995, the IRA, encouraged by its members, established a commission to investigate the role and status of reading specialists in schools. The commission was given two tasks: (1) analyze the literature and research about the role of the specialist and (2) conduct a survey of members to determine what reading specialists were actually doing in schools. That work is reported in two articles found in *The Reading Teacher* (Bean, Cassidy, Grumet, Shelton, & Wallis, 2002; Quatroche, Bean, & Hamilton, 2001). The work resulted in a position statement: *Teaching All Children to Read: The Roles of the Reading Specialist* (IRA, 2000b). Because of the many changes in the role of reading specialists in the decade from 2002 to 2012, that national survey was replicated. Below I summarize some of the findings of the recent study and compare them with the earlier study.

Comparison of the National Surveys of Reading Specialists

There is an old expression: "The more things change, the more they remain the same." However, in this instance, although there were some similarities in the roles of reading specialists, there were also differences in the responses to the two surveys. Survey results were similar in the following ways. First, in both surveys (Bean, Cassidy, et al., 2002; Bean, Kern, et al., 2015) respondents tended to be white and female; they were also experienced educators, with most having served as classroom teachers before accepting reading specialist positions. Second, respondents to the earlier survey and to the recent one indicated that they have dual roles: they instruct students and they also support teachers in providing instruction for students. Third, reading specialists continued to work in both classrooms and also in pullout settings, with 40% in the recent study indicating that they taught exclusively in pullout settings. Fourth, reading specialists have an important role in administering and analyzing assessment results, and also in assisting teachers in using those results for instructional decision making. Finally, the percentage of reading specialists overall serving at the secondary level was still small.

However, the differences between responses to the surveys were quite distinct. First, leadership is an important aspect of the role of reading specialists regardless of title. In the recent survey, we were able to categorize respondents as falling into one of four distinct role groups: reading specialist, interventionist/reading teacher, literacy coach, and a small group that self-identified as supervisors. In the recent study, we found that all but 11.3% of these respondents spent some time supporting the work of teachers. In other words, reading specialists as a whole, regardless of what position they have in schools, tend to have leadership responsibilities that call on them to be able to work effectively with adults as a means of improving literacy instruction.

Second, there was also more of a focus on collaborative work, not only with teachers but with their reading specialist colleagues and with other specialized professionals (e.g., special educators, librarians, counselors, psychologists). In fact, two key findings in the recent study were that (1) respondents were not the sole reading specialist in the school and generally worked collaboratively with others who served in a similar role and (2) they were not the sole reading instructor for the students with whom they worked. Both of these findings have important implications for reading specialists in terms of their ability to work collaboratively with others.

Third, although the percentage of respondents in both surveys who worked at the secondary level was similar, a larger percentage of respondents in the recent survey who self-identified as literacy coaches worked at the secondary level, supporting teachers in their classroom instructional efforts. In other words, more reading specialists at the secondary level self-identified themselves as coaches.

Fourth, most respondents in the recent study indicated they had multiple roles, that is, they taught students, supported teachers, led professional development efforts, and so on. It was clear, also, that their positions were subject to change depending on funding, district initiative, changes in leadership or school demographics, and so forth. Such a finding requires reading specialists to be nimble and able to adapt quickly and thoughtfully to meet the demands of their new roles and responsibilities. And again, reading specialists must possess the communication, interpersonal, and leadership skills that enable them to work with others to respond to the changing environment and culture.

Finally, respondents across all groups indicated they would feel better prepared if they had more educational experiences enabling them to assume leadership responsibilities in the school; such leadership included the ability to work effectively with adults, both individually and in groups, and to facilitate and lead the development of the reading program. In other words, respondents wanted more experiences that enabled them to work with adult learners, especially those thought to be resistant, in ways that promoted changes in instruction; lead groups as they worked collaboratively to make instructional decisions; and facilitate the change process in schools. These findings from the recent survey have implications for the content in this book that focuses on the leadership role of reading specialists—not only with teachers and other specialized personnel in the schools but with administrators, families, and community leaders and agencies.

One of the disturbing findings of both the 2002 and the 2015 surveys was the virtual absence of men and minority groups among the reading specialist population, a problematic finding given the importance of role models for students who are male or of a minority group. The increased numbers of literacy coaches at the secondary level seems to reflect the growing interest in and concern about instruction in the content areas and the focus on the Common Core State Standards (CCSS; National Governors Association Center for Best Practices & Council of Chief State School Officers [NGA & CCSSO], 2010), especially those standards that address literacy instruction in the various disciplines.

So, has the world of the reading specialist changed? We suggest it has. Although the various roles may vary—from instructional through coaching and leadership—all those in reading specialist roles need leadership, interpersonal, and communication skills that enable them to work effectively in schools as they exist today. The emphasis in schools on shared leadership, in which school personnel are "learning together, and constructing meaning and knowledge collectively and collaboratively" (Lambert, 1998, p. 5) have made schools places of learning for both adults and students. Such schools rely on teacher leadership and engagement in developing a common vision, developing expectations for students, and making instructional decisions. Often, the reading specialist serves as one of the informal leaders in schools (Bean & Lillenstein, 2012; Camburn, Rowan, & Taylor, 2003).

The Value of Reading Specialists in Schools

A study by Bean, Swan, and Knaub (2003), in which they interviewed reading specialists who had responded to a 2002 study, provided some answers to the question about the value of reading specialists. In the study, reading specialists in schools identified as exemplary were interviewed and then their principals were sent a follow-up survey. Principals in these schools were extremely positive about the importance of the reading specialists to the success of their reading programs, with 97% indicating that specialists were "extremely" or "very important" to its success. The specialists in these schools were experienced teachers (all but one of them worked directly with students), all also served in a leadership role, and all saw the leadership role as an essential part of their work. These specialists identified the following characteristics of the ideal reading specialist:

- Teaching ability
- Knowledge of reading instruction
- Sensitivity to children with reading difficulties
- Knowledge of assessments
- Ability and willingness to fill an advocacy role
- Ability to work with adults
- Knowledge of reading research
- Lifelong learners
- Ability to provide professional development
- Ability to articulate reading philosophy
- Energy

THINK ABOUT THIS

Which characteristics do you believe are most important? Why? The qualifications include those relating to knowledge, skills, and dispositions of reading specialists. Are there others that you would add?

Figure 1.1 illustrates the many different roles of reading specialists. The content of this graphic was influenced by the IRA (2000b) position statement on the role of the reading specialist and the work of Galloway and Lesaux (2014); it differs, however, in that it puts leadership in a central position, that is, as an important set of knowledge, skills, and dispositions affecting all roles of reading specialists. As in the IRA position statement, *support for student learning* is at the center of the graphic, as it is the ultimate responsibility of all reading specialists. The various tasks or responsibilities of reading specialists are identified as follows: working with students, teachers, families/communities, data, and facilitating school change. In the following chapters, the responsibilities of reading specialists in each of these categories are explored and ideas for working effectively are provided. Reading specialists will not necessarily have major responsibilities in each of these categories; they may focus on working with students and adults, or they may spend much of their energy facilitating school change by leading programmatic or

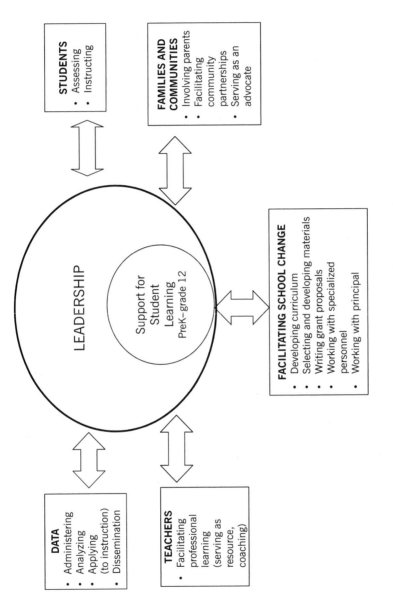

STUDENTS
- Assessing
- Instructing

FAMILIES AND COMMUNITIES
- Involving parents
- Facilitating community partnerships
- Serving as an advocate

LEADERSHIP

Support for Student Learning
PreK–grade 12

FACILITATING SCHOOL CHANGE
- Developing curriculum
- Selecting and developing materials
- Writing grant proposals
- Working with specialized personnel
- Working with principal

DATA
- Administering
- Analyzing
- Applying (to instruction)
- Dissemination

TEACHERS
- Facilitating professional learning (serving as resource, coaching)

FIGURE 1.1. Roles of the reading specialist.

11

curriculum development efforts. However, even with designated major or primary responsibilities in one category (e.g., delivering instruction to students), most often they will be expected to perform tasks related to other categories (support teachers, develop family involvement programs, administer assessments). Hence, the complexity of the role of the reading specialist and importance of being nimble!

WHERE WE ARE: THE 21ST CENTURY

There are several factors that have affected the role of the reading specialist, in addition to the emphasis on shared leadership. These include the focus on teacher performance and quality instruction; high-level literacy standards that call for literacy instruction, not only in the English language arts but in the content areas; focus on assessment as a basis for instructional decision making as a means of serving all students; a greater emphasis on preschool education; professional development for teachers, including literacy coaching; and, finally, the economic climate in the United States that has affected school spending and school resources. Each is discussed below.

Teacher Performance

The recognition that high-quality instruction is related to student learning has led to a call for teachers who are better qualified and prepared to teach reading—and with that call came recommendations for a focus on evaluating teacher performance, not just to identify teachers who may be experiencing difficulties but to provide professional learning experiences for them. Reading specialists or literacy coaches are often called on to assist novice teachers or those who have been identified as needing additional support. This movement has had its critics, generally because of controversy about which tools (e.g., observations, portfolios, student learning, self-report) can best assess teacher learning, but also because of the ways in which the results have been reported and used.

Rigorous Standards for English Language Arts and for Literacy in the Various Academic Subjects

Almost all states have adopted the CCSS developed by the NGA and CCSSO (2010) and others have adapted those standards, or developed sets of standards they believe will prepare students for college and career. Such standards require a new way of teaching that emphasizes the integration of reading with the other language arts, especially writing, and highlight the need for shared responsibility of all teachers in developing literacy skills. Teachers in the content areas, especially at the secondary level, will need to develop an understanding of how to help their students comprehend the informational texts of their discipline. Reading specialists who work in schools implementing these standards will need skills that enable them to work effectively, not just as teachers of struggling readers but with content-area teachers who are being asked to incorporate reading and writing strategies into their instruction as a means of developing student learning of academic content. The CCSS have been accompanied by an emphasis on literacy instruction for the adolescent learner, given current results on both state and national assessment measures, and the recognition that there is much that can be done to improve instruction at the middle and secondary levels.

Assessment as a Basis for Instructional Decision Making

The use of data to make instructional decisions has influenced what specialists do in schools. Specialists often help teachers administer and analyze test data throughout the year, and most importantly, they are responsible for helping teachers think about how to use these test results to differentiate instruction through the use of different materials, approaches, and/or small-group instruction. However, at times, the emphasis on accountability has led to "teaching to the test," and reading specialists (as well as classroom teachers) found themselves in the position of providing narrow, focused instruction only. In a more positive vein, the focus on accountability has made it critical that reading specialists understand how to assess reading growth, interpret results of various assessment measures, and communicate results to others. The RTI legislation (IDEIA, 2004) encouraged schools to use an approach different from the traditional discrepancy approach for identifying students with learning difficulties. RTI supports early intervention to reduce the number of students qualifying for special education by promoting differentiated instruction as a means of improving success of all students. This initiative necessitates collaboration among classroom teachers, reading specialists, and special educators with each professional bringing to the table ideas for how to make instructional adjustments. Classroom teachers can receive instructional support from reading specialists (e.g., a reading specialist may be responsible for providing supplemental comprehension instruction to a small group of students). For example, the reading specialist may provide explicit instruction on how to summarize or how to predict to students who seem to have difficulty even after the classroom teacher has presented these lessons to the entire class. Or the specialist may be assigned to deliver specialized or targeted instruction to a small group of readers who seem to be making little or no progress in the classroom, even after modifications have been made by the classroom teacher. Thus, the instructional role of the specialist will continue to be important, but it may require different responsibilities from those expected of reading specialists in the past.

Preschool Instruction

The research supporting literacy and language activities at preschool levels as a means of reducing or eliminating future literacy and learning problems has generated a great deal of focus on the instruction that goes on in preschool and day-care settings. Currently, the federal government is providing funding to assist states in building, developing, and expanding voluntary, high-quality preschool programs in high-need communities. Such programs will require preschool teachers to be well prepared and for better transition programs bridging preschool and kindergarten. Thus, the need for well-prepared reading specialists and literacy coaches who can work cooperatively with preschool educators to ensure there is a better understanding of what students need to know and do when they arrive in kindergarten—and so kindergarten teachers have a better idea of what students are learning in preschool settings. This movement also calls for more partnering among all individuals and agencies involved in the education of young children: parents, teachers, preschools, libraries, and community agencies.

Professional Development for Teachers

All of the initiatives described above have led to an increasing focus on providing effective professional learning experiences for teachers who are being asked to change the ways they teach. And research evidence about effective professional development suggests that such professional development be job embedded, ongoing, subject based, and provide for active learning. Such professional development has led to an increased emphasis on coaching in schools, and often a change in the role of many reading specialists across this country, with some who originally worked only with students now focusing on improving classroom instruction by supporting teachers. This new role of coaching requires individuals to have not only an in-depth knowledge of reading instruction and assessment, but in addition, knowledge of adult learning and excellent interpersonal, communication, and leadership skills. This movement has generated consternation for some reading specialists whose "first love" is working with struggling readers, or who feel unqualified to serve as coach.

The Economic Climate in the United States

Given the economic climate in the United States, funding has been reduced not only by the federal government but by states, and even local districts. Some schools then found it necessary to eliminate coaching positions (Bean, Dole, Nelson, Belecastro, & Zigmond, 2015). As mentioned by Steinbacher-Reed and Powers (2011/2012), often reading specialists were assigned these coaching tasks: they analyzed data with teachers, modeled, and co-taught; their role was changed so that they worked with both students and teachers. Again, reading specialists found themselves having multiple responsibilities, ones for which they may not have been prepared.

WHERE WE ARE GOING: A CRYSTAL BALL?

Although all the issues mentioned above will most likely continue to influence the role of reading specialists in the near future, there are several other factors that will affect the role in the coming years. First, I suspect that we will see some changes in how reading specialists serving as literacy coaches are prepared and in how they work in schools—given the results of research, including the national survey described previously (Bean, Kern, et al., 2015). The emphasis on providing professional development for teachers continues to gain momentum and schools across this country regardless of location, poverty, or achievement status, have begun to think about effective and cost-effective ways to offer such learning to their teachers. Thus, although some have continued to fund coaches, other schools have used different approaches: They have asked their reading specialists to teach struggling readers and work with teachers; they have established professional learning communities (PLCs) that promote collaborative learning; they have established schedules that provide teachers with time for discussion about assessment and instruction. Schools have been creative in thinking about ways that they can best use the talents and experience of their teaching staff to develop schools as places of learning for adults and students (Bean & Swan Dagen, 2012).

   In other words, there are many individuals in schools who are coaching or mentoring teachers: literacy/instructional/academic coaches, peers, teacher leaders, reading specialists, interventionists, and so on. Therefore, regardless of title, these specialized professionals need to have the skills, knowledge, and dispositions that enable them to serve in a leadership role. The revised Standards for Reading Professionals (IRA, 2010b) have the potential to help those preparing reading specialists to understand better the multiple tasks of assessment, instruction, and leadership.

A second initiative, however, that will most likely affect the ways in which reading specialists work in schools is technology. Reading specialists will need to be more knowledgeable about and able to evaluate the software that is available, and understand the influence of the "new literacies" on students, especially adolescent readers. Furthermore, they must understand how to use the capabilities of the computer and the Internet to help students become critical readers. Moreover, technology will continue to influence the ways in which reading specialists themselves are prepared for their positions; I suspect that there will be more opportunities for reading specialists and reading coaches to receive at least some of their preparation through online programs. Such online instruction will also affect the ways that reading specialists provide instruction to teachers with whom they work. Teachers have become accustomed to gaining information via the Internet rather than attending face-to-face meetings.

A third issue that will affect the role of reading specialists is that of the increasing diversity of students in classrooms across the country, specifically students whose primary language is not English. Between 1979 and 1999, the number of language-minority students in the United States nearly doubled from 6 to 14 million and it is predicted that the percentage of children who arrive at school speaking a language other than English will continue to increase (Kindler, 2002). Classrooms in today's schools are becoming more diverse, with more students of color, English learners, and high-poverty students. According to the National Clearinghouse for English Language Acquisition, by 2025 approximately one of four students will be an English learner. In 1990, 4.3 million children had one immigrant parent; this increased to 8.7 million in 2008 (*www.ncela.ed.gov*). Moreover, many children in the United States live in poverty, and these students can be found in both urban and rural areas. Because these second-language learners are demonstrating significantly lower levels of academic achievement as compared with native English-speaking students in the United States, classroom teachers and reading specialists need to be able to teach in ways that enhance the language and literacy learning of these students.

Finally, as we learn more about school change and the need to work with others if we are to improve schooling for all, there is recognition of the importance of collaboration, not only in the school setting but also with external partners (e.g., parents, community agencies, universities). Reading specialists must have the necessary knowledge and skills to work collaboratively to build those partnerships. This focus on collaboration, and on what is a new wave of school reform (Swan Dagen & Bean, 2014), will also affect the ways in which reading specialists work in schools.

Reading Specialists in Middle and High Schools

Given the increased attention to adolescent literacy, several chapters in this book include a section devoted specifically to reading specialists serving students and teachers in middle and high schools. In these sections, additional information is provided that highlights issues especially relevant for those specialists. As mentioned previously, literacy or instructional coaches are being hired at the middle and secondary levels with their primary responsibility that of working with teachers. However, at times, these schools will have both a reading specialist and coach, or they will have a reading specialist serving dual roles (i.e., teaching students and supporting teachers). Mason and Ippolito (2009) provide an excellent description of four roles of reading specialists in middle and high schools. First, these professionals can administer and analyze assessment tools that they or other teachers use for instructional decision making. Second, they can support the content-area teachers by providing professional development about literacy, modeling, or co-teaching with them; in other words, they assume coaching responsibilities. Third, they can work with special educators to assist students with learning differences or difficulties; in other words, they may be involved in working with an RTI team about how best to address the learning needs of students. Finally, they may be involved in creating and evaluating the literacy program at the middle or secondary levels, helping to select or develop programs, materials, or instructional strategies. In other words, they serve multiple roles that will differ, depending on the context in which they work, their job descriptions, availability of other personnel, and so on. The bottom line is they have an important role in improving the literacy learning of adolescents and, in order to fulfill that role, they must be able to work collaboratively with their colleagues.

THINK ABOUT THIS

Do you agree or disagree with the factors that have been identified above—relative to how reading specialists might function in schools? Which of the factors have affected you personally? Are there factors that you think should be added?

SUMMARY

The role of the reading specialist has continued to evolve over the past decades. Currently, we are experiencing a greater emphasis on leadership responsibilities across all roles. Some changes in roles have occurred in response to research findings about reading instruction and assessment practices. Other changes have emerged on the heels of criticism about the results of compensatory programs that lacked congruence between classroom and supplemental instruction. New emphases in reading instruction and increased demand for scientifically based reading instruction have created demands for reading specialists to assume an increased leadership role. Reading specialists, however, will continue to fill multiple roles that require individuals to have an in-depth knowledge of reading instruction and assessment and the ability to work well with other adults. The increased emphasis on professional development, improving literacy instruction for all students, preK–12, and technological capabilities will generate the need for new skills and new roles. Moreover, reading specialists will need to have an understanding of how the organization in which they work affects what they do and how they can collaborate with others to create changes that facilitate student learning.

ADDITIONAL READINGS

Bean, R. M., Kern, D., Goatley, V., Ortlieb, E., Shettel, J., Calo, K., et al. (2015). Specialized literacy professionals as literacy leaders. *Literacy Research and Instruction, 54*(2), 83–114.—This article provides the results of a national survey of specialized literacy professionals; it suggests that these professionals have many leadership responsibilities in schools.

Galloway, E. P., & Lesaux, N. K. (2014). Leader, teacher, diagnostician, colleague, and change agent: A synthesis of the research on the role of the reading specialist in this era of RTI-based literacy reform. *The Reading Teacher, 67*(7), 517–526.—These authors synthesized current research about the work of today's reading specialists and found that these personnel served as both an instructor of students and in a supportive role to teachers.

Mason, P. M., & Ippolito, J. (2009). What is the role of the reading specialist in promoting adolescent literacy? In J. Lewis (Ed.), *Essential questions in adolescent literacy: Teachers and researchers describe what works in classrooms* (pp. 312–336). New York: Guilford Press.—In this chapter, the authors describe four key roles of reading specialists in secondary schools. They highlight ways these specialists can support efforts of teachers in various disciplines.

Reflections

1. What skills and abilities do you think are essential for working successfully as a reading specialist in an instructional role? Leadership role? Assessment role?
2. With which role are you most comfortable? What concerns do you have about the other roles?
3. What are the implications of the following issues for reading specialists and their role: placement in the middle or secondary school; increased emphasis on working with preschool providers; focus on rigorous, high-level standards; teacher performance?

Activities

1. Analyze your own skills in relation to the three areas of expertise required of reading specialists: instruction, assessment, and leadership. Write a summary of your thoughts, indicating your strengths and where you think you may need to gain additional experience or knowledge.
2. Interview a teacher to gain his or her perceptions about the role of the reading specialist/literacy coach. You may also want to interview a principal (and a reading specialist/literacy coach), using the same questions.
3. Interview a reading specialist, asking questions about how he or she fulfills responsibilities in the following areas: instruction, assessment, and leadership. You may want to use the questions in the following section.

Interviewing Reading Specialists

1. What are your responsibilities as a reading specialist? (Ask the person to describe what he or she does in his or her school/program.)
2. How do you determine the goals and content of your instruction? (Ascertain *what*—and *who*—determines the instruction.)
3. Which assessment instruments do you find to be particularly helpful in assessing students' needs?
4. How do you use assessment results?
5. In what ways do you serve as a resource to teachers? Do you have any other coaching responsibilities, and if so, what?
6. If you were able to develop your own assessment program, what would you emphasize or change?
7. What are some of the major difficulties experienced by students in your school?
8. In what ways do you facilitate parent involvement?
9. What are the major issues you face as a reading specialist?
10. How well prepared were you for the position you now hold?

CHAPTER TWO

Working with Students

An Overview of the Instructional Role

Key Questions

- In what ways can reading specialists communicate and collaborate with classroom teachers?
- What possible approaches for collaborative teaching between reading specialists and classroom teachers are available, and what advantages or disadvantages are there to each?
- What do reading specialists need to know in order to work in schools that use an RTI framework?

This chapter discusses approaches that have been used successfully by reading specialists in teaching struggling readers—from working in pullout programs to working with teachers in the classroom. In this chapter, I also provide an overview of the RTI initiative, given its relevance to reading specialists.

Although reading specialists have multiple responsibilities, one most often associated with the role of the reading specialist is teaching students, especially those experiencing difficulties learning to read. Classroom teachers, who have multiple demands on them, value having reading specialists provide supplemental support to students with specific needs. Moreover, as mentioned in several studies, reading specialists themselves value the instructional role (Bean, Cassidy, et al., 2002; Bean, Kern, et al., 2015; Bean, Swan, & Knaub, 2003). Reading specialists gain a better understanding of what is occurring in classrooms and often can establish credibility with teachers when they have teaching responsibilities.

There is no single model of the instructional role for reading specialists to follow. Those who work in Title I programs may find themselves in classrooms, in pullout models, or both. Those at middle school and secondary levels often focus on reading in the content areas, and although they frequently work in the classroom with content teachers, they may also have responsibility for teaching classes of students needing supplemental reading support. Often reading specialists work with small groups of children; however, there are also times when these specialists work with individual students (e.g., Reading Recovery [Clay, 1985] or Success for All [Slavin, Madden, Dolan, & Wasik, 1996]).

What is essential is that the reading specialist who is responsible for teaching struggling readers understands the critical elements necessary to promote reading success for these students. Foorman and Torgeson (2001) provide an excellent summary of the research on effective classroom instruction and on effective instruction for children at risk for reading failure. They identify three critical components of instruction for struggling readers: such instruction "must be more *explicit and comprehensive*, more *intensive*, and more *supportive* than the instruction required by the majority of children" (p. 206, original emphasis). They describe the need for both cognitive and emotional support. In other words, these students need instruction that provides more scaffolding to help them complete tasks successfully, and in addition, they need "encouragement, feedback, and positive reinforcement" (p. 209). The importance of emotional support for all students cannot be understated, and such support is especially critical when working with adolescent students whose poor sense of self and feelings of academic inadequacy may limit their willingness to participate in literacy activities. When reading the sections below, think about how reading specialists can organize their instructional work to best address the needs of struggling readers. In the vignette in this chapter, Mark, an elementary reading specialist whose primary responsibility is delivering instruction to students, describes his work. Note the ways he organizes his schedule and how he communicates and collaborates with teachers in his school.

WHAT READING SPECIALISTS NEED TO KNOW ABOUT WORKING IN AN INSTRUCTIONAL ROLE

Collaboration

Regardless of the approach or the location of the instruction, to be effective, reading specialists must communicate and collaborate with teachers who are providing the "first line" of instruction to students. Only if the reading specialist knows what the classroom teacher is doing, and vice versa, can the most appropriate instruction be provided for students. Much has been learned about the problems that typically arise when struggling readers are faced with fragmented instruction that increases their confusion—and anxiety. Likewise, adjustments need to be made so that these readers are not asked to do the work required by both the classroom teacher and the reading specialist. Certainly, having students use their recess time to complete class assignments, or to take their work home because they didn't finish it, can have a negative effect on students' attitude toward reading and school. In scheduling, specialists should avoid taking these students away from subjects such as art or gym, or from participating in special classroom activities (e.g., a movie, or community speaker).

Reading specialists and classroom teachers have been ingenious in finding ways to communicate and collaborate. Often this is done "on the fly," since schools do not always provide the time essential for such planning. Indeed, this lack of collaborative planning time was one of the greatest concerns of reading specialists who participated in the national survey conducted by the Commission on the Role of the Reading Specialist (Bean, Cassidy, et al., 2002); getting time to work with teachers was also identified as a challenge in the recent national study (Bean, Kern, et al., 2015). When Ogle and Fogelberg (2001) asked reading specialists to describe a successful collaboration and the reasons for its success, respondents highlighted the importance of an effective school climate or culture that permits teachers to experiment with new ways of teaching. The reading specialist, with the classroom teachers, have an important role in creating environments that facilitate and reward collaboration. In the following sections, I discuss practical ideas for promoting collaboration.

Written Communication

Simple forms that can be completed by both teachers and reading specialists enable them to determine quickly what is being emphasized by each in a particular week or unit. These forms also serve as a paper trail that can be useful in decision making as well as to provide detailed information to parents and other educators (see Figure 2.1). Some teachers actually share or exchange copies of lesson plans. Reading specialists can ask teachers to identify the skills or strategies they are working on that week and can plan their lessons to coincide with them (e.g., students are working on distinguishing between fact and opinion, or being asked to verify their responses to questions by doing close reading). The reading specialist can then plan lessons that are more explicit or have more scaffolding for those students who need additional work with those aspects of literacy instruction.

Date: Week of _____

Teacher: _____ Grade: _____

Selection/unit being read? _____
_____

Key words being taught? (Attach list, if available.) _____
_____

Emphasis on specific skills or strategies? _____
_____

Any specific request about my role with in-class instruction? _____
_____

What day(s)/time would be best for our in-class sessions? _____
_____

Are there any students about whom you have concerns? _____
_____

Any specific scheduling issues (field trips, assemblies)? _____
_____

Comments:

FIGURE 2.1. Communication form.

Oral Communication

SCHEDULED MEETINGS

School districts have designed many different approaches to providing needed planning time for teachers and reading specialists. For example, specialists may meet with grade-level or subject-area teachers once a week or bimonthly during a designated planning period. During these meetings, participants can discuss common needs and particular issues, and they can talk about specific students who may need supplemental help. They can make decisions about who will do what with whom and when! One of the advantages of these meetings is that reading specialists and teachers learn from each other; such meetings also tend to encourage teamwork among teachers and specialists. As one reading specialist said, "We need to know what is going on. Are teachers planning to show a movie or making a change in what they are teaching? All of this affects my schedule. So, the planning meeting is very helpful." Moreover, these meetings foster the notion that students are the responsibility of all teachers—not only the classroom teacher or the reading specialist. Too often, in the past, classroom teachers believed that they had little or no responsibility for teaching struggling readers; rather, it was the reading specialists' task to teach those students. Another value of these meetings is that reading specialists will be involved in ways that affect the learning of all students, from those who are excellent readers to those experiencing difficulty. With the advent of RTI, more and more schools are developing creative ways of providing meeting times for teachers.

Common planning time for a grade level and for subject-area teams has become "common" in school districts as a means of making short-term decisions. Some schools provide for planning time during the school day and others incorporate a 30-minute planning time in the morning before students arrive. In one primary school (grades K–3), the school schedule includes a grade-level planning meeting of 45 minutes once every other week with reading specialists and other specialized personnel; teachers can use that period for their own planning during the other week. To assist with long-range planning, the district may provide time for reading specialists to meet with individual teachers or groups of teachers to discuss data results several times a year. Some hire substitute teachers to manage classrooms while the reading specialist meets with teachers. For example, in one school district that is implementing an RTI program, substitutes are hired for 1 day every marking period (four times a year); they teach classes while the reading specialists and teachers from each of the grade levels meet for 90 minutes to review assessment data and make instructional decisions about content, grouping, and how the reading specialist will support the teachers at a specific grade level. In another school, grade-level meetings designed to discuss data are held five times a year: four substitutes are hired and they teach for half a day in the four classrooms at a specific grade level while the specialized literacy professionals and a math coach meet with the teachers. In other words, each grade-level team has half a day to meet with specialized literacy professionals to discuss students' progress and changes in groupings or instruction. Although these approaches may seem costly, they provide the opportunity for in-depth discussions about specific students and how personnel can collaborate to meet student needs. The meetings also provide professional learning opportunities as reading specialists and teachers share ideas about resources, materials, and various approaches for differentiating instruction.

Reading specialists may also meet with individual teachers either before or after school, or during a designated time for teacher planning/ preparation. However, some teachers may be reluctant to give up their own planning time; school leadership may need to negotiate with teachers' unions or associations so that opportunities for interaction between teachers and specialists are an expected aspect of the school day or week.

INFORMAL CONVERSATIONS

There may be opportunities to talk briefly when students are working independently. However, this is not an approach that allows for long periods of discussion, since teachers need to be available to teach, assist—or watch—as students are working. Many times teachers talk informally during their lunch break or in the halls. Knaub (2002), in her study of collaborative work between specialists and classroom teachers, found that teachers and reading specialists who worked together became familiar with various types of lessons (e.g., Cunningham & Hall's [1994] *Making Words*) and were able to coordinate their teaching effectively and with little planning. Knaub (p. 50) coined the phrase "impromptu partnering" to convey the ease with which reading specialists and teachers often collaborate. We found this same sort of conversation occurring between literacy coaches and teachers; such "opportunistic" discussions provided the basis for later, more intentional work (Bean, Belcastro, Jackson, Vandermolen, & Zigmond, 2008).

Support from Administration

Without administrative support, there is less chance that meaningful collaboration will occur. Research findings indicate that principal leadership is essential for promoting the work of reading specialists and literacy coaches (Bean, Dole, et al., 2015; Matsumura, Sartoris, DiPrima Bickel,

& Garnier, 2009). Schedules that provide teachers and reading specialists with opportunities to plan and policies and procedures that encourage collaboration are necessary for developing effective programs. Likewise, reading specialists need schedules that enable them to be in specific
classrooms during the teaching of appropriate subjects. Even the placement of students needs to be considered carefully. As noted by Ogle and
Fogelberg (2001), in some schools, struggling readers at the same grade
level are placed in two or three classrooms only so that they can receive
services from the reading specialist. Administrators can also show their
support by providing staff development for all teachers participating in
collaborative teaching. It is not sufficient for reading specialists alone to
understand how to work collaboratively; all teachers can benefit from
experiences that heighten their understanding of what collaboration
means and how to do it. This is especially important as schools attempt
to implement programs that meet the recommendations of the RTI initiative, which requires collaboration among classroom teachers and other
available specialized personnel (e.g., reading specialists, special educators). Finally, principals show support by being involved, attending at
least some or part of the meetings of reading specialists and their teacher
colleagues, and having an understanding of what the issues and challenges are for reading specialists in their instructional role.

Clear Procedures

Both classroom teachers and reading specialists must know and understand their roles in the classroom; the lack of clear procedures can lead
to problems. Reading specialists may feel as though they have no clear
instructional responsibility and therefore "float" around the classroom,
trying to anticipate what might be helpful. This type of role seems to
generate the feeling in reading specialists that they are "aides" in the
classroom and that their expertise is not useful or valued. Classroom
teachers also experience frustration because they do not know exactly
why the reading specialist is present. Only with the establishment of
clear expectations can teachers both enjoy and recognize the benefit of
an additional person in their classrooms. However, establishing those
clear expectations is not easy, given the culture that tends to exist in
schools, that is, teachers are assigned a group of students and are responsible for the academic success of those students. Teachers have been
accustomed to teaching in isolated settings, planning and implementing
instruction that they deem best. Figure 2.2 identifies questions that the
classroom teacher and reading specialist can ask each other as they think
about how to work together. Given the focus in schools on RTI, there
is much more co-teaching in schools today and teachers are becoming

	Yes	No
1. Do we come to class with prepared materials/ideas?	_____	_____
2. Do we signal our students to come to us when it is time?	_____	_____
3. Do we follow through on plans made at joint planning sessions?	_____	_____
4. Do we provide feedback on students' lessons to each other regularly and frequently?	_____	_____
5. Do we bring materials to joint planning sessions?	_____	_____
6. Do we share new strategies with the other teachers?	_____	_____
7. Do we engage in self-reflection after teaching a lesson?	_____	_____
8. Do classroom teachers try to help the reading specialist "fit in" with the flow of the classroom?	_____	_____
9. Do we invite feedback on students/lessons from each other?	_____	_____
10. Do classroom teachers share expectations for student behavior?	_____	_____
11. Do we try to keep a schedule? (Does the reading specialist arrive on time? Does the teacher plan to be ready for the collaborative lesson?)	_____	_____
12. Do we discuss other classroom teachers/reading specialists or students with others in a professional manner?	_____	_____
13. Do we "keep up" on reading instruction information and read professional journals?	_____	_____
14. Do we demonstrate respect for each other?	_____	_____

FIGURE 2.2. Questions to ask between teacher and reading specialist.

more accustomed to having other adults in their classrooms. However, given that reading specialists are "visitors" in teachers' classrooms, they must respect the experiences, management style, and organizational preferences of individual teachers. In other words, to be effective, reading specialists should differentiate the ways in which they work in teachers' classrooms. Some teachers may prefer to take a leadership role in making decisions about what the specialist can do and with whom, some will relinquish that role to the specialist, while others will work more collaboratively and want to plan together. Flexibility is key! (More about this in Chapter 4 on leadership.)

THINK ABOUT THIS

Would you feel comfortable using the questions in Figure 2.2 in a conversation with teachers? How can you use these questions effectively?

The following scenario describes how Shala, a reading specialist, and David, a third-grade teacher, planned their lessons for a week, using a framework that builds on the classroom instructional program. It also discusses how Shala works with some of David's students in a pullout setting to provide supplemental instruction for them (see Figure 2.3). The schedule calls for Shala to be in this classroom 3 days a week— Monday, Wednesday, and Friday—for 30 minutes each day. This week, the class is reading the selection *Mom Can't See Me* (1990) by Sally Alexander. David and Shala team teach to introduce the selection on Monday, focusing on vocabulary and prior knowledge. Then, to help students who are working with vocabulary in pairs, both the reading specialist and teacher circulate around the classroom. Shala also takes 5 minutes to talk with a new student about his previous school experience and to listen to him read a grade-level text so that she and the teacher have a better idea of the child's reading performance.

On Tuesday, the entire class reads the selection together and participates in a discussion with the classroom teacher. Students are also assigned to various learning centers where they are given activities that relate to their specific needs while the teacher monitors their work (Shala had helped David design these centers by providing him with ideas and resources). While the students are working in centers, David provides 20 minutes of supplemental instruction to a small group of three students who need more explicit instruction focused on decoding multisyllabic words. (During this center time, Shala works in a pullout setting with two students from David's class and three students from another third-grade classroom who are having decoding difficulties. She is providing

Monday	Tuesday	Wednesday	Thursday	Friday
In class (30 minutes)	*Pullout*	*In class (30 minutes)*	*Pullout*	*In class (30 minutes)*
Team teach (introduction to selection). Participate in guided and independent practice (monitor with teacher).	Targeted instruction for several groups of third-grade students (two from David's room).	Targeted, small-group instruction based on student needs.	Targeted instruction for several groups of third-grade students (two from David's room).	Targeted, small-group instruction based on student need; monitor with teacher.

FIGURE 2.3. Shala's weekly schedule with David and his students.

instruction that is more explicit, structured, and multisensory to help these students develop stronger decoding skills; these students also do partner reading in each lesson so that they have opportunities to apply what they are learning to actual reading.)

On Wednesday, the goal is fluency practice. Three groups are formed, with Shala working with a group of students identified as needing additional assistance with reading the text, the classroom teacher working with another group, and the third group engaging in partner reading. Shala asks students in her group to read and reread a specific section of the selection. First, she models fluent reading (and disfluent reading); she then has various students read the section orally (e.g., the boys, the girls, the students with red shirts). She also reviews some of the concepts and understandings that were addressed in the discussion during the previous day. Students in David's group also read orally, but his group is focused on finding and reading parts of the selection that answer specific comprehension questions.

On Thursday, the classroom teacher presents a specific skill suggested in the core reading program anthology to the entire class and also introduces a writing task to the students: "Write a letter to the author telling [her] what you liked about the story and raising questions that you would like to have her answer." Students again are assigned to centers; David monitors their work and also spends about 15 minutes providing supplemental instruction to a small group of students who need some reinforcement of the vocabulary taught that week. (And again, as she did on Tuesday, Shala meets with the same five students in a pullout setting to work on their decoding skills.)

On Friday, students continue to write the letter and they are also given time to read additional materials that are available in the classroom. The reading specialist and teacher are holding conferences with students, helping them to think about what they have written and how they might revise or edit their work. The focus is on writing a friendly letter to an author. For 10 minutes, Shala, the reading specialist, also pulls aside a small group to review strategies for identifying multisyllabic words because she and David had noted that some students were having difficulty with such words.

Shala and David use a mutually agreed-upon framework in planning each week's lesson so they don't need extended meetings to make decisions about the week's instruction. Shala knows that she is going to help students as they work with vocabulary on Mondays (she may also work with a small group to do some review work); on Wednesdays, the focus is on rereading the selection, and Shala often works with the group experiencing the most difficulty; on Fridays, there is an emphasis on some follow-up activity (e.g., writing, art, or creative dramatics). Shala assists with this activity, or she may work with a small group to provide additional reading practice or review specific strategies or skills. Then she also helps students in David's classroom by providing the intensive support they need by pulling them from their classroom and working with them in a small-group setting. This set of procedures is, of course, only one example of how the reading specialist and teacher may work together. Many different approaches can be used; the approach selected may depend on the curricular demands or the needs of the students.

THINK ABOUT THIS

What do you see as the strengths of this framework? Do you have any concerns about it? What skills and abilities do the reading specialist and classroom teacher need to make this framework effective? What other procedures do you think might work?

APPROACHES TO COLLABORATION

In this section, I describe five approaches to collaboration that are based on the literature (Bean, Trovato, & Hamilton, 1995; Cook & Friend, 1995) and on observations made of reading specialist interns and classroom teachers (Bean, Grumet, & Bulazo, 1999). Some of the approaches require in-class teaching, whereas others might occur either in class or away from the classroom; all require collaborative planning. Table 2.1

TABLE 2.1. Approaches to Collaboration

Model	Advantages	Potential problems/dilemmas	Location
Station or center teaching	• Students have opportunity to work with both teachers • Attention to individual/group needs or interests • Small-group work • Teachers have some choice (utilizes teacher strengths and interests) • Teachers share responsibility for developing and teaching	• Time-consuming to develop • Noise level in classroom • Organizational factors • Management factors	In class
Targeted teaching	• Focuses on individual or group needs • Individual or small group • Targeted instruction • Uses strengths of teachers to meet needs of students	• The need to know both classroom reading program and specialized approaches • Rigid grouping	Either in class or pullout
Parallel instruction	• Pacing/approach can vary • Small-group instruction • Same standards/expectations for all students • Easier to handle class	• May not meet needs of students • Noise level in classroom	Generally in class (can be pullout)
Teach and monitor	• Same standards/expectations for all students • Immediate reinforcement or help from monitor • Opportunity to do "kidwatching" (assessment) • Teachers can learn from each other (demonstration)	• One teacher may feel reduced to aide status • Lack of attention to specific needs of children	In class
Team teaching	• Same standards/expectations for all students • Uses strengths of both teachers • Teachers share responsibility • Students have opportunity to work with both teachers • Attention to individual/group needs or interests • Small-group work	• Lack of common philosophy or approach to instruction	Generally in class

provides a summary of the approaches and lists the advantages as well as potential problems of each (Bean, 2009).

Station or Center Teaching

Both reading specialists and teachers can develop stations or centers for teaching, based on the needs of the students and their own expertise or interests. Such stations can be used to provide independent work for some students while the specialist and teacher are teaching others, or a teacher, specialist, or instructional aide can be assigned to work with students at a center. The classroom teacher might be responsible for leading a center on writing, while the reading specialist guides a review center for phonics or vocabulary development. This enables both teachers to work with all students as they rotate through the centers, giving the reading specialist opportunities to learn more about what readers of all abilities can do, and also preventing students from thinking the reading specialist works with "struggling" readers only. Such centers can be used one or more times a week, thereby facilitating a flexible, heterogeneous grouping of students. Activities provided in the center can be such that students rotate through all centers (writing center, listening center), or tasks can be differentiated and students may be assigned to specific centers (phonics center for students who need additional practice, fluency center). The best centers include activities that provide for the differentiated needs of students and promote independent work. For older students, one center can be developed that uses Internet capabilities, if there is access to a computer in the classroom. One of the advantages of learning centers is that teachers can design activities for areas of literacy in which they have specific expertise or interest. They can also focus their energies on a specific area of reading, thus reducing preparation time. Although the development of activities for centers is time-consuming, once developed, they can be used at future times or in different classrooms. Moreover, activities can be shared across grade levels. Some key resources for center activities at the elementary levels include Florida Center for Reading Research (*www.fcrr.net*) and Diller's (2005) *Literacy Work Stations for Grades 3–6*. Many suggestions for learning centers can be found on the Internet (e.g., *www.teachersdiscovery.com*; *www.pininterest.com/learningcenters*). Centers can be useful at the middle and high school levels for promoting student engagement and motivation; they can be used effectively by content-area teachers who want to provide various interactive activities for students (See *http://frauspam.wikispaces.com/file/view/Learning+Centers+in+High+School.pdf* for an example of how a teacher of foreign language planned centers for her classroom.)

To implement centers effectively, teachers need to have excellent organizational and classroom management skills. Furthermore, teachers and specialists must work collaboratively. Some teachers may have difficulty with the noise level that occurs in their classrooms as the centers are functioning; hence the need for collaboration in establishing classroom rules for moving through the centers. In the beginning of the year, teachers and specialists may choose to use just one or two centers, helping students to understand how to function in such centers, the rules for moving from center to center, and so on.

Targeted Teaching

Classroom teachers who have responsibility for a large number of students may not be able to focus or target instruction to the extent necessary for some students to achieve success. The reading specialist can address specific needs of individual or small groups of students by selecting supplemental materials that provide for reinforcement of learning by adjusting the level of material used, practicing fluency with material at students' instructional level, or reteaching a skill or strategy. They may be using a specific reading program developed for students who are having difficulty learning to read (e.g., Wilson Reading System [Wilson, 1996], Reading Recovery [Clay, 1985], or Read 180 [Scholastic, 2002]). Students who need additional exposure to the vocabulary of a story (perhaps even before the story is introduced) may be grouped for instruction, while other students work on their writing projects or do independent reading. In one school district, reading specialists work with selected primary children individually for short 10-minute mini-lessons, asking them to read orally, working with a word or words that present difficulty for them. The specialist next provides opportunities for students to compose a sentence that can be read, cut into strips, reordered, reread, and taken home for practice (along with the book that has been read). In another school, in the intermediate grades, reading specialists work with small groups of students who need additional support with comprehension; their major focus is helping students understand and use specific comprehension strategies such as those described in *Explaining Reading: A Resource for Explicit Teaching of the Common Core Standards* (G. Duffy, 2014). At the high school level, reading specialists may work with students who need more help with study skills or with reading their science textbook. They may also be assigned to teach two or three classes of students who have been identified as needing reading support; these students most often are required to take this class, possibly in lieu of an elective or study hall. Although the reading specialist generally takes responsibility for targeted lessons, at times the classroom teacher may want to teach some of these lessons while the specialist works with other students.

Parallel Instruction

Parallel instruction provides opportunities for reducing the number of students in one group, thereby providing opportunities for differentiated pacing and feedback based on student needs. Both teachers teach the same lesson and the same content but with a different group of students. For example, both teachers may have students reread the story orally, but there may be much more scaffolding by the teacher working with students who are having difficulties reading that selection (e.g., teacher reads more of the selection while students listen, but offers opportunities for students to read aloud). Or, if there is a focus on comprehension, in one group the teacher may provide more opportunity for group discussion while in another group there might be more explicit instruction about a specific reading strategy (e.g., using prediction before, during, and after reading). Parallel instruction, done in the same classroom, can be difficult because of the noise level, with two direct lessons occurring at the same time. Although students seem to adjust nicely to the noise, teachers tell me they have difficulty adjusting to two simultaneous activities going on around them. There are times that the reading specialist can take the students to another room, if one is available.

Teach and Monitor

In this approach, one teacher presents the lesson while the other moves around the room, helping and supporting children who need assistance. As mentioned previously, it is this approach that has created frustration for some reading specialists who feel that they have become nothing more than aides in the classroom. When the reverse occurs and the reading specialist assumes the instructional role, a few classroom teachers may see this as a time for them to complete other tasks—marking papers or calling parents—causing concerns for reading specialists who notice this type of behavior. Nevertheless, there are many opportunities and advantages for such teaming in the classroom. For those working with young children, an extra pair of hands and eyes can be beneficial. For example, reading specialists may teach a lesson requiring first graders to manipulate letter cards as they "build words." The classroom teacher can monitor, making sure children have the right cards in the right place. Likewise, writing and reading workshops may require monitoring (and conferencing) by both teachers. Another advantage of this approach is that classroom teachers can observe the reading specialist using a specific strategy with which they may not be familiar. If the classroom teacher is teaching, the reading specialist can observe students with reading difficulties and note how they behave in a group setting ("kidwatching").

Team Teaching

Team teaching may include aspects of each of the models described above. In this model, both teachers plan how they will conduct instruction, whether for a particular lesson or over time. The previous scenario of the third-grade teacher and reading specialist (David and Shala, respectively) describe several approaches to collaboration. Both teachers have specific roles based on their expertise and interests. Each works with the entire group as well as with small groups or individuals within that group. Such collaboration requires time for planning, a good working relationship between the two individuals, and common beliefs/ideas about reading instruction and classroom management. At the secondary level, team teaching can be especially effective as a result of using the respective "expertise" of the content-area teacher and the reading specialist.

HELPING STUDENTS SUCCEED IN THE CLASSROOM AND DEVELOPING NEEDED SKILLS AND STRATEGIES

One of the dilemmas faced by reading specialists is that of determining where to put their focus: on helping students succeed in the classroom, or helping students to develop literacy skills/strategies that are areas of need? There is no simple answer. In fact, the only solution is that of doing *both*. Students who are reading below grade level and struggling with the material in their classrooms deserve to receive the help they need so that they can achieve some degree of success. This is especially important in today's schools, given the diversity in backgrounds, skills, and literacy levels of students. For example, English learners, with some additional support and scaffolding of vocabulary instruction, may be quite successful in a content-area classroom. Furthermore, with the emphasis on rigorous, high-level standards, students who struggle to read may need more explicit instruction when they are asked to read grade-level material, or when they are required to do close reading of text. At the same time, students can benefit from opportunities to work in small groups or individually, so that the reading specialist can review and reteach the specific skills with which these students are having difficulty. The What Works Clearinghouse (*http://ies.ed.gov/ncee/wwc*) reports the effectiveness of various intervention programs (e.g., Reading Recovery [Clay, 1985] or Read 180 [Scholastic, 2002]).

Focus on Classroom Success

The need for congruence between classroom and reading specialist instruction is recognized as important when working with struggling readers (Allington & Shake, 1986; Walp & Walmsley, 1989). Allington (1986) decried the fact that struggling readers, who are least able to make accommodations, may experience two separate and distinct instructional programs. Reading specialists can promote congruence by reteaching or reviewing a specific skill or strategy important for classroom performance. They can also provide additional practice with specific vocabulary words needed for a selection, guide students in repeated readings of selections, and help with specific assignments.

Although this emphasis is important in the primary grades, it is especially essential for students at upper levels where they are using reading to learn new concepts in various subject areas. What skills and abilities will help the middle school student read and comprehend his or her social studies textbook more effectively? What are the note-taking skills and review strategies that students in a biology class can use so that they are prepared for the unit test? When reading specialists address these questions, they most likely will work in the classroom with the content teacher to promote successful classroom learning.

Focus on Meeting Specific Needs

Students who have not learned various skills or strategies need to have opportunities to develop them; otherwise, they may always have difficulty with reading. Thus, for students in the intermediate grades who have weak phonic skills, targeting instruction on those skills can be extremely useful. Likewise, if students are assigned to read from textbooks that are above their reading level, they need many opportunities to read silently and orally in books that are at or slightly below their instructional level. In other words, although students can be provided with the scaffolding they need to read "difficult texts," they also need opportunities to read text at their instructional level as a means of developing fluency and gaining confidence in their ability to read (Allington, 2013; IRA, 2013; O'Connor et al., 2002). The bottom line is that struggling readers need opportunities to achieve success—to build on what they know and can do. The reading specialist who designs lessons that address the needs of students, provides them with opportunities to practice what they are learning, and creates a desire—not only to learn to read but to read independently—can make a difference in students' literacy learning.

Reading specialists at the secondary level may wish to organize a specific class in which they work with small groups of students who are struggling with reading. During that class, they can alleviate some of the difficulties the students are facing by reviewing or reteaching specific strategies or skills. For example, such students may benefit greatly from lessons that help them learn various Latin and Greek roots and how to improve their vocabulary with such knowledge. Such lessons should help students see the relationship between what they are learning in this small-group setting and the subjects they are taking. No matter the emphasis of the specialist, students must be helped to see the relevance of what they are learning and how it can help them to read effectively and achieve success in their classrooms.

Response to Intervention

What, Why, and How

A federal initiative that has had a major impact on how schools differentiate instruction for all students is RTI (sometimes thought of as response to *instruction*). This initiative, which emerged from the reauthorization of IDEA (IDEIA, 2004) has implications for how schools identify and work with students who are experiencing learning difficulties. The IRA, in its position statement about RTI, views it as a "comprehensive, systematic approach to teaching and learning designed to address language and literacy problems for all students" (2010a, p. 2). It is not a program nor does it promote one approach to teaching and learning. Rather, the goal of RTI is to reduce the number of students being identified as needing special education, by providing early identification of needs and immediate intervention. Mesmer and Mesmer (2009, p. 283) discuss five important steps in the RTI identification process: (1) establish benchmarks for literacy performance and appropriate assessment measures to identify students at risk; (2) implement scientifically based interventions for those who need them; (3) monitor the progress of students receiving intervention; (4) provide more intensive interventions for students who continue to need help and continue to monitor progress; and (5) if a student is not making progress, begin a decision-making process to determine eligibility for special education. Such a program requires involvement of all the professionals: classroom teachers, reading specialists, and special educators. It also requires schools to think differently about how reading instruction occurs in schools. Moreover, implementation can be more successful when there is a literacy team that leads the effort by discussing assessment results, scheduling, grouping, and instructional decisions (Bean & Lillenstein, 2012). Schools often use a multilevel model for differentiation similar to the three-tiered model developed at the University of Texas at Austin (2003). As illustrated in Figure 2.4, such a framework might include the following:

• *Tier 1:* high-quality comprehensive instruction at the classroom level that should meet the needs of most students in that classroom. Most frequently, schools adopt some sort of core program that is used by all students, although some schools have developed their own "home-grown" program. This instruction should include whole-class, small-group, and individual instruction and is generally provided by the classroom teacher. In the example above, Shala, the reading specialist, assists

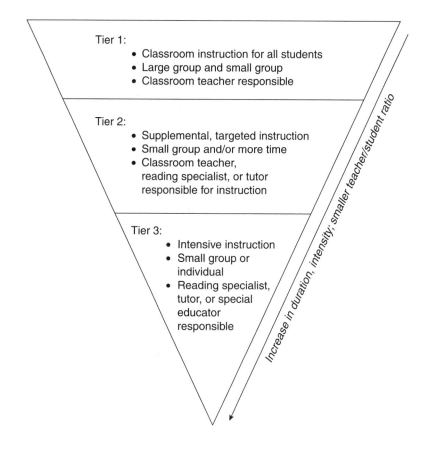

FIGURE 2.4. RTI framework.

teachers with their Tier 1 instruction by working in the classroom with them.

• *Tier 2:* supplemental instruction that can include small-group work and often additional time. This instruction is an extension of the Tier 1 instruction; it provides for needs-based, explicit and structured reteaching, and additional practice. Most often, additional time, often 30 minutes a day for 3–5 days a week, is provided for Tier 2 instruction. Schools plan for this instruction in different ways. In some schools, all students participate during Tier 2 time in small-group, differentiated instruction, with some students receiving interventions and others, enrichment activities. Students may be regrouped across classrooms based on need (e.g., group working with fluency, another with comprehension). In other schools, students who need Tier 2 instruction receive it during a nonreading period. Often this instruction is provided by a reading specialist or a tutor prepared to implement such instruction.

• *Tier 3:* intensive instruction that requires additional time, most often individual, or very small group. This instruction may be provided by the reading specialist or another professional who has specialized preparation. In some schools, Tier 3 instruction is provided by the special education teacher for students who are not responding to Tier 2 instruction.

All three tiers necessitate careful assessment of skills and progress monitoring to determine students' success and needs. Schools have developed problem-solving or literacy leadership teams to discuss assessment results and their implications for instruction. Assessment is discussed more thoroughly in Chapter 9.

Some Issues and Questions

Much has been learned about RTI and its potential for improving students' literacy learning, for helping schools identify at a younger age students with possible reading problems and providing the necessary interventions to prevent further difficulties, and ultimately reducing the number of students identified as needing special education. However, there are still some unknowns and a need for additional research about what type of framework works best in what situations. Important questions include, What sorts of Tier 2 instruction are best for students? How long should students receive Tier 2 instruction before being recommended for Tier 3 instruction? Does the number of tiers make a difference? For example, how soon should students be recommended for special education placement? As Shanahan (2008) indicates, "there are lots of variants in what counts as RTI. . . . There are three-tiered RTI models and four-tiered models, and even with those models not everyone agrees as to what the different tiers may refer to" (p. 106). A question also arises as to whether these tiers are linear, that is, must a student go through each tier, or can a student go from Tier 1 to Tier 3, skipping Tier 2? In other words, is important support being denied students because they must go through each of the tiers before receiving the intensive instruction needed by them?

Another important question addresses the use of RTI in middle and high schools: What sorts of programming is possible at these levels for schools wishing to use an RTI model for these adolescent readers? More work has been done at the elementary level, although some secondary schools are attempting to use RTI as a framework for supporting their struggling readers (H. Duffy, 2009; Samuels, 2009). One key resource for those working at the middle and high school levels is the National Center on Response to Instruction (*www.rti4success.org*). At that site, there are suggestions and resources for all levels, and there is also a section that provides many resources focused on RTI at the secondary level.

What should be obvious is that classroom teachers alone—even the very best—would be hard-pressed to meet the expectations of this approach. The demands are great in terms of assessment and instruction. Reading specialists as well as school leadership must become familiar with the goals of RTI so that there is a clear understanding of what it means, and does not mean. As stated by Allington (2006), some schools think they can address RTI by purchasing three different reading programs, with students at Tier 2 participating in two of the programs, and students identified as needing Tier 3 instruction, actually participating in three programs! Such an approach flies in the face of what is known about congruent instruction. Allington suggests that the keys to successful implementation of RTI requires schools to build in additional time and/or more personalized instruction to improve upon or extend classroom reading instruction. Moreover, RTI requires experts such as reading specialists who can "identify just where the reader has gotten off-track and then . . . design instruction that moves the reader back onto an accelerated track of development" (p. 20). This does not negate the possibility that students may benefit from a special (and different program), especially those at Tier 3. This type of intervention would reflect the notions in the IRA position statement *Making a Difference Means Making It Different* (2000a). But if such programs are used, "there should be clear articulation about how such an approach complements or reinforces what is being taught in the classroom" (Bean, 2008, p. 20).

One final question about RTI relates to how it "fits" with the current emphasis on CCSS or the high-level college and career standards adopted in many states. Specifically, the standards identify or establish outcomes, that is, the knowledge and skills expectations for all students; they do not, however, provide information about how schools can address the needs of diverse learners (e.g., English language learners [ELLs], special education, high poverty). By using an RTI framework, schools can determine what students have and have not learned, and the instruction and interventions necessary for them to achieve the expectations of the standards.

In the following section, I discuss an issue that has generated controversy in the past for reading specialists, that is, whether instruction should be in the classroom of the students or in pullout situations. Given the RTI initiative, having multiple teachers in the classroom has become more accepted, although actual implementation is still problematic. Most frequently, there is a need for both in-class and pullout instruction, and determination of the location of supplemental and intensive instruction—as well as who teaches those students—is dependent on the context of the school, including its human resources and the needs of struggling readers.

PULLOUT OR IN-CLASS INSTRUCTION: IS THAT THE QUESTION?

In the recent national survey of reading specialists (Bean, Kern, et al., 2015), we found that pullout instruction was present to the same extent as it was in the earlier survey (Bean, Cassidy, et al., 2002), that is, about 40% of the reading specialists indicated delivering instruction outside the classroom. It appears that schools now recognize that both pullout instruction and in-class instruction have their merits and both are used in schools. In-class instruction is useful because it provides help to students in their own classrooms, supporting the notion of inclusion. At the same time, the success that has been attributed to various tutoring programs, such as Reading Recovery (Clay, 1985) and the tutoring component of Success for All (Slavin et al., 1996), has led to an increase in programs in which students are tutored individually and away from their classrooms.

In this section, I discuss the benefits and limitations of each setting and what is needed if each is to work. Table 2.2 identifies bridges and barriers of in-class, pullout, and combination models as described by principals, teachers, and reading specialists (Bean et al., 1995). The benefits of these models can be thought about in three ways: What are the advantages for students? What are the advantages for teachers in terms of implementation? and How does each model improve classroom instruction as a whole?

TABLE 2.2. Instructional Setting: Identification of Bridges and Barriers

Setting	Principals	Reading specialists	Classroom teachers
		Bridges	
In class	• *Provides more opportunities for collaboration, cooperation, and communication.* • Provides less isolation for students.	• *Provides more opportunities for collaboration, cooperation, and communication.* • Could serve more students.	• *Provides more opportunities for collaboration, cooperation, and communication.* • Provides congruence. • Discourages the labeling of children.
Pullout	• *Provides students with a place and opportunities to feel special.* • Serves more students.	• *Provides a special environment for young students.* • Requires collaboration and cooperation to be successful. • Provides positive learning experiences in small groups.	• *Provides a comfortable environment in which students can try new strategies.* • Provides opportunities for students to develop positive self-esteem and self-confidence. • Provides special/individualized attention for students.
Combination	• *Provides the flexibility to do what is best for the students.*	• *Provides flexibility of setting when students' needs are better met outside of the classroom.* • Provides flexibility for personality and philosophical differences between specialist and teacher.	• *Provides flexibility to change settings when necessary.* • Mirrors the needs of the people and children involved.
		Barriers	
In class	• *A reading specialist acting in the role of an aide.* • Reading specialist permitted to work with Chapter 1 students only.	• *A reading specialist acting in the role of an aide.* • Increases the distractibility of students. • Collaboration, cooperation, and communication are difficult.	• *A reading specialist acting in the role of an aide.* • Team teaching is difficult. • Encourages a pullout model within the classroom.

(*continued*)

TABLE 2.2. *(continued)*

			• Improper scheduling provides no time for cooperative planning.
		• Provides little flexibility for personality and philosophical differences between specialist and teacher.	
Pullout	• Reading specialist's room is in an undesirable facility. • Could serve fewer students.	• Teacher penalizes student for going to Chapter 1—such as making up work during recess.	• Resentment on the part of students for being pulled out— they miss a lot of classwork. • Does not fit integrated approach. • Improper scheduling provides no time for cooperative planning. • Promotes labeling of students.
Combination	• None expressed.	• None expressed.	• None expressed.

Note. Italicized text indicates trends across groups. From Bean, Trovato, and Hamilton (1995, p. 211). Copyright 1995 by Taylor & Francis. Reprinted by permission.

In-Class Models

Benefits

In-class instruction is much more efficient in that students are not pulled from their classroom, so they lose neither time (for travel to instruction) nor focus (the emphasis is on what is needed in the classroom). Furthermore, there may be less stigma when students are not pulled from their classrooms; in other words, students are not identified as "different" from others. Additionally, students who are not targeted for assistance also may benefit from the instruction occurring in those classrooms.

When an in-class program is working effectively, teachers often feel that they learn from each other and that the quality of instruction is greater as a result of the sharing of ideas and materials. Some instruction is much more effective with two teachers in the classroom—for example, writing or reading conferences, monitoring work of young children who are using manipulatives, and content teacher and specialist co-teaching to address the literacy and content needs of students at the secondary level. By working in the classroom, the reading specialist can observe how the targeted students perform in this setting.

Over time, communication and collaboration between the two teachers occur more naturally, with each having a better understanding of the other's expectations. And importantly, the reading specialist and teacher accept responsibility for the reading performance of all students in the classroom. The emphasis during the past several years on the use of data to make instructional decisions has led to even more emphasis on the in-class model, with various educators (e.g., reading specialist, special educator, paraprofessionals) present in the classroom to support the classroom teacher in differentiating instruction for students.

Potential Problems

Given the benefits discussed above, why have in-class programs in some schools been problematic? As mentioned previously, past traditions and our current model of schooling have not promoted such collaboration and shared teaching. We are more accustomed to the traditional model in which each teacher is responsible for his or her classroom. As we discuss each of these potential problems, we consider them in relation to students, teachers, and classroom instruction.

Some students may have difficulty learning in a whole-class setting and may need the privacy and quiet afforded by a pullout model. They may also need more intensive work in a one-to-one situation. Likewise, the in-class setting may not afford opportunities to work on the skills/strategies that particular students need; rather, the focus may be on helping students to achieve in that particular classroom. Moreover, students may still be identified as "different"—especially if *pullout* has simply been changed to *pull aside* or *pull back*!

Probably the greatest difficulty with in-class programs is that of differing and conflicting philosophies of teaching or even classroom management. Some teachers do not appreciate (and cannot tolerate) the noise and activity that an additional teacher brings. Neither teacher may have the knowledge and skills necessary for undertaking such a venture. This problem is especially likely to occur when mandates are issued and teachers and specialists are thrust into such programs without the necessary professional development. There are also concerns that reading specialists are not used appropriately or are assigned to so many classrooms and students that they cannot work efficiently or provide *enough* support to students.

Finally, some classrooms are too small or contain so many students that the specialist cannot work effectively. In some schools, reading specialists are not provided with a place to work effectively with students in the classrooms or they find themselves moving from one section of the classroom to another, trying to find a place in which to conduct their lessons.

Critical Factors for a Successful In-Class Program

1. Teachers and reading specialists have consistently stressed the importance of scheduling common planning time so that they can implement a successful in-class program. Although some reading specialists and teachers, over time, learn to plan effectively via written communication or "on the fly," these approaches are not as effective as two or more teachers sitting down and planning together.

2. Both the reading specialist and the teacher must be willing to "share" the students. This willingness occurs only when the two have respect for each other and are able to agree on, and enforce, consistent rules for classroom management and student behavior. The two teachers must also talk openly with each other about their beliefs and instructional practices. Such conversations can lead to successful compromises regarding how the in-class model operates.

Pullout Programs

Benefits

One of the benefits of pullout instruction is that students, when pulled, get the specific instruction that they need (e.g., strategies for improving their comprehension skills, word-attack skills) in a small-group or individual setting, where they can focus on what they are learning. There is evidence that individual tutoring (Pikulski, 1994; Wasik & Slavin, 1993) and small-group instruction are beneficial to students (Elbaum, Vaughn, Hughes, & Moody, 2000; Manset-Williamson & Nelson; 2005; Sackor, 2001) and that such instruction, when provided by a well-prepared teacher, can improve students' reading achievement. Classroom teachers may feel that they can better focus their instruction to address the needs of the remaining students. Reading specialists can focus their instruction; they do not have to worry about creating a distraction in the classroom and they have the materials they need to implement their lessons.

Potential Problems

One of the criticisms of the pullout model is that students lose time as they move from one room to another. One reading specialist commented: "I've had to develop an incentive program to encourage children to arrive at my room on time. It's amazing how they can dawdle as they move through the halls, stopping at the water fountain, the bulletin board, or just wandering along." Another criticism is the stigma that occurs when students leave their classmates to receive special instruction. At times, classroom teachers have been critical of the pullout model, feeling that students are missing important instruction, or disliking the disruption that occurs when students leave or enter the classroom. The anecdote in Chapter 1 (pp. 4–5) speaks to teacher concerns about pullout programs. Reading specialists too may feel that they are less aware of what is going on in the classroom, both in terms of how specific students perform and how teachers are presenting the literacy curriculum to their students. Finally, especially at the secondary level, students may have little success in transferring what they are learning in these pullout classes to the work that they do in the content area.

Salinger, Zmach Tanenbaum, Thomsen, and Lefsky (2008), in discussing the impact of several intervention programs at the ninth-grade level, found limited results and identified several difficulties with such programs, including problems with overreliance on commercial programs. Research about intervention or pullout programs at the secondary level, as well as research about programs in which content teachers work more closely with specialists or reading coaches, is a definite need.

Critical Factors for a Successful Pullout Model

In order for pullout models to work, there must be careful planning and collaboration between the reading specialist and classroom teachers. Reading specialists should be aware of what is occurring in classrooms, even though they are teaching students away from the classroom. One suggestion is that reading specialists spend some time in the classroom, observing students and teacher instruction. This experience provides the reading specialist with a better sense of how his or her students perform and behave when in a large-group or classroom setting. Moreover, it should be clear as to whether the instruction received in the pullout setting is supplemental or serves as the core program for students.

IDEAS TO FOSTER EFFECTIVE COLLABORATION IN INSTRUCTIONAL ROLES

Regardless of whether the reading specialist works in a pullout setting or goes into the classroom (or both), the following ideas have been helpful to reading specialists in fostering effective collaboration.

1. *Time.* Teachers appreciate the fact that the reading specialist is in their classroom as scheduled (even if the teachers are not quite ready for him or her). In talking with teachers about reading specialists, one of their primary complaints was that specialists did not arrive in their classroom when expected. Arriving and leaving on time are critical, as is adhering to the schedule when taking students from the classroom.

2. *Be prepared!* Have everything needed to teach a lesson, including magic markers, scissors, dictionaries, books for practice, and so on. If going into the classroom, do not assume that the teacher will have the material needed—or be willing or able to take the time to find it. Reading specialists who teach in classrooms have developed ingenious systems for organizing and carting materials, from using luggage with wheels to movable carts to milk carton containers.

3. *Discuss and establish responsibility.* The reading specialist and classroom teacher must decide early in the process who will be responsible for giving grades, writing report cards, and making telephone calls to parents about student performance.

4. *Offer to help.* As the reading specialist with expertise, think of ways to be helpful in the classroom. Perhaps the teacher is covering a special unit in which students need to take notes—this would be a great time to give a mini-lesson on note taking to the entire class. Or the teacher may be doing the midyear assessments with his or her students and needs some help with students who have been absent.

5. *Meet your commitments.* Teachers have difficulty when reading specialists make changes in their plans, even if there are legitimate reasons for such changes (e.g., attend an Instructional Support Team meeting to discuss the needs of a specific student or a meeting requested by the principal). These unforeseeable occasions do happen, but to the degree possible, reading specialists should alert the teacher as soon as they can and make arrangements to reschedule.

6. *Be flexible!* Although the reading specialist may be on time and prepared, teachers and their classes may not be ready or even present. Assemblies, fire drills, health examinations, and many other events compel teachers to change or adjust their plans. These occurrences are, of course, frustrating to the reading specialist but may not be avoidable. *Adjusting* is the only helpful response. If some change needs to be made in the lesson (e.g., the teacher did not complete yesterday's lesson and wants to work with the entire group), the reading specialist can volunteer to assist by helping the students who may have difficulties completing the task or try to rearrange his or her schedule so that the plans can be implemented at a different time. Or it may be a time that the reading specialist returns to his or her office or room to do some additional planning, or to assess a child who is new to the school.

7. *Discuss the progress of the students with whom you are working.* This is especially important when working with students in a pullout setting. Let teachers know what students are learning and the success they are having. Such conversations help teachers better understand the

needs of these students, and may open the door to more extended discussions about what can be done in the classroom to facilitate learning.

READING SPECIALISTS AT THE MIDDLE
AND SECONDARY LEVELS

Reed, Wexler, and Vaughn (2012) noted key differences between RTI at the elementary and the secondary levels. First, there is more of a focus on remediation rather than prevention, given that many of these students have already been identified as needing support. Second, there may not be a need for universal screening, given the available extant data that can be used for making instructional decisions. In other words, more time can be devoted to instruction rather than to assessment. Moreover, students can quickly be assigned to less or more intensive remediation programs. At the same time, these authors indicate the need for ongoing follow-up and progress monitoring.

I now describe some important ways of working in RTI programs at the secondary levels. First, the secondary role may require more of a focus on supporting the instructional efforts of content teachers, that is, co-teaching with teachers of social studies, science, and math, as well as English language arts. This role requires reading specialists to have a solid understanding of disciplinary literacy and how to work with content-area teachers to teach students "the language and ways of reading and writing in each of the particular disciplines . . . the history teacher understands the particular ways that language and text 'works' in the field of history" (Anders & Clift, 2012, p. 175). In fact, the focus on disciplinary literacy requires a critical shift that asks reading specialists to translate the generic literacy practices with which many are familiar (e.g., anticipation guides, graphic organizers) into more discipline-specific variations (Messina, 2013). Several key resources include *Adolescent Literacy* (Ippolito, Steele, & Samson, 2012) and *Developing Readers in the Academic Disciplines* (Buehl, 2011).

Second, reading specialists may be assigned to teach small groups of students who are struggling with reading, perhaps using an RTI framework. However, as stated previously, such scheduling is not easy at the upper levels. Secondary schools have been creative in their efforts to develop and implement RTI. Some have adopted intensive programs for students (e.g., Read 180 [Scholastic, 2002] or Language! [Green, 1996]). Other schools have developed tutoring centers or provide after-school support while others have focused their efforts on providing professional development, often with coaching, to help content-area teachers provide high-quality instruction. What has been learned is the need for school leadership and professional development for all involved, and an ongoing commitment to meeting student needs. But there is still much to learn about the implementation of RTI at the secondary level, and the extent to which such efforts are effective.

SUMMARY

Although most reading specialists have instructional responsibilities, the way in which they fulfill them may vary. One key to enacting an effective instructional role is collaboration. Reading specialists must know how to work collaboratively with their colleagues to ensure effective instruction for students. There are many different ways of working collaboratively, some of which are more effective when working in the classroom and others more appropriate in pullout settings. Deciding where to work (in class or pullout) is not the key question about instruction for struggling readers. Rather, the reading specialist with teachers and the principal must think about and identify instructional goals for students and how best to achieve those goals. Given this information, schedules will need to be developed that enable reading specialists to best meet the needs of students in the specific context or climate of the schools in which they work. Moreover, the increased emphasis on RTI as a framework for providing differentiated instruction to meet the needs of all students has generated the need for reading specialists to work even more collaboratively with their colleagues in planning and implementing effective instructional programs for all students. Developing and implementing such a schedule is described more fully in Chapter 3.

ADDITIONAL READINGS

Bean, R. M., & Lillenstein, J. (2012). Response to intervention and the changing roles of schoolwide personnel. *The Reading Teacher, 65*(7), 491–501.—After visiting five schools implementing RTI, Bean and Lillenstein describe ways in which roles of specialized literacy personnel have changed, with much more emphasis on collaborative decision making and shared leadership.

International Reading Association. (2010). *Response to intervention: Guiding principles for educators: A position statement.* Newark, DE: Author.—This position statement provides information about RTI, what it is, its guiding principles, and supporting resources and references.

Shanahan, T., & Shanahan, C. (2012). Teaching disciplinary literacy to adolescents: Rethinking content-area literacy. In J. Ippolito, J. I. Steele, & J. F. Samson (Eds.), *Adolescent literacy* (pp. 40–59). Cambridge, MA: Harvard

Educational Press.—In this chapter, the authors discuss the importance of content-area teachers helping adolescents move beyond basic and intermediate reading skills to more discipline-specific reading skills.

Reflections

1. What do you think are the skills and abilities that reading specialists need if they are to work effectively in the classroom? In pullout settings? Both?
2. What skills and abilities do teachers need to work with reading specialists? In what ways are the skills and abilities needed by reading specialists and teachers the same? Different?
3. What types of lessons or instruction would work best with each of the approaches to collaborative teaching?

Activities

1. Observe a reading specialist in an in-class setting. Write a description of what he or she and the classroom teacher are doing. Which approach or approaches to collaborative teaching are used? What are your responses to these approaches?
2. Observe a reading specialist teaching students in a pullout setting. Write a description of what he or she is doing with students. (Be sure to ask the specialist how he or she made decisions about the instruction.)
3. In small groups, discuss the vignette below, reflecting on what Mark brings to the reading specialist role; identify three important "take-aways" from that vignette. Share work of small groups with the whole class.

Some questions to think about:

What lessons can be learned about the role of the reading specialist from this vignette?

In what ways does Mark serve as a leader?

What questions come to mind after reading this vignette?

MARK: EDUCATION AS MY SECOND CAREER

I had been an attorney before and largely enjoyed it. After a number of years, however, I found myself questioning whether the practice of law was for me. Idealistic as it may sound, I wanted to help people. Was practicing law allowing me to do that? And if so, was I helping those most in need? So I became an elementary teacher.

During the first 2 years as a teacher, I grew a bit frustrated watching some students struggle. As important as their time in the general classroom was, it didn't always seem to be meeting their needs. Some students were called on to read text at levels too difficult and they never seemed to catch up with their peers. Instruction was geared toward where the students were supposed to be, instead of where they were. As such, it was not very effective. It mattered enormously to me that I be effective. And so I became a reading specialist and now work in a charter school in Pittsburgh. Approximately 98% of the students are of color and approximately 80% are from low-income families. I work with all of the K–5 classrooms.

My two major responsibilities, for which I am assisted by a full-time paraprofessional, are interventions and organizing and maintaining small-group guided oral reading. Small-group reading, which is in addition to classroom reading instruction, involves all students in second through fifth grades. Over time, we have developed a system in which each class is divided into four groups (or a grade that has two classes, into seven groups) and, in the overwhelming majority of cases, the group is led by an adult—either the classroom teacher, classroom aide, my assistant, or me. Even specialty teachers participate.

Decisions about how to group students into reading groups and about who to work with during interventions are largely informed by data. We use a combination of DIBELS and AIMSweb assessments administered to all students at the beginning, middle, and end of the year, and on a more regular basis (i.e., monthly, for those who struggle). In addition to using data to make decisions, I take into account comments by teachers and my own observations. At the beginning of the year, the classroom teacher and I work together to divide the class into groups. Occasional adjustment of students in groups may take place during the school year.

Guided oral reading is the core instructional component of these reading groups. Groups are scheduled for 25 minutes, 4 days per week (3 days in the case of fifth grade). Group leaders are instructed that during small-group reading, students must be reading, discussing, or writing in response to what they have read. No worksheets! During this period, I always lead one of the groups myself, usually a group of strugglers. Reading groups take up most of my morning schedule.

There are primarily two sets of materials used for reading groups. First, the reading series provides leveled weekly readers aligned with the week of instruction, as well as second-grade decodable readers that focus on one or two specific phonic elements. In general, strugglers and younger students are more likely to use materials from the series. These materials allow for much rereading of texts, a practice supported by research and also by the Pennsylvania Core Standards.

In addition, we have gradually acquired, over 16 years, a large number of chapter books ranging greatly in subject matter, genre, and readability. Older and more advanced students usually read chapter books appropriate for their abilities and interest. In all cases students are asked questions about what they are reading. Questions tend to be open-ended to help students develop a coherent understanding of the text. I provide most of the materials to each of the group leaders, except on the occasion when a classroom teacher wants to take on that job. We read a balance of fiction and nonfiction. For nonfiction, we often read from the Who Is/Who Was series, biographies of individuals and groups. We also read from many different fiction texts. Among my favorites are *Holes* by James Sachar, *Because of Winn-Dixie* by Kate DiCamillo, *The Watsons Go to Birmingham—1963* by Christopher Paul Curtis, and *Danny, the Champion of the World* by Roald Dahl. I am also a fan of the My Weird School series by Dan Gutman, involving the protagonist, third grader, A. J., and his nemesis, Andrea. Also, I have rewritten about 10 books as Readers' Theater plays. I generally have the group read the entire book and then reread the play version. I do this because the students really enjoy these books and because I know that repetition will enhance word recognition and fluency. This strategy can be used with any chapter book that contains a lot of dialogue and the approximate right number of characters. Retyping is time-consuming, but then I have the script as a resource forever.

I work closely with all K–5 teachers and assistants, along with my own assistant, and the specialty teachers who help with reading groups. I provide and organize almost all of the resources for reading groups. When group leaders are using 1- or 2-day decodable readers or leveled books, I e-mail a weekly schedule to everyone involved. When group leaders are using chapter books, from time to time I check in with them. Students in struggling groups alternate approximately once per month with me and once per month with their own classroom teacher so that both of us are directly working with them on a regular basis.

My other primary responsibility is interventions for struggling students, which often take place in the afternoon. My assistant and I implement interventions in kindergarten through fifth grade. Again, we use the results of assessments to make decisions about students with whom to work. Monthly progress monitoring results occasionally help us "graduate" students from interventions and bring in new students who have slipped. In kindergarten, interventions are generally one-on-one. From first through fifth grades, interventions are usually in groups of two or three, depending on scheduling issues and the number of students per grade needing help in the allotted time. Readers' Theater generally works better with slightly larger groups.

Leadership

My role in the school is an interesting one. I'm not exactly a teacher, not exactly an administrator. But I do have leadership responsibilities. I am in regular contact with all of the teachers and staff who work with K–5 students and/or lead a reading group (currently, 26). I send out assessment data to leaders the moment I have complied it, and talk with them about the implications for instruction and groupings. When necessary, I try to find some time at the beginning of the day, during their prep periods, or at the end of the day to touch base. When a significant issue arises, I set meetings with grade levels and promise that no meeting will last more than 15 minutes. From a time-management perspective, I keep in mind that balancing the time I work with teachers and the time I work with students is an ongoing issue. It is a fast-paced, rapidly changing day filled with emotional highs and the occasional low.

I believe that, particularly for newer teachers, I have had a positive impact. The degree and intensity with which I am sought out by teachers varies. Some teachers feel comfortable talking with me at great length about individual students. Others are comfortable knowing that I am available as a resource to answer questions about instruction in general. All teachers interact with me about the students from their classrooms who I work with directly. Many appear grateful that I have helped to provide clear pathways for their instruction and scheduling. A few teachers share their own ideas for whole-class instruction with me ahead of time and ask for feedback. On a few occasions, I go into a general classroom to model a lesson or provide a mini-lesson simply because it's more efficient to do so in a whole class than with a few students at a time. I coach first-grade teachers in phonics and reading of decodable text for 30 minutes per week, and work with kindergarten teachers more informally. In short, in addition to overseeing reading groups and providing intervention, I support teachers in a variety of ways, large and small.

Success!

I particularly enjoy working with younger students because they usually make tangible progress with intervention. For example, I worked with one particular student one-on-one the entire kindergarten year, focusing mostly on phonics. Earlier in the year, she had showed some spark, but by the middle of the year, she seemed to reach a plateau. She was not sounding out words and reading words as successfully as I had hoped. I knew, and formal assessment results started to demonstrate, that she was not progressing as quickly as I had initially expected.

We continued on with an emphasis on phonics and reading text at her level. I had occasion to be able to work with her a bit over the summer after kindergarten. By then, the spark seemed to have returned. She developed the ability to read words (at least most CVC words) accurately and automatically. A casual observer would likely not see her as a struggling reader anymore. What I was particularly pleased about was that she recognized there were some words she knew so well she could simply read as units, but knew to take the time to sound out other words, when she had to.

What, if anything, did I do right? I think the short answer is that she and I simply stuck with it. I continued the instruction, did not allow frustration to derail her or me, and eventually she began to display the success and confidence that she had lost in the middle of her kindergarten year, showing big improvement in accurate and automatic word recognition with accompanying progress reading text. There really is no magic bullet. It's simply good instruction, ample time on task, a positive attitude and, perhaps, a dash of luck.

MARK BECK, MEd
Elementary Reading Specialist
Manchester Academic Charter School
Pittsburgh, Pennsylvania

CHAPTER THREE

The Instructional Role

Initiating, Implementing, and Evaluating

Key Questions

- What are the factors reading specialists need to consider when implementing a supplemental instructional program?
- What makes scheduling a complex task for the reading specialist?
- In what ways do the instructional roles of reading specialists at the elementary, middle, and high school differ? In what ways do these differences require different knowledge and skill sets?

Chapter 2 provided a broad overview of the instructional role, focusing on the need for collaboration, approaches to collaborative teaching, and the strengths and limitations of two settings for instruction (i.e., in class and pullout). It also discussed the RTI initiative and what it means for reading specialists. This chapter explores ideas and issues that reading specialists need to address at various stages (e.g., starting a new supplemental program, developing and scheduling a program at the beginning of the year, ongoing implementation issues, and evaluating results of the supplemental program). In order to develop and implement an effective program, reading specialists need to understand (1) the culture of the school, (2) the importance of congruence between their instruction and that of the classroom teacher, and (3) approaches to scheduling that permit effective use of their time. The instructional role of reading specialists at the primary or beginning reading level, intermediate or middle school level, and the high school level is examined, and the need for obtaining feedback or evaluating the supplemental program is explored.

DEVELOPING THE PROGRAM

In most instances, newly hired reading specialists step into a program that is already developed and most likely understood by faculty at the school. Reading specialists, in fact, are often funded by Title I funds (No Child Left Behind [NCLB], 2001), which is the largest source of federal funding for elementary and secondary education. In 2009–2010, more than 56,000 public schools used Title I funds and 21 million students were served (U.S. Department of Education, 2000b). Eligibility and implementation requirements provide schools with specifics about implementation and evaluation of these Title I programs. However, there are situations in which reading specialists do have responsibilities for changing or modifying the existing program. This has certainly occurred during the past several years as schools have implemented approaches that address RTI guidelines. Also, reading specialists often are involved in developing a schedule for themselves at the beginning of the year—a schedule that enables them to see eligible students in an appropriate context and have time to plan with and support teachers.

Before reading specialists can establish their schedules, however, they must have access to the schedules that have been developed for grade levels or teachers with whom they will work. In many schools, reading specialists work directly with the principal or Title I coordinator to develop this school schedule; if so, then they may be able to provide input about how the schedule affects their ability to work with students, or at least, have an awareness of what the parameters are in terms of their own scheduling.

Getting the Evidence

Regardless of the type of program under consideration by the school administration, reading specialists and others associated with possible changes should have an understanding of the research and the requirements of the funding stream for the supplemental or compensatory program. It is also helpful if they share this information with classroom teachers who will be directly affected by the program. The information discussed in Chapter 2 should help reading specialists think about the student population in their school and the advantages and limitations of pullout and in-class programs. In order to develop these compensatory or supplemental programs, evidence is needed about effective literacy instruction and also about assessment, which tools to use, how to interpret for instructional decision making (see Chapter 9), and how to plan to meet student needs in a specific school or context.

Sharing the Evidence

As mentioned above, classroom teachers should be involved in the decision-making process. They should have opportunities to read the literature and talk with their colleagues and the reading specialists about the specialized instructional support program. Getting teacher input about concerns and being receptive to their suggestions will ensure a greater possibility of teacher buy in and receptivity. When schools are considering program changes, it is helpful for reading specialists and teacher leaders to visit programs in other schools. The opportunity to see a program in operation can often alleviate any fears or anxiety that teachers and specialists may have about programmatic changes.

Getting Started

If there are major changes in any program, the best way to start is "slowly." One can begin by recruiting teachers at a specific grade level to work with the reading specialist in a different way. For example, given the current emphasis on high-level, rigorous standards, and the need for a curriculum that provides opportunities for inquiry and integration of learning experiences, a team of second-grade teachers might decide to use its core program differently (at least for one unit). They may try to relate the selections in the unit about animals to what students are learning in social studies, science, and math, and to provide more writing, listening, and speaking experiences. They may require additional reading of informational text or ask students to write a short "research report." The reading specialist may work in a slightly different fashion with this grade-level team than with other teams. Over time, it may be that teachers at additional grade levels, with the leadership of the principal, decide to move in this direction. The pilot with one grade level offers opportunities for teachers and the reading specialist to identify and solve any problems with the new program design.

In recent years, a combination of in-class and pullout programs has become much more prevalent and teachers are more accustomed to having another adult in the classroom. Yet, some teachers are still uncomfortable with having another adult in the classroom and to be effective, reading specialists will need to function in different ways in different classrooms. Different strokes for different folks! Some compare working in the classroom to a marriage—there must be give and take, compromise—and the recognition that progress does not occur in a straight line! There will be highs and lows! When working with teachers to implement an in-class program, reading specialists can establish readiness by giving teachers choices about how the program will function, what part of the reading block the reading specialist will support, and exactly how the reading specialist will support instruction (e.g., working with a small group of struggling readers during the rereading time; preparing specific activities for use at a learning center and then being responsible for that center during instruction). Also, if working in the classroom is somewhat new to teachers and to the reading specialist, starting with volunteers is an option. Often, when teachers see that the program is an effective one for students, they become more comfortable with the proposed change.

As mentioned, given the focus on accountability and RTI, teachers are becoming more accustomed to working collaboratively with many different support personnel, not only with the reading specialist but with special educators, volunteers, and paraprofessionals. Therefore, teachers tend to be more accepting or at least resigned to the fact that their students may receive instruction from other adults.

Ongoing Professional Development

Providing professional development for classroom teachers and reading specialists about how to collaborate and to work effectively in the classroom can be especially helpful. The school district may choose to bring in someone from outside the district who is familiar with the work of reading specialists or the importance of collaboration in providing for the instructional needs of all students. Or a reading specialist and a classroom teacher who are working together could discuss and share with other teachers the work that they are doing in the school. They may also invite other classroom teachers to observe them as they are working together in the classroom. Teachers may be asked to read pertinent materials, for example, *Response to Intervention: A Position Statement* (IRA, 2010a); in this document, which describes important notions about RTI, there is a strong statement about the importance of collaboration. The document also calls for a school-level decision-making team that includes teachers and specialized personnel, such as the reading specialist. It also indicates the importance of providing adequate time for communication and coordination to ensure the development of a coherent, comprehensive literacy program. Other possible articles that discuss collaboration between reading specialists and teachers (e.g., Ogle & Fogelberg [2001] or Bean [2001]) provide ideas to help develop a deeper understanding of ways to promote a culture of collaboration.

Regardless of whether specialists are responsible for developing a new program, working with a school administrator who is undertaking such an effort, or working in an established program, they must consider the culture of the school and classrooms, the need for congruence between classroom instruction and special reading programs, and scheduling that maximizes the use of their time. These areas are discussed in the next sections.

THE CULTURE OF THE SCHOOL AND CLASSROOMS

Given that reading specialists generally work with many different teachers in a school, they need to become familiar with the school culture (i.e., its norms or ways of being). What are teachers expected to do relative to bus and lunch duty? In what ways do teachers share materials or resources? Reading specialists should also develop a working relationship with the principal, given the key leadership role of that position. This may mean meeting with the principal on a regular basis, perhaps once a week, or sending him or her a weekly summary of work being done with teachers. It also means communicating with principals about any issues or concerns relative to scheduling, students, assessment results, and so on. A lack of understanding or agreement between the reading specialist and the principal regarding the specialist's role can create serious problems. In Reading First in Pennsylvania, reading specialists serving in the role of literacy coaches indicated that they were successful in their roles only if a principal understood and supported them in their efforts (Carroll, 2007; Zigmond & Bean, 2008). For example, the principal who lacks knowledge about the importance of collaboration may not arrange schedules that facilitate planning between specialists and classroom teachers. Or a principal who asks reading specialists to evaluate or supervise teachers, especially those who are experiencing some teaching difficulties, may generate situations that limit the specialists' effectiveness in working collaboratively with teachers. In a study of schools implementing RTI effectively, we found that strong principal leadership was essential and required the principal to have an understanding of RTI and be involved in implementation efforts by attending meetings of the leadership team, discussing results of assessment data with literacy leaders, and in general, supporting the efforts to differentiate instruction for all students (Bean & Lillenstein, 2012). Most of all, principals were responsible for setting the tone, that is, establishing a climate that provided opportunities for school personnel to collaborate, one in which they felt safe in making their concerns known, and one in which their views were listened to with respect.

Reading specialists too should listen to and respect the views of teachers. Teachers who are not accustomed to an in-class approach may not be receptive initially to the presence of the reading specialist in their classrooms. Teachers may not understand how they can or should function when there is another adult in the classroom. Some teachers have difficulty "giving up" their students; they are accustomed to providing all of the instruction in the classroom. I am reminded of one teacher who told me how she planned for a specific story (one that she loved), including the "costume" she wore to introduce the story and the dramatic entrance that she made! Lacking an understanding of how an in-class model might work, she was distraught to think that some of her students would not have an opportunity to be part of her planned experience. Teachers who are insecure in their role might be threatened by the presence of another professional in the classroom. On the other hand, most teachers, given the staff development needed to learn how to teach collaboratively and the rationale for such instruction, are willing to try the new procedures, and again, given the demands in today's schools, more and more teachers are becoming accustomed to partnering with others.

Reading specialists and their teaching partners need to think carefully about the many different issues related to effective collaboration, especially if co-teaching in the classroom is planned. Cook and Friend (1995) identify nine different topics that reading specialists and teachers might discuss on a regular basis: instructional beliefs, when and how to plan, parity issues, confidentiality issues, noise levels, classroom routines (instructional and organizational), discipline, feedback, and pet peeves.

THINK ABOUT THIS

What questions would you raise regarding each of these topics? What are your beliefs about each of these that would affect how you work with students? Think about how you might talk with a teacher about each of these issues and what you might learn!

Congruence or Alignment

As mentioned in the previous chapter, one of the concerns about pullout instruction is the lack of congruence or alignment between the instruction provided by the reading specialist and that provided by the classroom teacher. Such congruence is important for helping students achieve in their own classrooms, which gives them a sense of self-worth and satisfaction (i.e., "I can do it!").

In a seminal article, Walp and Walmsley (1989) discuss three types of congruence: philosophical, instructional, and procedural. They indicate that the easiest form of congruence to achieve is *procedural,* where teachers decide when and how they are going to work together in the classroom. How many times per week and for how long will the special-ist be there? What are the classroom management procedures? Who will teach what section of the lesson? How often will the reading specialist meet with classroom teachers? How will they share information about students?

Instructional congruence is more difficult to achieve, given the need for both teacher and reading specialist to think reflectively about the strategies and skills needed by students, how the teachers will present them, and what materials they will use. Questions such as the following can be asked: "How will the specialist work with specific students; for example, what materials, approaches, and activities?"; "What data are available to provide information to make decisions?"; and "What will the classroom teacher be doing and with whom?"

Philosophical congruence is most difficult to achieve. When teach-ers working in the same school have similar goals and objectives for each grade level, many times they are able to compromise or agree on an approach that is best for students. But if a teacher has deep-rooted beliefs about how reading should be taught and these beliefs are not congruent with those of the reading specialist, these two educators may have diffi-culties working together. For example, a classroom teacher who is deeply committed to using a core program in a very structured way, with much whole-class instruction, may have difficulty working with a reading spe-cialist who is promoting more differentiation of instruction with stations or centers in the classroom, small-group work, and opportunities for students to interact with one another.

Furthermore, in addition to differences in beliefs about instruction, teachers and specialists may have differences of opinion about how students should be disciplined or in procedures for classroom manage-ment. Reading specialists have indicated concerns about some teachers' low expectations of students with learning problems and the disrespect shown toward these struggling readers. It is difficult for reading spe-cialists to work in a classroom in which such behavior occurs, given that they have little authority or opportunity to intercede or change behavior.

Walp and Walmsley (1989) make clear that reading specialists and teachers within a school need to discuss the term *congruence* and what it means. They indicate, for example, that congruence may *not* mean "more of the same," nor does a "different" approach necessarily hinder congruence (p. 366). In fact, in some schools implementing RTI pro-grams, students who are having more serious difficulties (often those identified as needing Tier 3 instruction) are taught using a more explicit approach; for example, the Wilson Reading System (Wilson, 1996) or the Sonday Reading System (*www.winsorlearning.com*). The key to effective congruence may be the ability of the teacher and specialist to discuss and share knowledge about their philosophical or theoretical approaches to reading instruction and why certain approaches to reading instruction may differ, depending on students' needs and abilities.

THINK ABOUT THIS

What do you think can be done when there are philosophical differences between teacher and specialist in their beliefs about reading or their approaches to classroom management?

The answers to this question are not easy or definitive. Sometimes the specialist can make a difference just by serving as a model. The fact that the reading specialist is an advocate for struggling readers may also make a difference. If there is serious concern about how teachers treat students, specialists may need to consult with supervisors regarding what can or should be done. Specialists, too, must have someone with whom they can share their experiences and problems. Overall, teachers and specialists alike want to do their best to help students learn; therefore, it is infrequent that specialists find themselves in unworkable situations. Nevertheless, they should be aware that such a situation can occur.

Making a Schedule

There is no easy solution for developing an effective schedule. It depends on the number of students with whom the reading specialist is required to work, the number of classrooms in which these students are placed, and the type of program the reading specialist wants or is expected to develop. It also depends on the time allotted to the reading specialist for instruction. In some schools, reading specialists are assigned to instruction for every period of the day (except for the usual planning period and lunch). In other schools, reading specialists work with students for part of a day, and the remainder is used for various other activities, such as working with teachers or addressing assessment needs. Developing a schoolwide schedule is a huge undertaking. Reading specialists don't want to remove students from recess, physical education, music, or art, for reading instruction. Nor should students miss content-area instruction, if at all possible. In many schools, reading instruction—both core and targeted instruction—occur during the language arts block; often, some students receive targeted interventions, perhaps from the reading specialist or another teacher, while other students are participating in enrichment activities.

An effective schedule requires an effective use of time, space, and resources, both human and material (Canady & Rettig, 1995). At the beginning of the year, think about the overall or big picture. When will assessment be scheduled? Common planning time or data meetings? Time for interventions? Moreover, decisions about schedules have to be made so that personnel function in ways that take advantage of their skill strengths (e.g., the classroom teacher with a background in teaching the gifted may have responsibilities for working with enrichment activities during Tier 2). Again, common planning time is critical as it provides for making changes based on student progress and needs. Useful resources about scheduling include *Elementary School Scheduling: Enhancing Instruction for Student Achievement* (Canady & Rettig, 2008), *Scheduling Strategies for Middle Schools* (Rettig & Canady, 2013), and 'The Power of Innovative Scheduling" (Canady & Rettig, 1995). Information is also available at *www.schoolschedulingassociates.com.*

When there is only one reading specialist in a school, the time available for teaching students multiple times a week is limited. In the study of reading specialists in exemplary schools, the number of students with whom reading specialists worked varied from 20 to 80, with a mean of 52 (Bean, Swan, & Knaub, 2003). Certainly, the specialist assigned to 20 students can design a schedule that is very different from one responsible for working with 60 students. Issues include how the reading specialist can provide the following important aspects of intervention support:

- Intensity (frequency with which he or she meets with students)
- Size of group (individual or small group)
- Specific needs of students

Below are specific questions that reading specialists can ask themselves:

- How often in a week can the reading specialist meet with certain students (how should this vary, given the specific ages or difficulties of students)?
- Which students can be grouped together because of similar needs?
- Which students should be taught in a pullout setting?
- In which classrooms can the reading specialist function effectively (or for what part of the literacy block can the reading specialist function within the classroom)?

Below, I describe the schedule of one reading specialist, Katie R., who works in a primary school with a literacy support team that includes a reading specialist intern, a paraprofessional, a math coach, and Katie. The team develops and negotiates a schedule with participating teachers. Figure 3.1 illustrates Katie's schedule for September. Note that she delivers Tier 3 instruction to several grade-level groups using My Sidewalks, an intervention program (available from Pearson Education). This Tier 3 instruction generally takes place during a 30-minute period devoted to intervention/enrichment (I/E); students are pulled from their classrooms for this instruction. Katie also co-teaches 4 days a week with four different second-grade teachers. The teacher and the needs of their students guide Katie's work. In some classrooms, she takes half the class and leads the guided reading part of the literacy block while the teacher does the same with the other students (parallel instruction). In other classrooms, she may facilitate literacy centers, often planning a phonics or reading strategy center. Some of this work is determined by the day of the week she is in each teacher's classroom. So, if she is in a room on a Tuesday, she would conduct the first read of a story using guided reading. If she is in the classroom on a Thursday, she would generally lead a literacy center.

Katie also delivers Tier 2 instruction to groups of students at the first- and second-grade levels; during this time, she teaches lessons that address specific needs of students. The other students may be involved in an I/E lesson or she might pull the students from their morning meeting time. Katie goes to a kindergarten classroom for 5 days a week where she and the teacher lead or facilitate students' work at literacy centers. Katie also has one 30-minute period for planning, coaching, or assessment purposes each day. She and the math coach have a 40- or 45-minute planning meeting with each grade level every other Wednesday. Each member of the team has a similar teaching schedule. This schedule changes slightly each month, depending on student needs or concerns about the current scheduling. Teachers are involved in the conversation about these changes, often during the grade-level planning sessions, and then each grade-level team receives a schedule indicating when they will be receiving reading support service, which team member will be working with them, and which students are scheduled for pullout instruction. Students are seen frequently for Tier 2 and Tier 3 instruction; Katie is able to be in the classrooms of teachers 4 or 5 days a week. This is possible because there are several specialized literacy professionals available in the building. (The district partners with a local university preparing reading specialists and the intern works alongside Katie, learning from her in an apprenticeship position; at the same time, the intern is taking classes in the evening at the university.)

What makes this program work effectively are (1) the planning meetings that provide for communication among all involved; and (2) the written information that is provided by the reading support team to the teachers, informing them each month of the services that they will

September

Time	Monday	Tuesday	Wednesday	Thursday	Friday
8:00–8:30	BUS DUTY	BUS DUTY	BUS DUTY	BUS DUTY	BUS DUTY
8:35–9:05	Grade 1 Sidewalks #1	Grade 1 Sidewalks #1	Planning/Coaching/ Assessment	Grade 1 Sidewalks #1	Grade 1 Sidewalks #1
9:05–9:35 Grade 3 I/E	Grade 3 Sidewalks #1	Grade 3 Sidewalks #1	Grade 3 Sidewalks #1	Grade 3 Sidewalks #1	Grade 3 Sidewalks #1
9:35–10:20		Grade 2 Language Arts Push In — Day 1: Planning Day 2: Teacher 1 Day 3: Teacher 2; Day 4: Teacher 3 Day 5: Teacher 4 Day 6: Read-Aloud Test: small group			
10:20–10:50 Grade 2 I/E	Grade 2 Pull Out #1	Grade 2 Pull Out #1	Grade 2 Pull Out #1	Grade 2 Pull Out #1	Grade 2 Pull Out #1
10:50–11:20 K I/E	Kdg Push In Teacher A	Kdg Push In Teacher A	Kdg Push In Teacher A	Kdg Push In Teacher A	Kdg Push In Teacher A
11:20–11:35	Planning/Coaching/ Assessment	Planning/Coaching/ Assessment	LUNCH 11:20–11:50	Planning/Coaching/ Assessment	Planning/Coaching/ Assessment
11:35–12:05	Grade 1 Pull Out	Grade 1 Pull Out	11:50–12:35 Grade 2 Team Planning	Grade 1 Pull Out	Grade 1 Pull Out
12:05–12:35	LUNCH	LUNCH	12:35–1:20 Grade 3 Team Planning	LUNCH	LUNCH
12:35–1:50	Planning/Coaching/ Assessment	Planning/Coaching/ Assessment	1:20–2:05 Grade 1 Team Planning	Planning/Coaching/ Assessment	Planning/Coaching/ Assessment
1:50–2:20	Grade 2 Pull Out #2	Grade 2 Pull Out #2	2:05–2:50 Kdg Team Planning	Grade 2 Pull Out #2	Grade 2 Pull Out #2
2:20–2:50	Grade 1 Sidewalks #2	Grade 1 Sidewalks #2		Grade 1 Sidewalks #2	Grade 1 Sidewalks #2
2:50–3:15	BUS DUTY	BUS DUTY	BUS DUTY	BUS DUTY	BUS DUTY

Grade 1 Pull Out
Tier 2
5 students

Grade 3 Sidewalks #1
Level C
Tier 3
5 students

Grade 2 Pull Out #1
Tier 2
4 students

Grade 1 Sidewalks #1
Level A
Tier 3
4 students

Grade 2 Pull Out #2
Tier 2
4 students

Grade 1 Sidewalks #2
Tier 3
2 students

be receiving during that month. Also, this schedule was developed to limit taking students from special subjects or from content-area instruction. Most of the Tier 2 and Tier 3 literacy instruction occurs outside of the literacy block unless the specialist or another team member is in the classroom working with students. Katie indicated that the ways in which the support team works in the classroom with teachers differs slightly, depending on teacher style and preferences. Some teachers want the reading specialists to work only with students with the greatest needs, while others want to work with those students themselves (in a smaller group setting); in that instance, Katie works with students who are reading above grade level to further develop their literacy learning and expose them to more challenging text. Still another teacher likes to use the time to run centers and have the reading specialist introduce the phonics skill for that week. Almost always, the reading specialist team member helps the teacher divide the class into smaller groups.

WORKING AT VARIOUS LEVELS

In the following section, I describe the work of three reading specialists, each working at a different level. It will become obvious that the roles they fill have many similarities, even though there are also differences in how the specialists schedule their time and where they put their emphases.

Yvonne: A Reading Specialist in the Primary Grades

Yvonne is a certified Reading Recovery teacher and also serves as a reading specialist for kindergarten and first-grade students in one school in her district. During the afternoon, as part of her Reading Recovery role, she works with four first-grade students who have been identified as needing individualized support. She follows the procedures and strategies required as part of the Reading Recovery program, seeing each student for 30 minutes a day.

In the morning, Yvonne schedules her time so that she can work in the classrooms of the three kindergarten and first-grade teachers (see Figure 3.2). She also meets with each grade-level team once every 2 weeks, during which time she and the teachers discuss (1) the specific skills, strategies, and content that teachers will be presenting; (2) any data the teachers have about students; and (3) specific students who are experiencing difficulty and what instruction might help them.

Yvonne works in each of the first-grade classrooms three times a week. On 2 days, she assists the classroom teacher who is presenting an

Time	M	T	W	Th	Fri
8:30–9:10	Gr. 1-A	Kdg. A	Gr. 1-A	Kdg. A	Gr. 1-A
9:15–9:55	Gr. 1-B	Kdg. B	Gr. 1-B	Kdg. B	Gr. 1-B
10:00–10:40	Gr. 1-C	Kdg. C	Gr. 1-C	Kdg. C	Gr. 1-C
10:45–11:15	Planning Time				
11:20–12:10	Lunch				
12:15–3:30	Reading Recovery/Planning/Preparation Period				

FIGURE 3.2. Yvonne's schedule.

activity-based phonics lesson to the whole class; this activity requires children to manipulate letter cards on their desks. She walks around helping individual students who are having difficulty. In one of the first-grade classrooms, she conducts the lesson so that the teacher, new to the district, can learn the procedure. In this classroom, the teacher monitors the students' work. Often, if there is time after this mini-lesson is completed, Yvonne pulls aside a few students and asks them to read material in which they can apply the skills they are learning. (The other students write their new words in a journal or complete assigned work.) One day, Yvonne works with a small group that needs additional review of the skills taught that week. While she is teaching that group, the teacher is either holding reading conferences or teaching another group that may also need additional help with some strategy or skill. The groups change each week, depending on the needs of the students.

In the beginning of the year, in the kindergarten classrooms, Yvonne and the teachers focus on phonemic awareness activities. Either she or the teacher teaches the lesson while the other assists and reinforces the students' work. These lessons last only 15 minutes. Then Yvonne works in one of the centers that has been set up in the classroom, generally assisting students who have been identified as needing help with letter recognition or concepts of print. Yvonne also helps when there is a writing activity, taking dictation as students tell her what they want to say. Yvonne and the kindergarten teachers have also agreed that there is a small number of students in each of the kindergarten classrooms who would benefit from additional small-group or Tier 2 instruction for more focused oral language and vocabulary experiences. Yvonne is revising her schedule so that she can work with these six students for 15 minutes, 2 days a week, using a form of interactive reading, ELL Storybook Intervention, that she read about in the Walpole and McKenna book *Differentiated Reading Instruction: Strategies for the Primary Grades* (2008).

THINK ABOUT THIS

What do you think are the strengths of this plan for the reading specialist? What do you see as potential problems with Yvonne's schedule? In
what ways is Yvonne supporting the professional growth of teachers?
How can Yvonne change her schedule to make room for this small-
group instruction with kindergarten students?

Greg: A Reading Specialist at the Intermediate Level

Greg works in a setting where the intermediate teachers, grades 4–6,
teach either the language arts block or math, science, and social studies.
His major role is to provide instruction for struggling readers. At the
same time, the principal has asked Greg to serve as a resource to teachers and has allowed him to develop a schedule that provides him with
that opportunity (see Figure 3.3). Greg works in the classrooms two
times a week with the six teachers responsible for teaching the language
arts block. This schedule necessitates careful planning so that when he
is in the classroom, he can work productively. During his time in the
classrooms, Greg works with small groups needing additional support
with vocabulary or comprehension skills. He may also assist by holding
conferences with students about their writing. On Fridays, Greg's schedule allows him to work where needed. He may work with students who
have special needs or with teachers who are addressing a specific issue
or topic (e.g., outlining). He also uses this time to assess students about
whom the teachers are concerned.

Greg works with the content-area teachers to help them incorporate
literacy instruction in their content teaching. He has gone into classrooms to work with students on study skills or to conduct mini-lessons

Schedule	M	T	W	Th	F
Period 1	Gr. 4-A	Gr. 4-B	Gr. 4-A	Gr. 4-B	float
Period 2	Gr. 5-A	Gr. 5-B	Gr. 5-A	Gr. 5-B	float
Period 3	Gr. 6-A	Gr. 6-B	Gr. 6-A	Gr. 6-B	float
Lunch					
Period 5	Work with math/science/social studies teachers, assessment/ planning with teachers				
Period 6	Same as period 5				
Period 7	Planning				

FIGURE 3.3. Greg's schedule.

requested by the teachers. He did a lesson on writing a research report (how to organize it) for the sixth graders who were given this assignment in social studies. He also did a demonstration lesson, introducing the students and the teacher to the "know, want to know, learn" (K-W-L) strategy (Ogle, 1986) as a means of activating prior knowledge, and creating enthusiasm and an organizational framework for the unit on machines and how they work (for the fifth-grade science teacher). At times, Greg plans with the various content teachers during his afternoon periods. He is now planning to work with Kelly and Jesse, the sixth-grade social studies teachers who, after attending workshops on the CCSS, decided that they wanted to improve students' learning by giving them opportunities to talk in small groups about what they have read. Greg shared the chapter "Discussion in Practice: Sharing Our Learning" (Erdmann & Metzger, 2014) and after reading and discussing it, the three of them developed plans for next steps. Together they planned lessons that the two teachers would implement in their individual classrooms. On Day 1, students would read the chapter and see an accompanying video about the contributions of the Romans to western civilization. On the following day, students would be randomly divided into groups of five, so that they would be sitting with students they generally didn't sit with. They would then engage in a 15-minute discussion, using several open-ended questions that had been developed by their teachers. Afterward, students would present a summary of their discussion to the entire class. Greg would be there on the second day, so that there would be two teachers in the classroom, moving around, encouraging, and monitoring the work of students. They agreed that they would meet after the lessons were taught to debrief and decide what did and did not work. They would then continue their planning, focusing on ways that they could improve students' discussion behaviors and student understanding of the content.

THINK ABOUT THIS

What skills do you think are essential if Greg is to be successful in this situation? What problems does Greg face with this schedule? What are your responses to the work that Greg is planning to do with Kelly and Jesse? (Who is taking the lead?) Why is the work that Greg is doing likely to succeed? Any possible pitfalls?

Brenda: A High School Reading Specialist

Brenda is the *only* reading specialist in a large high school, making her job a difficult one. She has a flexible schedule, except for three periods each day when she teaches small groups of ninth graders who scored at a low level on a reading assessment measure given at the beginning of the school year, or those recommended by teachers as needing help to pass the state competency test given in the spring. During the other periods, Brenda makes arrangements to work with a small number of teachers while they are teaching a specific unit. She believes that spending more time in a particular classroom (perhaps almost every day while the unit is being taught) gives her the opportunity to become better acquainted with the students and their needs, and with the teaching style and goals of the classroom teacher. Recently, content-area teachers had attended several workshops about the CCSS, and following those sessions, Leon, one of the history teachers, asked Brenda to work with him when he taught the 4-week unit about American democracy. Brenda and Leon reviewed the unit in the text, discussed Leon's goals for the unit, and then decided that they would work together to help students become more familiar with the structure of their textbook as a means of learning how it contributes to a deeper understanding of the content. Students would also cite information from the text to justify or validate their responses to questions that Leon had asked them to consider.

After talking with Leon about the history text and its components, Brenda taught a mini-lesson, highlighting various organizational aspects of the textbook, ways in which the author identified important information, and how students might take annotated notes that would improve their understanding of the text. The two teachers then team taught a lesson on voting rights and responsibilities; Leon identified several key questions and students worked in groups of three to discuss the questions and then locate and identify the pages on which the answers to those questions were found. After the small-group session, Brenda and Leon held a discussion with the entire class in which students discussed their answers, going back into the textbook to justify their responses. The students were then assigned to read an article about the ways in which African Americans in the South in the early 1960s were prevented from voting and the efforts of college students to register individuals to vote. Brenda and Leon planned to ask students, after a class discussion, to write a summary of what they learned, using information from the text and from the article that they had read. For this unit, Brenda and Leon focused on several of the standards from the CCSS for Literacy in History/Social Studies (grades 9–12), especially those related to integrating and evaluating multiple sources of information read, and writing summaries based on relevant and sufficient evidence (CCSS Initiative, 2010).

Brenda's other responsibilities include assessing students at the request of teachers and working informally with teachers who want to talk to her about students or instruction that facilitates students' understanding of text material. Brenda also shoulders the major responsibility for making presentations to faculty that help them understand how integrating literacy strategies specific to their discipline can improve student learning of content. Next month, she will give a short presentation to the science department teachers about how to make better use of the diagrams and data in their textbook. She will also meet with science and social studies teachers together to discuss the ways in which they could help students gain a better understanding of the vocabulary specific to those disciplines.

Brenda is a member of the school's leadership team and just this past week, they discussed the importance of literacy across the curriculum as a means of improving student learning overall. The school has the opportunity to participate in a funded project in which volunteer teachers and members of the leadership team could attend workshops on literacy and how it can improve content-area teaching. Brenda is excited about this opportunity and the chance to work more closely with teachers from the various academic disciplines, but she wonders how she will be able to manage this work, given her teaching responsibilities.

THINK ABOUT THIS

What skills and abilities do you think Brenda needs to be successful in her position? One of Brenda's difficulties is finding the time to work with all the teachers who have requested her assistance. What suggestions or recommendations would you make to Brenda? What are some possibilities that Brenda can consider that may enable her to work more closely with teachers as they begin to implement this new approach to content-area teaching?

READING SPECIALISTS AT THE MIDDLE AND HIGH SCHOOL LEVELS

What should be obvious from the schedules of the reading specialists described above is that all, primary through high school, have some instructional responsibility. All need to know how to work with struggling readers either individually, in small groups, or as a whole class. And all need to know how to work collaboratively with the classroom teacher to identify student needs regarding what is required in the classroom curriculum and which strategies or skills the students might need to become successful readers. Furthermore, those working at the middle and high school levels need to have a deep understanding of adolescent literacy and adolescent learners. In the 2012 Adolescent Literacy position statement of the IRA, adolescent literacy is defined as "the ability to read, write, understand and interpret, and discuss multiple texts across multiple contexts" (IRA, 2012a, p. 2). The document also highlights the importance of literacy specialists or coaches who can work both with readers who need additional support and collaboratively with the content-area teacher to improve disciplinary-specific literacy instruction. In the position statement, the reading/literacy specialist or coach is seen as possessing knowledge about general literacy strategies; at the same time, it is expected that content teachers, familiar with their discipline, will be better able to identify the information to be learned, the questions to be asked, and "how texts specific to the discipline are structured, and how to evaluate the accuracy, credibility, and quality of an author's ideas" (p. 6). In other words, the IRA recommends the need for collaboration between the reading specialist and the content-area teachers. In order to fulfill their roles, reading specialists at the high school level serve more in a resource capacity or as a coach for teachers than in a direct instructional role (Bean, Kern, et al., 2015; Henwood, 1999–2000). Henwood, a high school reading specialist, defined her role as a collegial one, indicating that she did not want colleagues to regard her as an expert giving advice: "Instead, I needed to be considered a partner in improving the learning of all students, one who complemented the teacher's knowledge of content with knowledge of the learning process that I possessed as a reading specialist" (1999–2000, p. 317). Chapter 4 provides additional information about serving as a resource to teachers.

Too often, however, there are no reading specialists in middle and high schools. However, multiple factors call for specialized literacy professionals who have the expertise to work at these higher levels with teachers and their students: the high expectations for students that require them to be college and career ready; the increasing complexity and availability of multiple forms of literacy, including traditional print materials and digital text; and the diversity and variability of students in schools today (i.e., English learners, students from high-poverty backgrounds). Reading specialists can perform the following tasks at these levels:

- provide tutorial or intervention service.;
- collaborate with content area teachers to provide discipline-specific literacy instruction that will enable students to succeed and become self-sufficient learners;
- assess students' reading and writing—and teach them to self-assess their reading and writing;
- teach the general literacy strategies relating to vocabulary, fluency, comprehension, and study skills;
- relate literacy practices to life-management issues such as exploring careers, examining individuals' roles in society, setting goals, managing time and stress, and resolving conflicts; and

- offer reading programs that recognize potentially limiting forces such as work schedules, family responsibilities, and peer pressures. (IRA, 1999, p. 8)

This list of services should be useful to specialists who are working in middle and high schools as they think about their own job descriptions and how they function in the schools. The vignette in this chapter, written by Toni, a reading specialist at the middle school level, elaborates on the positive aspects and the challenges of her position. She highlights the importance of understanding the "adolescent," the difficulties of scheduling, and the challenges of working in an inclusive program. Toni also discusses the leadership roles of her position involving not only working with teachers but writing the Title I proposal for the school district. Maintaining a sense of humor, being flexible, and having patience appear to be three important traits for success in her role.

GETTING FEEDBACK (EVALUATING THE PROGRAM)

Reading specialists who are willing to listen to the comments of teachers and who seek regular feedback as a means of improving what they do will be able to make the adjustments that enable them to be more effective in their roles. For example, midway through the year, the reading specialist might ask teachers to complete a simple questionnaire that raises questions important to the successful functioning of the program (see Figure 3.4). Or the reading specialist might choose to talk with individual teachers about the program. The specialist may also want to discuss the program with a supervisor or the principal and other specialists. Reflecting on what has been successful and what has not is an important process for program improvement. A more formal evaluation might involve analyzing the impact of the program on the students. At the end of the year, reading specialists can review the achievement data on the students with whom they have worked. How much progress have these students made? Has the program been a successful one for them? If so, in what ways? Chapter 9 provides ideas for assessing student performance.

SUMMARY

Reading specialists must be able to initiate new programs and work effectively in those that are ongoing. They may be assigned to work in an instructional role at various levels in the schools. Regardless of the

Dear Teacher:

I am interested in getting feedback from you about the program that you and I are implementing. Both of us want to help students learn to read successfully. So, I'd appreciate your response to the following questions. If you would feel more comfortable discussing these with me, I would be happy to sit down and talk with you.

1. Have you seen any improvement in the performance of struggling readers in your classroom?

     None   Some   A lot

Please elaborate:

2. Have you seen any improvement in the attitude of struggling readers in your classroom?

     None   Some   A lot

Please elaborate:

3. How easy has it been to create a schedule that enables us to work together?

     Easy   Not easy

4. What can be done to make scheduling easier?

5. What has been the most positive part of our working together?

6. What has been the most difficult aspect of program implementation?

7. Any suggestions for program improvement?

Thank you,

_____

Reading Specialist

FIGURE 3.4. Getting feedback from teachers.

level at which they work, specialists need to have an understanding of the culture of the schools to which they are assigned and a good working relationship with school personnel. Likewise, given the need to work collaboratively with teachers, the issue of instructional congruence is an important one; struggling readers need experiences that will help them integrate and apply what they are learning from several teachers or subjects. Reading specialists at all levels must be experts on reading curriculum, instruction, and assessment. Reading specialists at the upper levels need to have an understanding of how students use reading to learn, using texts from many different sources. At all levels, specialists must be able to work collaboratively with other adults. Getting feedback from those with whom they work can provide a basis for program improvement.

ADDITIONAL READINGS

International Reading Association. (2012). *Adolescent literacy: A position statement of the International Reading Association.* Newark, DE: Author. Available at *www.reading.org/Resources/ResourcesbyTopic/Adolescent/Overview.aspx.*—This document provides detailed information, defining adolescent literacy and providing a summary of the essential elements of an effective adolescent literacy program. It identifies additional adolescent literacy resources that can be accessed online.

Wixon, K. K., & Lipson, J. Y. (2012). Relations between the CCSS and RTI in literacy and language. *The Reading Teacher, 65*(6), 387–391.—These authors discuss the impact of the CCSS on the implementation of RTI in schools. They view the higher expectations of the CCSS as resulting in greater variability in student learning and increased need for differentiated instruction.

Reflections

At what level would you feel most comfortable working? What qualifications do you have that made you choose that level? What skills and knowledge would you need to work at that level?

Activities

1. Ask a reading specialist to share his or her schedule with you. How similar is that schedule to the ones described in this chapter? What are the specialist's views about his or her schedule (e.g., any problems, why the schedule developed in that way, what is helpful about the schedule)?

2. Discuss the following scenario with other reading specialists or classmates. As a reading specialist, you have been assigned to work in the classroom with several intermediate-grade reading teachers. You have heard other teachers talk about one of them, Frank, as a really tough teacher who makes his students "toe the line." You see yourself as a teacher who "lets kids have some fun." You give students permission to talk informally and share personal stories, believing that struggling readers need a low-risk environment in which to succeed. You are worried! What do you think you should do? (Remember, there is no right answer in this situation; what might work best as you begin your work with Frank?)

Some questions to think about:

What lessons can be learned about the role of the reading specialist from this vignette?

In what ways does Toni serve as a leader?

What questions come to mind after reading this vignette?

TONI: A JOB IN CONSTANT FLUX, OR FOLLOW THE BOUNCING RED BALL!

After working as an elementary reading specialist in a primary building (grades K–3) for 17 years, I was transferred to the junior/senior high school to work predominantly with middle school (seventh- and eighth-grade) teachers and students. All of the pictures, love notes, smiles, and hugs from primary grades are gone—only to be replaced by "Do we have to?" "This is stupid," and "I don't want to do this" (Hmm . . . there is now Attitude with a capital *A*). So what is life like as a middle school reading specialist? While the day-to-day job differs greatly, kids are still kids, reading is still reading, and teachers are still teachers. My goal is, and always has been, to keep my focus on the kids—and do the very best I can to best remediate/help/support them. (Asked often—what level is "easier"—primary/intermediate/middle/high? The answer is *no* level is "easy"; each level is different.)

Challenges

Scheduling is a different animal at the middle school level. While time (AHH— TIME, TIME, TIME!!) is a major challenge/obstacle at all levels, the lack of and inflexibility of this commodity seems magnified at the middle school level. The bell rings every 43 minutes, kids come and go, and there is no "downtime" like study halls in my district, making access to students difficult. Unlike my elementary experience, I have very little input at this level regarding what the schedule will look like—administration decides (wish I had more input here). Most of my time is spent in an inclusive setting, working with teachers and students during the language arts block, which is two periods long: 90 minutes total. During this time reading, writing, and grammar are taught. Inclusive work, particularly with adolescents, is practical. While the kids know who struggles and who does not, shining a spotlight on those struggling (by pulling them out) can be counterproductive. Nevertheless, there are some significant drawbacks to inclusion (even with two teachers—how can we successfully address the wide range of

77

abilities, needs, deficits, and behaviors displayed by the adolescent hormone-crazed students?). Add to this—finding time to plan with teachers and adjusting to a variety of teachers' attitudes, approaches, and styles—the job of reading specialist gets even more demanding (but herein lies both challenges and opportunities: how can I help?). There are times I feel like little more than an aide walking around the room; at other times, the planning of and execution of lessons can be differentiated, engaging, effective, and downright fun and exciting! Remember—keep the focus on the students.

Pullout support was tried for a period of time (as directed from administration). Students were pulled 2 days a week (out of chorus or band) to attend a reading support period. There were some obstacles/drawbacks to this arrangement: (1) students did not have to "work" in band/chorus so did not want to leave there and come to work for me; (2) my time with them was not graded, so it didn't count; and (3) student attitude was not positive, so they felt they were in the "dumb" class. From my perspective, two periods a week (even with small groups of students [six to eight]) just was not enough time to effectively address the varied academic deficits. However, there were some positive outcomes from this model. I had the opportunity to form positive connections with some of the students and support their language arts instruction (reviewing, reteaching, and providing additional practice), thereby improving their language arts grades. I also became an advocate for them with some of their other teachers. However, since the goal of the pullout sessions was to improve test scores on the PSSA, and this pullout time did not improve test scores, it was eliminated and my schedule went to full inclusion.

Instruction and Assessment

During inclusion time, instruction and assessment are driven by a curriculum focusing on the CCSS and the state test administered in grades 7 and 8 (not bad in theory but tough in practice!). The majority of the assessments administered are curriculum based—tied directly to the skills being taught in any given unit. Teachers do adapt, in varying degrees, the class assignments and assessments. Being in the classroom provides an opportunity to provide some input into the planning/differentiating of instruction and assessment (more input sometimes than other times and more input with some teachers than other teachers). An important aspect of my job is to build the teacher's repertoire of activities and approaches for use both now and in the future. I also compiled some PSSA test-prep types of assessments to prepare students for the format and vocabulary used on the state test. These assessments were administered first as a shared/guided activity and progressed to a graded individual-type assessment. Questions missed often provided focus for future instruction as well as a time to address some basic test-prep-type strategies. The only summative assessment given, in addition to the state test, is the STAR assessment: a computer test giving a basic reading level for each student. These results were helpful in getting an overview of the student performance and some handle on growth. Teachers willingly administered these tests (short—only about 20 minutes and computer-generated results), but the coalition of data and the sharing of the results were basically my responsibility. This test is administered to students in the district, grades K–8, three to four times a year, and does provide an overview of each individual student and the progress made over time in the general area of reading. Having these data to share with both language arts teachers and content-area teachers provided a chance to advocate for some of the struggling readers as well as offering the opportunity for the "ongoing" professional development I do at this level.

Leadership

At an elementary level, I did more "formal" professional development (e.g., presentations). At this level I find PD to be more of the ongoing discussions with teachers about students, strategies, expectations, and differentiation. Professional development opportunities come up often. It's a matter of staying updated about state mandates, testing requirements, new reading research, and ready to seize opportunities to share information and connect it to current instruction. Opportunities to share information (aka informal PD) with administration also arises and I look for and take advantage of these opportunities.

Another area that has been part of my job responsibilities is to coordinate the federal programs for the district: Title I and Title IIA. Knowing the federal regulations, completing a grant application, working collaboratively with teachers, parents, and administrators are skills I use routinely. Writing grants to secure funds to accomplish specific tasks (e.g., dinner for parents along with an informational meeting, teacher professional development conferences) is valuable, given money is always an issue (along with time!).

Some Final Thoughts

At a primary level there is an urgency, pressure, and a feeling of great responsibility to make sure the students learn to read—MUST get those foundational skills—and it really is up to us, as teachers, to make sure that students are being taught in a way that is effective, productive, and appropriate for each child. At a middle school level, some of that responsibility for learning shifts to the students: they need to put forth the effort and thought but they also still need to be taught in a way that is effective, productive, and appropriate. Many times I saw the middle school students as just "big" little kids but with raging hormones and enormous social pressure. I had the unusual situation of working with students in the K–3 building and then working with them again in the junior/senior high building—something that was both rewarding and discouraging. Seeing students who had been at great risk in the primary grades, now successful and flourishing in middle school, was incredibly rewarding—the hard work and focused instruction provided by a cadre of teachers worked and a child's life had been changed—AMAZING!! On the other hand, some other students continued to struggle—and now their frustrations and lack of successes were being exhibited in very nonproductive ways—UGH!! Weak skills, social pressure, and increased academic demands create a "perfect storm" for inappropriate behaviors and conflicts with teachers and fellow students (What can I do to help them at this point?). I relish the successes and work as hard as I can to address the challenges. Receiving accolades from middle school students is extraordinary. One student wrote on my board "I love you Dr. Saul"—I took a picture of it and referred back to it on tough days! As with most of us in the field of education, the students who come back and tell you that in some way you positively affected their lives make all the challenges (student need, limited time, student attitude/motivation) and hard work worth it. Tackling challenges and successfully helping kids—ahh . . . what a great calling.

Lessons Learned

- The biggest lesson I learned when going to a predominately inclusive position, is to sit back for a bit, to observe, and get to know the teachers' styles and approaches and then tread lightly—always being supportive and NOT judgmental.

- DO NOT attempt to make major changes quickly. Set priorities and make changes a little bit at a time and work to establish credibility. Once credibility and trust are established, the environment to effect change is set—while still moving slowly

Toni Saul, EdD
Middle School Reading Specialist
Allegheny Valley School District
Cheswick, Pennsylvania

CHAPTER FOUR

Leadership of the Reading Specialist

What Does It Mean?

> Ultimately, your leadership in a culture of change will be
> judged as effective or ineffective not by who you are as a
> leader but by what leadership you produce in others.
> —FULLAN (2001a, p. 137)

Key Questions

- How is leadership defined in this chapter?
- What communication skills are essential for those in reading specialist roles?
- In what ways can reading specialists work with groups to facilitate teacher learning and overall school improvement?
- In what ways can reading specialists serve as a resource to teachers?

This chapter discusses qualities and characteristics of effective leaders, ideas for working with groups, and serving as a resource to others. Other chapters also address aspects of leadership: Chapter 5 focuses on professional development; Chapters 6 and 7 on coaching as a specific approach to serving as a resource to teachers and providing "job-embedded" professional development; and Chapter 8, the development of school reading programs.

Words similar to those in the quote above have often been used to describe or define individuals in leadership positions. They emphasize the effect that the actions of leaders can have on those with whom they work, creating an enthusiasm for learning and empowering others in ways that enable them to grow professionally and personally. The reading specialist functions as a leader, whether working primarily with students, coaching, or coordinating programmatic efforts. However, although the instructional role of the reading specialist is a given—accepted by administrators, teachers, and reading specialists themselves—less clear-cut are the leadership responsibilities assumed if the reading specialist is to have an impact not only on individual students but on the school as a whole. Yet, in today's schools, it is even more urgent that reading specialists as well as other teachers recognize and accept their role as leaders. Shared leadership and collaboration among teachers are integral to successful schools in today's world. All leaders must understand the culture of their organization and work with others to develop that culture so that it meets the needs of its members (e.g., teachers and students).

As mentioned in Chapter 1, leadership is an essential aspect for all reading specialists, regardless of their title, responsibilities, and tasks. In their respective roles, they can exert an influence on the overall reading program and literacy learning of all students in the school. In fact, as discussed in a previous chapter, in a study of reading specialists in exemplary schools (Bean, Swan, & Knaub, 2003), 100% of the principals in those schools indicated that specialists were important to the success of the reading programs overall; they were leaders in their schools. In follow-up interviews with some of these reading specialists, they described the many ways they served as leaders, performing activities such as serving as a resource to teachers, conducting professional development workshops, leading curriculum development efforts, and working with other professionals and community members to improve students' achievement. All but one of the reading specialists interviewed had instructional responsibilities; nevertheless, in varying degrees all were very much involved in leadership activities.

In the national study of the role of reading specialists (Bean, Kern, et al., 2015), leadership was also identified as being an important aspect of their role. Respondents in that study indicated they were expected to serve as leaders and as such needed much more preparation about how to lead—to inspire and involve others in the school as a means of building capacity. Moreover, those reading specialists who served as coaches highlighted the importance of possessing excellent leadership, interpersonal, and communication skills. These skills and competencies are described fully in the revised Standards for Reading Professionals (IRA, 2010), which placed more emphases on this leadership role, given the call for shared or distributed leadership in schools (Bryk, Sebring, Allensworth, Luppescu, & Easton, 2010; Spillane, Halverson, & Diamond, 2001).

WHAT IS LEADERSHIP?

Those who write about leadership define it in many different ways. Some think of leadership in terms of the position that a person holds (e.g., the principal). Others see it as synonymous with control or influence, suggesting that anyone who can influence or persuade others to behave in specific ways has leadership qualities. For example, teachers may be influenced by an experienced teacher who is well respected by peers for his or her ability to teach and willingness to offer solutions or direction to others about various school issues (e.g., "We need to make sure that the reading core program we adopt provides lots of good ideas about vocabulary instruction"). Others see leadership as a set of behaviors; an individual can be a leader by exhibiting certain behaviors associated with leadership, such as solving problems creatively, obtaining commitments from others, or resolving conflicts. Certainly, specific traits or characteristics enhance leadership (e.g., ability to communicate well with others, effective interpersonal skills). Likewise, style (e.g., democratic, laissez-faire, authoritative) can influence the way in which one leads. A specific principal might be characterized as demanding or known as someone who leads in a top-down manner (authoritative); another principal might be someone seen as having a democratic style (i.e., involves teachers in decision making and aims for consensus of teachers for solving problems). Another might relinquish leadership—perhaps in an area such as literacy, to another individual such as the assistant principal or a literacy coach—and be viewed as laissez-faire.

Leadership in this text is defined as any activities or set of activities associated with working with others to reach or accomplish a common goal, that of improving student learning, especially literacy learning. In other words, leadership is seen as a process, not as a set of traits or styles. It is closer to the notion of distributed leadership as defined by Spillane and colleagues (2001) who indicated that leadership is more than the action of one individual; rather, it is the interactions that occur between and among individuals. In other words, leadership is shared and distributed among personnel in different ways, depending on the context, the situation, and individual competencies. So, in one school, the literacy coach might assume major leadership responsibilities for the literacy program given that the principal has little background in that area and relies on the coach to lead literacy efforts. In another school, the principal, with a reading specialist certificate, might serve as the leader of a team of reading specialists and coaches who work collaboratively to make decisions about instruction, grouping, and assessment. In yet another school, the literacy coach might work with the teacher who has expertise in using technology in the classroom, asking him or her to lead efforts to enhance teacher knowledge and capability to use digital tools for project learning as a way to address language arts standards. In this case, the literacy coach as a leader involves and empowers the teacher with expertise to serve in a leadership role; leadership is distributed and shared. In other words, there are multiple ways to distribute leadership in a school; what is important is that leadership is distributed or stretched so that all have opportunities to serve in such a role. As stated by Lambert (1998), everyone in the school setting has "the potential and right to work as a leader" (p. 9), and informal leadership in schools can greatly influence school change efforts.

In fact, reading specialists most often are expected to lead by influence. Most reading or literacy coaches, employed as instructional rather than administrative personnel, do not have the "authority" to require teachers to make changes. Most often they suggest, recommend, or nudge teachers to make instructional changes. And, although some reading specialists or literacy coaches regret that they do not have the authority to require compliance, Knight (2007) and Toll (2004, 2005), knowledgeable experts of coaching, view the coach's role as collegial rather than evaluative, supervisory, or authoritative.

Those reading specialists whose major responsibility is instructing struggling readers also function as leaders. Say, for example, the school wants to select a new reading textbook. The reading specialist has worked in classrooms with teachers and is well aware of the strengths and limitations of the current textbook. He or she is also familiar with most of the available series, has experience in serving on textbook-selection committees, and knows the research on reading instruction. The reading specialist, therefore, may well be the best person to serve in a leadership role on a committee to select a new textbook. Another reading specialist may take the lead in helping several new teachers who have questions about the most effective ways to use flexible grouping in their classroom, whereas a reading specialist at the middle or high school level may lead the study group meetings being scheduled to discuss literacy across the curriculum. Leaders are those who promote positive change and inspire and empower others to participate in the process. They lead not only by the power of persuasion but by the power of example. As Covey (2004) states, "Leadership is communicating to people their worth and potential so clearly that they come to see it in themselves" (p. 98). In other words, leadership sets into motion leadership in others.

In *Lead Simply: How to Create That Special Team of People*, Sam Parker (2012) discusses three key aspects of leadership helpful to reading specialists in schools. Think about how you might actualize each of these key aspects of leadership in your work.

- *Model*. Lead by example: be enthusiastic, focus your energies.
- *Connect*. Be an active listener, encourage an open flow of ideas.
- *Involve*. Share responsibility.

CHARACTERISTICS AND QUALIFICATIONS OF EFFECTIVE LEADERS

"I think everyone can be a leader. The key is for people to see themselves as being someone who can make a difference."
"One of the important things about leadership is being yourself!"
"True leaders are loyal to those who are under them."
"You have to be reliable. When you tell someone you are going to do something, you need to do it!"

THINK ABOUT THIS

Think of a leader you know and respect. What qualifications or traits does he or she exhibit? What impact does/did that individual have on your behavior? Do you agree with the four statements above about leadership? Why or why not? What traits or characteristics do you associate with effective leadership?

The statements above reflect thoughts about characteristics of effective leaders. What is key however, is that in schools, everyone—teachers, specialists, and administrators—can serve in a leadership role. When a teacher chairs a committee to select a new textbook, he or she is assuming a leadership role. When reading specialists sit down with a new teacher to discuss how to teach struggling readers in the classroom, they are serving in a leadership role. So too, when teachers work with a group of volunteer tutors or with student teachers assigned to them for their field experiences. The following five characteristics are seen as contributing to effective leadership: ability to communicate, teamwork, empowerment, goal seeking (having a vision or direction), and respect for others.

Communication Skills

Active Listening

Seek first to understand, then to be understood.
—COVEY (1989, p. 235)

I have had opportunities to have informal conversations with coaches, and not just literacy coaches, but life coaches, executive coaches, and even a health coach! Invariably, when asked what they believe is the most important attribute of a coach, they respond, "Being a good listener." Covey, in his book *The 7 Habits of Highly Effective People* (1989), presents this notion as one of the important principles designed to help individuals work with each other effectively. Of course, we know how to listen; we do it all the time! However, as Covey (2004) indicates, too often, individuals listen from "within their own frame of reference" (p. 192). He describes a listening continuum that includes "ignoring, pretend listening, selective listening, attentive listening, and empathic listening—only the highest, empathic listening, is done within the frame of reference of the other person" (p. 192). Too often, we listen from our own frame of reference because we are busy evaluating, interpreting, or preparing our responses rather than trying to understand what the person is attempting to communicate. Active listening is one of the key skills of an effective leader. It shows respect and creates trust, essential for effective communication. The following behaviors contribute to active listening:

1. *Focus on the speaker's message.* Listen to the message for both content, what the speaker is saying, and feelings. Look for cues that indicate how the speaker feels (e.g., facial expression, body language, posture). For example, a teacher who is telling the reading specialist about the negative classroom behavior of a particular student, in describing the behaviors, may be feeling confused, unhappy, or even angry about the situation. The active listener attempts to understand both the content and the feelings behind the message. An understanding of content and feelings can be helpful to the reading specialist in making a decision about how to respond.

2. *Test your understanding by rephrasing in your own words what you heard the speaker say.* In other words, try to put yourself in the place of the speaker; what are his or her views or perspectives. You may also need to ask questions, especially when you are not certain that you have understood the message. Covey (1989) suggests that the listener (a) mimic content (i.e., repeat what is said), (b) rephrase content, and (c) rephrase content and reflect feelings (pp. 248–249). In other words, there is a need to *clarify* and *confirm* what we are hearing as well as acknowledge the perceived feelings.

3. *Provide nonverbal indications of active listening.* Effective listeners understand the importance of nonverbal indicators of active listening: They smile and acknowledge that they are listening by nodding in agreement. They sit in ways that show their interest in the subject and in the listener. Some researchers have indicated that much of effective

listening has to do with these nonverbal aspects. Think about an experience you've had, perhaps in talking with a salesperson, or trying to get information when your airplane flight has been canceled. It's very easy to determine whether that individual is engaged in active listening. The speaker is much more willing to carry on the conversation when there is evidence of active listening.

4. *Encourage elaboration.* When listeners are asked to "say more," or to expand on what they are saying, they are more likely to share in-depth their concerns or issues. They will also be more likely to trust the individual with whom they are speaking. Sometimes speakers need encouragement to provide additional information or assistance in organizing their thoughts so that the message is clear. Miller and Miller (1997, p. 92) provide three examples of how to invite elaboration: giving a gentle command ("Say more), open-ended question ("Anything else?"), and a statement ("I'd like to hear more").

5. *Stay away from interrupting the speaker or finishing sentences*! In their book *Joining Together: Group Theory and Group Skills*, Johnson and Johnson (2003) emphasize the importance of nonevaluative listening, indicating that one of the barriers to effective communication is the tendency of individuals to make judgments as they are listening to a speaker. Have you ever found yourself thinking about your reply while another is speaking? Or interrupting a speaker before he or she has finished a sentence? Such behavior is not part of active listening; it not only limits the listener's understanding of the message but can create a negative attitude on the part of the speaker.

Clear, Congruent Speaking

Johnson and Johnson (2013, pp. 132–133) provide important insights about sending messages. Their list is adapted below.

1. *Own messages by using first-person-singular pronouns.* If you have a particular feeling or opinion about an issue, make certain that you indicate this directly, for example, by saying, "I really have problems with ability grouping; these are the reasons."

2. *Make your verbal and nonverbal messages congruent.* As mentioned previously, nonverbal communication is important. Even though you may have a positive message to relate to others, a frown on your face or lack of expression may reduce the impact of that message to others. Listeners attend to more than words: They notice the tone and the non-verbal cues. I remember vividly an interesting experience in observing a second-grade teacher. As she led the students through the lesson, she

never smiled or expressed any emotion, even when she complimented certain students on their performance. This behavior confused me because I did not sense any real connection between the students and this teacher. I wondered whether students were receiving mixed messages or even a single message that this teacher had little enthusiasm for the subject she was teaching or a sense of caring for her students. As we talked after the lesson, the teacher mentioned to me that she was not very expressive. Then she said, "I just have a permanent frown on my face. My students understand that I care." In other words, she was well aware of the nonverbal message that she sent, but she also believed that her students saw past that message. I wondered, however, about the impact of this behavior on students, especially those who were struggling in her classroom. How do you feel when you are with others in a group meeting and when you say something, an individual in the group seems to be frowning? What are your reactions to this?

3. *Ask for feedback about the message.* Taking the time to ask listeners to restate your message or to ask for questions tells you whether you and your listeners are "on the same page" and whether any confusion exists. In any group session, you might end by summarizing what you heard (e.g., here are the ideas that you identified about how to improve our writing program; did I miss anything?).

THINK ABOUT THIS

Think about your own communication skills. What are your personal strengths? Possible trouble spots? What communication qualities do you appreciate in others? Use the questions in Figure 4.1 to help you respond to these questions.

Teamwork

None of us is as smart as all of us.
—BLANCHARD, BOWLES, CAREW,
AND PARISE-CAREW (2001, p. 60)

The ability to work as part of a team is an especially important competency for reading specialists because most frequently the leadership role is one of influence rather than authority. In other words, the reading specialist must be able to motivate others to work together to improve the school reading program. Reading specialists often work with groups or teams of teachers (e.g., committees, grade-level groups, subject-area groups). The following standards can be used in shaping effective teamwork:

1. Am I an active listener? Do I listen to understand both the content of the message and the associated feelings or emotions?

2. Do I provide nonverbal indications of active listening (nodding in agreement, smiling, encouraging elaboration)?

3. Do I use strategies to make sure that I "understand" the words of the speaker (rephrasing or paraphrasing, asking speaker to clarify)?

4. Do I build on what the speaker is saying (responding in a way that indicates I am listening)?

5. Do I facilitate conversations that indicate teacher and I are co-learners or working together to solve a problem?

6. Do I summarize what I have heard (or ask the teacher to summarize) as a means of facilitating understanding?

FIGURE 4.1. Effective Communication: Questions for Coaches to Consider. From Bean, R. M., in *Rebuilding the foundation: Effective reading instruction for 21st century literacy* (T. Rasinski, Ed.), Bloomington, IN: Solution Tree Press. Adapted with permission.

- The atmosphere is comfortable and relaxed.
- All feel as though they have an important role in the group, and all participate.
- Group members listen to one another.
- Leadership shifts from individual to individual, depending on experience or expertise.
- The group works effectively as a unit to achieve its tasks.
- Group members are conscious of how the group is functioning (i.e., they are aware of the interpersonal and communication skills between and among group members).

I recommend Johnson and Johnson's *Joining Together* (2013) for those who want to read more about working with groups. They discuss in a clear manner the importance of attending to both *task* and *maintenance* responsibilities of a group, as described by Hersey and Blanchard (1977). That is, there is a goal to be met, and group members need to work in ways that enable them to focus on that goal. If the group is not staying on *task*, someone in the group must remind members of their goal; often this is the designated leader. At the same time, the leader must also be conscious of the importance of *maintaining* a climate that enhances the members' ability to work comfortably and effectively with one another. Ideas and comments made by members should be received in a receptive manner; all members must be encouraged to participate in the conversation.

In working with groups, remember that it takes time for members to think and work as a group, and to move from divergent to convergent thinking. Often, leaders become disappointed or disillusioned when, after one or two meetings, it appears as though no progress is being made. All groups go through what Kaner, Lind, Toldi, Fiski, and Berger (1996, p. 20) call "a groan zone," before they begin to function effectively.

Empowering Others

The most effective schools are those in which teachers feel as though they have a voice in what happens; they feel a sense of ownership or empowerment. There are several ways in which leaders can empower others. First, they can recognize the work of others, thus identifying colleagues as leaders. They can also encourage others to actively participate, thus promoting leadership behaviors. For example, the reading specialist may ask an individual teacher to lead a workshop session in which he or she discusses classroom management. In a group setting, the reading specialist as leader may solicit ideas and thoughts of particular group members, especially those who tend to be reticent to speak but who often have great ideas to share. The reading specialist can also provide opportunities for decision making that require group consensus or participation. For example:

> "We've come up with three different ideas about how we want to promote parent involvement in our schools. Let's talk about each of these, and what they mean in terms of planning and implementation. All of us as a group need to decide whether we will attempt to do all of these or will focus on just one. After listing pros and cons, we should try to come to a consensus as to our future direction."

Achieving Goals: Having a Vision

This characteristic of effective leadership is what some would call "the bottom line": the ability of the leader to help others to first decide upon goals or a vision, and then work with the group to reach them. Without a sense of direction, a goal, or a vision, little can be accomplished. When a decision is needed (e.g., about materials or a curriculum issue), the leader must be able to work with others in ways that ensure one is made. First and foremost it is essential to establish (1) a clear understanding of the goal to be achieved and (2) a commitment of the group to achieving that goal. In addition, leaders must make certain that those with whom they are working have the skills and resources they need to achieve those goals. Finally, there must be recognition and support every time a step is taken that moves the group toward goal achievement.

Respect for Others

Effective leaders respect those with whom they work. They seek and value the ideas of others; they recognize their own limitations. So, although effective leaders have a sense of vision and work aggressively to reach that vision, they are also respectful of the views of others. They are honest and fair in their dealings with their colleagues. Leaders who are seen by colleagues as "having all the answers" will soon find themselves without anyone to lead! Moreover, there will always be diverse perspectives when working with others; effective reading specialists accept this diversity and recognize that those with diverse views can help others think more creatively about various problems and solutions. Remembering that all individuals have different ways of making sense of the world can enable you to react differently to individuals, to practice a new form of compassion and connection (Berger, 2012). In other words, conflicts are not necessarily personal but the results of an individual's attempt to make sense of a situation from his or her perspective.

WORKING WITH GROUPS

All reading specialists, regardless of role, will find themselves working with small groups (e.g., grade-level or subject-area teams, curriculum committees, professional learning communities). The specialist may be the leader of the group, and on other occasions a member of the group. In either case, an understanding of basic group dynamics and how to conduct a group meeting are critical for the group to work effectively. By taking into consideration the following steps, meetings should be more productive with less grumbling about them being a waste of time.

Planning and Preparation

Planning includes setting goals for each meeting, preparing the agenda that assists in meeting these goals, and handling logistics for the meeting itself. Any informational items that do not need discussion can be prepared for distribution or sent to participants prior to the meeting. It may be productive to spend the first few minutes of a meeting, especially the initial meeting of any group, on helping the group to become acquainted (or reacquainted) with one another. Group leaders may want members to introduce themselves, share some personal information, or discuss their views about working on the task to which they are assigned. The agenda should be structured so that items of priority are identified first; a specific amount of time can be designated for each item so that those at the bottom of the agenda are also addressed. Part of initial planning includes providing for the place in which the meeting will be held. If the meeting is a large one and information is being presented, a classroom setting with rows of desks may serve as the venue. But if group participation is desired, the room must be one in which participants can sit in a circle and see and hear one another. The physical space matters! Often it helps if refreshments are provided, especially if the meeting is an after-school one (a common occurrence). All materials needed for the meeting should be at hand (e.g., handouts, flip charts). Planning also includes making decisions about how records are kept and disseminated. For some meetings, it might be important to keep minutes so that there is a permanent record of decisions made.

Establishing Norms for Group Behavior

The time spent in establishing rules or norms for group behavior is well spent; otherwise, the group may flounder as it attempts to make decisions or handle uncomfortable situations in which individuals are at odds about a specific issue. If possible, such norms are better established at the beginning of the school year or when a group is being formed. Otherwise, a leader may have to work to redirect the process if the group is working in a dysfunctional manner (e.g., only two of the six language arts teachers do most of the talking and, in fact, make the decisions in terms of scheduling and grouping; the other four leave the meeting "rolling their eyes" and feeling as though their voices are not being heard). Norms for the following may need to be addressed:

- What processes for decision making will be used (e.g., consensus, voting)?
- What roles are needed for effective group functioning (e.g., Is there a need for a note taker or a facilitator?; Will leadership change each meeting)?
- How will conflict be addressed?
- How will the group make certain that all members have opportunities to be heard?

Although a working group tends to develop its own set of rules and behaviors, the leader plays an important role in helping the group decide on these and then to follow them. It is also wise to post these norms or rules and review them before starting a meeting. It may also be helpful if the principal works with the reading specialist during some initial meetings of the group to establish those norms. Figure 4.2 provides a sample of what a list of norms might include, although the best way to proceed is to ask the group to establish its own norms. The leader can talk with the group about what they value when they attend meetings, asking members to identify ways of working that make meetings effective (e.g., members arrive on time).

Attending to Task and Relationship Aspects

Accomplishing goals or tasks is of key importance for both leader and team members! (Who has not heard grumbling about useless meetings in which items are discussed, rehashed, and then discussed again at the next meeting?) At the same time, members must be sensitive to the way in which the group is working so that all feel valued, participate, and assume a sense of responsibility for group achievement. This is not always easy, and some meetings will be better than others. One of the most effective ways to build a sense of "esprit de corps" is to take time at the end of the session to talk about what went well and how the group might modify its behavior to improve its work.

Working with Disruptive Group Members

There may be individuals in some groups who are difficult to work with—they do not want to be in the group, they are not accustomed to working with groups, or they antagonize others because they are unwilling to listen to others' ideas. Perhaps individuals such as those described below (adapted from Parrott's book *High-Maintenance Relationships: How to Handle Impossible People* [1996]) have been members of groups with whom you have worked:

- Begin and end the meeting on time. (Everyone arrives on time!)
- Have a focused agenda.
- All participants have an "equal voice."
- Be civil—agree to disagree.
- Be an active listener.
- Challenge ideas—not people.
- Presume positive intentions of team members.
- Make decisions by consensus.

FIGURE 4.2. Norms for team behavior at grade-level meetings.

- The Critic—constantly complains about whatever is being discussed (e.g., "Why are we talking about changing our schedules again?").
- The Wet Blanket—negative and pessimistic about new ideas or suggestions (e.g., "That will never work!").
- The Control Freak—wants to direct and control the decisions that will be made; tends to talk a great deal and loudly; not inclined to listen to ideas of others; pushes for specific decisions to be made.

There is no simple answer to working with such individuals. However, there are some techniques that may be effective in dealing with, say, George, who tends to be a critic. First, setting norms for appropriate group behavior as described above is key to changing or at least minimizing the effects of George's disruptive behavior. Second, within a group setting, the leader can often reduce disruptive or hostile behavior by giving George permission to express his frustrations or feelings. For some, having the opportunity to vent reduces or eliminates future negative behavior. Third, if all else fails, the leader may want to talk with George privately and describe the behavior about which he or she is concerned, asking, at the conclusion, whether there is anything the leader or the group can do to assist him in working more effectively with other members. Finally, we need to remember that each of us can at times be a difficult group member, depending on the topic or our own emotional state at the time.

Planning Again!

A meeting should not end without taking the time to summarize what has been achieved and to make plans for the next meeting. Various members may be asked to take responsibility for handling one or more tasks before the next meeting. It is helpful to send notes or minutes of the meeting to members, highlighting major decisions and reminding them of the tasks that need to be accomplished before the next meeting. And again, taking the time to reflect on what worked well during the meeting provides a starting point for the next meeting. Two key questions to be asked at the end of the meeting are "What have we learned?" and "Where are we now?"

THINK ABOUT THIS

Notice the ways that Katy (see "Voices from the Field" in this chapter) works with her team of teachers and how she facilitates grade-level meetings. In what ways does Katy provide for both task and maintenance behaviors?

The ideas presented above are important for reading specialists who have major responsibility for developing or coordinating school reading programs (see Chapter 8). Books that may be useful to those who frequently work with groups include Johnson and Johnson's *Joining Together: Group Theory and Group Skills* (2013), Kaner and colleagues' *Facilitator's Guide to Participatory Decision-Making* (1996), or Parker's *Lead Simply: How to Create That Special Team of People* (2012).

THE READING SPECIALIST AS LEADER

Each reading specialist will handle leadership responsibilities in a slightly different way, depending on (1) job descriptions and opportunities, (2) the degree of fit between his or her personality and a leadership role, (3) his or her leadership skills and abilities, and (4) the school context. Note the different leadership roles reading specialists in the vignettes in "Voices from the Field" assume: some have full-time leadership roles (Celia, Karen, and Wendy) and the others, who have more responsibility for working with students, find themselves functioning as leaders throughout the school day or week. Reading specialists who work with children for six periods a day have less opportunity to assume leadership roles but can still serve as leaders as they interact with individual or groups of teachers. The new reading specialist, with little experience, may not yet be ready to handle complex or large-scale leadership roles but can work with a mentor to gain experience with such tasks. All reading specialists need to have not only an awareness of their own leadership skills and strengths but an understanding of how to serve as an effective leader. Certainly, the culture of the school (e.g., opportunity for a leadership role, teachers' receptivity to working collaboratively) will influence the ways in which reading specialists address the leadership role.

As mentioned previously, Hersey and Blanchard (1977) provide a useful way of thinking about leadership in their discussion of situational leadership. They suggest classifying the actions of leaders into *task* actions (e.g., achieving the goal) or *maintenance* actions (e.g., moving the group along in the discussion or taking into consideration the feelings and competencies of group members). They purport various combinations of leadership can be effective, depending on the makeup of the group: How motivated are members to accomplish this task?; How knowledgeable are members? When group members do not have essential knowledge or skills, the leader must engage in high-task behaviors to keep the momentum flowing. Hersey and Blanchard suggest that in these instances, the leader may need to spend more time telling or transmitting information. The leader may also need to convince the members that they can accomplish the job (i.e., selling).

In groups where participants have a great deal of knowledge and are eager to work on the designated task, the leader can work in a different manner, serving as a participant in the group or even delegating responsibility. Imagine the following situation, for example: You are working with a group of experienced teachers who have different views and perspectives about the reading program they are currently using in their school. Their task is to identify criteria that they can use to select new material. All are eager to get new material, but there are some strong opinions about what constitutes effective reading instruction and agreement is not imminent. Your role (most likely) is to help the group discuss the salient points in an effective manner while remaining sensitive to the different viewpoints and making certain that all members understand that their thoughts are valued. This group is eager to accomplish the task, and the members have much experiential knowledge. At the same time, they need a leader who can focus them on maintenance or relationship actions that help them to listen, respect different views, and learn from others.

One can also think about task and relationship behaviors when working with individual teachers. For example, if a reading specialist meets with a teacher who is concerned about the comprehension that he or she is providing for his or her third-grade students and asks for help in making instructional modifications or changes, it is obvious this teacher is eager for help. Building a relationship will most likely not take much effort; rather, the focus can be on the task of providing this teacher with effective ideas for teaching comprehension.

THINK ABOUT THIS

How comfortable would you be in your leadership role in the situation with experienced teachers whose task is to select new materials? What difficulties do you foresee in working with this group? What essential skills would you need for working with the third-grade teacher who is seeking information about teaching comprehension?

The following section describes ideas for ways in which the reading specialist can serve as a resource to others. This leadership role is an informal one that can be used by most reading specialists, regardless of experience or job description.

SERVING AS A RESOURCE TO TEACHERS

• *Inform teachers of new ideas and materials.* Such information does not need to be formally presented in a group meeting. Reading specialists can circulate key journal articles to interested teachers and administrators. They can also summarize articles in interesting ways and place them in faculty mailboxes. For example, after reading several articles about fluency or teaching comprehension strategies, a reading specialist can develop a flyer summarizing key instructional ideas and send this (electronically or in print) to teachers (see Figure 4.3 for an example). The flyer can even include some ideas about how the reading specialist might be able to work with teachers to implement the strategies. Teachers tend to appreciate these short summaries that alert them to some possible ways of improving classroom instruction for their students. When new material arrives at the school, reading specialists can inform teachers such material is available and volunteer to "try out" the material with a selected group of students. They can take new children's books to specific teachers, suggesting that their students might enjoy reading them. Sometimes it is helpful to talk about professional issues at lunch or before or after school. For example, the reading specialist might comment, "So, what do you think about the article in the paper questioning the effect of retention? How does that fit with the policy that we have in our school?"

• *Spread the word about effective teaching and teachers: Encourage shared leadership.* As mentioned earlier in this chapter, a major task of a leader is enhancing the capacity of others to lead. So, when a novice teacher asks for help with grouping, the reading specialist may identify one or two teachers who are especially talented in planning for the instructional needs of groups of students. After seeking permission from those teachers, the reading specialist can suggest the novice teacher observe in those classrooms (with the reading specialist taking over the class of the visiting teacher) or, if possible, the reading specialist can observe along with the novice teacher. If so, the reading specialist can, in a postobservation conference, highlight salient aspects of the grouping in the lesson observed. The reading specialist is serving as a resource since he or she has a better sense of what teachers are doing in their classrooms and who might be especially effective with specific approaches or strategies. At the same time, he or she is sharing and developing leadership capacity in others.

• *Focus on the student.* Most teachers want every child in their classroom to be a successful reader. Often, teachers have tried many different strategies to help various children—sometimes with little success. Therefore, one key approach to serving as a resource to teachers is helping them implement strategies that may improve reading performance of one or more students. During a staff development project in which I served as a resource to teachers in one school, one of the tasks that I most enjoyed was helping a new teacher learn several effective strategies

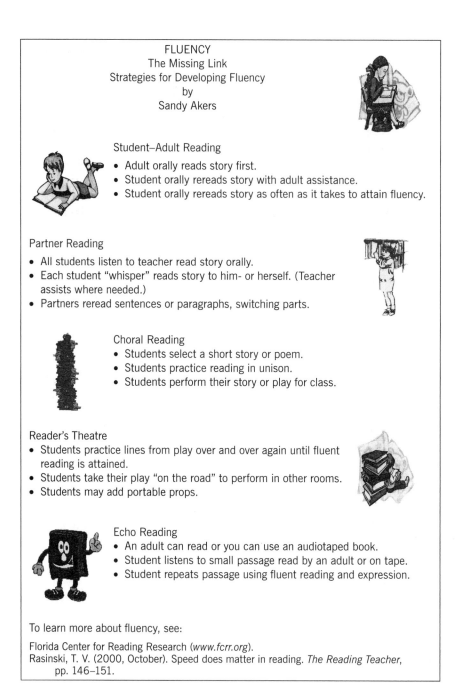

FLUENCY
The Missing Link
Strategies for Developing Fluency
by
Sandy Akers

Student–Adult Reading

- Adult orally reads story first.
- Student orally rereads story with adult assistance.
- Student orally rereads story as often as it takes to attain fluency.

Partner Reading

- All students listen to teacher read story orally.
- Each student "whisper" reads story to him- or herself. (Teacher assists where needed.)
- Partners reread sentences or paragraphs, switching parts.

Choral Reading

- Students select a short story or poem.
- Students practice reading in unison.
- Students perform their story or play for class.

Reader's Theatre

- Students practice lines from play over and over again until fluent reading is attained.
- Students take their play "on the road" to perform in other rooms.
- Students may add portable props.

Echo Reading

- An adult can read or you can use an audiotaped book.
- Student listens to small passage read by an adult or on tape.
- Student repeats passage using fluent reading and expression.

To learn more about fluency, see:

Florida Center for Reading Research (*www.fcrr.org*).
Rasinski, T. V. (2000, October). Speed does matter in reading. *The Reading Teacher*, pp. 146–151.

FIGURE 4.3. Student brochure. Reprinted by permission from Sandra R. Akers, Reading Specialist, Butler Area School District.

for improving the decoding abilities of her students. We reviewed assessment data and discussed several strategies, including Cunningham and Hall's (1994) Making Words technique. I then agreed to do a demonstration lesson of that procedure. I also gave the teacher her own copy of Cunningham and Hall's book *Making Words*. The teacher was very excited about the approach and invited me to observe her as she taught. The children were now learning a great deal—and she was excited about their success—and her own.

• *Be available and follow through on your commitments.* Unless reading specialists are "seen" in the schools, there may be little chance of serving as a leader. It is easy to find tasks to attend to, such as paperwork or administrative duties, that take specialists away from classrooms. When reading specialists take the time to stop in and visit teachers, post the days on which they will be at a specific school (if they travel), or volunteer to help teachers if they see an opening, they are leaders. Effective reading specialists also eat with their colleagues or visit the teacher lounge on a regular basis so that they get to know teachers on a more personal level, as well as a professional level. Often interactions between the reading specialist and teachers occur informally or "on the fly." Teachers may stop the specialist in the hallway or the lunchroom to ask a question that opens the door to more in-depth conversations at a later time. One literacy coach describes how her interaction with teachers increased when her office was moved from near the principal's office to near the students' bathroom (Bean & DeFord, n.d.).

Equally important is providing follow-through on every commitment made. Usually, teachers do not understand or appreciate cancellations, even when they appear to be unavoidable; for example, the principal may ask the reading specialist to attend a district meeting about the literacy program. Certainly, there are times when reading specialists may need to cancel or make changes in their schedules, but every effort must be made to assure the teacher that the commitment will be honored at a later time. The teachers should also be informed as soon as possible if there is to be a change in the schedule. Also, reschedule as soon as possible. Lack of follow-through will quickly destroy the credibility of the reading specialist. Teachers may soon decide that there is little they can expect from the reading specialist and will close the door, literally and figuratively, to future interactions.

• *Be flexible.* Flexibility is an especially critical quality because often creative and effective ideas emerge in the moment, as the reading specialist works with a specific teacher or teachers, and their implementation usually requires "on-the-spot" adjustments to planned work. These ideas may come from the reading specialist or the teacher. The most effective reading specialists quickly think of ways that they can facilitate the development and implementation of these ideas, rather than thinking of reasons why such ideas are impractical. In discussing leadership, Colin Powell said, "You don't know what you can get away with until you try" (Harari, 2002, p. 65). In other words, reading specialists are most effective when they look for ways to make things happen.

Flexibility is also important in terms of working with individual teachers. For example, the reading specialist may be able to serve as a coteacher in the classroom to implement guided reading with one teacher because that teacher is receptive to working with another adult in the classroom. With another teacher, the reading specialist may provide materials and suggestions about guided reading, giving that individual an opportunity to think about the approach and how it might be implemented. In another instance, the reading specialist and teacher may plan the lesson together, and after the teacher implements the lesson, the two educators meet together to talk about the results and next steps.

• *Be a willing helper!* There are times when teachers are overloaded and can use some additional help from the reading specialist (e.g., getting ready for the annual parent evening, classroom assessment responsibilities, report card time). Reading specialists who are willing to assist teachers, even if in a small way (e.g., helping to post student work, assisting with the assessments) will develop better relationships with teachers and ultimately find them to be more willing to listen to ideas that may require some changes on their part. In the vignette in this chapter, written by Katy, a part-time coach, she describes the ways she helped teachers at the beginning of the year by developing materials for them (see "Voices from the Field" below).

A RESOURCE FOR SPECIALIZED PROFESSIONALS

As mentioned in Figure 1.1 (see Chapter 1) reading specialists often work with specialized personnel in schools. RTI or similar models for differentiating instruction and the focus on data as a source of decision making call for much more collaboration in schools. In a recent study of schools implementing an RTI approach, one finding showed a greater emphasis on working collaboratively to identify student needs and make decisions about how to support teachers (Bean & Lillenstein, 2012). Collaborative teams included professionals such as reading specialists and literacy coaches, special education teachers, speech teachers, counselors, and psychologists. The principal also met frequently with these teams, but was not always the team leader; frequently the reading specialist or coach was responsible for leading the team efforts. The group met to make decisions about how to improve literacy instruction for the students in their schools, discussing results of assessment, grouping possibilities, and instructional approaches. All meetings ended with action plans: Who was going to do what, with whom, and when?

Such teams of course may also include teachers of the arts, librarians, and physical education instructors, as well as others. What is important is that those responsible for teaching students receive the same message so they can plan for coherent and coordinated instruction. Although many schools have implemented teams to discuss students with special needs, there should also be informal conversations among these educators. Too often, children with special needs receive multiple and possibly conflicting intervention strategies because of the lack of communication among the educators involved with them. Educators can learn from one another about the various approaches used to improve reading performance. For example, speech teachers are often well prepared to teach phonemic awareness to young children. Likewise, special educators may appreciate information about the various approaches to teaching reading that the reading specialist can share with them. Special educators, in turn, often have well-designed behavior management programs or instructional strategies that they can share with others.

In addition to working with educators who work with students who have special needs, involvement with others—such as art teachers, librarians, and so on—can promote improvement of reading for all students in the schools. Music teachers can teach songs that help young children develop their phonemic awareness skills. The arts program can be used in the upper grades as a means of expanding and enhancing students' thematic learning in the various content areas. The librarian can be a source of information about book availability and work with teachers to promote student interest and motivation to read. Recently, the IRA (2014) in collaboration with other organizations released a position statement about the importance of leisure reading and the impact it can have on students' literacy learning. In that document, the importance of partnering with school librarians is highlighted.

Interactions with school psychologists may also be an important part of the reading specialists' role, not only to obtain test information about students but to learn more about the child and to share information that may assist the psychologist in getting a more complete picture of a specific student. Often, the type of assessments that reading specialists administer help psychologists gain a more specific understanding of the child's instructional needs in relation to literacy. Hoffman and Jenkins (2002) conducted interviews with a group of reading specialists to learn more about their interactions with school psychologists. They found that these reading specialists had some collaborative experiences with the school psychologists, but that scheduling time for interactions was a problem. They also talked about the importance of establishing good personal relationships and knowing more about how to collaborate effectively.

A RESOURCE FOR ADMINISTRATORS

Principals set the tone and establish the conditions to enhance the work of the reading specialist; without their support, reading specialists will have difficulty performing their role effectively. As stated by Bean and Lillenstein (2012), "the principal served as the central person for promoting a risk-free environment, . . . facilitating shared responsibility and accountability" (p. 497). Although many principals, especially those in the elementary school, have an in-depth understanding of reading instruction, some do not; given their multiple responsibilities, many do not have adequate time to devote to the leadership of the reading program. They may rely on the reading specialist in their school for specific information about how the school as a whole is doing (e.g., achievement scores in the areas of reading: decoding, comprehension). Principals may also need to be informed as to whether there is a need for additional professional development in the area of reading for specific teachers (e.g., content-area teachers in the high school want to know more about discipline-specific literacy instruction). In other words, when reading specialists inform the principal about their activities and solicit support (e.g., changes in scheduling, need for supplemental materials, digital resources), they will be better able to do their job more effectively. Reading specialists, in addition, should make themselves available to the principal, responding to the principal's requests for information about the reading program. Some principals schedule meetings with the specialist once a week; others prefer to receive written updates from the reading specialist on a regular basis. Because principals are busy with many different responsibilities, reading specialists may need to initiate interactions, perhaps sending brief e-mail messages summarizing key points about literacy instruction or assessment.

SUMMARY

Reading specialists all have leadership responsibilities, but these differ depending on job opportunities, experience, and the technical skills of the specialist. Such skills include having the ability to (1) communicate with others, (2) work with teams, (3) achieve goals, (4) empower others, and (5) work in a respectful way with others. The leadership role for reading specialists is often one that requires leading by influence and will differ, depending on the context in which one works. All reading specialists can serve as a resource for teachers, administrators, and other professionals involved with struggling readers.

ADDITIONAL READINGS

Bean, R. M., Swan, A. L., & Knaub, R. (2003). Reading specialists in schools with exemplary reading programs: Functional, versatile, and prepared. *The Reading Teacher, 56*(5), 446–455.—This article describes the results of a study of reading specialists and principals in schools identified as having an exemplary reading program. All reading specialists had leadership responsibilities. Principals indicated that reading specialists had an important influence on the effectiveness of the reading program.

Barth, R. S. (2013). The time is ripe (again). *Educational Leadership, 71*(2), 10–16.—The author discusses why teacher leadership has not been prevalent in schools, the potential for increased teacher leadership, and the rationale for promoting it.

Reflections

1. How would you assess your own leadership skills? What do you see as your strengths? Weaknesses?
2. Why is the leadership role of the reading specialist an important one? Why do you suppose that some reading specialists see it as one of their most difficult tasks?
3. Think about a group with which you have been involved recently. What was the leader's style? How did the leader help the group to work effectively?
4. Jot down ideas about how you might actualize the three elements (pp. 84–85) identified by Parker (2012); then discuss your ideas with others.

Activities

1. Interview a reading specialist to determine what leadership roles he or she assumes. Ask the specialist to identify what skills are needed to perform such tasks and what challenges exist.
2. Attend a group meeting. Think about the leadership style of the leader. How did the group achieve its goals? In what ways did the group exhibit its ability to work together as a team?

3. Discuss the following scenario: What leadership style would be most effective, given the characteristics of the teacher?

   A new first-grade teacher has told you that she is having no difficulties teaching her students, is enjoying her experience, and does not need any specific help from you, the reading specialist. However, you have been in her classroom and have noticed some classroom practices that indicate that she has very little knowledge of how to teach phonics.

4. In small groups, discuss the vignette below, reflecting on what Katy brings to her role as literacy coach; identify three important "take-aways" from that vignette. Share the work of small groups with the whole class.

Some questions to think about:

What lessons can be learned about the role of the reading specialist in this vignette?

In what ways does Katy serve as a leader?

What questions come to mind after reading this vignette?

KATY: KINDERGARTEN TEACHER AND COACH

As hard as it is for me to believe, this fall I will start my 25th year in education. As I reflect on those years, there have been, as one would expect, ups and downs, ebbs and flows, growth and learning. The tears of my first year gave way to determination and grit that, over the years, have wiped away my fear of failure and the insecurities I had about my ability or, more often, my inability to be an effective educator. That determination grows stronger every year and motivates me to do my best with teachers and for children every day.

Motivated was the way I began last September. My job was twofold: teach reading in my kindergarten class half the day and work with K–2 reading teachers the other half supporting them in teaching literacy. I shared a room with another coach/teacher who had the same schedule: teach kindergarten math and coach K–2 math teachers. This had not been done at the school before so we were pretty much on our own to make it work within and outside our classroom. Our principal was supportive of the work that needed to be done, but relied on the two of us to take a leadership role in deciding how we would work with teachers. The prospect was exciting, but daunting. I was responsible for the learning of 25 kindergarteners and 12 adults.

I knew this position was for only 1 year—our funding did not last beyond that. As a result, I recognized the large amount of work I had to do in a short amount of time. Sheryl Sandberg wrote in her book *Lean In*, "Leadership is about making others better as a result of your presence and making sure that impact lasts in your absence" (2013, p. 157). In my mind, "leadership" was synonymous with "coaching" and this became my mantra for the year. I constantly asked myself how I could best use my time and energy while I was working wih teachers so the effects would last after I was back in a classroom full time.

Although I had taught with most of the teachers I was working with for at least 2 years, I thought I still needed to develop a new level of trust between us because I wanted them to let me into their classrooms with the confidence that I was there to build them up and never tear them down. We have had coaches in the district for many years and, unfortunately, because of the actions of a few, a level of mistrust between teachers and coaches had formed in some places. Based on previous experience, I know the best way to a teacher's heart is to take something off his or her plate—identify a need they have and take care of it for them. I began with flashcards. First-grade teachers wanted short-vowel flashcards. Second-grade teachers wanted one- and two-syllable long-vowel flashcards. Although no one disagreed about the need for them, the time it was going to take to make them was not a top priority. So I typed, mounted, laminated, and cut them for each teacher. They were so appreciative. I felt like it sent a message: I understood all of the demands on their time and I was there to help in any way I could.

Our school is on a 6-day schedule. One day during the 6-day rotation each team meets as a grade-level learning community for 70 minutes—homeroom and first period. Special subject teachers, who are not assigned a homeroom class, are responsible for picking up a designated class from breakfast, keeping them during homeroom, and teaching them during first period. Scheduling the meetings during first period gave us the ability to add on the 25 minutes from homeroom. Excuses about not being prepared and/or being late were minimized because the meeting was first thing in the morning and no one saw their students before the meeting began.

My coaching partner and I decided early on that we would do weekly rotations of mornings and afternoons. For example, I would teach kindergarten in the morning for an entire week while she performed her coaching duties. The next week I coached in the morning and taught in the afternoon. This worked best because our teaching time evened out—there was more teaching time in the morning schedule than in the afternoon—and we would each be able to attend the weekly grade-level meetings approximately every other week. It was important for us to attend each K–2 grade-level meeting because they were the genesis of our work. The impact the meetings had on teacher learning and teacher practice was amazing. These meetings also helped the two of us set the agenda for our work.

Data-Informed Decision Making

I used to think I believed in data-driven instruction. I recently read Deborah Meier's phrase "data informed" in Diane Ravitch's book *The Death and Life of the Great American School System* (2010). That resonates with me much more. We call our grade-level meetings data teams, but that term always seemed too narrow as a way to describe the work that actually takes place. We used data from tests as one way of looking at children, but we also used student work, teacher observation, and personal anecdotes. This broader picture brought each student to life. We did not see them as numbers on a page, but as real living, breathing, learning individuals. As we began to have more complete pictures of each learner, we were better able to address their needs.

In order to get us away from looking strictly at the numbers, early in the year I asked each teacher to bring a writing sample from every child. They could choose or create any assignment, but each child had to have a sample. I brought a copy of their class list to our next meeting and a hat with the numbers 1–30 on individual slips of paper in it. I wanted us to look at a random sample of student work so I had each teacher choose a number from the hat and find the child who corresponded with that number on his or her class list. We pulled samples from five different children and discussed their work. We talked about what we wanted to see in each sample. That led to questions and dialogue about the appropriateness of each task. We talked about what we saw and what we didn't see—children were misspelling sight words they should have mastered, punctuation was nonexistent, correct use of capital letters was inconsistent, some students wrote one long run-on sentence, the first paragraph was indented incorrectly.. ..We made a list of everything. The more comfortable teachers became, the more samples they brought into the discussion. We prioritized student need(s) from the list we created. For example, although we do not teach skills in isolation, we did talk about the importance of sight words versus indenting each paragraph. In a sense, which gives us the most bang for our buck? We connected reading and writing—if they can write sight words, it seems most likely they will also be able to read them. We didn't always agree on the priority of things, so each teacher chose something from the list to work on over the next 6 days and more work samples were brought to the next meeting. This cycle led to discussions about teacher practices and reflection on what worked, what didn't, and why. I was available between meetings for anything a teacher needed—planning, co-teaching, modeling, observing to give feedback, creating supplies, hearing stories about lessons . . . whatever was necessary to further the work. The meetings were routine in many ways so teachers knew what to expect and what was expected of them, but were flexible enough so real issues that came up in classrooms could be discussed and the teacher went away with some sort of solution or, at least, suggestions for how to attack the problem. I also knew what my work was. As a result, I could organize my time so I was not overwhelmed by my coaching and teaching duties.

Team Meetings

Although we developed a routine for the meetings, the work wasn't always smooth or easy. Teachers weren't always comfortable sharing the work of their students and they weren't always willing to try something new. Suggested strategies that were outside of our managed curriculum were sometimes seen as rebellious recommendations and not welcome in certain classrooms. The fact that teachers see the work of their students as a reflection of them as teachers instead of using it as a reflective tool to inform their work was, at times, a barrier to the growth of individuals. The only way I saw to resolve the issues was consistency and time. At the end of every meeting, we explicitly stated what the expectations were for each team member before the next meeting. I was certain to honor the work they did at the next meeting, no matter what other important questions or concerns had come up between meetings. By holding everyone accountable for completing the work they agreed to, we set standards and expectations for our time together. I believe that when teachers understood that they didn't always have to agree, different approaches and philosophies were accepted and appreciated and the basis of our work was the student products they brought with them. They began to value the process and fully invest in the time we spent together.

One teacher, Kelley, had a major shift in her thinking and teaching this year. She has been teaching for 4 years, never taught the same grade level 2 years in a row and has been furloughed at the end of each school year. This uncertainty took its toll on her. She wondered why she worked so hard without the reward of job security. Her attitude of indifference was very clear. It was a struggle to get her to the grade-level meetings on time without a list of excuses. She was a step-by-step curriculum follower and didn't see the need to discuss anything because the curriculum told her what to do and when to do it. Late in the first quarter of the school year another teacher asked some questions about reading behaviors he was seeing with a few of his students. It turned into an in-depth conversation with the team. Each teacher had questions and observations to share. Kelley was quiet at the beginning, but she slowly entered the conversation by saying she was seeing the same behaviors in her students. At the end of the meeting, she stated that the conversation made her think differently about how she was working with some students. She asked me several questions throughout the week and brought concerns to the whole group at our next meeting. Her team shared background thinking, materials, and strategies to try. She tried one and saw success. She tried another and saw more success. She took baby steps with her class and with her team. She didn't let setbacks derail her. She began to use the curriculum as a foundation and put more thought into what her students needed to reach the goals she had for them. She admitted that she was afraid of venturing into unknown territory, but with the support of her team, she felt successful and empowered to try things she had never done before. She now sees herself growing as a confident teacher who can make sound decisions for her students.

William Ayers quoted Lillian Weber in his book *Teaching toward Freedom*: "They begin school an exclamation point and a question mark; too often they leave as a plain period" (2004, p. 41). She was talking about students, but the same could be said of teachers. My job as a coach is to be one of the people who keep teachers excited and passionate about their work, yet continuously prod them to ask good questions in order to understand the art and craft of our profession. Facilitating change, being an instructional leader, is the heart of what we do. In order to do this I need to know each teacher as a learner and be willing to work with him or her where he or she is. I can't impose my thinking and my expectations on teachers. I need to find out what their goals are and work with them toward those. As Max DePree wrote in *Leadership Jazz*: "Efficiency is doing things right. Effectiveness is doing the right things" (1992, p. 130). Baby steps help us see the growth embedded in the learning process and show us the effect of the right things we are doing. We can't get everything done at once, but planting seeds that will continue to develop in our absence is the essence of coaching—the core of our true effectiveness.

KATY CARROLL, EdD
Teacher and Coach
Pittsburgh Public Schools
Pittsburgh, Pennsylvania

CHAPTER FIVE

Professional Learning

The New Professional Development

Professional development is not about workshops . . . it is at
its heart the development of habits of learning . .
—FULLAN (2001b, p. 253)

Key Questions

- What are the essential factors in an effective professional
  development program for teachers?

- What are the essential differences between the terms *professional
  development* and *professional learning*?

- In what ways can teachers become involved in active professional
  learning?

In this chapter, I discuss research findings about professional development (PD), professional learning communities (PLCs) as an approach
for improving teacher practices and student learning, and standards as
a foundation for professional development. Also, I describe the elements
of context, process, and content, and how they affect the development
of professional learning (PL) experiences. I conclude with specific ideas
about leading and evaluating professional development initiatives, using
the terms *professional development* and *professional learning* inter-
changeably, often using PD to refer to earlier literature and research and
PL to refer to new thinking about how to enhance teacher learning in
schools today.

Michael Fullan (2001b) in the quotation above identifies an important notion about the PD of teachers: Teachers must be internally

motivated to learn more about being effective at the craft of teaching, to become lifelong learners. Thus, the new title of this chapter is inspired by the recently developed *Standards for Professional Learning* (Learning Forward, 2011), which signal the importance of PL based on the day-to-day realities of classrooms and focused on improving student learning. No longer is the emphasis on educators being the recipient of something "done to or for them." Rather, the focus is on teachers being proactive in their own learning by being involved in collaborative learning, shared leadership, and decision making at the school level. This does not mean that gaining information through workshops or school meetings is meaningless, but rather teachers have a much different role in what happens in those workshops or meetings and in the follow-up activities that are provided.

PD in the past tended to be standardized, based on transmission of information, short term, and at times irrelevant to what teachers needed to do to improve their practices. Sessions provided by schools or districts tended to be offered schoolwide, generic, and lacking the intensity and focus to affect teacher practices or student learning. Often, PD was seen as a quick fix or silver bullet; it was based on a "one-size-fits-all mentality." Once teachers had attended a specific workshop or workshops, it was expected they would change their teaching practices and student learning would improve. New research about adult learning, school change, and leadership has stimulated new ways of thinking about PL, however.

Reading specialists often have important roles in supporting these PL opportunities. They lead workshops to provide information about effective literacy instruction or assessment and they facilitate grade-level or departmental team meetings, helping teachers think about instruction for a specific grade, academic subject, or component of literacy. They also assist in the development of curriculum, or they coach, suggesting resources, coplanning and co-teaching, modeling, observing, and providing feedback to individual teachers about their literacy instruction. They serve an important role in facilitating shared decision making and teacher leadership as they work collaboratively with their colleagues. Key to reading specialists' PD efforts is their ability to work with school leadership, especially the principal who establishes the conditions for promoting teacher learning.

REVITALIZING THE WASTELAND

Concern about and interest in literacy instruction, from national to local levels, have led to calls for improving teacher knowledge and performance in teaching literacy. Moreover, we now have evidence that quality teaching is the single most important variable contributing to student learning (Darling-Hammond, Wei, Andree, Richardson, & Orphanos, 2009; Hanushek, 1992; Rivkin, Hanushek, & Kain, 2005). In fact, having three or four good teachers in succession can be especially important for students and, likewise, having several weak teachers in a row can negatively influence students' learning (Center for American Progress and the Education Trust, 2011).

According to Snow and colleagues (1998), all teachers need support and guidance throughout their careers, not just novices, but those who have been teaching for extended periods of time to assist them in updating their knowledge and instructional skills. As Louisa Moats puts it: *Teaching Reading IS Rocket Science* (1999). In that publication, the writer indicates teachers must be experts in order to teach reading effectively. They must know a lot about their subject matter and the instructional strategies that will enable them to provide the best literacy experiences for their students. Given the diversity of our society, they must also have a deep understanding of their students, their experiential backgrounds, and cultural heritage.

Yet as mentioned, PD, as it had been conducted in schools, has generally been considered the wasteland of education (Little, 1993). Teachers have been introduced to, and sometimes bombarded with, information about new projects or activities that happen to be in fashion at a specific time, often before there was research evidence to establish the innovation as effective. At times, initiatives were placed in schools without attention to the implementation process, that is, the support and resources that teachers needed so that the innovation was implemented as intended. As Fullan (1991) discussed, there was often an implementation dip, with teachers having difficulty using new ideas to which they had been introduced. Often, without support and ongoing feedback, these new instructional approaches did not become part of the teachers' repertoire. Joyce and Showers (1995) called for creating change in schools using a PD system that was "far more powerful and pervasive than the one that exists" (p. 5).

THE STATUS OF PROFESSIONAL DEVELOPMENT: WHAT WE KNOW FROM RESEARCH

Previous research on PD indicates that participation in such efforts can change teachers' attitudes and practices and even improve student achievement (Desimone, Porter, Garet, Yoon, & Berman, 2002; National Institute of Child Health and Human Development, 2000; Sparks & Loucks-Horsley, 1990; Taylor, Pearson, & Rodriguez, 2005).

In Taylor and colleagues' (2005) study of PD in schools implementing a school change framework, greater growth was seen in students' reading achievement in schools that had high implementation, and also, greater effects were seen when the results were examined after 2 years. Three recently published reports provide key information about the status of PD in the United States (Darling-Hammond, Wei, Andree, Richardson, & Orphanos, 2009; Jaquith, Mindich, Wei, & Darling-Hammond, 2010; Wei, Darling-Hammond, & Adamson, 2010). Four key findings of these reports are:

1. Teachers value PL experiences, especially those meaningful to them in their daily work.
2. PD not connected to teachers' classroom teaching had little impact on teaching or student learning.
3. Teachers had few opportunities for sustained PD experiences, that is, short-term workshops were most common; opportunities for collaboration decreased between 2002 and 2004.
4. State policies and systems that helped to improve PD for teachers include standards for PD, accountability and monitoring of PD efforts, units in the state that provide PD for districts, and resources for schools.

There is probably little to disagree with in these findings, however, several are disappointing; it appears not much has changed in how PD is provided in schools today. Yet, over the years, evidence about the criteria for quality PD has been growing; in a recent report on teacher development, Darling-Hammond and colleagues' (2009, pp. 9–11) identified four critical elements of PD initiatives. They must:

1. Be intensive, ongoing, and connected to practice.
2. Focus on student learning and address the teaching of specific curriculum content.
3. Align with school improvement priorities and goals.
4. Build strong working relationships among teachers.

WHAT IS PROFESSIONAL DEVELOPMENT?
WHAT IS PROFESSIONAL LEARNING?

In the recent *Handbook of Professional Development in Education*, Lieberman and Miller (2014) describe two competing models of PD. The prevalent model in schools today is the training model of in-service teacher education, in which teachers receive information, often through workshops; these informational sessions are (or should be) followed by some sort of coaching or feedback efforts. Most often, this model is a top-down approach, determined by the district (e.g., we need to improve comprehension) or even the state (e.g., all schools will learn how to implement RTI). Although such in-service efforts have merit, it is difficult for them to take into account the specific context in which an initiative is being implemented or what is known about how adults learn. The new paradigm, PL as growth in practice, emphasizes the following: a focus on the specific problems of the classroom and school, meaningful collaboration and engagement with ideas, and opportunities for teachers to reflect about their problems and to develop solutions for them. It requires teachers develop habits of learning so they become lifelong learners. One approach to this growth-in-practice paradigm is PLCs. Other approaches similar to PLCs call for schools to function as places of learning, where there are opportunities for teachers to work collaboratively and focus on addressing problems specific to the students in their school and classrooms. I discuss PLCs and some of the factors important for their success below.

THINK ABOUT THIS

What type of PD have you participated in—school mandated, volunteer, group, or individual effort? Which has been most useful and why? Would you define these activities as promoting you as a learner? Have you had opportunities to participate in a PLC and, if so, what are your responses to this type of learning?

IMPROVING PROFESSIONAL LEARNING: SCHOOLS AS PLACES OF LEARNING

PLCs can be defined as "groups of teachers who meet regularly for the purpose of increasing their own learning and that of their students" (Lieberman & Miller, 2008, p. 2). Members of a PLC learn from one another in their efforts to improve student learning. Vescio, Ross, and Adams (2008) identified five essential characteristics of PLCs: (1) development of shared values and norms, (2) focus on student learning, (3) reflective dialogue among teachers, (4) making teaching public, and (5) collaboration among educators at the school. However, instituting successful PLCs is not easy. Wood (2007) describes the challenges faced by a district that attempted to implement PLCs: an overemphasis on the process rather than a focus on student learning, resistance by teachers and administrators to the required cultural changes, and lack of time and support. In other words, there is a danger in PLCs that teachers (without leadership) will focus more on the protocol or group activity than they will on what they can learn to facilitate student learning. In order for PLCs to be effective, then, the school must be prepared to begin a journey that requires participants to learn how to hold meaningful conversations that focus on key topics related to instruction and assessment. Teachers need time to talk about and collaborate on important issues related to teaching and assessment; there must be leadership guiding them in these collaborative efforts, and support and understanding from school administration for this work. PLCs can be more effective if the principal is a member of the team, working alongside teachers.

Recently, my colleague Allison Swan Dagen and I (Swan Dagen & Bean, 2014)) described this emphasis on PL as a means of addressing "the collective ability and capacity of teachers in a school to address challenges and solve problems that enable the organization to become more effective in . . . improving student learning" (p. 44). In other words, to increase overall school performance, more must be done than to improve individual teacher skills and competence; rather, the focus should be on helping teachers work together toward a common vision, and participate in decision making and shared leadership as a means of achieving their goals. So, regardless of whether a school indicates that it has or does not have formal PLCs, it should establish itself as a place where both student and adult learning are valued, and where there is an emphasis on teachers working together to analyze data, make decisions about instruction, and participate as leaders in the school.

STANDARDS FOR PROFESSIONAL LEARNING

One of the sources of information that can drive PL in a school is the standards in the recently revised *Standards for Professional Learning* (Learning Forward, 2011), which include seven dimensions: learning communities, leadership, resources, data, learning design, implementation, and outcomes. In an earlier publication (National Staff Development Council, 2001), three key elements of effective PD were described: context, process, and content. I use these three elements to discuss PL as it applies to literacy instruction in schools.

Context

The creation of a successful PD plan must be based on the context in which it is to be implemented. Several questions must be addressed:

- What are the literacy goals and needs of the students in the school? What do teachers need to know and be able to do to address these goals and needs? What are teachers' attitudes about change? What are the experiences, skills, and abilities of the teachers who will implement the plan?
- Is the culture in the school one that is receptive and eager to change? Do teachers work together in a collaborative fashion and focus on the ultimate goal of improving student learning?
- Does the leadership in the school support and advocate for PL for teachers?
- What resources are available from the administration and the community?

In one school, faculty may be receptive to new ideas and ready to make changes in how they teach literacy. In other schools, more preliminary work may be needed before the actual program can be implemented. Often it is necessary for the leadership team to think about current practices and what may need to be eliminated before new practices can be instituted. One of the common complaints of teachers, and rightly so, is that they are always asked to add to what they are doing—in an already filled day!

Other legitimate issues include concerns about various practices that do not seem to fit together, that are incongruent with each other, or lack support or resources at the school level for a district-mandated practice policy. These issues need to be discussed by key personnel and teachers if the PD effort is to be successful. Specifically, this area of context focuses on improving teacher quality by establishing the conditions by which they can work collaboratively to achieve agreed-upon goals.

Process

In thinking about processes, school personnel must address the following questions:

- What data are available that will support learning of both teachers and students? Are demographic, perceptual, process, and outcome data used to make decisions? (See Chapter 9 for a description of these types of data.)
- Does the plan for PL consider the research and theories about adult learners as well as that about change in schools, including research about implementation? The research described in Rohlwing and Spelman (2014) led to the principles for adult learning in Figure 5.1, which reading specialists can take into consideration when preparing PL experiences for teachers.

- Value meaningful learning—that can be used!
- Value connections—being able to connect new learning to what they already know.
- Appreciate opportunity for active learning and interaction with others.
- Put a high value on self-efficacy (learning must take place in a risk-free environment).
- Appreciate some control over own learning.
- Are responsive to internal motivation.
- Learn in different ways and at different paces.

FIGURE 5.1. What we know about adult learning.

Guskey (2000) identifies seven different models or processes to consider when planning PD experiences: training, observation/assessment, involvement in a development/improvement process, study groups, inquiry/action research, individually guided activities, and mentoring. Some of these models are more effective than others in specific contexts. Often a PD plan is based on a combination of models. For example, in a large-scale, state-funded PD initiative that I codirected (Swan Dagen & Bean, 2007), teachers attended workshop sessions throughout the year and were asked to develop a focus or action research project, based on the needs of their students. Teachers also administered informal assessment tasks to determine the literacy strengths and needs of their students. Furthermore, they were observed implementing various strategies and given feedback about their instruction. In this project, called LEADERS (Literacy Educators Assessing and Developing Early Reading Success), external coaches were responsible for helping teachers understand the various strategies and they assisted in implementation efforts. Attempts to generate teacher learning included individual choice about a focus project; promoting teacher efforts to interpret and use the results of assessment, and discussing their literacy instruction with them; planning strategies to promote changes that would enhance student learning; and finally, visiting them in the classroom and providing feedback about their instruction. Opportunities for teachers to work in groups were also an integral part of the project.

In addition to various processes for PD, there are also different sources of PD, including state education departments, districts, or even school-based PD. States that receive grants from the federal government or from foundations are often required to offer PD for educators in their schools, including teachers, specialized professionals (e.g., coaches, special educators), and administrators. Districts often offer PD for all schools in their district; for example, if the district decides it will use a specific core reading program, every faculty member responsible for reading instruction will participate in the PD efforts for that program.

In this case, the PD experience is often one developed or provided by "outside experts."

In other instances, district personnel may develop a literacy program based on standards that they themselves have developed or adopted and then provide the necessary staff development (perhaps using both internal and external experts). These initiatives, whether "homegrown" or based on a commercial program, have the advantage of focus, given that all teachers are provided with the staff development they need to use the specific approach.

In initiatives in which selected teachers volunteer to participate in a specific program, one of the strengths is the enthusiasm of those who volunteered. On the other hand, such initiatives are likely to spawn several problems. The district or school may not completely understand or support what these teachers are doing; there may be multiple initiatives in the district, causing confusion for volunteer teachers who may be receiving mixed messages. In some instances, volunteers are not certain of what they have agreed to do!

Individual teachers can attend various workshops or conferences and read journals or books that help them make changes in their instructional practices. These individuals, as described by Joyce and Showers (1995), are the "gourmet omnivores"; the 10% of teachers who are always seeking to improve. These teachers are always looking for ways to do a better job of teaching students; they are truly lifelong learners. Still, they may have a difficult time using these newly learned approaches, which may be different from those recommended or required for use in the school, and the teachers again may receive little or no support for their efforts.

Process often gets short shrift as teachers receive PD that some call "flavor of the month" or "drive-by efforts." Successful PD plans generating teacher change have several process-related characteristics in common:

1. *Focus.* Too often, schools have multiple PL efforts going on at one time and teachers have difficulty determining what it is they should emphasize in their teaching. To be effective, however, PL should be aligned with the goals or standards of the district or school. Then with full-speed ahead and laser-like precision, PL activities should be focused on achieving those goals! Collins in his book, *Good to Great* (2001), relates achieving success in business to the parable of the hedgehog and fox. The fox, in attempting to catch the hedgehog, uses multiple and varied approaches, while the hedgehog has one simple approach to survival: that of rolling up into a ball with a "sphere of sharp spikes, pointing outward in all directions" (p. 91). Guess who wins every time! The moral of the story: focus on what you can do best, what you are passionate about, and what can help you achieve your goals (i.e., learning for all students).

2. *Duration.* Effective programs are long-term or sustained endeavors. They may begin with a workshop in which teachers learn various strategies, but the program continues throughout the year with opportunities for teacher practice, inquiry, and reflection.

3. *Opportunities for feedback.* Teachers need opportunities to talk about what they are implementing, what works, and questions/concerns they have about implementation. The development plan should include a built-in mechanism to help teachers as they implement new strategies. Individuals with expertise can visit teachers and help them by demonstrating or observing practices and then taking the time to discuss aspects of the work. Such coaching is supportive rather than evaluative. (Coaching as a PD tool is discussed in Chapters 6 and 7.)

4. *Embedded into the classroom practices of teachers.* When the PD effort is one closely related to what teachers do every day in teaching and assessing students, there is a much better chance the initiative will succeed. One of the ways that this "fit" can be accomplished is to have teachers who have been able to implement a particular strategy effectively present their work to other teachers. Teachers appreciate hearing from those who have actively been able to "do it" in their classrooms, and they value seeing these teachers in action. Also, when teachers work together in a group to carefully study the results of data from assessment measures and the work of their own students, powerful changes can occur in instructional practices.

5. *Sense of recognition.* Acknowledge teachers for the work they do. Recognize those who have "expertise"; for example, such teachers can demonstrate for others or assist others in implementation. When teachers feel a sense of accomplishment and empowerment, they contribute significantly to the success of the initiative. They make creative and specific suggestions for how the initiative can work more effectively, and they encourage other teachers to use the new strategies.

Content

PL must ultimately result in both changes in teacher performance and in student learning; such changes should reflect efforts to achieve specific curriculum goals or standards. So, the question addressed in this text is, What do teachers need to know and be able to do to provide the most effective literacy instruction for their students? Reading specialists responsible for PD have multiple resources that they can access to address this question.

Important sources of information about content are the individual state standards; in some states there may be the CCSS, and in other states, standards may have been adapted or developed by the states themselves.

Regardless, this source of information is critical for determining literacy content. Research findings also provide evidence about the effectiveness of approaches to teaching literacy. All reading specialists should be familiar with the What Works Clearinghouse (*www.whatworksclear-inghouse.gov.edu*) as a source of information. This website contains information about various programs and approaches, and a summary of the research studies that provide evidence about their effectiveness for students. There are also district standards aligned closely with state standards; these standards may be written for specific levels (elementary, secondary) or they may be grade specific. They provide important guidance for planning PD for teachers in a specific school or district. A useful resource for helping teachers implement instruction based on the CCSS is *The Common Core Coaching Book: Strategies to Help Teachers Address the K–5 ELA Standards* (Elish-Piper & L'Allier (2014).

THINK ABOUT THIS

Read the vignette written by Celia in this chapter (see "Voices from the Field"). Think about the ways that Celia, in her work, exemplifies the five process-related characteristics described on pages 118–119.

DESIGNING EFFECTIVE PROFESSIONAL LEARNING EXPERIENCES: TIME FOR TEACHERS

During the past several decades, I have been involved in a number of PD efforts, both as a reading specialist for a school district, and then as a university faculty member partnering with schools and their teachers in literacy projects. In all these endeavors, teachers have been enthusiastic about learning and passionate about their work with students. When they were treated with respect, had some choice about their learning experiences, and most of all, saw results for the students with whom they worked, they continued to use what they learned, and most of all, became lifelong learners. However, in some of these endeavors (especially in large districts), my colleagues and I were not able to address the larger issue of overall organizational structure and change (e.g., the district may not even have been aware of this particular literacy initiative in a specific school or schools). Granted, we made some changes, we influenced individual and small groups of teachers, but overall whole-school or districtwide change eluded us. Also, although we had some impact on principals who were involved with these PD opportunities, even these principals were unable to affect change to the extent there was a tipping point, generating greater student learning overall.

Yet, overall change in teacher learning is critical if we are to provide effective education for all students. As described in the Time for Teaching report (National Center on Time and Learning, 2014), three major movements require that we change the ways in which we prepare and provide learning experiences for teachers. They include current emphasis on rigorous, high-level standards such as CCSS; the recent emphasis on evaluation of teachers and teaching; and the fact that the core of teachers in schools today are younger and less experienced. The report discusses five implications for practitioners in schools interested in improving PL of teachers. They include:

1. Assess current PD practices and teacher time use.
2. Consider program models that enable additional time for teacher collaboration.
3. Align benchmark assessments, standards, and curricula, and share relevant, timely data with teachers.
4. Support the development of a cadre of instructional leaders and coaches in schools.
5. Expand opportunities for teachers to develop and share expertise.

In this report, there are detailed descriptions of 17 schools and the ways in which they were able to successfully implement PL and influence teacher practices and student learning. According to the report, these schools spent much more time on both classroom instruction and PL experiences than schools on average. They were committed to creating overall change in their schools by focusing on teacher learning as a major ingredient in ensuring an effective educational program for all students.

THINK ABOUT THIS

What PL experience has been most useful to you (you have learned a great deal and are able to use what you learned in your teaching)? What process characteristics were part of that PL experience?

GUIDELINES FOR DEVELOPING, LEADING, AND EVALUATING AN EFFECTIVE PROFESSIONAL DEVELOPMENT PROGRAM

1. *Know the goals and needs of the school and its teachers.* As indicated previously, an understanding of the context is essential. If the reading specialist has responsibilities for implementing a long-term

PD program in his or her district, that program should be based on a needs assessment or some sort of plan and vision (e.g., the district has decided to improve literacy instruction by supporting content-area teachers in their efforts). For additional information, especially when the PD is being offered in a school the reading specialist is not familiar with, talking with school administrators or teachers, visiting the school, or observing in the classrooms can also be helpful. Lyons and Pinnell (2001) provide an excellent list of characteristics to look for in the school culture (see Figure 5.2).

2. *Hold sessions in environments that are conducive to learning.* In the LEADERS initiative (Swan Dagen & Bean, 2007), we designed the room in which we held sessions to look like the classrooms that we expected teachers to have: there were learning centers, reading and writing areas, and student work on the walls and bulletin boards. The room was equipped with tables, providing opportunity for group work and discussion. The environment was a comfortable one, enabling participants to interact as a community of learners. (Every so often, we had to work in a classroom with individual desks set in rows, and the differences in the interaction and attitude of participants were remarkable!)

Think about the physical needs of the participants. Plan for breaks and refreshments, as needed. My initial work with PD was done with a colleague who always said, "Feed your group!" Although we chuckled about that statement, teachers who come to a Saturday workshop or who attend a PD meeting after school really need—and enjoy—light refreshments. It not only meets an actual physical need but also provides an opportunity for social bonding.

3. *Recognize the learning styles and needs of adults.* As mentioned, teachers, as adult learners, bring to the learning experience a variety of experiences, skills, and knowledge that influence how new ideas are received and the degree to which they acquire and implement new skills. They bring with them their multiple roles and responsibilities, not only as teachers but also as parents, homemakers, and so on. They bring the many experiences they have had in life and work, as well as their feelings or emotions associated with past learning experiences. Teachers participate in PD for monetary incentives on occasion but more often because they hope to gain concrete and practical ideas that will enhance the learning outcomes of their students (Guskey, 1986). Indeed, Guskey (1986) reported evidence that positive change in "learning outcomes of students generally precedes and may be a prerequisite to significant change in the beliefs and attitudes of most teachers" (p. 7). Change is gradual for most teachers and requires a well-developed, long-term effort. Guskey

1. As you enter the building, what do you see?

2. Is there a welcoming atmosphere?

3. Is the building as a whole clean and attractive?

4. Is the school office a welcoming place where people are acknowledged and helped?

5. Are the classrooms, cafeteria, office, and library clean and attractive?

6. Do staff members speak respectfully to students and do students talk in respectful tones to one another?

7. What is happening in the yard or playground? Are students playing? Are teachers interacting with students?

8. Are the students and their community a visible part of the school? Is student work displayed and valued in the corridors, office, library, and other gathering places?

9. How available are books? Can students find books to read in places besides the library?

10. Is the principal accessible? Does the principal interact in a friendly way with students, staff members, and visitors?

11. Do people in the school talk with one another? What do they talk about? Do they talk about their work?

12. Are professional development books and materials available?

13. Do teachers have a place where they can meet and work together? Is it attractive and welcoming?

14. When asked about the school, what do people say? Are their comments positive?

15. When asked about the students in the school, what do people say? Are their comments positive?

16. When asked about the parents and the community, what do people say? Are their comments positive?

FIGURE 5.2 What to look for in the school culture. From Lyons and Pinnell (2001). Copyright 2001 by Heinemann. Reprinted by permission.

(p. 9) also discussed several characteristics of effective staff development efforts: (a) the new program or approach should be presented in a clear, explicit, and concrete manner; (b) personal concerns of teachers must be addressed; and (c) the person presenting the program should be credible, articulate, and able to describe how the practice can be used by teachers. Even then, some teachers may leave the meeting not convinced that the new ideas will work for them; at best, they will try them!

Some suggestions for making effective presentations to adults are listed in Figure 5.3. These suggestions come from my own experience and from *How to Run Seminars and Workshops* (Jolles, 2001), a book useful for those making presentations to groups.

1. Create an atmosphere conducive to adult learning; it should be relaxed, yet businesslike. Seating should be conducive to discussion and interaction. Breaks and refreshments should be planned.

2. Stimulate and maintain interest. Use visuals to reinforce learning; tell stories; ask questions of the group or use small-group activities.

3. Involve participants to engender interest and increase retention. In addition to small-group activities and questioning, the learner can ask participants to perform some tasks.

4. Set goals and inform participants (i.e., What do you expect them to know or do when the session is over?).

5. Show enthusiasm and use your voice effectively.

6. Plan your session so that you know how much time you will give to each segment.

7. Create a strong beginning and ending. This is where you capture the attention of the group and what the group will remember when they leave!

FIGURE 5.3. Making effective presentations.

4. *Use a variety of activities and approaches, especially those that require active participation on the part of those attending.* People learn best by "doing," and opportunities for individuals to think about, reflect, and discuss various aspects of literacy will enhance learning. Approaches that have been successful include the following:

- *Study or book groups.* When teachers are involved in activities meaningful to them, they become more engaged in the process and generally more willing to apply what they are learning to their classroom practices. Participation in a study or book group puts teachers in charge of their own learning, providing them with materials they can read, reflect, write about, and discuss with others. Groups may be formal ones established by the school district, or they may function informally, with a group of teachers deciding what they will read, and when and how often they will meet. Often there is a designated leader for each meeting who facilitates the discussion by thinking of questions and activities that may be appropriate for the material to be discussed. A resource that may be helpful is the brief on leading study groups published on the website of the Literacy Coaching Clearinghouse (*www.literacycoachingonline.org*). Walpole and Beauchat (2008), in this brief, highlight several important points: Work with participants as a co-learner, provide for choice and voice, and facilitate opportunities that enable members to make personal connections. For example, hold discussions about how ideas being discussed might be implemented in classrooms, and the challenges that teachers might face, or the resources that they might need.

• Thibodeau (2008), a literacy specialist, writes about the study group she led with a volunteer group of high school content teachers who taught a number of different subjects (e.g., English, geometry, algebra). The group met for an introductory meeting in the summer and then held meetings once a month for 2 hours after school for a year. As she states, the group learned "with and from one another" (p. 56); moreover, the teachers made changes in their instructional practices and felt their students benefited from the literacy strategies being taught in the classrooms.

• *Analyzing student work.* In the LEADERS initiative, teachers brought samples of their students' work and discussed them with others who taught at the same grade level but in different schools. This activity always generated much discussion and reflection, with teachers able to think about how well their students were doing in comparison with those in other classrooms. More important, teachers discussed which strategies and activities were helpful in promoting successful performance.

• *Analyzing student assignments.* Often, this activity can complement the analysis of student work. Teachers who teach a similar subject at one grade level (e.g., English literature) can share the assignments that they ask students to complete to meet the same standard or objective. Teachers may be surprised when they see the differences in expectations across classrooms. Matstumura's text *Creating High-Quality Classroom Assignments* (2006) provides helpful ideas for those wishing to delve more deeply into this approach to PD.

• *Use of videos (classroom practices).* There is no doubt that "seeing is believing." Although we often modeled new strategies for teachers in workshops, they always appreciated seeing us demonstrate specific strategies with their students. In the beginning, we used videos that had been developed for other purposes; as we continued with LEADERS, we were able to show videos made by teachers participating in the project. In one high school participating in a PD initiative, individual teachers agreed to have their lessons recorded and then participated in a group discussion with other teachers, discussing the ways in which the lessons exemplified active engagement of students (the focus of the PD initiative in this school). This was a group of teachers who enjoyed working with one another and not threatened by making their teaching public! Often, videos are available on state department websites (e.g., the Georgia Department of Education has modules and videos focusing on various aspects of literacy education, from beginning reading through instruction for adolescents). Videos are often available on various Internet websites but should be reviewed carefully to determine quality.

• *Use of technology.* Technology can be used in many different ways to enhance PD efforts. It can be used to facilitate communication, to obtain valuable information, or to serve as the primary provider of PD. In a recent large-scale initiative in Pennsylvania, participating teachers in school districts were released from instruction and attended webinars that had been developed by state content specialists—without leaving their school site! These types of experiences are becoming more and more frequent as technology improves and as school personnel learn to use such technology effectively. In the LEADERS project, we developed a website that participants could access and a private listserv that teachers could use to communicate with others. Also, the Internet has provided individual teachers with opportunities to locate resources to learn more about various aspects of literacy. They can obtain professional resources or practical ideas, including lesson plans or activities. They can also participate in webinars about literacy instruction. Several examples of valuable websites include:

> Alliance for Excellent Education: *alliance@all4ed.org*
> Education Week: *educationweek.org*
> International Literacy Association (formerly the International Reading Association): *www.reading.org*
> Read, Write, Think: *www.readwritethink.org*
> Reading Rockets: *www.readingrockets.org*
> National Council of Teachers of English: *www.ncte.org*
> Florida Center for Reading Research: *www.fcrr.org*

Technology has had an effect on several large-scale literacy initiatives. In Pennsylvania, teachers and coaches in Reading First participated in a series of online courses on effective primary reading instruction and coaches could also take courses on coaching (*www.learningscience.org*). Florida also offered a series of online experiences for teachers in grades PreK–12 (Zygouris-Coe, Yao, Tao, Hahs-Vaughn, & Baumbach, 2004). In the Classrooms of the Future initiative in Pennsylvania, whose goals were to improve the ways in which teachers at the secondary level used technology, coaches in the initiative participated in webinars, blogs, and forums to enhance their knowledge and to communicate with others. One of the exciting aspects of this large-scale project was that project leaders could hold regional meetings in different locations and provide information to all participants by using technology. Such efforts, using technology, can provide opportunities for more differentiated, teacher-centered, self-directed models of teacher learning.

• *Action research.* When teachers are given opportunities to identify and then answer their own questions about students' learning, they become the ultimate professional. They implement best practices and then assess their effectiveness. In LEADERS, we created a simple framework based on four questions for helping teachers think about their action research projects:

> What do your students need to become better readers or writers?
>
> What activities or strategies are you going to use to help students succeed?
>
> What was the outcome? What effect did your intervention have on students?
>
> What have you learned about yourself and your teaching?

Teachers summarized what they knew by writing a brief summary and developing a poster that illustrated their responses to each of the questions. Teacher research generates ongoing learning and may facilitate change in classroom practice. Teachers interested in such activities can be encouraged and supported in their efforts. They can discuss their work with other teachers in faculty meetings, write a short column for the school or community newspaper, collaborate with others to investigate a specific issue, or as in LEADERS, develop posters that display evidence of their work and its effect on classroom performance.

• *Reflection.* Give teachers opportunities to discuss and reflect on what they have done in their classrooms. They can keep logs or be given opportunities to talk informally with their peers about their experiences. One of the greatest opportunities for reflection is after teaching a lesson (discussed further in Chapter 7).

5. Provide opportunities for teachers to receive feedback about implementation in the classroom. In LEADERS, whenever coaches observed teachers, they met with them to discuss the results of the observation (discussed further in Chapter 7).

6. Provide for evaluation of the PD initiative. Both formative and summative approaches to PD are essential. *Formative,* or ongoing, evaluation provides opportunities for modification, adaptation, or change. *Summative* evaluation, which addresses impact and results, enables the developer to determine the effect of the PD effort on individuals and on the system as a whole. Guskey (2000) identified five levels of evaluation:

participants' reactions, participants' learning, organizational support and change, participants' use of new knowledge and skills, and student learning outcomes.

In LEADERS, we used the following techniques for addressing each of the levels:

- *Level 1: Participants' reactions.* Questionnaires at end of each workshop; midyear focus group.
- *Level 2: Participants' learning.* Teacher content test (pre–post).
- *Level 3: Organizational support and change.* Interviews/questionnaires with principals and teachers.
- *Level 4: Participants' use of new knowledge.* Classroom observations.
- *Level 5: Student learning outcomes.* Pre–post tests developed by project team and administered to students.

In Figure 5.4, we provide a rating scale that can be used to assess the PD initiatives in a specific school or district (Bean & Morewood, 2007).

SUMMARY

In this chapter, I discussed the importance of PD as well as some of the limitations of PD as it has been implemented in schools. Research about effective PL and about PLCs as an approach to improving teacher learning was described. Standards for PL were identified followed by a discussion of context, process, and content elements as important considerations in developing any PL initiative. In the final section, I presented guidelines for developing, leading, and evaluating an effective PD initiative in a school or district.

ADDITIONAL READINGS

Thibodeau, G. M. (2008). A content literacy collaborative study group: High school teachers take charge of their professional learning. *Journal of Adolescent and Adult Literacy, 52*(1), 54–84.—The author discusses the approach she used for facilitating a study group with a group of high school teachers and its effects on teaching practices.

Williams, S. S., & Williams, J. W. (2014). Workplace wisdom: What educators can learn from the business world. *Journal of Staff Development, 35*(3), 10–12, 14, 20.—Identifies effective practices common in business and education to promote employee or teacher learning (e.g., mentoring is key; collaboration gets results).

Rating Scale

3	High implementation
2	Partial implementation
1	Not an established part of the comprehensive professional development program or plan.

Content

Score	Description
	School has coherent set of literacy goals and standards across grade levels that can be used as a framework to guide professional development. (Standards for literacy performance at each grade level have been identified, e.g., what should students know and be able to do?)
	Curriculum and instructional practices are evidence based.
	Curriculum and instructional practices set high expectations for all students.
	Curriculum and instructional practices to be emphasized relate to needs of students as determined by multiple sources of data.
	Opportunities enable teachers to gain in-depth understanding of the theory and research underlying practices (why something is important).

____/15 Total

Collaboration and Sense of Community in the School

Score	Description
	Teachers have decision-making role in how they learn what is necessary to achieve goals set by the school.
	Teachers in school are given opportunities to work together, interact, network, learn from one another (e.g., grade-level meetings, study groups, etc.) in a collegial manner.
	There is a focus on the value of parents and their role as members of the community.
	Teachers are recognized for the work that they do.
	Teachers have opportunities to serve as leaders in planning and implementing professional development activities.

____/15 Total

(continued)

FIGURE 5.4. Professional development for promoting school change in literacy. From Bean and Morewood (2007, pp. 381–382).

Duration and Amount of Time

Score	Description
	Professional development programs are ongoing (over time) and give teachers opportunities to develop in-depth understanding of the content to be learned.
	Teachers have ample contact hours related to the PD topic.

____/6 Total

Active Learning

Score	Description
	School makes use of new technologies in helping teachers achieve their professional goals.
	Teachers use information from their classrooms and students in their professional development work (e.g., they use data, review student work samples, do lesson study).
	Activities are differentiated according to teacher needs and styles of learning.
	Teachers have opportunities to participate in inquiry-based activities that necessitate critical thinking, application, and reflection.
	Teachers have opportunities to practice what they are learning with their peers or in small groups.

____/15 Total

Application and Feedback Opportunities

Score	Description
	Teachers have opportunities to apply what they are learning in their classrooms.
	Teachers interact with their peers about their experiences in a risk-free environment and reflect on what they are doing.
	Feedback is geared toward supporting and guiding teacher practices (it is not evaluative).
	Teachers are recognized for what they know and do.
	Teachers have opportunities to self-evaluate and reflect on their work (e.g., video, etc.).

____/15 Total

FIGURE 5.4. (*continued*)

Reflections

Discuss with your classmates PD in which you have participated. What activities did you find to be most useful? What, in your view, was least useful?

Activities

1. Interview an administrator at your school about the PD plan for teachers in the school, especially as it relates to literacy instruction. Think about whether that plan addresses context, process, and content elements. Use Figure 5.4 to help you think about questions that you might ask the administrator.
2. Prepare a PD session for your classmates (or for the teachers in your school), in which you introduce them to one new idea or strategy. Use information from the guidelines in this chapter to develop that presentation. Ask the participants to evaluate the session, using a short questionnaire. Then self-evaluate your performance, reflecting on the ideas presented in this chapter.
3. In small groups, discuss the vignette below, reflecting on what Celia brings to the reading specialist/literacy coach role; identify three important "take-aways" from the vignette. Share work of small groups with the whole class.

Some questions to think about:

What lessons can be learned about the role of the reading specialist in this vignette?

In what ways does Celia serve as a leader?

What questions come to mind after reading this vignette?

CELIA: MY JOURNEY FROM STUDENT TO TEACHER TO LITERACY COORDINATOR

Although I was recently appointed coordinator of literacy grades K–6, I served as a district literacy coach in District U-46 for 6 years, and in this vignette, I discuss that role. District U-46 is the second largest school district in Illinois, with two early learning sites, 40 elementary schools, eight middle schools, and five high schools. It covers 90 square miles and serves over 40,000 students in grades PreK–12. The population of the district is 50% Hispanic, 31% white, 8% Asian, 6% black, 6ow income, and 25% ELLs. I attended school in this district since I was 5 years old. I did my student teaching there and got my first teaching position as a first-grade bilingual teacher there as well. After 8 years as a classroom teacher, I became a Reading Recovery teacher and served in that capacity for 5 years. During a summer professional development I was leading, two administrative interns recruited me to join their ranks as a district literacy coach.

My Role as Leader

As a district literacy coach, I provided instructional leadership in several ways. One of my primary responsibilities, with other coaches, was to provide professional development for over 3,500 teachers. We were fortunate, in that we had funds from a grant enabling the district to release teachers for 2 full days, once in the fall/winter and a second time in the winter/spring. Teachers cycled through the professional development with other teachers from their grade level or content area. So, for example, all first-grade teachers attended the same professional development with their colleagues on 1 of 3 days in a given week. After the full day of professional development, teams of two coaches visited each school site, where a floating sub was provided so each grade-level team could meet with the coaches to ask and answer questions, as well as have a facilitated work session for about an hour.

The district professional development was structured with district guidance about best practice and district needs. Typically the first half of the day was whole group to ensure all groups received the same information. Small-group activities and cooperative work were always included to engage the participants. During the second half of the day, teachers could choose from a menu of offerings; sessions focusing on ELLs and special education student needs were always included as choices.

The district literacy coaches then met with administration, who gave us guidance for the professional development. The coaches worked cooperatively to determine who would be responsible for presenting each follow-up session and then each person or team planned their professional development sessions. For the site-based sessions, teams of coaches were assigned to schools in order to provide consistency in support. The goal of these follow-up sessions was to support the needs of each team of teachers as determined by teachers and site administrator.

In addition to this systemic professional development, district literacy coaches provided one-on-one coaching support by request. Teachers who chose to request support from district literacy coaches submitted a simple form and coaches then followed through with activities that met the needs of the individual teacher (meeting, modeling, observing, and providing feedback). During these sessions we found when we were modeling for teachers, it was best if the teacher had a task to complete while observing (e.g., taking notes and raising questions about what they were observing to guide the follow-up conversation). We created a simple T chart labeled "What I Noticed/Questions I Have." This led to richer and more focused conversations that could truly impact the teacher's understanding.

Instruction

In my role as a district coach, I didn't have specific instructional responsibilities, that is, I was not assigned to teach students during the day. However, as a coach, by modeling, I had opportunities to provide instruction for students. One of the most frequent requests for modeling was in the area of guided reading. Though it was tricky to plan an effective guided reading lesson for students with whom you have not been working, I first met with teachers, asking questions (e.g., "At which level are the students reading?"; "What reading strategies have you already taught and on which one would you like me to focus the lesson?"; "What resources do you have available for guided reading?"). Once I had a good idea of what the teacher had done and where he or she was headed, I discussed the importance of book selection: the book must not only be at the instructional level of the students, it must lend itself to the strategy being taught (e.g., if I wanted primary students to use picture cues, the book must contain excellent picture cues. If I wanted intermediate students to visualize the piece of text, it must contain language causing the reader to create a mental image). Once we selected a book, I walked the teacher through the reading and rereading of the text, always keeping in mind, "What will the students do when they reach this challenge and how can I facilitate the use of the reading strategy on which I am focusing?"

After planning and modeling the lesson cooperatively with the teacher, we debriefed the lesson. I asked questions such as "What do you think went well? What do you think I could change?" Referring teachers back to their observation notes I asked, "What did you notice? What questions do you have about what you saw?" I also shared with the teacher any decisions I may have made that were in response to the students and not planned for in the lesson. However, one thing I was sure to emphasize was the importance of sticking to one focus, ensuring any deviations from the planned lesson continued to support the lesson focus.

Assessment

Our district uses the Fountas and Pinnell Benchmark Assessment System in English and Spanish in order to determine students' text level in kindergarten to sixth grade. In my role as a district literacy coach, I offered staff development in how to administer the assessment, as well as how to use the information to guide instruction. One of the greatest challenges with this assessment is interrater reliability. For years, the district literacy coaches have provided professional development sessions for administering, scoring, and using the assessment. Yet we still have a great variance between teachers in our district. This is still an ongoing effort for us.

Schedule

District literacy coaches don't have a predetermined schedule. It is constantly changing because of districtwide professional development schedules, required meetings, training, and teacher requests for coaching. One of the most important qualities in being a district literacy coach is flexibility. Since we work with teachers, we must frequently be available before and after school hours when the teacher is available to have conversations that support learning.

Greatest Challenges

Without a doubt one of the greatest challenges in my role as a district literacy coach was communication. I can't tell you how many times I provided information to a room full of a hundred teachers and it seemed like each one heard something different. I have come to realize the great influence of a person's background knowledge and perspective in shaping the message heard. Of course, how closely they were listening also played a role! To help overcome this challenge, I put key points in writing. With the use of technology, I was able to do this without killing a forest.

Since my primary role was that of a leader who provided professional development, another challenge I encountered were teachers who felt they knew everything and you were wasting their time. Or the teacher who thought your professional development was another fad and they could just do the same thing they had always done until the fad went away. Cynical and close-minded teachers are one of the great challenges of being a district literacy coach. Fortunately, there are only a small number of these teachers in the profession.

A Success Story

An administrator shared with me her concerns about a second-year kindergarten teacher's assessment scores. According to her assessment results, all but one of her students qualified for summer intervention. I had worked with the teacher on a few occasions the previous year and agreed that there must be some mistake. I e-mailed the teacher requesting a meeting to go over the results. She invited me to her classroom the next morning. Another coach and I went, so that while I talked with the teacher the other coach could cover the classroom. We discovered that the teacher had indeed made a mistake and thought she was recording the student's independent level instead of their instructional level.

However, while I was there an administrator joined us and shared other concerns about this teacher's classroom environment and the lack of student work, rigor, and writing. The teacher began to cry. Fortunately, her students had just left for their library time with the other coach supervising them. I assured the teacher that she wasn't in trouble and I was only there to support her. We created a plan for me to come back and model some lessons for her, as well as observe a writing lesson and give her feedback. We also contacted other kindergarten teachers that she observed with me so that we could discuss the instructional strategies they used and reflect on their classroom environments.

A few weeks later, I returned to the teacher's classroom to find a much less stressed teacher who had implemented what she had learned. She realized the effectiveness of thoughtful instruction and high expectations and her students were engaged and building upon the foundation she had established with them. In my role as the district coach, I have learned often teachers just need a little bit of focused instruction and reassurance they are on the right path. I also learned that while administrators may mean well, their mere presence may intimidate teachers.

Things I Have Learned

- You can't please all of the people all of the time.
- For effective coaching, you must build a trusting relationship.
- Be honest: if you don't know the answer to a question, say so and then go find the answer and return with it.

- If you start with the willing, others will join when they see the student motivation and success.

- Focus on the students; all teachers want their students to succeed.

- Take care that you allow some struggle, as that is how people learn and change (I like the story of the little boy that tried to "help" the butterfly out of the cocoon, only to learn that the butterfly couldn't fly because it is the struggle of getting out of the cocoon that strengthens the wings for flight).

CELIA BANKS, MEd
Coordinator of Literacy K–6
School District U-46
Elgin, Illinois

CHAPTER SIX

Coaching

Improving Classroom and School Literacy Instruction

A good coach will make [his] players see what they can be rather than what they are.
—ARA PARSEGHIAN (former football coach, University of Notre Dame)

Key Questions

- In what ways can literacy coaching be helpful in supporting teacher and student learning?
- How can the interactive framework of coaching inform the work of coaches?
- What knowledge, skills, and dispositions are essential if coaches are to be effective?
- In what ways is coaching at the elementary level similar or different from coaching at the secondary level?

In this chapter, I present an overview of and discuss the rationale for coaching in schools, providing a definition and a summary of guidelines based on research. This is followed by a description of an interactive framework of coaching; I also describe qualifications for successful literacy coaches, followed by a section comparing coaching at the elementary level with the secondary level. The chapter ends with a list of possible activities coaches can use in working with individual and groups of teachers; in Chapter 7, I describe in more depth activities for working with individual teachers and provide examples of each. We know much more now than we did a decade ago about coaching; thus, there are two chapters on coaching. Moreover, those reading specialists who coach or want to know more about coaching can find information in the other chapters in the book equally important, especially discussions about assessment, professional development, and leadership.

Although literacy coaching was "very hot" during the years of Reading First and the government's fiscal support for coaches in every school (Cassidy & Cassidy, 2009), there has been a reduction in the number of coaches in schools during the past several years. Budgetary constraints faced by districts as well as the lack of substantial evidence about the effectiveness of coaching as a means of improving teacher practices and student learning have contributed to this decrease in coaching positions (i.e., Does coaching make a difference?). However, coaching continues to be one of the key approaches to improving teacher practices and ultimately, student learning, especially with initiatives such as RTI, the emphasis on more rigorous, high-level standards, and the evaluation of teacher performance. School personnel recognize that teachers need ongoing professional learning to be able to make the changes necessary to implement these initiatives effectively. The Time for Teaching report (National Center on Time and Learning, 2014) mentioned in Chapter 5 calls for support for a cadre of instructional leaders and coaches in schools to enhance teacher learning.

At the same time, perhaps the emphasis should be on coach*ing*; not coach*es*. Schools may ask teacher leaders or reading specialists to coach; they may bring in outside experts. A principal who visits teachers to provide support and guidance rather than to evaluate their performance, coaches. In other words, there seem to be fewer full-time educators dedicated to coaching. For example, a reading specialist might spend most of the day teaching struggling readers but also assume responsibility for coaching teachers to assist them in providing quality classroom instruction, similar to what Mark does (see "Voices from the Field" in Chapter 2). In some schools, reading specialists have been asked to change the way in which they work, moving from primarily an instructional role to a coaching role, perhaps without having the necessary preparation to handle coaching responsibilities successfully. These coaches are then required to learn on the job—sometimes a painful way of gaining essential skills and competencies.

COACHING: WHY AND WHAT?

One criticism of professional development programs is the lack of ongoing support for implementation efforts. Without such support, teachers may have difficulty implementing the strategies or approaches to which they have been introduced and choose to revert to more familiar teaching procedures. For this reason many schools, when they adopt new approaches, provide coaching for their teachers. Furthermore, in various federal and state legislation (e.g., Reading First and Striving Readers), there was support for or even requirements that implementation efforts include a coach in the schools. One state, South Carolina, passed legislation requiring a literacy coach in every elementary school. Essentially, coaching is an approach to job-embedded, ongoing professional development focusing on authentic and meaningful learning experiences. L'Allier, Elish-Piper, and Bean (2010), in summarizing research about literacy coaching, identified these seven guiding principles: coaching requires specialized knowledge, time working with teachers is the focus of coaching, collaborative relationships are essential for coaching, coaching supporting student learning focuses on a set of core activities, coaching must be both intentional and opportunistic, coaches must be literacy leaders, and coaching evolves over time.

As you read this and the following chapter, each of these guiding principles are discussed in more depth. *Coaching* seems to be the right term to use for this supportive work with teachers, especially if we think about the definition of a coach as an individual with expertise who provides guidance or feedback that enables someone else to become more proficient. Even as we think of the great football coaches—Vince Lombardi (Green Bay Packers), Chuck Noll (Pittsburgh Steelers), and Ara Parseghian (University of Notre Dame)—we think of individuals who were not only able to teach in the traditional sense but were able to inspire and motivate their players to do their very best and to live up to their potential. In Nater and Gallimore's (2006) book about John Wooden, the legendary basketball coach at the University of California, Los Angeles (UCLA), they detail the teaching methods that made him a great coach and teacher: "teacher respect, motivation, self-improvement, deep subject knowledge, preparation, and transferring information" (p. xiv). According to these authors, Wooden thought of himself "first and foremost as a teacher" (p. xiii).

THINK ABOUT THIS

The title of the Nater and Gallimore book is *You Haven't Taught Until They Have Learned: John Wooden's Teaching Principles and Practices* (2006). What do you think this title means? Do you agree with it? Do you think it relates in any way to literacy coaching and, if so, how?

    Reread Ara Parseghian's statement at the beginning of the chapter. Agree? Disagree? How would this statement apply to the work of a literacy coach in schools?

So it is with literacy coaches: Their job is to work with teachers in their schools and to help them do their very best to facilitate student learning. Teachers may be novices, needing a great deal of feedback or guidance, or they may be more experienced, having taught for many years. Experienced teachers may benefit from feedback about new approaches, or they may need reinforcement, reassurance, recognition, or even some motivation that promotes ongoing student learning. Both new and experienced teachers may have learners in their classrooms whom they are struggling to teach (e.g., English language learners, students with special needs) and would appreciate an opportunity to learn more about how to work with them.

However, those who write about coaching and educators in the field do not always define the word *coach* in a similar fashion. To some, literacy coaches are teachers who coach children, enabling them to do better. Others see them as teachers with expertise in reading (often, reading specialists) who have multiple responsibilities, from working with paraprofessionals or community agencies to working with teachers in the role described above—primarily responsible for providing support and guidance—so that classroom instruction for students is effective. Others see them as individuals who may not have literacy expertise, but have the ability to guide teachers to think more deeply about their practices.

The coaching role can vary, therefore, depending on the job requirements of the coach or reading specialist. Some literacy coaches have explicit and well-defined job descriptions and know what they can—and cannot—do. At the same time, some reading specialists also coach but in a less formal way. They serve as a resource to teachers by providing materials or suggestions for working with struggling readers; they attend or lead study group meetings, conduct professional development workshops, or sit and listen to teachers who want to reflect about how to improve their instructional practices. They also lead meetings in which they and teachers discuss results of assessment measures and make decisions about instruction. In the vignettes in the "Voices from the Field" sections of this book, all writers, whose titles differ, have leadership responsibilities and they coach. Celia, Wendy, and Karen are full-time coaches and identified as such. Mark's role is primarily instructional, but he is available to work informally with teachers. Toni also works primarily with students, but has key leadership responsibilities and also supports teachers' instructional efforts in a middle school context. Katy works half time as a coach and half time as a kindergarten teacher. Again, they exemplify the many different ways in which the reading specialist role is enacted. And most likely, there are many more variations in how reading specialists participate in coaching activities!

VARIATIONS IN DEFINITIONS OF COACHING

Although I focus on *literacy* coaching in this book, in some schools, coaches have a broader or different role. For example, there are instructional and curriculum coaches who are responsible for working with teachers in different subject areas. There are also technology, math, and science coaches who are responsible for supporting teachers' work in those areas. Much of what is discussed in this book has relevance to those broader or different coaching roles; however, given the purpose and audience of this book, I focus on literacy coaching. Various authors have defined coaching in slightly different ways. For example, read the two definitions below, and think about how the views of these authors would affect the role of literacy coaches in schools.

THINK ABOUT THIS

What are the views of the following authors about the goals of coaching and its focus? What do you think each position requires in terms of qualifications?

> [A]n experienced teacher who has a strong knowledge base in reading and experience providing effective reading instruction to students, especially struggling readers. In addition . . . has been trained to work effectively with peer colleagues to help them improve their students' reading outcomes . . . (Hasbrouck & Denton, 2005, p. 1)

> The role of the coach is the same in every domain . . . develop a relationship with me, develop expertise so that you would know how to help me, plan for my success, communicate your confidence in me and my potential, help me find the very best in myself, and in the end, step out of the way so that I could claim the change as my own. (Burkins, 2007, p. 5)

In Hasbrouck and Denton's (2005) definition, there is an emphasis on student learning, specifically reading achievement, and a focus on the need for a strong reading background for the coach. In Burkins's (2007) definition, there is more of a focus on the importance of teacher learning and growth, and on the teacher as the source of ideas for coaching. Both definitions provide important insights into coaching—and to the variations that exist in its definition. In other words, the nature of coaching is complex. Given that, I propose an interactive framework of instructional coaching that may help those interested in coaching— coaches, teachers, administrators, researchers, and those who prepare reading specialists—think about the factors that affect how coaching is implemented in a given school.

AN INTERACTIVE FRAMEWORK
OF INSTRUCTIONAL COACHING

As shown in Figure 6.1, there are three specific elements—the model, the context, and the coach—that affect how coaching will be defined, implemented, and evaluated within a given school. These elements overlap and interact with one another and each is affected by the other. I discuss each of these below.

Models of Coaching

McKenna and Walpole (2008) describe coaching as a continuum, from soft to hard. They define soft coaching as responsive, invitational, and nonconfrontational. Generally, those who advocate soft coaching focus on coaching as a means of guiding teachers in thinking about their instruction; they are responsive to teachers' needs and goals. In other words, the coaching is teacher centered (see Figure 6.2). Hard coaching is based on the perspective that there are some approaches to teaching that are more effective than others, and it is the coach's role to assist teachers in implementing these approaches effectively. Often, this sort

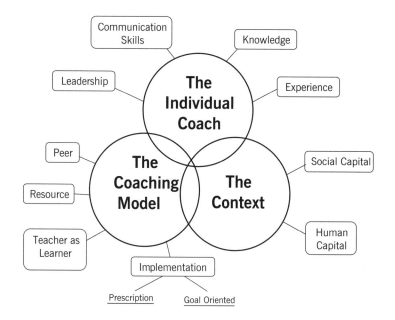

FIGURE 6.1. An interactive framework of literacy coaching.

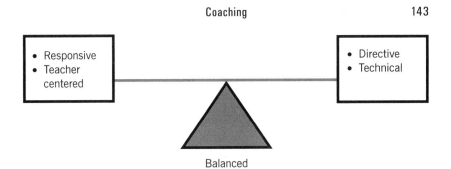

FIGURE 6.2. Continuum of coaching.

of coaching is directive and considered to be synonymous with fidelity to implementation (i.e., Is the teacher implementing the program as designed?). Frequently, coaches are focused on developing the technical skills of teachers. However, coaches may move between hard and soft coaching, providing what Ippolito (2010) calls balanced coaching. The seesaw provides an appropriate metaphor: in one conversation, coaches may begin by being directive, and then offer teachers the opportunity to identify their needs, reflect on their work, and assist in making decisions about next steps, or vice versa. Coburn and Woulfin (2012) in their longitudinal study on coaching in a large-scale reading reform effort found coaches in this initiative used a balanced approach: they were directive, helping teachers make expected changes in instructional practice; at the same time, they responded to teacher requests that addressed specific needs. I identify below four general models of coaching that may be implemented within a school. Think about where they fit on the continuum.

Peer Coaching

In this model, colleagues work with each other to provide feedback and support. This model, proposed by Joyce and Showers (2002), was one of the original approaches to coaching, and emphasized that both coach and teacher were of equal status. In a given school, the language arts teachers in a middle school might decide to implement literature discussion groups, and after attending a workshop and reading resource materials, observe one another as they facilitate such discussions. Joyce and Showers in 2002 revised their procedures for peer coaching by omitting feedback as a coaching component. Too often, feedback given by peers became evaluative or supervisory in nature rather than supportive, and therefore incongruent with the concept of peer coaching. Also, Joyce and Showers redefined the meaning of coach. According to them, "the one teaching is the 'coach' and the one observing, the 'coached'" (p. 89). In other words, the coach models for the other teacher who then is expected to talk briefly about what he or she observed and then apply the learning in instructional practice. Schools may adopt peer coaching to develop teacher leadership and encourage collaboration among teachers. Given the recent emphasis on teacher collaboration, there has been an increased interest in peers working together, visiting one another's classrooms, and then holding follow-up discussions of what was seen. Wendy, a district instructional coach, uses walk-throughs, enabling teachers to visit classrooms of other teachers, discuss what they saw, and think about how they can apply what they learned to their own classroom practices. Wendy's use of walk-throughs is described in more depth in the vignette in this chapter.

Resource Model

This model is one in which there is much flexibility. Often, in addition to working with students, the reading specialist supports teachers in many different ways. My interest in the resource role (and in coaching) began when I became a reading specialist and was permitted to write my own job description (Bean & Wilson, 1981). The assistant superintendent indicated that I could define my own responsibilities. (If you ever have that opportunity, take it! It's a chance to put all you have learned into practice.) In my role, I had opportunities to work with novice teachers who wanted my assistance in how to organize their reading groups, teach phonics or comprehension, differentiate instruction, and so on. I also worked with teachers who had concerns about their struggling students and wanted additional ideas about how to help them succeed. And, I was privileged to work with several high school teachers who wanted to incorporate literacy into their content teaching. I also worked with a high school reading specialist and together, we started a program in which high school struggling readers tutored elementary students who were having difficulties learning to read. As one of my responsibilities, I chaired a language arts committee that was charged with developing a comprehensive reading program for the district. In other words, there were opportunities for working with both individual and groups of teachers and to influence overall school change. The key notion of this role is that the reading specialist or coach generally responds to requests from teachers or administrators, although there are always opportunities to initiate activities. By being proactive, reading specialists can seek out possibilities that might exist (e.g., the reading specialist might note that students in several fourth-grade classrooms are experiencing comprehension difficulties and indicate that he or she would be willing to model some ideas about how to work with these students).

Teacher as Learner

In this model, the goal of coaching is to support teachers in achieving their own goals and facilitate teacher learning. This focus on teacher as learner respects the individual goals of teachers, highlights the importance of reflective practice, and provides for personalized or individualized coaching. The goal of this model is to enhance teachers' ability to self-manage, self-monitor, and self-modify (Costa & Garmston, 2002, p. 21). Toll's (2006, p. 13) "fresh alternative" model and Costa and Garmston's (2002) cognitive coaching model both emphasize the importance of listening to teachers to understand their concerns, interests, and needs. This model gives a key role to teachers who are expected to identify their own goals and, to the degree possible, be knowledgeable about their own strengths and needs; it supports the notion that teachers are capable of identifying what they need to learn to improve classroom instruction. However, teachers differ in their knowledge and their ability to be self-analytical; moreover, the goals of individual teachers may not be focused on those identified by the school as important for change and improvement.

Implementation Model

I divide this model into two categories: prescriptive and goal oriented. In my view, these two types of implementation are ones that have existed most frequently in schools during the past decade. They are a reflection of the accountability and standards movement that stresses the importance of student achievement or learning. Both highlight the importance of implementing particular approaches, strategies, or programs appropriately; both require that coaches have content expertise as well as an understanding of the coaching process. There are differences between the two types, however.

PRESCRIPTIVE

In this type of implementation model, there is little opportunity for teacher choice in strategies, materials, or approaches. The program selected requires teachers to follow certain procedures—at times, scripted—and the coach's role is to make certain that teachers can and do use those approaches in their classrooms (i.e., there is fidelity to implementation.) There has been criticism of this type of implementation model because of its focus on teachers as *technicians* rather than as professionals who are capable of making decisions about what the students in their classrooms need and how to provide it. Moreover, teachers may feel these prescriptive programs limit their ability to make necessary instructional changes required when students are experiencing difficulties or not learning. On the other hand, this approach to instruction (and coaching) addresses the need for all students to have equal access to what a school or district has adopted as an "appropriate" approach for teaching reading; coaching can help teachers implement that program or approach as stipulated by the developers. In a paper written for the United States Agency for International Development (USAID, 2014), I acknowledged that in some situations where there are inexperienced staff with minimum understanding of literacy instruction, the reading materials used may be scripted in nature, and coaches may need to focus, *initially*, on developing teachers' technical skills. The goal, however, is to move beyond a focus on technical skills to one that helps teachers grow as professionals.

GOAL ORIENTED

In this type of implementation model, there is more opportunity for choice, although there are specific goals that have been identified by the school and/or a literacy framework that has been adopted. For example, in Pennsylvania, teachers and coaches in schools in the Pennsylvania High School Coaching Initiative (PIIC) attend classes offered by the Penn Literacy Network (*www.gse.upenn.edu/pln*) a professional development program based on an evidence-based literacy framework emphasizing the importance of literacy across all subject areas. Many strategies are introduced, all emphasizing the importance of co-constructed learning and active engagement. Teachers can be selective in terms of which aspects of the framework would be useful in their classrooms (e.g., active engagement strategies, self-questioning), and coaches support teachers in achieving *their* individual goals as a means of achieving school goals. Wendy's vignette in this chapter exemplifies a coach using a goal-oriented model; the district identified a vision, its goals, and the initiatives needed to accomplish those goals. Wendy's role is to provide the leadership to generate change in the entire district K–12.

The model selected affects how coaches work—which teachers the coaches work with and *how* they work with those teachers. For example, in an implementation model that is prescriptive, the coach will most likely decide whether teachers are implementing a program "correctly" and will work with teachers who are not doing so. In one school, the principal stated empathetically to the coach: "I want you to focus on working with two teachers who are experiencing difficulty—a new teacher and one who seems to have problems with implementing the curriculum." In a resource model, coaches will have much more flexibility, most often relying on requests of individual teachers or encouraging teachers to work with them. In a teacher-as-learner model, coaches will develop a personalized coaching plan for teachers based on goals and needs identified by the teachers. What is intriguing to consider are the different views that teachers may have of coaching, depending on the model.

THINK ABOUT THIS

How might teachers relate to the coaching that they would receive, depending on the model? What do you see as the advantages and potential difficulties with each of the models? Develop a matrix with the following headings—Advantages, Difficulties—and discuss with others your views about each of the models.

The Context of the School

Recent research highlights several key factors about conditions that must exist in a school if coaching is to be effective. First is the need for support at the district level as well as at the school level; when districts have multiple initiatives that cause confusion among teachers and coaches, or there is a lack of support for the coaching effort, there is little chance that coaching will be effective or sustained. Second, and as important, is the key role of the principal in understanding why coaching is important *and* in supporting the work of the coach (Bean, 2011; Fixsen, Naoom, Blasé, Friedman, & Wallace, 2006; Matsumura et al., 2009; Wanless, Patton, Rimm-Kaufman, & Deutsch, 2013). All reading specialists/literacy coaches should communicate with principals on a regular basis, seek advice, and provide information about what is needed for effective reading instruction. The type of communication can differ, depending on the preferences of the principal. There can be set times for meetings, perhaps weekly, or coaches can summarize in writing their weekly activities and highlight issues or topics to be addressed by the principal. For example, a coach may be concerned about dissension in the third-grade team, with several members unhappy about the decision to make changes in student grouping. In this case, the reading specialist can request a conversation with the principal to discuss the problem in general and talk about ideas about how to resolve this difficulty. Third, reading specialists/literacy coaches should develop ways to build teacher support and understanding of the coaching initiative—to develop a sense of trust—so teachers do not see coaches as monitors or evaluators but as individuals who can work with them to improve student learning. Wendy, being new to the high school, knew one of her first responsibilities was to establish a sense of trust between the teachers and herself.

Finally, one of the key factors affecting coaching is the climate or culture in the school. There are two important constructs that underlie context or culture: one is social capital and the other, human capital. Leana and Pil (2006) discuss two types of social capital: internal and external. *Internal* social capital relates to the interactions and relationships among teachers, administrators, and others that promote a common and shared vision within a school setting. Positive internal social capital includes the following: sense of responsibility for all students, belief that all students in a school can learn, high expectations, and sense of common goals for students. Leana and Pil, in their study of schools in a large urban school district, found significant relationships between what they defined as internal "social capital" in schools and improved student achievement.

External social capital refers to the links between the school setting and its community. In this case, teachers and administrators work collaboratively with parents and with various agencies to promote student learning. This is exemplified by efforts to inform, seek information, and support from parents. (This topic is discussed in Chapter 10.)

Human capital refers to the human resources existing in schools: the teachers, their educational experiences and talents, and the additional personnel who support instructional differentiation (e.g., reading specialists, librarians, literacy coaches, speech and language therapists, school psychologists, special educators). A stable staff, where there is little turnover among teachers, is an aspect of human capital. Literacy coaches can build on the work of the previous year and not have to "begin again" with a large number of new teachers. Finally, as mentioned above, the principal is also an important human resource; his or her understanding of and support for the literacy coach's role are important to the success of the coach. The principal also has a key role in building external social capital or a sense of community by reinforcing and supporting the work of teachers and reading specialists/coaches.

The kind of work coaches can do and the outcomes they can achieve are often related to the context or culture of the school in which they work; that is, the norms or ways things get done! Too often, these norms are unspoken and difficult to discern. Listed below are some issues that can create difficulty *or* be a source of support for coaches.

- Work issues related to contract agreements.
- Teacher experiences and/or beliefs about students, learning, and teaching.
- Leadership issues.

- Number of professional development initiatives, some of which may not align with others in the schools.
- Clarity of and support for the coaching role by administrators and by teachers.

There are other issues, of course, and each organization has its own set. In the previous chapter, Figure 5.2 lists questions that help you think about the culture of a school. Described below are two situations that highlight how culture can positively or negatively affect the work of the coach. What is your response to each of these scenarios?

THINK ABOUT THIS

In Brown Middle School, the principal and teachers met together to discuss the test scores in the various content areas, including social studies, science, and reading. The content-area teachers were concerned about the test scores and indicated a need to learn more about how to help students with the literacy demands of their discipline. After much discussion, the principal and teachers decided it would be advantageous to change the position of Ms. Smith, the reading specialist, from one in which she worked with students only to one that provided her with time to also work with teachers. The principal agreed to modify the teaching schedule for the reading specialist and also to provide common planning time for teachers of a specific discipline. Ms. Smith, who had worked in the school as an English teacher and then as a reading specialist, had the credibility and respect that enabled her to work collaboratively with teachers in the school.

In Green Elementary School, the principal had written a grant to support the work of a literacy coach, with an emphasis on an approach to reading instruction different from that used by the teachers. The teachers were surprised when the principal met with them and introduced the coach, who had not worked in the district, but had been a reading specialist for a number of years in a neighboring district. The principal explained that the coach's responsibility was to "help them improve their teaching of reading." Although the literacy coach met with grade-level teachers on a regular basis, much of what she was asking them to do was contradictory to what their current reading series promoted. Teachers became frustrated with trying to incorporate two different approaches to reading instruction in their classrooms and the literacy coach was even more frustrated because the district reading program, according to the district supervisor, was the approach that teachers needed to use.

Where were the differences in the conditions in the schools in terms of their readiness for coaching? Talk with others about those conditions—and about the factors that would promote a successful coaching initiative. What could be changed to promote a better coaching initiative in Green Elementary School?

The Coach

The IRA (2004), in its position statement on coaching, indicated the qualified coach is one who has teaching experience at the grade level at which he or she coaches, experience in working with adults, excellent interpersonal and leadership skills, and reading specialist certification. In their brief, "Qualifications for Literacy Coaches: Achieving the Gold Standard," Frost and Bean (2006) agreed with those qualifications, but also indicated too often such well-qualified individuals are not available. School districts must choose the best possible candidate, and then provide the experiences and staff development to support that individual. Such on-the-job training is not the best approach to use but at times it is a reality, and inexperienced coaches may need to begin slowly, learning the content and process of coaching while they are working with and building relationships with teachers. A helpful approach to on-the-job training is to have new coaches join a network of coaches so they can learn from the experiences of others. They may also be assigned to a mentor coach available to answer questions, provide moral support, and serve as role models for them.

Even the best-qualified coaches must recognize that their beliefs, styles of teaching, and personalities influence how they work with and perceive others. Kise, in her book *Differentiated Coaching: A Framework for Helping Teachers Change* (2006), explains all of us have our own preferences for organizing our lives and approaching our work. Some coaches may be extremely well organized and detail oriented; in their classroom teaching, they had explicit rules and regulations for managing their classrooms, believing students needed the structure of routines in order to learn effectively. These coaches may find it difficult to walk into classrooms where there is a much more laissez-faire approach to classroom management and organization, even if the teachers in those classrooms are considered to be excellent teachers and students are learning! What is critical is coaches understand their preferences and those of the teacher—and recognize and value the differences. After a presentation that I gave on coaching, two coaches came up to me, chuckling. They worked together in the same elementary school and it was clear they enjoyed their work. As one of them told me, "I'm like a bulldog; I never give up—I'm tenacious." The other coach said, "And I'm like a big, old Labrador retriever, nurturing and supporting teachers." They went on to tell me it was obvious to them that teachers in the school seemed to have a preference for one or the other, and this was fine with them. In other words, they knew their own strengths and their tendencies, and recognized the same in teachers in the school. Not all schools, however, can offer a choice of coaches to teachers so it is important for coaches to understand how their personal style, communication skills, and so on, can have an impact on those they coach, and accept that they will be able to work more easily with some teachers than others.

Characteristics of Effective Coaches

Below, I highlight four important qualifications of literacy coaches, based on the coaching literature and research.

1. *Know your stuff.* As one principal put it, it is a given—literacy coaches need to have excellent, up-to-date knowledge of literacy instruction and assessment, and the research that undergirds that knowledge. Coaches need this knowledge in order to analyze the lessons they see and identify the relevant aspects of instruction for discussion with the teacher. Those who have a deep understanding of their field are able to "see" things that novices or those with less understanding may not see. An analogy might be a golf instructor who quickly sees that the student is bending his or her arms (not good), not keeping the lower body stable and balanced, or making some other mistake. Likewise, the literacy coach can readily observe, for example, (a) when a teacher moves so quickly through a lesson that students are experiencing difficulty understanding what is being taught, or (b) where the teacher might have stopped to check for understanding or provided additional examples of a specific concept or skill as a means of giving additional scaffolding to students. Clearly, reading specialists must be learners themselves, reading the current literature and research, attending conferences and workshops. Reading specialists can maintain their own professional libraries and join professional organizations so that they remain knowledgeable (see Chapter 12 for more about the reading specialist as a lifelong learner).

2. *Experience.* Literacy coaches are more effective if they have had successful experiences as teachers. Although longevity is not an issue, literacy coaches should have experiences that build credibility with classroom teachers and enable them to feel empathy for the teachers' many responsibilities. Some can transcend the need for experience, but in the long run, reading specialists benefit from having worked with classrooms of students with diverse needs and interests.

3. *Ability to work with adults.* When we talk with coaches about how prepared they were to fulfill their roles, many of them tell us they felt comfortable with the content (literacy instruction and assessment),

but less comfortable with knowing how to work with adults. An understanding of adult learning is essential. As mentioned in Chapter 5, adults come with previous experiences and beliefs influencing new learning, want their learning to be meaningful to them, require multiple exposures to help them see the value of the new initiative or idea, and have busy lives and don't want to waste their time.

4. *Effective interpersonal and leadership skills.* To function successfully as a coach who has responsibility for observing and giving feedback to teachers, the reading specialist must have excellent interpersonal and communication skills. Coaches must be good listeners, be able to empathize with the teachers, and provide balanced feedback that reinforces excellent teaching behavior and provides ideas for improvement. They must also be able to develop a trusting relationship with the teachers whom they coach, so that their feedback is valued. Essentially, coaches must be able to get their messages across to their colleagues (i.e., the teachers in the classrooms). (See Chapter 4 for more information about interpersonal, communication, and leadership skills.)

Identified below are principles that should be taken into consideration when one is involved in coaching activities.

1. *Share your plans and ideas with teachers.* Teachers should understand what coaching means and what it does not mean, why they are involved, and how it will benefit their students. Teachers need to understand that the coaching process is not an evaluative one, but rather one that strives to help them be more effective. To the degree possible, invite teachers to participate in the coaching process as they will be more receptive to the process.

2. *Obtain teacher input.* Take time to hear and respond to teachers' concerns. Focusing the coaching on addressing teachers' needs will make it more likely that the coaching will be received positively by teachers.

3. *Provide necessary support.* Once the coaching process begins, provide the resources teachers need to make changes in their classroom instruction. In other words, if a coach or teacher identifies a specific need (e.g., additional training or supplemental material), such support should be provided.

4. *Take time to develop the trust needed to be an effective coach.* Begin with those who are eager and willing to participate. By working with teachers who are receptive, coaches themselves will be more relaxed and can use these initial cycles as opportunities to practice their "coaching" and communication skills. One builds trust by maintaining

confidentiality. Coaches who talk with others, especially administrators, about what they have seen in classrooms will not be seen as supportive. Teachers will be less likely to respond in a positive manner.

Summary of the Interactive Framework of Instructional Coaching

In sum, coaching does not occur in a vacuum. Successful coaching requires a context in which the conditions are conducive to coaching, a coach who has the skills and abilities to work within that environment, and an understanding of the model of coaching being implemented. When coaching does not seem to be effective, think about each one of these dimensions: Is the school one in which there is support, understanding of, and even enthusiasm for coaching?; Has "readiness" for coaching been established?; Does the coach have the skills, knowledge, and abilities that enable him or her to work within that context?; and Is the model of coaching understood and is it appropriate for the teachers in that school?

Comparison of Coaching at the Elementary Level with the Secondary Level

Ippolito and Lieberman (2012) discuss differences that exist between coaching at the elementary and secondary levels. They suggest that goals of schooling as well as the culture of the school create a different set of challenges for coaches. First, elementary school teachers are focused on building foundational skills (i.e., helping students develop the language, literacy, and thinking skills necessary for learning to learn). Teachers at the secondary levels generally have a more laserlike focus on teaching students the content of their disciplines—what students need to know about American history, the human organism, geometry, and so on.

Second, teachers at the elementary school level tend to have a deeper understanding of literacy (reading and writing); teachers at the secondary level are generally subject-area specialists with less knowledge of how important literacy is to the development of content-area skills. Thus, elementary teachers may be more receptive to coaching that focuses on literacy and how it can be integrated into instruction (in both language arts classes and in the content areas). Teachers at the secondary level may need to be convinced of the importance of such instruction.

Third, coaches may find it easier to find time to work with teachers at the elementary level, with more opportunities for flexible scheduling. At the secondary level, the tight schedules and the fact that teachers work with many different students may create a more difficult or at least a different coaching situation.

Finally, and probably most difficult, when coaches, who often have elementary school backgrounds, begin their work with secondary content-area teachers, they may need to establish their credibility. Teachers may question what these literacy coaches know about the adolescent student or about the unique aspect of teaching the disciplines, and rightfully so. Coaches who come to the secondary school with little knowledge of a discipline (science, social studies) will have to work collaboratively with the content-area teachers, with each contributing to the development of lessons built on disciplinary literacy appropriate for a specific content area.

At the same time, although these differences exist, there are some similarities. The process of coaching is the same: one must be able to work effectively with groups, hold positive problem-solvingconversations with teachers, provide feedback in ways that respect teachers' values and beliefs, and so on. Indeed, Ippolito and Lieberman (2012) suggest that differences "may be more a matter of degree than of fundamental difference . . . " (p. 69).

Given the culture of the secondary school and the focus on working with teachers of the disciplines, school leaders have generated various ideas for implementing coaching initiatives. Some encourage effective disciplinary-area teachers at the secondary level to become certified as reading/literacy specialists or to seek advanced literacy preparation that enable them to serve as coaches for their colleagues. Others have suggested that literacy coaches with elementary school backgrounds focus on working with department chairs or teacher leaders at the secondary level to help them gain a better understanding of literacy; these secondary leaders would then serve as coaches for teachers in their particular disciplines. What is critical is that school leaders select literacy coaches who have the leadership and interpersonal skills that enable them to work effectively with teachers of the disciplines. There are individuals who can transcend their lack of secondary experience, but they will need the support of administration as well as the ability to work well with adults to be successful. Several resources useful for literacy coaches who work at the secondary level include *Standards for Middle and High School Literacy Coaches* (IRA, 2006), *(Re)Imagining Content Area Literacy Instruction* (Draper, 2010), and *Developing Readers in the Academic Disciplines* (Buehl, 2011).

ACTIVITIES OF COACHING

There are many different coaching activities that can be used to support and guide instructional efforts in schools (see Figure 6.3 for a list.

Group Activities

- Developing, locating, or sharing resources with teachers (written or oral).
- Meetings with grade-level or subject-area teams to discuss assessment, instruction, curriculum, student work, teacher assignments, and so on.
- Leading committee work (developing curriculum, preparing materials).
- Leading or participating in study groups to discuss specific materials read by the group.
- Leading or participating in more traditional types of professional development workshops.
- Participating in lesson study (Stigler & Herbert, 1999) with groups of teachers.
- Assisting teachers with online professional development.
- Coaching on the fly (COTF)—unscheduled meetings with groups of teachers (e.g., discuss students, scheduling, family involvement).

Individual Activities

- Coplanning lessons.
- Problem-solving conversations with individual teachers (about specific students, assessment, instruction, etc.).
- Modeling.
- Co-teaching.
- Observing and providing feedback.
- Combination—coaches may combine modeling, co-teaching, and observing while working with teachers in the classroom. (Coach is generally in the classroom for an extended period of time.)
- Coaching on the fly (COTF)—impromptu meeting with a teacher to discuss topic of importance to that teacher (a specific student, test scores, etc.).

FIGURE 6.3. Coaching activities.

These activities are divided into group and individual activities. Coaches may also assist teachers by providing direct service to students—that is, assessing students who may have been absent or helping teachers with ongoing progress monitoring, or teaching a group of students for a predetermined amount of time—but the focus in this chapter and in Chapter 7 is on coaching activities.

In an article written in 2004, I categorized coaching activities according to levels of intensity or risk (Bean, 2004); this list can also be found in the IRA (2004) position statement on the role and qualifications of the reading coach in the United States. Some activities are more informal and create less anxiety for teacher and coach (e.g., an informal discussion about a specific student experiencing difficulty), while others may be of greater risk or intensity (e.g., observing and providing feedback about the teacher's instruction).

THINK ABOUT THIS

In looking at the activities identified in Figure 6.3, which of those would you feel most comfortable doing? Least comfortable? Which do you think would be most threatening to teachers? Least threatening?

In Chapter 7, I discuss coaching activities that are focused on working with individual teachers. Group activities are discussed in Chapters 4 and 5. Although reading specialists who serve as coaches may not be involved in all of the activities described in Figure 6.3, reading specialists will, at different times, need the knowledge, skills, and abilities to undertake these responsibilities.

SUMMARY

In this chapter, I discussed the "what and why" of literacy coaching. This was followed with the presentation of an interactive framework of literacy coaching consisting of three important components: the coaching model, the context, and the coach. After discussing characteristics of effective coaches, I identified principles of coaching. I concluded by identifying the many different activities coaches may use as a means of working with teachers and others in their schools.

ADDITIONAL READINGS

Bean, R. M., & Eisenberg, E. (2009). Literacy coaching in middle and high schools. In K. D. Wood & W. E. Blanton (Eds.), *Literacy instruction for adolescents: Research-based practice* (pp. 107–124). New York: Guilford Press.—The authors describe coaching at the secondary level and discuss its effectiveness. They then describe a statewide, secondary-level, instructional coaching initiative in Pennsylvania, and conclude with guidelines for coaching at this level.

L'Allier, S., Elish-Piper, L., & Bean, R. M. (2010). What matters for elementary literacy coaching: Guiding principles for instructional improvement and student achievement. *The Reading Teacher, 63*(7), 544–554.—Guiding principles about literacy coaching based on research findings are presented; examples of how the research findings can be applied to practice are described.

Skiffington, S., Washburn, S., & Elliott, K. (2011). Instructional coaching: Helping preschool teachers reach their full potential. *Young Children, 66*(3), 12–19.—The authors describe coaching initiatives in several Early Reading First projects, elaborate on their interviews with teachers and coaches, and then present lessons learned about coaching at this level.

Reflections

1. Think about a school with which you are familiar and its readiness for coaching (as described in the interactive framework of coaching). What are the conditions that would make coaching easy or difficult?

2. How comfortable would you be in a coaching role? What experiences, knowledge, and skills do you possess to be an effective coach? What do you think you need to do to improve?

Activities

1. Select a book on coaching and read to identify how the author(s) define coaching. Does the definition align with any of the models of coaching described in this chapter?

2. Develop with a group some interview questions that could be asked of a literacy coach. Relate those questions to the interactive framework of coaching.

3. Shadow or follow a literacy coach for a day and then be prepared to discuss what you saw. What coaching activities did you observe?

4. In small groups, discuss the vignette below, reflecting on what Wendy brings to the reading specialist/literacy coach role; identify three important "take-aways" from the vignette. Share the work of small groups with the whole class.

Some questions to think about:

What lessons can be learned about the role of the reading specialist/coach in this vignette?

What key characteristics make Wendy an effective reading specialist/coach?

What questions come to mind after reading this vignette?

WENDY: COACHING AT THE DISTRICT LEVEL

My teaching career began about 20 years ago at the Clearfield Area School District, a rural district consisting of 190 professional staff and 2,300 students (53% of our students receive free and reduced lunch and 4% are minority students). In our district, I worked as a reading specialist at the elementary level for 16 years, as an elementary literacy coach for 1 year, and for the past 3 years, was asked to shift my focus to include the middle and secondary levels. I then became an instructional coach for all K–12 teachers in our district. What I do each day has shifted somewhat from year to year depending on the needs of the school district. The coaches, curriculum director, and administrators meet regularly to discuss district priorities and instructional focus areas. For the past several years, teachers in our school district have been involved in a variety of initiatives to increase student engagement, which include the use of formative assessments and cooperative learning.

When my coaching role shifted to include the secondary level 3 years ago, I began to focus my daily coaching activities on student-engaged instruction and finding a way to mesh the initiatives in the district. To accomplish this, I facilitated learning days (professional development sessions) with all K–12 teachers, using a metacognitive instruction framework developed by our district; this framework focuses on the goals and activities of several district initiatives. The professional development sessions highlight student engagement strategies and learning walks *during* each session. Teachers are asked to reflect on their teaching practices and set goals following these sessions. My coaching often involves working with teachers to help them think about the goals they have set to become more effective educators. It's exciting to hear the conversations and reflections that influence practices as a result of our learning sessions. I developed my own protocols for these walks based on goals we had established.

On a day-to-day basis, I work with teachers to analyze data and plan instruction based on those data, provide one-on-one coaching, design effective instruction that engages students, meet with administrators, coordinate and lead teachers on learning walks/classroom visits, attend professional development sessions, create a coaching newsletter for teachers, facilitate book study sessions—and implement sessions stemming from these book studies. (Book study sessions typically involved reading and discussing books together. Then as we implemented ideas from the books we were reading, we would do learning walks, and also hold meetings via Skype from locations throughout our school district. This made it easy for teachers to be in different locations, share what they were implementing, and discuss the most effective practices.) Below I provide a daily schedule that illustrates my many responsibilities, although there is not really a typical day!

8:00–8:45	Meet with elementary teachers via Skype regarding the implementation of *The Daily 5* structure as part of a book study implementation
9:00–10:30	Grades five and six reading data—analyze data in preparation to meet with teachers about next steps
10:30–11:15	Model interactive writing lesson—grade-one classroom (debrief to follow)
12:30	Visit eighth-grade classroom during a class period to offer feedback for classroom management
2:00	Meet with a seventh-grade geography teacher during his or her planning period to design a lesson incorporating student engagement strategies

Creating a Schedule

My schedule is very flexible. Since I work in a K–12 capacity and my focus is providing professional development, my schedule is often based on what I am planning to do with individual teachers. Initially, I schedule the professional development sessions with groups of 8–10 teachers at a time, throughout several weeks in the fall and again in the spring. Then I make decisions based on formative assessments and teacher reflections during and following the professional development sessions. I meet with teachers for a variety of purposes and build my schedule around what is needed and teacher requests.

For the past 2 years, there have been two coaches in our district. One coach has focused on math and one on literacy, but both address unified effective instructional practices overall. We work together to plan and deliver professional development sessions. We work separately, however, in our one-on-one work with teachers; yet, we continuously collaborate and problem solve to make our interactions with teachers as effective as possible.

Greatest Challenges

One of the greatest challenges has been shifting from the elementary to the secondary level. I had worked at the elementary level for my entire teaching career and when I was asked by the superintendent to shift my focus to include the secondary level, I was unsure of how to begin. Since the teachers at that level had not worked with a coach in the past, it was challenging to help teachers understand my role as a coach. They really did not know what I was there to do or what I could do! I explained my goal was to collaborate with them in increasing student engagement in learning and thinking. I made sure they knew I was not a supervisor nor did I have evaluation responsibilities. I tried to make our relationship informal and comfortable. I did not know many teachers at the secondary level, so I began by trying to connect with teachers on a personal level, listening closely to what they said about their interests and hobbies. I initiated learning walks, which were very well received. Teachers were willing to give up their planning time to be able to watch one another teach and reflect on effective practices; often this type of classroom visit was a first for them!

The shift to the secondary level has also been one of the most rewarding aspects of my coaching experience. Teachers were very receptive and willing to discuss effective instruction, visit one another's classrooms, reflect together, and change instructional practices to be more engaging and effective for students. As a result, students are more engaged in the process of learning, grappling with ideas, and working together to problem-solve and share their thinking. Even though this shift was challenging, the results have been extremely rewarding.

Success!

I believe that establishing learning walks in our schools has been one of the most powerful and rewarding parts of my coaching experience. Teachers were extremely curious to see what others were doing in their classrooms and were willing to give up their planning time to participate in learning walks. Some teachers commented that for the 30-plus years they had been teaching, they had never before had the opportunity to watch other teachers in action and were grateful to have the experience. During my second year at the high school, 46 teachers agreed to participate in learning walks.

Because the learning walk implementation at the high school was so successful, we were able to establish a culture in which teaching was made public within our high school first, then the middle school, and more recently our elementary schools. It has become commonplace to visit classrooms, focusing on a specific area, or strategy, or structure, and to reflect on our own practices. Shifting from talking about what we do, to actually being able to notice effective instructional practices in action, is when we impact our own instruction.

This too, has provided me with a way to follow-up with teachers as a means of supporting their efforts to become more effective educators. For example, following a learning walk where we focus on effective questioning, a teacher might set a goal of creating a more student-centered questioning culture within the classroom. My follow-up work with that teacher would involve collaborating to design lessons enabling him or her to accomplish that goal; that is, the classroom would be one where students were asking and answering questions and involving one another in dialogue. I may model such a lesson or we may co-teach, and then we would debrief and reflect together about the effectiveness of the lesson.

Another success story has to do with helping to initiate and create a common vision in our district K–12. There is a general ease with which we can talk to one another and visit classrooms to reflect on teaching practices. Students are now engaged; rather than getting information, they are part of the process of learning and problem solving together to make meaning. In walking through the hallways and in classrooms, you can't help but notice the shift in the teaching and learning culture—a shift to a passion for learning with students being in the forefront of learning.

Results

Instructional coaching has been a challenging, yet rewarding experience. Through creating a common vision throughout our K–12 schools, shifting the focus of coaching to the secondary level, initiating learning walks, and integrating student engagement initiatives in our school district, we have seen some promising results. At the secondary level, we have seen a shift in room arrangements from rows to small groupings that enable student interaction. There has been an increase in this type of classroom arrangement; in 2011–2012, 42% of secondary classrooms were arranged in ways that facilitated student collaboration, while in 2013–2014, 75% of the classrooms had such seating arrangements. Also, we now observe multiple student engagement strategies used in over 90% of classes. Previously, students were asked questions that generated one-word answers but are now being asked to explain their thinking or to cite evidence for their answer. At our high school where the initiative and learning walks first began, we experienced a double-digit jump in reading proficiency scores from 63 to 75% after the first full year of providing professional development for all staff.

One of the most striking, although harder to quantify, change has been in the culture of our buildings. As you walk the halls of our schools, there is a learning culture where teachers are willing to visit one another's classrooms, ask each other questions, and reflect on their own practices in order to grow as an educator. Increasingly, teachers are organizing their classrooms so that students are sharing their thinking, clearing up one another's confusions, debating, problem solving, and taking charge of their own learning. These shifts in culture and practice are the most important changes needed to prepare our students for the expectations of the Core Standards and to be ready to compete in a global society.

WENDY SALVATORE, MEd
Instructional Coach (K–12)
Clearfield Area School District
Clearfield, Pennsylvania

CHAPTER SEVEN

What Coaches Do
to Improve Instruction

Working with Individual Teachers

Key Questions

- In what ways can reading specialists develop a trusting relationship between teachers and themselves?
- What ideas are useful for the coach when starting a new school year or a new position?
- In what ways can coaches work with individual teachers? What guidelines facilitate each of these activities?
- How can feedback to teachers be provided so that it is received positively?

In this chapter, I begin by discussing ways reading specialists, new to coaching, can develop the relationships necessary for them to be successful in their work. This is followed by sections that highlight the work of coaches with individual teachers. In previous chapters, I described the work that coaches do with small groups, such as grade-level teams, disciplinary teams, or interest groups, and also the more traditional and large-group professional development sessions to support teacher learning (these aspects of coaching are discussed in Chapters 5 and 6). Also, Chapter 4 provides additional information about communication, an important aspect of effective coaching.

THE READING SPECIALIST AS COACH: GETTING STARTED

In a study of coaches in Reading First schools in Pennsylvania (Bean et al., 2008), we found some schools employed coaches who were new to the school, while others selected coaches who had been teachers in that school. Both sets of coaches saw advantages and disadvantages to this selection process. Coaches new to a school felt that they came to the position without any previous bias about the school and its staff; teachers likewise had no prior experiences with the coach on which to base judgment. On the other hand, these coaches had no sense of any "land mines." They had to work quickly and effectively to gain an understanding of the culture of the school, including learning about students who attend the school, and teachers' knowledge and beliefs about language, literacy, and learning.

Most coaches who were hired from within felt as though they had the credibility and respect necessary to do the job and, in addition, understood the cultural dynamics in the school. They also understood that their prior experiences at the school could be helpful in some ways, but detrimental in others. Some experienced resentment given they were leaving the teacher ranks or because they had competed for the position with another colleague..

What all coaches new to the position recognized was that they had to begin *quickly* establishing themselves in this role, and at the same time, move *slowly* enough that they could develop a sense of trust between teachers and themselves. Some ideas for getting started follow:

1. *Be accessible.* A new coach needs to be seen, walking the halls, or stopping by classrooms to talk with teachers. All coaches and especially those new to the school should post their schedule and identify their availability; such a schedule can also provide space for teachers to "sign up" for a conversation, request resources, and so on. All teachers should have an e-mail address and telephone number for contacting the coach. As mentioned in a previous chapter, even the location of the office is important. Bean and DeFord (n.d.) describe the comments of one coach who talked about the importance of location, indicating that she had much more opportunity to talk with teachers when her office was moved from near the principal's office to near the students' bathroom! Coaches who keep their office doors open, who have instructional materials available for teachers to borrow, and who are willing to participate in professional conversations will have an easier time developing that important sense of trust. Some coaches like to keep some treats in their offices; teachers who come in to talk often enjoy a small piece of chocolate or a cup of tea or coffee.

2. *Initiate activities and seek responsibilities.* New coaches have at times indicated they aren't sure what to do or how to start getting involved. In the beginning weeks of school, several approaches might be useful. New coaches can write an introductory letter describing their

backgrounds and then identify some ways in which they might work with teachers. Or a new coach can develop a reading room, perhaps in the coach's office, that includes professional and instructional materials, and invite teachers to visit the room to borrow materials. Another coach might schedule informal conversations with each teacher, suggesting that such a conversation will help the coach develop a more in-depth understanding of the students in each classroom, their abilities and needs, and how the coach might help teachers address those needs. Figure 7.1 describes ideas for this conversation and suggests possible questions the coach might ask the teacher. Some coaches have asked teachers if they could teach a mini-lesson in the teachers' classrooms or read to the students to get to know them (since the coach will be in the classroom at different times during the year). And, of course, coaches at the beginning of the year can help teachers as they attempt to conduct the initial assessments often required in schools. Your mantra might be Be proactive! For example, if a teacher mentions wanting to do more with writing instruction, but "isn't sure how to begin," suggest some reading materials, schedule a time to talk about those materials with the teacher, or volunteer to work with the teacher to plan lessons, and so on. In other words, seize any opportunities there for the taking. Carpe diem!

Schedule a time to meet with each teacher individually in a comfortable situation and when it is convenient for the teacher to talk. Below is a suggested framework for the conversation.

1. **Breaking the ice.** Share with the teacher some information about yourself—your goals as a coach, your background (if new to the school). Talk with the teacher about his or her background, interests. Sometimes, there are pictures on the teacher's desk of grandchildren, vacation trips, or pets that can spark a short conversation.

2. **Setting a goal.** Establish the reason why you are holding these conversations: Get to know the teacher's goals for the students; learn more about the students in the classroom and their strengths and needs.

3. **Suggested questions:**
   a. "What are your goals for your students this year (think about broad goals of the reading program)?"
   b. "What are the skills and abilities of students in terms of achieving the goals? How can I help you learn more about your students?"
   c. "What strategies/approaches seem to work for you and help you achieve your goals? What keeps you from achieving your goals?"
   d. "What resources would be helpful to you?"
   e. "In what ways can I be helpful?"

FIGURE 7.1. Questions for an initial conversation with teachers.

3. *Develop a sense of trust.* As mentioned in Chapter 6, some activities of coaches are seen as more threatening (e.g., observing and giving feedback) than others. To help teachers understand coaching is meant to be supportive and nonevaluative, take time to develop a sense of trust between the teacher and yourself. Spending time with teachers in the lounge or eating lunch with them provides opportunities for informal conversations about topics important to them—their hobbies, families, pets, favorite music, and so on. Share information about yourself. These informal conversations can help to develop relationships and indicate you care about them as individuals.

Starting the position by serving as a resource to teachers is often helpful. Katy, in writing about her work as a literacy coach, talks about making materials for teachers and how that helped her to establish positive relationships with them (see "Voices from the Field" in Chapter 4). But so too, is maintaining *confidentiality.* In almost all cases, what coaches see and hear when they talk with teachers or visit their classrooms must remain between teacher and coach, although there may be a few instances when a situation affects the well-being of a child or children, and in that case, confidentiality does not apply. Likewise, coaches will hear things from administrators that are not to be shared with teachers. This does put coaches in a difficult spot; as one coach said, "We're in limbo or purgatory. Neither fish-nor-fowl."

4. *Start with the willing.* Although coaches may be required to work with all teachers in a school, if possible, begin with volunteers (i.e., teachers who seem eager for or request coaching support). By working with volunteers, coaches can hone their own skills in a supportive environment. Moreover, the word often spreads . . . "Coaching was very helpful!" Although starting with eager and willing teachers can be helpful, coaches should not stop there. In order to effect school change, they must continue to seek opportunities to work with all teachers in the school, although they will not work with all teachers in the same way nor to the same extent.

THINK ABOUT THIS

Which of the above ideas do you think are most useful for a new coach? Are there others that might work well?

Coaching Activities with Individual Teachers

In the following section, I describe ideas and activities for working with individual teachers. Decisions about coaching activities need to be made intentionally, taking into consideration the following: teacher goals, choice (How would the teacher prefer to work with you?) and teacher needs (What would work best to help the teacher improve instruction?) Often, coaches use the following sequence of activities as they work over time with teachers: I do (model), we do (co-teach), and you do (observations). Although this is a reasonable way to work, it's often wise for coaches to observe in the classrooms first as a means of learning more about the teachers' students. To the degree possible, involving the teacher in deciding how to proceed helps the coach establish a more collegial relationship and enhances teacher receptivity to coaching and coaching suggestions. Celia, a literacy coach, writes about how she responds to a teacher's request as a means of determining follow-up activities, indicating how the decision about activities is made together (see "Voices from the Field" in Chapter 5).

DEMONSTRATING OR MODELING

One of the most important means of coaching is demonstrating or modeling specific behaviors or strategies. As mentioned previously, Fullan (1991) described the "implementation dip" that often occurs.. Specifically, he discusses the fact that even after teachers have attended workshops or presentations about effective programs or approaches, their successful implementation of what they learned remains an issue. So, if the goal is to have a teacher learn to use a specific strategy (e.g., Beck & McKeown's [2001] "Text-Talk") as a means of exposing young children to challenging text, the coach may decide to model that approach while the teacher observes. In the LEADERS project, described in Chapter 5, participating teachers indicated that demonstration lessons were extremely helpful. When they observed another individual using a specific approach or strategy, especially in their classrooms with their students, these teachers felt as though they had a much better understanding of how to implement that strategy. Some guidelines for doing such demonstration lessons follow:

1. Establish a purpose for the modeled lesson and learn as much as you can about the students and the instruction in that classroom. Celia, in her vignette, discusses the questions she asks teachers as she prepares to model a lesson (see "Voices from the Field" in Chapter 5).

2. Plan with teachers so that they have some role in the lesson, assisting children or conducting a small part of the lesson. This active involvement creates more interest and understanding on the part of the

teacher—as well as commitment. One effective coach always gave the teacher a role in the modeled lesson (e.g., "I would like you to keep an eye on Roberto and Chelsea while I teach. Generally they have difficulty following directions. Perhaps if you sat next to them, it would be helpful"). Prior to the modeled lesson, coaches can frame questions with teachers to discuss or reflect on what happened during the lesson (i.e., student responses and reactions).

3. Provide teachers with a protocol that assists them in focusing their attention on the lesson they are watching. Such a protocol can be quite simple, perhaps a chart with three columns addressing the following: What is the coach doing?, What are the students doing?, and What questions or comments do you have? In some instances, coaches may want to provide protocols that contain information about the specific steps in the instructional strategy being modeled (e.g., procedures for teaching a word-building lesson).

4. Discuss the lesson with the teacher as soon as possible after teaching it. Reflect with the teacher on the effectiveness of the lesson. Did I achieve my goals, and if not, why? What went well? What could have gone better? Be certain to address those questions that created the need for modeling in the first place! Be honest in sharing with the teacher unexpected aspects of the lesson (e.g., handling of a behavior problem). Few lessons are perfect and teachers will feel more comfortable working with a coach when they see that the coach also can have difficulty with a disruptive student or elicit little response from students, despite earnest efforts to stimulate interaction. Give teachers opportunities to ask questions, reflect, and make comments as well.

5. Address next steps. There should be some type of follow-up to the modeled lesson. Such follow-up could include observing the teacher presenting the same type of lesson that was modeled as a means of determining what the teacher learned. At the same time, there may be teachers who are uncomfortable with this step and the coach may need to do some co-teaching to create a sense of a partnership or co-ownership of the lesson. Likewise, the coach may also coplan a similar lesson with the teacher, but not observe until the teacher has had an opportunity to teach such a lesson several times. There is more than one way to follow-up with a modeled lesson; often the coach needs to follow the lead of the teacher (i.e., What makes sense for him or her?).

A few cautions: Some teachers may not require modeling; moreover, they may want the coach to work in a different way with them (e.g., helping them coplan a lesson). Second, modeling of a specific strategy or approach in all classrooms may not be time efficient. Instead, coaches may want to model in one third-grade classroom and find ways to invite the other third-grade teachers to observe that lesson (e.g., the principal or other personnel may work with the other third graders). Another option is for the coach to produce a video of a modeled lesson in one classroom and then share and reflect on the lesson with a group of teachers during a follow-up group meeting. Finally, the goal for coaching is to move the teacher toward independence; therefore, be cautious when teachers are interested only in having you model for them!

COPLANNING

As mentioned previously, coaches need to understand where the teacher is in terms of readiness for coaching. Some teachers may welcome the coach if he or she is willing to help the teacher plan one lesson, several lessons that focus on developing a specific strategy or skill, or a unit of work (e.g., planning integrated lessons addressing the CCSS). For example, the coach and teacher may want to work on lessons that help students understand how to participate in structured discussions to enhance comprehension. Coplanning may include lessons introducing students to key ideas about participating in a discussion and the various roles that they can assume (e.g., leading, facilitating, recording); other lessons may include looking at the materials of instruction and deciding the key questions to ask and where the best "stops" are for asking those questions. The coach and teacher can schedule follow-up meetings where they discuss reactions to and reflections about the lessons. Such coplanning can precede coach observations. These professional conversations can promote teacher learning; they can be conducted with individual teachers or with a group of teachers. Coplanning can be useful because it builds a collaborative relationship between coach and teacher, and also helps the coach gain a deeper understanding of what teachers know or think about the lesson, literacy learning, and their students.

PROBLEM SOLVING

Problem solving with teachers can be a fulfilling and productive activity for coaches. Critical issues that teachers are facing at the time can be addressed (e.g., difficulties of one student in the classroom, management issues, working with multiple groups, how to implement a specific strategy, or how to talk with the parents of a struggling reader). Collegial problem solving can help the coach and the teacher make key decisions about next steps for both teacher and coach. Teachers may make changes in grouping of students or try new management strategies. Follow-up coaching activities may be initiated (e.g., the coach may agree to model or to co-teach). Essentially, this coaching activity is an important approach for developing a relationship of trust, relies on the teacher to provide important information about the problem to be discussed, and requires the coach to be an excellent listener and ask questions that lead toward solving the problem. (See Chapter 4 for information about communication skills.) Often, reading specialists who do not have the formal title of coach are involved in this type of coaching activity—helping teachers think about an issue they are facing and how to solve it.

OBSERVING

An effective coaching approach to professional development is observing the work of teachers and providing feedback. By observing, coaches can see what is occurring in the teaching/learning process, provide reassurance, suggest alternative strategies, and in general, work *with* the teacher to improve classroom practices. Observations, however, are too often synonymous with evaluation because too often that has been their primary purpose. In fact, in an attempt to reduce anxiety on the part of the teachers, in some initiatives, coaches are requested to refrain from using the word *observing*; rather, they use the term *visiting* to describe their work. In the coaching cycle described below, the focus is on facilitating the teacher's growth and the coach is seen as a resource. Figure 7.2 outlines a cycle for coaching similar to the models proposed by Costa and Garmston (2002), and Glickman (1990). The four steps in the cycle include planning, observing, analyzing/reflecting, and conferring. In the following sections, each of the four steps is described, with examples from several coaching cycles. (Appendix A provides a template to be used as a summary sheet for the planning, analysis, and postconference steps. By using a summary sheet like this, coaches can keep track of their work with individual teachers, observe progress, and reflect on next steps.)

Planning

Planning is an important first step. Walking into the classroom without a focus is similar to traveling in an unfamiliar city without a map and trying to get from one location to another—there are many different directions to take and many different means of transportation. Likewise, with observation. The planning conference enables the coach and the teacher to discuss important issues as listed below.

Step 1: Planning

Talk with the teacher, using the following questions: What are the goals for the lesson? What does the teacher hope to gain from the experience? In what ways should data be collected?

Step 2: Observing

Observe in the classroom, focusing on the aspects that have been jointly agreed on in the planning meeting.

Step 3: Analyzing/reflecting

Both coach and teacher think about the lesson that has been observed. The coach analyzes data from observation and identifies topics/issues for discussion. The teacher generates questions and ideas for discussion.

Step 4: Conferring

Coach and teacher meet to discuss the lesson, using data obtained in steps 2 and 3. The goals of this step are to reflect with the teacher about the lesson (Were lesson goals accomplished and in what ways can the lesson be improved to meet student needs?) and to obtain a commitment from the teacher about possible changes or modifications in classroom practices.

FIGURE 7.2. Coaching cycle.

- What are the goals of the lesson? ("I'm teaching a series of lessons that address the standard about comparing and contrasting the structure of two different texts.")
- What does the teacher expect students to be doing during this lesson? What student outcomes are expected? Is there anything the coach should know about the students? The lesson?
- What does the teacher hope to learn from the observation? What is the focus of the observation?
- What is the best means of obtaining the information needed to address the teacher's goals?
- What are the procedures to be followed? (Where should the coach sit? How long will the coach stay?)

The planning session provides an opportunity for building trust and promoting reflection. It enables the coach to gain information about the class, lesson, and teacher. For example, this may be the first lesson the teacher has taught using a particular strategy, or perhaps there is a student with special needs who just arrived 2 days ago. One planning meeting between a second-grade teacher and a coach went as follows:

Sally, a second-grade teacher, had planned a lesson to address standards relative to writing, specifically, informational writing, and wanted Teresa, the coach, to provide her with feedback about the lesson. Sally and Teresa agreed that Teresa would observe, noting the procedures that Sally used in teaching the lesson. They agreed that Teresa needed to focus on the students to determine whether they understood and were involved in the lesson. Teresa indicated that she would take careful notes of what students were doing and saying; she would also "script" part of the lesson, to record what Sally and the students were saying at significant points in the lesson (i.e., what did Sally say to guide students and how did students respond to Sally's questions?). Sally reminded Teresa that she would be working with the entire class and that her class was not familiar with informational writing. This would be a lesson introducing a sequential framework to the class. They agreed on a time and place for the observation.

Observing

There are many different frameworks or systems that can be used for collecting data during observations. There are simple checklists that indicate the presence of some behavior or event (e.g., student work is displayed) or scales that describe to what extent something is present (e.g., student work is displayed not at all, a little, or a great deal). There are observation systems that are specific to the strategy or skill being taught (e.g., What should be included in a lesson on close reading?) and there are those that are more general, addressing key elements of effective literacy instruction at a specific level. Observers can also script teacher verbal behavior as a means of obtaining data. Some of these techniques are comprehensive and time-consuming, others, less so.

At the present time, many states or districts have developed or adopted observation frameworks for teacher performance evaluations. Most frequently, these frameworks are general, that is, not specific to one content area (e.g., importance of active engagement with various grouping arrangements; teachers will ask high-level questions). However, the reading specialists or coaches in a district, with teachers, may use those frameworks to develop an observation system for their informal classroom visits of literacy instruction. Such modification can provide for consistency of and a focus on well-defined expectations for classroom instruction. When teachers are aware of observation protocols and, have some involvement in selecting or developing them, there is likely to be more acceptance of their use.

Observation Protocols

In this section, I describe four observation protocols that may be useful to coaches as a starting point. The observation form in Figure 7.3 was used in the collection of data for an evaluation project in which we observed classroom literacy instruction in grades K–8 (Bean, Eichelberger, Turner,

Name: _____ Grade: _____ School: _____ Subject: _____

Instruction

Evidence of:

_____ student engagement
_____ clarity of explanations/directions
          (helping students understand)
_____ modeling/coaching/scaffolding
_____ flexible grouping

Specific strategies observed:

Comments:

Classroom Management

Evidence that the teacher:

_____ uses positive reinforcement
_____ exhibits positive-feeling tone
_____ establishes clear expectations for behavior
_____ establishes routines that students understand

Comments:

Literate Environment

Evidence of:

_____ student work around the room
_____ classroom libraries
_____ places for small-group work (reading center,
          learning centers, etc.)
_____ print-rich
_____ standards/expectations for students

Grouping

whole class
small group
pairs
individual
other: _____

Materials

text
student writing
board/chart
worksheet
computer
games
other: _____

Teacher Interaction

telling/giving information
modeling
recitation
discussion
coaching/scaffolding
listening/watching
reading aloud
checking work (monitoring)
other: _____

Student Response

reading
reading turn-taking
talking
listening
writing
manipulating

Code: 0 = not at all evident; 1 = evident sometimes;
         2 = evident most of the time; 3 = evident throughout

Comments:

Time Period	1	2	3	4	5	6
Students on task						
75% or more students on task						
50–75% students on task						
Less than 50% students on task						

FIGURE 7.3. Classroom Observation Form.

& Tellez, 2002). This form was influenced by the work of Taylor and Pearson (2002); several of the categories and specific behaviors from their school change classroom observation scheme were adapted for use. The form can also be useful for thinking about the dimensions to be observed (e.g., instruction, materials, classroom management).

The observation protocol in Figure 7.4 was adapted from a protocol used to observe in Reading First classrooms (K–3); the adapted version can be used to observe reading instruction across the elementary grades. It provides observers with specific descriptors of what they might expect to see when observing reading instruction and also a scale used to determine the extent to which specific indicators are present in the classroom or seen during the observation period. (Appendix B describes an observation protocol used for observing in content areas in upper elementary, middle, or high schools. This protocol provides information about how the teacher facilitates learning, the literacy activities of students, and information about grouping and materials used.)

The observation protocols described previously can be used when observing several different aspects of lessons. However, as mentioned, observers who are visiting classrooms to see how well teachers are implementing a specific skill or strategy (e.g., Text-Talk; Beck & McKeown, 2001) may choose to develop a protocol that describes explicitly what is expected. Or if a school has a literacy framework emphasizing specific strategies, then the literacy coach may choose to develop an observational protocol focused on those strategies. For example, Thibodeau (2008), a literacy coach, worked with several secondary content-area teachers and taught them several literacy strategies to be used before, during, and after reading text selections. In that case, an observation protocol can be developed addressing elements of those strategies.

There are also open-ended observation systems requiring much skill on the part of the observer, but at the same time, providing meaningful information about what is happening in the classroom. The one described below requires coaches to describe what is happening by scripting what they hear and see. Using paper and pen or a laptop computer, the coach records exactly what is going on in the classroom. The end product provides the coach with "data" to be shared with the classroom teacher (e.g., "Here's what the students were doing when . . ."). Specific steps are summarized in Figure 7.5. The advantage of this type of scripting is that "actual" behaviors and language are recorded rather than an interpretation or judgment about what is seen (as occurs when the observer makes a judgment, using a scale from 0 to 3). This open-ended scripting can be conducted for part of a lesson (e.g., for a 10-minute period when the teacher is interacting verbally with students). So, if the goal of the observation was to focus on student and teacher talk, the scripting

Teacher: _____ Grade Level: _____
Date: _____ Time Begin: _____ End: _____
Students Present: _____ Lesson Focus: _____

Materials: (Check all that apply)

Textbook	Group: (Check all	Adults: (Check all	Student Teacher
Board/Chart	that apply)	that apply)	Teacher Intern
Computer	Whole Class	Teacher	Other: _____
Worksheet	Small Group	Reading Specialist	
Student Work	Pairs	Reading Coach	
Other: _____	Individual	Instructional Aide	

Protocol to be used as a guide. Scale to be completed after the observation has been completed.

Scale:	Great Extent (3)	Some Extent (2)	Minimal Extent (1)	Not Observed (0)
Classroom Environment: Print Rich				
Classroom Library Is Accessible *Students are able to gain easy access to the library in the classroom. Books are eye level.*	☐	☐	☐	☐
Library Has Wide Variety of Books/Genres *Library includes informational, pleasure, poetry, language play, reference materials, etc.*	☐	☐	☐	☐
Reading and/or Writing Strategies Are Displayed *Strategies posted are informative tools designed to promote classroom learning.*	☐	☐	☐	☐
Reading Spaces Are Inviting	☐ yes ☐ no			
Learning Centers Are Evident	☐ yes ☐ no			
Student Work on Display Inside/Outside	☐ yes ☐ no			

Scale:	Great Extent (3)	Some Extent (2)	Minimal Extent (1)	Not Observed (0)
Classroom Management/Climate				
Maintains Positive Learning Environment *Interactions are respectful and supportive. Tone and atmosphere are encouraging.*	☐	☐	☐	☐
Encourages High Level of Student Participation *Teacher facilitates active engagement of students during lesson.*	☐	☐	☐	☐

FIGURE 7.4. Observation protocol. From Bean, Fulmer, and Zigmond (2009). Adapted with permission from the authors.

Maintains Effective Behavioral Routines *Clear expectations are established by teacher and internalized by students. Minimum time is spent in transitions.*	☐	☐	☐	☐
Maintains Robust Literacy Routines *Teacher facilitates strong literacy routines that are recognized and understood by students.*	☐	☐	☐	☐
Preserves Student On-Task Behavior *Teacher consistently facilitates student engagement during reading instruction.*	☐	☐	☐	☐

Scale:	Great Extent	Some Extent	Minimal Extent	Not Observed
	(3)	(2)	(1)	(0)
Instructional Practices Introduces and Reviews Concepts/Skills Clearly *Teacher develops concept or skill plainly and accurately. The concept or skill introduced is evident.*	☐	☐	☐	☐
Differentiates Literacy Instruction *Teacher appears to use individual student literacy performance in planning instruction. Literacy learning is structured for small groups or individual students.*	☐	☐	☐	☐
Facilitates Text Comprehension *Teacher helps students to make connections to targeted concepts; activates student background knowledge; engages students in high-level thinking activities; encourages students to make predictions; summarizes, retells, or makes use of graphic organizers to organize their thinking.*	☐	☐	☐	☐
Engages in Coaching/Scaffolding *Teacher provides corrective feedback by prompting the student in an effort to encourage the student to arrive at the correct answer independently.*	☐	☐	☐	☐
Highlights Significance of Reading Process *Teacher emphasizes the reading and writing process and the use of strategies; "A good reader sees the parts of words to help him or her decode. A good reader/writer does . . ."*	☐	☐	☐	☐

FIGURE 7.4. (*continued*)

*Models Skills/Strategies *Teacher demonstrates a particular skill or strategy to students.*	☐	☐	☐	☐
*Provides Guided Practice *Teacher supports students in practicing targeted skill or concept. Teacher provides opportunities to practice literacy learning.*	☐	☐	☐	☐
*Provides/Monitors Independent Practice *Teacher has students practice targeted concept/skill individually and monitors by giving feedback when needed.*	☐	☐	☐	☐
*Provides Application Activities *Teacher has students apply targeted concept to new learning for problem solving and independent learning. Students take responsibility for their own literacy learning.*	☐	☐	☐	☐

*Gradual release of responsibility model (GRRM; Pearson & Gallagher, 1983).

FIGURE 7.4. (*continued*)

during the 10 minutes would provide evidence about the type of question or statement being raised by the teacher, how the teacher responded to students who responded correctly or incorrectly, and the quality of student response. Teachers are generally fascinated when they see actual evidence of their teacher-talk. It does take time to learn to observe using this approach. However, with practice it becomes an effective means of collecting information to share with teachers. (See Appendix C for a form for using this approach.) Rather than taking such extensive notes, in some schools teachers are willing to review videos of their teaching with a coach or reading specialist so they can see and reflect on their teaching, student behaviors and responses.

Some summary points about observations follow:

• Focus. It is not possible to observe everything that is going on in a lesson. Therefore, making a decision about the focus of the observation is essential; if possible, that focus should be determined jointly by both coach and teacher.

• Be objective. While observing, be sure to indicate what you are seeing without being judgmental.

• Be sensitive to the fact that being observed may create anxiety for teachers; students too may behave differently because of the observer in the room.

1. Upon entering the room, spend several minutes doing an environmental sweep and collecting information about number of students, literacy environment in the room, and seating arrangements. You may want to draw a picture of the classroom.

2. Using blank sheets of paper, divide the sheet into two sections with a line down the middle, with "Teacher" in the left section and "Students" in the right section.

3. Begin identifying what is occurring in the classroom. If there is classroom discourse (i.e., the teacher is interacting with the students), try to jot down key phrases or words that the teacher and the students are saying. You may also want to identify whether specific students are responding. Remember to note whatever is especially relevant to the focus or goal identified in the planning session. For example, if the teacher wants the coach to attend to levels of questions, then recording the specific questions is important. If the teacher wants the coach to observe whether students are actively involved, then the coach would need to attend to that dimension of instruction.

4. When the teacher is serving as a facilitator (walking around classroom assisting students), the coach can focus on what students are doing, or not doing, as well as what the teacher is doing or saying.

Example of a script:

Teacher	Students
Walking around helping students, answering questions.	Students are all writing in their journals.
Helps child by asking him to read what he had written in journal.	One student has head down and is not writing. (OC: task too difficult?)

5. Every 5 minutes, draw a line under what you have written so that you have some indication of how long various activities have lasted and when they occurred. Sometimes, you may want to draw a line when an activity changes; for example, the teacher has finished reading a story and is now beginning to ask questions about the selection.

6. Mark "OC" (observer's comment) when there are events in the lesson about which you want to talk with the teacher or have questions. For example, mark "OC" next to the note, "Student refused to do work" and note query, "Can't do?"

7. Every 5 minutes or so (when it seems appropriate), it is wise to stop writing and just look around the classroom. It is easy to become so immersed in the writing that you miss some of the nonverbal and physical interactions.

FIGURE 7.5. Observation system for data collection.

- When entering a classroom, remain as unobtrusive as possible, finding a spot to sit and observe without interrupting the flow of the lesson. Talk with teachers prior to the lesson about whether they are going to introduce you. Generally, ask teachers to promptly make the introduction so that you can quickly and quietly go to a seat where you can observe without causing any disruptions.

- If the teacher asks you to interact with the students and the lesson, you may choose to join in and help teach the lesson. (Teachers can learn a great deal by having coaches work with them, and because the coach's goal is to be helpful, this modification may be what is needed at this time.) However, the coach may also return to observe at another time, asking the teacher to assume full responsibility for teaching the lesson.

- Leave a small sticky note when you leave, thanking the teacher and indicating that you look forward to talking with him or her. Sometimes a positive comment, such as "I enjoyed listening to the students tell what they would do in that situation!" can lessen teacher anxiety about the observation and the follow-up conversation.

Analyzing/Reflecting

Each step of the coaching cycle is an important one; however, the step of analyzing and reflecting is critical, for without it, there is little chance of making an impact on teacher learning and performance. Reflection is not only the purview of the coach but also the teacher. Before meeting for a postconference, both literacy coach and teacher can think about what occurred in the lesson, and especially how the questions raised in the preconference or planning stage were addressed. Also, teachers can be asked to think about the lesson, and to jot down a few ideas or questions for the postconference.

It is here, in the analysis phase, that the coach can make good use of the observation checklist, scales, notes, or scripts that were used during the observation. These provide excellent information that can be shared with the teacher during the conference. What levels of questions were asked? What steps did the teacher follow in teaching the strategy? How many students (and who) were not involved during the lesson? Going back through the data and thinking about answers to the following questions enable the coach to plan a strategy for the postconference to be held with the teacher.

- What are the key points to raise? (Are they related to the goals set by the teacher? How important in terms of possible impact on student learning?) You may choose to summarize some of the key points on a template similar to the one in Appendix A.

- How does the coach want to start the conference? (Does the coach start with identification of some strengths? Should the coach ask the teacher to discuss his or her views?) Thinking about how to begin a conversation can be very helpful in getting the discussion moving in a positive direction.

- What changes would best improve the instruction in that classroom? (Are the changes doable [e.g., does the teacher have the skills to implement suggested changes]?) Have teachers decide on one or two priority goals. Identify the support needed by the teacher to implement any changes.

- How can the coach be helpful? What approach might be best in working with this teacher (co-teaching, coplanning, etc.)?

Conferring with the Teacher

The postconference should occur as close in time to the observation as possible, not only to allay the teacher's concerns but also because recall and memory of what occurred are much better. However, the analysis and reflection steps are important and should not be eliminated. It's helpful to talk briefly with teachers immediately after an observation, thanking them for the opportunity to work with them, making a positive comment about some aspect of the lesson (e.g., the classroom environment, one student's performance), and identifying a time for the postconference.

One goal of the conference is to promote teacher reflection to the highest degree possible, focusing on teacher and student behaviors (Who was doing what?), comparing actual and desired behaviors, or considering reasons why these occurred or did not occur. Another important goal is the generation of future plans: What can the teacher take back from the conference to improve classroom instruction? Another is to assess the effects of the coaching experience: In what ways was the experience helpful—and what comes next?

Coaches need to be cognizant of the individual strengths, experiences, and learning styles of teachers. Using this knowledge, coaches can think about what stance to take in talking with teachers: coach as mirror, as collaborator, or as expert (Robbins, 1991).

The Coach as Mirror

In this instance, the teacher is self-reflective and quickly assumes a leadership role in the conference. The coach then serves to confirm and validate what the teacher articulates. These types of conferences generally move along quite easily because these teachers recognize whether they have achieved their lesson goals, why or why not, and often can suggest possible solutions to any problems. The coach then serves as a mirror by reflecting back to the teacher specific examples that indicate support for what the teacher is saying. Both teacher and coach talk about possible next steps. In the example below, the coach is working with an experienced kindergarten teacher who analyzes her own behavior and sets future goals for herself.

> KINDERGARTEN TEACHER: I lost the group after about 15 minutes. They were really with me until I started asking various questions about the main character. I don't think they lost interest in the story; I think they were sitting too long. I wonder if I might have asked several of them to . . .
>
> COACH: Yes, I think you're right. After about the third question, when you were trying . . .

The Coach as Collaborator

In this case, the literacy coach and teacher work together to determine the strengths and possible weaknesses of the lessons. They are both struggling to identify what was especially effective and what may have been done better.

> SEVENTH-GRADE SOCIAL STUDIES TEACHER: It seems to me there has to be a better way to get more students involved in the discussion. The same students are always raising their hands, while the others wait for them to reply.
>
> COACH: Let's talk about this. Remember that chapter about holding effective discussions in the classroom in Kylene Beers's book *When Kids Can't Read: What Teachers Can Do* (2003)? Let's think about the recommendations she makes. One suggestion was that students talk to each other before . . .
>
> TEACHER: Oh, yes! I remember; that's a great idea. Another thought I had was to ask students to generate questions for other students. Let's talk about how I might do that.
>
> COACH: Terrific idea; I think your students would really enjoy the challenge of that.

The Coach as Expert

In some instances, especially with novice teachers or teachers who are attempting a new approach for the first time, the coach may need to serve as expert, using directive coaching, and providing information to help teachers understand whether they are implementing various strategies or approaches effectively.

> FIFTH-GRADE TEACHER: So, when I was trying the K-W-L, I wasn't sure what I should do after students identified all they knew about turtles. Exactly how should I move to the W step?
>
> COACH: I think you did a great job! You had the students review what they knew, and then you commented: "Wow, we know a lot, but it appears that there is still much more to learn. For example, I wondered what the differences were between land turtles and sea turtles? What are some things you are wondering about?" You can help to jump-start the students by modeling for them, providing them with one or two examples of what they might want to learn. Often this will help them generate additional ideas.

In any single conversation with a teacher, coaches may find themselves moving from one stance to another, especially as the teacher raises questions or generates ideas. For example, the coach may begin the conversation using a more collaborative stance, but when the teacher asks for explicit guidance, may need to proceed by providing expert advice. The key is language—how we talk with others influences the results of any conversation. In Chapter 4, many ideas about effective communication are described. Just as a reminder here—being a good listener really matters!

This postconference session often serves as the planning step for the next cycle! For example, in the planning session described previously in this chapter, Teresa, the coach, talked with Sally, the teacher, about observing a mini-lesson on informational text. After observing, Teresa held a postconference, during which she and the teacher talked about next steps.

> Teresa said to Sally, "Overall, your students seemed to be able to arrange the sentence strips correctly; they really understood the sequence of making a peanut butter sandwich. What do you think the next steps might be; how can you move your students along?" Teresa asks the teacher to generate some ideas to try in the next lesson. The coach then asks, "Sally, you also raised some concern about Juan and Maria, two EL students who seemed to be somewhat puzzled. I agree, they seemed to have some difficulty following your directions. I wonder whether it would be good to work with them in a smaller group so that they get more opportunity for support and scaffolding. What do you think?" They agreed that it

would be helpful if Teresa would come into the classroom and teach a similar lesson to a smaller group of students, including Juan and Maria, while other students were working in small groups at independent learning stations. Sally was excited about the opportunity to watch Teresa work with these students; she felt she would learn a lot by stepping back and "kidwatching."

Subsequent planning sessions can be short, once goals have been established for a teacher. Because of time constraints, planning may have to occur as you are conversing with the teacher before or after school or for several minutes during a planning period. Nevertheless, planning is important; it helps establish a common goal for coach and teacher and focuses the observation!

Below, I identify guidelines for holding feedback conversations so that they are respectful, allow for divergent thinking, and enable teachers to gain both the skill and will to make changes in their classroom practices.

GIVING FEEDBACK

The feedback that coaches provide to teachers may require they make changes in what or how they teach. If the teacher and coach together can identify those areas or behaviors in which change is desired (i.e., the coach as mirror or the coach as collaborator), then the feedback session is generally a productive and positive one. On the other hand, there are times when the coach has to be more directive in working with a teacher. Always, the desire is to provide feedback that is constructive and workable. Nevertheless, some teachers may react defensively and have difficulty accepting feedback. Providing feedback in a carefully balanced and respectful manner can help to alleviate defensive and negative reactions. Several suggestions follow:

1. *Be specific.* Telling the teacher the lesson was good, fine, or interesting is not constructive—it does not provide information the teacher can use to improve classroom practices. Instead the coach must be as specific as possible. For example, if the coach wants to reinforce the many ways the teacher has made the environment student friendly, he or she can describe specifically what was seen (e.g., many different kinds of books in places where students could readily access them; student work posted on the walls; a chart that read "You Made My Day," with students' names on it). Likewise, if the coach has concerns about an instructional aspect of the lesson (e.g., the teacher called only on the few students whose hands were up), the coach can show the teacher the data

from the observation showing who was called on and who wasn't. Or if teacher questioning was only at a literal level, even though the emphasis was on inferential thinking, the coach can share data with the teacher and they can analyze the level of questions together.

2. *Behave in ways that reduce defensive behavior.* It is natural for all of us to defend what we have done in response to what we perceive as criticism. Coaches can reduce defensive behavior in several ways. First, they can focus on describing what they observed rather than making a judgment about it and, to the degree possible, create a problem-solving situation (e.g., "I noticed that students were less attentive in the discussion part of the lesson than while reading the story. Let's talk about that. What do you think caused their inattention?"). Such an approach promotes collaboration and reduces the tendency for the coach to be perceived as the only one who has the answers. Second, coaches can acknowledge that teachers have unique experiences and knowledge; they know the goals they are trying to achieve and the personalities of the students with whom they work. They have their own perspectives about what occurred in the lesson. They can therefore contribute to the solutions or suggestions in ways the coach cannot. So, coaches might begin a postconference with a statement such as the following: "Tell me about your goals for the lesson, and let's talk about what you did to reach those goals."

3. *Provide balanced feedback.* Make certain the teacher clearly understands the issue or item under discussion and how it might be resolved. For example, if the teacher is providing opportunities for students to develop fluency but the students are reading books that are too difficult for them to read without making many errors, the coach needs to acknowledge what the teacher is doing (providing fluency practice for students). In addition , the coach should help the teacher understand how such practice can be more productive (e.g., the material should be at an instructional or independent level). Feedback can be divided into a two-step process, as follows:

- *Discuss the merits of what the teacher is doing* (e.g., the merits of providing fluency practice for students): "We know that in order to be effective readers, students need to have opportunities to practice reading. The use of partner reading is certainly an effective strategy, and so is repeated reading. It was great to see that happening in your classroom."
- *Identify the concern or area that needs changing*: "One of the ways that you can increase the effectiveness of the fluency practice you are providing is by changing the difficulty level of the material that students are using. What materials do you have available that

might be appropriate? Or, let's see what is available in the resource room."

In the example above, the coach was not critical of the teacher but instead relayed information on how the teacher could increase the effectiveness of a specific strategy. Balanced feedback should include specific information as to what is effective and what can be improved. Both the teacher and coach can explore ideas for how to address the issue being discussed as most often there is more than one solution to resolving an issue.

4. *Focus the feedback on one or two important possibilities.* Less is more! What is most important for the teacher to consider? How doable is it? Is it something that the teacher can do somewhat easily and achieve success? As a coach, think about what changes or modifications in instruction might make the biggest difference to students—what would make the teaching and learning more effective—and then focus on how and what the teacher needs to know in order to make those changes. Finally, provide the necessary resources, support, and scaffolding.

5. *Celebrate the successes of the teacher.* This suggestion is closely aligned with balanced feedback, but it deserves to be mentioned again. Although the coach is there to help guide improvement, there are most likely aspects of the lesson deserving of celebration (e.g., student work is displayed, there are many different reading materials available for students, the students are attentive and on task). All of us need positive reinforcement and the coach should acknowledge what has been especially effective in the classroom.

6. *Support the teacher in self-reflection efforts.* Even though this suggestion is last, it may be the most important. The old adage, "Give a man a fish and he eats for a day; teach a man to fish and he eats for a lifetime," is appropriate here. To the extent that the teacher can identify, address, and think about the lesson—its successes and how to improve it—the most likely it is that there will be follow-through in future practices. Such reflective behavior can be facilitated when the coach is a good listener and able to scaffold and build on the thoughts of the teacher.

Coaching can be a valuable approach to improving the literacy instruction in a school. It can also be a growth experience for both the coach and the teacher. However, given that schools have not generally focused on this type of supportive coaching, it takes time to build an atmosphere of trust and receptivity. In talking with an individual responsible for working with new teachers, I asked her what she thought were the most important components of effective coaching. She shared these comments:

1. *Confidentiality.* What is seen by the coach and said by the teacher always stays between them. Nothing should ever be repeated, criticized, or made fun of in the teachers' lounge, principal's office, or at a school function.

2. *Nonthreatening demeanor.* The coach is present as a colleague, not an evaluator. Bring to the conscious level all of the good things that are happening in the class and offer suggestions about other possible methods of presenting the information. The coach is not there to make a teacher feel incompetent!

3. *Focus.* It is always advantageous to have a mutually agreed-upon target to focus the observation. When the conference occurs, the coach is ready with multiple suggestions and questions designed to make the teacher think and grow professionally (personal communication, 2001).

One of the most difficult tasks for coaches is providing feedback to teachers because often they have been the peers of their colleagues or recognize they have no evaluative responsibility. Moreover, for many, confrontation or conflict is difficult. Although coaches may have little difficulty discussing the good points in a lesson, often they struggle when they have to raise issues of concern. Learning to do this in a respectful and clear manner takes time. An important point: *Put the focus on what needs to be done to improve student learning and the steps that can be taken to do so.* Learning to be a critical friend takes time and has to occur in a culture where teachers feel comfortable and value making their teaching public.

THE REALITY OF THE SCHOOL

Although many coaches would value the opportunity to work in a systematic way with teachers (e.g., going through the formal observation cycle, from planning through postconference), school schedules and multiple demands on the coach, as well as differing needs of teachers, create the need for other forms of coaching beyond those discussed previously. One is "on-the-fly" or opportunistic coaching (i.e., coaches make themselves accessible so that they can respond to the needs and requests of teachers). The other is "combination coaching" in which teachers and coaches work together in a somewhat seamless fashion, moving from modeling to co-teaching to observing, in the same lesson or literacy block. Coaches may also want to do walk-throughs either by themselves or with other school personnel (e.g., administrator, school curriculum director, special educator). Finally, coaches need to think about how to differentiate their coaching; such efforts will enable them to develop a workable schedule and be productive in their work with teachers. Each of these is discussed below.

On-the-Fly Coaching

In a study of coaches in Reading First in Pennsylvania (Bean et al., 2008), we found that frequently coaches spent short amounts of time conversing with teachers, specialists, librarians, and principals in the hallways, between classes, at lunch, or before or after school. Such conversations actually led to important work with these school personnel and below I provide some examples of what is meant by on-the-fly coaching.

> Fred, the coach, was stopped by Harry, a third-grade teacher, as they waited for their students to get off the bus in the morning. He wondered why the district was asking teachers to administer another assessment test, besides the one that was given every 6 weeks. What would be gained by giving this assessment? Fred and Harry spent about 5 minutes talking about the new measure and how it was different from the one that was currently being administered. Fred also told Harry that he would be happy to stop by and show him the informal measure and, if Harry wanted, to model the administration of it with several of his students.

> Fred walked with the librarian on their way to the staff development meeting that was to be held after school. The librarian was working with the sixth-grade science teacher on a unit about planets. She wanted to know what she could read that would help her understand this new emphasis on "informational text" and what she might do in her library classes that would be useful to the students in that science class. Fred indicated that he would e-mail her an article about informational text she might find useful. He also told the librarian he would be happy to spend some time discussing this with her during her planning period.

What is clear is that these on-the-fly meetings generate opportunities for more in-depth coaching and that coaches can take advantage of these quick, spontaneous conversations that come up on a daily basis.

Combination Coaching

In our work with Reading First coaches (Zigmond & Bean, 2008), we found that some coaches stayed in the classrooms of teachers for an extended period, working with them for an entire reading block of 90 minutes. During this time, they modeled, co-taught, and even observed.

Then later that day, or the next day, they discussed their work and planned for the next teaching segment. We saw this sort of coaching especially when teachers were new to the school or to teaching a specific grade level. Reading coaches tended to spend extensive amounts of time, over a short period of time, helping these novice teachers learn more about how to provide or differentiate instruction.

Walk-Throughs

During the past few years, leaders in schools have begun to make frequent, short visits to classrooms to get a better picture of what is occurring across the school. Often these walk-throughs are done by several individuals (e.g., a principal and curriculum developer, two teachers). One might describe a single observation as a snapshot or photograph and walk-throughs as a photograph album. Certainly, this description illustrates the advantages of such a coaching approach. If coaches walk through all the classrooms at a grade level (e.g., at least once a week), they will get a sense of the similarities and differences across the classrooms in instruction, environment, and management, which may help coaches as they work with teachers in grade-level meetings. They will get a sense of how a classroom functions over a number of visits. Also, another advantage is that teachers and students become comfortable with the coach in the classroom, especially if the walk-through is an informal, friendly event. If the coach is making a walk-through alone, the following suggestions may be helpful:

- Try to get an overall sense of what the classroom looks like (the environment).
- Listen carefully to the teacher to get a sense of what teaching is going on and what instructional strategies are being used.
- Also, in some classrooms, focus on the students to see what they are doing. Take time to stop by the desks of a few children: Do they understand what they are to do? Are they completing a task as expected? Ask students to explain what they are to do and why they think it is important for them to complete this task.

Most often, a simple "thank you" or a wave is sufficient when leaving the room, especially if coaches have informed teachers that they will be doing these walk-throughs on a regular basis. Teachers also appreciate it if the coach leaves a quick note (sticky notes are terrific) reinforcing something that occurred during the visit (e.g., "The kids really seemed to be enjoying the story today!"). The note might be addressed to the students: "Dear Students: I especially liked the 'good thinking' when

Mrs. Botte asked you to predict how the story would end! Wow, what clever ideas!"

Walk-throughs with an administrator, such as the principal, can be useful for several reasons: they enable the two observers to establish a common language and focus for the literacy work being done; they may also be instructive for administrators who may have less knowledge and understanding of literacy instruction than the coach. However, coaches need to be careful that these walk-throughs are not seen as evaluative by teachers (i.e., the coach and principal together are making judgments about teachers). When the culture of the school is one in which teachers expect visitors to come into the classroom, and visits occur routinely and as a natural part of the school day, it is less likely teachers will view walk-throughs in a negative manner. Wendy, in her vignette (see "Voices from the Field" in Chapter 6), describes the walk-throughs that became a regular part of the teachers' professional development program in their district. She and a group of teachers visit the classrooms of other teachers who have agreed to participate. These walk-throughs are always focused and teachers doing the walk-throughs are looking for examples of active engagement of students.

Differentiating Coaching: Building a Schedule

If coaches are to be productive in their work, they need to consider ways to work effectively with teachers; this means they need to differentiate what they do. Coaches might want to think about the following as they develop schedules. First, group coaching is efficient and effective and may reduce the number of teachers who need follow-up individual coaching. Such meetings may also help coaches identify exactly how they might work with specific teachers. For example, as a result of a fourth-grade-level meeting about improving academic vocabulary, the coach might do the following: provide specific journal articles or Internet sources to all teachers, facilitate a group meeting with teachers responsible for teaching social studies, or model a mini-lesson for a novice teacher who asked for more specific guidance. In other words, group coaching can serve as a source of information about next steps. Grierson (2011) described her study of professional development that involved both semimonthly, small-group professional learning sessions and also weekly individualized coaching. She concluded small-group meetings were not enough to promote meaningful teacher change; rather, the small-group sessions helped teachers identify goals to be addressed in follow-up coaching. The individualized coaching support helped teachers internalize what they learned during their small-group sessions. Celia, in her vignette (see "Voices from the Field" in Chapter 5), discusses the ways that she follows up on the large-scale professional development offerings in her district.

Second, coaches can take into consideration the preferences of teachers as to the coaching approach to be used. When individuals are given such choices, they may be more likely to accept and follow-through with the ideas provided through such activities. Therefore, if a teacher is hesitant about the coach coming into the classroom, coplanning a lesson might be a first step. Such coplanning can lead to a follow-up conversation between coach and teacher focused on the teacher's reflection about the success of the lesson. The coach does not stop there, however. Next steps might include modeling or co-teaching, or even observing. Ultimately, however, the coach may need to make a specific recommendation for the next steps, especially if the teacher does not seem to be making recommended changes or students in the classroom are not learning as expected.

SUMMARY

This chapter discussed the importance of coaching as an approach to providing professional development for teachers. Ideas for getting started as a coach were identified followed by specific suggestions for modeling, coplanning, problem solving, and co-teaching. A four-step cycle of planning, observing, analyzing, and conferring was described. Various protocols for data collection were identified, followed by a section on providing feedback to teachers. Finally, three variations on coaching procedures—on-the-fly, combination, and walk-throughs—were described, followed by ideas for differentiating coaching.

ADDITIONAL READINGS

Blachowicz, C. L. Z., Buhle, R., Ogle, D., Frost, S., Correa, A., & Kinner, J. D. (2010). Hit the ground running: Ten ideas for preparing and supporting urban literacy coaches. *The Reading Teacher, 63*(5), 348–359.—Describes a successful coaching initiative in urban schools and discusses 10 strategies that were essential to its success.

Grierson, A. (2011, April). *Walking the talk: Supporting teachers' growth with different professional learning.* Paper presented at the annual conference of the American Educational Research Association, New Orleans, LA.—The author discusses the results of a group-coaching study followed by one-on-one coaching, suggesting both types of coaching are needed to improve teacher practices.

Reflections

1. Given your experiences, how comfortable would you be observing in a class-room and providing feedback to teachers? What skills do you think you need to develop more fully?
2. Think about the four steps in the coaching cycle. Which would be the most difficult steps for you to implement? Why?

Activities

1. Go through a coaching cycle with a colleague. Think about the following after you have completed the cycle. What did you learn from the planning conference that affected the way in which you observed? In your analysis of the observation, what points did you identify as important to discuss with the colleague? In what ways did you provide feedback to the teacher? How successful do you think you were in conducting this coaching cycle? What would you do differently?
2. Try providing balanced feedback. Work with a colleague or a member of your class. Here are two scenarios to try. Remember to clarify what has occurred, provide specific feedback about the merits of a situation or behavior, and discuss ways to address any concern.

   Scenario 1. Carlos observed Frank, a sixth-grade social studies teacher, as he used an anticipation guide to introduce a new unit on the Civil War. He gave the class a sheet on which there were a number of facts about the war and asked them to indicate whether they agreed or disagreed with the facts. Immediately, hands were raised; students grumbled that they could not read certain words or that they did not know what to do. Frank told them to put the sheet in their desks and to open their books to the first page of the chapter.

   Scenario 2. Henrietta arrived to observe Greta, a third-grade teacher, who had indicated that she was trying to use flexible grouping in her classroom, but that students were not able to work independently. She wanted help from Henrietta because, at this point, as she stated, "These kids can't work independently." Now Greta was conducting guided reading with a group of six students. On the board was a list indicating what the other students should be doing: reading books silently, working on the computer, or doing worksheets. And some were actually doing those things. However, four or five students were wandering around, talking to others. Two had their heads on the desk and appeared to be sleeping. Every 2 minutes or so, Greta would look around, away from the group with whom she was working, and remind students firmly, "You know what you should be doing. Let's get to it!"

CHAPTER EIGHT

Developing a School Literacy Program

Facilitating School Change

> If knowledge is power, then literacy is the key to the
> kingdom.
> —IPPOLITO, STEELE, AND SAMSON (2011)

Key Questions

- What problems or issues do schools face in addressing schoolwide change?
- How does the focus on high-level, rigorous standards, such as the CCSS, affect literacy instruction?
- What do reading specialists need to know about curriculum development and the selection of materials used in a comprehensive literacy program?
- In what ways is technology affecting literacy instruction in schools?
- In what ways are school literacy programs affected by federal and state regulations and guidelines?

This chapter begins with a description of issues or problems that often prevent the development of effective literacy programs in schools and schoolwide change. A discussion about the value of a needs assessment process to develop a comprehensive literacy program follows. A section about using standards as a basis for curriculum development includes guidelines for curriculum development and information about adolescent literacy programs. Suggestions for selecting materials are presented. I also discuss technology and its value in helping students become critical readers. Given that schools must adhere to legislative requirements and accountability demands, a discussion about current state and federal educational initiatives is presented.

In previous chapters, the emphasis was the work of reading specialists at the teacher or classroom level. The goal of this chapter is to provide information and cultivate awareness about the role of reading specialists in developing and sustaining a comprehensive literacy program in the schools or district. Although improvements at the individual teacher or classroom levels are essential, they are not sufficient for overall large-scale program improvement. Reading specialists often lead or participate in facilitating overall school change efforts.

PROBLEMS OF EFFECTING LARGE-SCALE CHANGE

Educators involved in efforts to develop schoolwide literacy programs need to be aware of the barriers or issues creating difficulties in any school improvement or reform efforts. Fullan and Hargreaves (1996) identified six basic problems, each of which can be related to literacy program development: overload, isolation, "groupthink," untapped competence (and neglected incompetence), narrowness in teachers' roles, and poor solutions or failed reform (p. 2). Each of these, as they relate to literacy instruction, is discussed below.

Overload

Teachers are required to do much in today's schools. Not only must they have the pedagogical knowledge and understandings of their various subject areas or grade levels, they are also asked to teach students with special needs or serious discipline problems. Some work in schools where the student population is diverse, with large numbers of English learners or students from poverty backgrounds requiring teachers have skills, knowledge, and dispositions enabling them to work effectively with their students. Teachers may be asked to learn about and implement many initiatives or programs, some of which are not compatible. These initiatives may be driven by the funding available to school districts, with accompanying regulations and requirements. For example, in one district, a school had obtained funding to implement a program based on a form of individually prescribed instruction. At the same time, the district was attempting to implement a form of classroom management that recommended whole-class instruction, with provision for individual differences through multilevel tasks. Teachers were confused and legitimately frustrated in the face of administrative refusal to deal with their concerns; administrators contended that there was no problem in a marriage of the two initiatives. If that was not enough to cause problems, one of the schools embarked on a writing initiative that required teachers to attend professional development sessions *in addition* to the ones they were attending for the first two initiatives!

Isolation

A sentiment heard frequently is "It doesn't matter what I hear in school meetings; I just shut my door and do what I believe is best." Often, these statements are made with every good intention by teachers who have seen initiatives come—and go! In the past, schools tended to be organized around an isolationist perspective, with teachers assuming major responsibility for the 25 or more students in their classrooms, or at the secondary level, responsibility for the 180 or so students over six periods a day. At the present time, however, classroom teachers (K–12) are being asked to work with other teachers and specialized professionals to make decisions about how to provide the best possible instruction for students; such decisions require collaboration among grade-level or subject-area teachers. Teachers are being asked to share and review student data, both objective and subjective, as a means of designing appropriate instruction.

There is evidence such collaboration is important in building a school vision and in creating an environment in which teachers believe they have an important role in helping students succeed. In fact, results of studies (Hord, 2004; Leana & Pil, 2006; Supovitz, Sirinides, & May, 2010) indicate there is a strong relationship between achievement and the extent to which schools exhibit a strong sense of community or a collaborative commitment to effective instruction for all students. Supovitz and colleagues (2010), in fact, found both principal leadership and collaboration among peers in the schools influenced teacher practices and were related to student learning. Such a new way of thinking about teaching may be difficult for some teachers who must now share information about their teaching and their students with other personnel in the school. For example, teachers might need to discuss with a reading specialist who provides in-class instruction, ways that students might be grouped, a schedule that would work for both teacher and specialist, classroom management strategies, and specific ideas for instruction. Teacher and specialist must be able to plan, teach, and evaluate what they do on an ongoing basis. Often, there is a need for support and staff development experiences to help school personnel collaborate effectively.

Groupthink

As mentioned above, in today's schools, a great deal of emphasis is placed on developing communities or networks of learners, highlighting the importance of collegiality and collaboration in promoting school change. Although such efforts can be powerful forces for change, there are some downsides. Fullan and Hargreaves (1996) indicated the importance of continuing to support individual creativity and diversity while, at the same time, enhancing the ability of individuals to work together for change. Once a group establishes a norm or sets a direction, it may be difficult for the creative thinker to be heard. Such an individual may be thought of as reluctant or resistant to change. Yet this individual may be able to bring new perspectives and fresh insights to a specific issue.

Untapped Competence (and Neglected Incompetence)

Every educator in the school has the potential to contribute to an effective school literacy program and assume a leadership role in creating school change. When school administration limits the extent to which teachers participate in the change process, they decrease the school's potential for change, ignoring important ideas generated by teachers and creating situations in which there may be minimal teacher buy in and ownership of any new initiative. Teachers can provide key information about activities that work or do not work, instructional strategies they have modified so they are more effective for younger or older students, and management techniques that create an atmosphere in which learning can take place. When teacher knowledge and skills are acknowledged and valued, there is an accompanying sense of pride and ownership, enhancing what they do in their classrooms. At the same time, we must be honest and bold enough to challenge those few who are incompetent or who refuse to work with students in ways that promote learning.

Narrowness in Teachers' Roles

There is a call for teachers to serve as leaders in the schools in new and different ways. No longer do teachers have to leave the classroom to have leadership responsibilities. As schools change, teachers and reading specialists can serve as leaders in curriculum and professional development efforts, in spearheading efforts to select materials or change reporting procedures, and so on. When teachers are offered and make a commitment to accept major decision-making responsibilities, implementation of an initiative is greatly strengthened. Researchers (e.g., Dagen & Bean, 2014; Newmann & Wehlage, 1995; Saunders, Goldenberg, & Gallimore, 2009; Spillane, 2005; Vescio et al., 2008) describe the positive relationship between school achievement and schools functioning as professional communities in which teachers have a voice in decision making—where they too have leadership responsibilities. Teachers learn from one another and they value such learning; however, establishing the conditions for collaboration occurs over time and requires support from both school and district leadership.

Poor Solutions or Failed Reform

The lack of success of many school reform efforts in literacy can be attributed to a variety of reasons: ineffective, overly circumscribed solutions (e.g., a belief that one particular approach or program will create the changes in school performance, a mediocre program); lackluster or poor implementation (e.g., the selection of effective approaches or programs, but little effort given to helping teachers learn how to implement the program in their classrooms); or lack of sustainability (e.g., too many new initiatives, with little time to learn one well). At times, schools do not stay with an initiative long enough to make a difference. In the evaluation of Reading First in Pennsylvania, Zigmond and Bean (2008) found after 5 years that almost 80% of the Reading First schools had shown increases in the percentage of students reading at proficiency and a reduction in the percentage of students at risk. But for some schools, it took 5 years to reach this goal. Moreover, in other schools, problems were so complex (e.g., student absenteeism or mobility, weak leadership, teacher turnover) that reform efforts needed to be more comprehensive than a focus on literacy instruction alone. In a study of the sustainability of Reading First in two states, Bean, Dole, Nelson, Belcastro, and Zigmond (2015) found there was continued use of Reading First components (e.g., progress monitoring, date-informed instruction, dedicated reading block, flexible grouping) when there was teacher, principal, and student stability; buy in of the program; and funding enabling schools to support personnel such as reading coaches to assist with implementation efforts.

WHAT SHOULD WE DO?

Schools that have "beat the odds"—that is, have done better than expected, given the demographics of the school population—provide some direction (and inspiration) in efforts to make large-scale changes in our schools. According to Taylor, Pressley, and Pearson (2002), "Research on effective teachers and schools is surprisingly convergent" (p. 371). These schools employ teachers who have excellent classroom management skills and provide excellent literacy instruction, often involving small-group instruction for students. In these schools, teachers work collaboratively with reading specialists and other personnel, as well as with the parents of the students. Bryk and colleagues (2010), in their work with the Chicago Public Schools, illustrate the complexity of schools as organizations presenting a framework of essential supports. These include:

- Leadership as the driver of change. Principals have a key role in developing a shared vision and leading schoolwide change efforts.
- Schools have meaningful relationships with parents and local community agencies.
- Professional capacity. There is a focus on supporting faculty learning with the school as a place of learning for adults and students.
- A student-centered learning environment exists in schools; students feel safe and are provided with quality learning experiences.
- Curriculum and instruction are coherent and consistent. Guidance is given to teachers so that there is consistency in what students are expected to learn; teachers are given the tools they need to succeed.

Bryk and colleages (2010) indicate the importance of all these essential supports, comparing school change with "baking a cake." Without all of the ingredients, it's not a cake (p. 66). These essential supports are discussed throughout this book. In this chapter, the foci are on developing the literacy program so it is coherent and consistent, and providing guidance to reading specialists who may have important responsibilities for developing the school literacy program. I begin by discussing a needs assessment process as a first step for developing, implementing, and evaluating a comprehensive literacy program.

THINK ABOUT THIS

Think about a school with which you are familiar. To what extent and how does that school address each of the essential supports described above? What strengths does it have? What weaknesses? In what ways can a reading specialist work in this school to promote school change?

A NEEDS ASSESSMENT AS A FIRST STEP
FOR DEVELOPING A COMPREHENSIVE LITERACY PROGRAM

Figure 8.1 describes a framework for developing a comprehensive literacy program, beginning with a needs assessment resulting in a district comprehensive literacy plan document; the other stages illustrate steps to develop a school-based curriculum. The arrows go in both directions, given districts may back map, that is, study their current curriculum as a first step of the needs assessment process. They may also have a comprehensive literacy plan and be ready to use standards to develop the literacy curriculum. The district comprehensive literacy plan document serves as the basis for reviewing standards, establishing specific goals, and developing a scope and sequence plan (PreK–12). These initial steps provide the basis for decision making about curriculum, instruction, and evaluation.

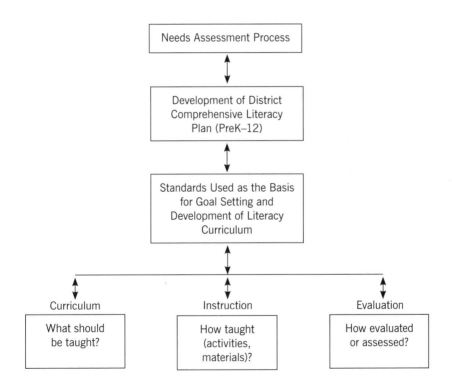

FIGURE 8.1. Framework for developing a comprehensive literacy program (PreK–12).

Conducting a Needs Assessment as a Basis for a Literacy Plan

The needs assessment provides an opportunity for educators to look at the current curriculum and determine whether it addresses the vision and mission of the school or district (Does it take you to where you want to be?). The results of the needs assessment can be used to develop a comprehensive literacy plan enabling educators to see the "big picture," that is, how well the district is achieving its goals, the consistency and articulation from level to level, and what needs to be done to improve literacy instruction across the board. In addition, involvement in the process can be an excellent learning experience, increasing knowledge of participants about the literacy emphasis at various levels, establishing a better relationship among teachers at those levels, and in general, helping to create a sense of ownership of the literacy program. The document also provides a written record to be used for curriculum development and selection of resources. Finally, it can be disseminated to the community and other stakeholders as a means of sharing information about literacy in the schools and generating support and involvement. Below I identify steps that may be useful to reading specialists involved in conducting a needs assessment and developing a comprehensive literacy plan for their school or district.

• Establish a literacy leadership team composed of educators from all levels (PreK–12), community members (representing business, community agencies) and families as a means of generating grassroots support and involvement. These stakeholders provide important insights about the culture of the community and how it contributes to school learning. Reading specialists are often asked to serve as members of such teams or to lead the effort.

• Use a process to identify the strengths and needs of the district overall and to establish priorities for moving ahead. There are many needs assessment documents available, often provided by states for use by districts; for example, the needs assessment tool developed by leaders of the Striving Readers initiative in Pennsylvania for use by districts submitting applications to receive a grant can be found at *www.iu17-2. pdesas.org/Main/News/390391*. Even districts that did not receive funding found the completion of the needs assessment to be useful to them. They learned a great deal about the overall status of literacy in their districts. Team members were surprised at how little they knew about literacy instruction at levels other than where they taught. Any district embarking on a need assessment process can modify available instruments to meet the needs of their district. Generally, a needs assessment will address the following components: standards and curriculum, assessment, instruction, professional development, partnerships with families and communities, and leadership. The questions in Figure 8.2 are important ones to consider when completing a needs assessment.

- Obtain the information needed to complete the needs assessment. According to Bernhardt (2013), four different sources of data are essential for thinking about schools and how they can meet the needs of their students. These include *student demographics* (Who are your students and what are their needs?), *perceptions* (including those of teacher, students, and community members), *school processes* (classroom practices, materials), and *student learning* (outcomes based on various assessment measures). In other words, test data are not sufficient; key information should be obtained from teachers, parents, and students as to their perceptions about literacy learning. Constituents may be interviewed, asked to complete questionnaires, or to participate in meetings to discuss their views about the literacy program in their school. Observations in classrooms as well as an analysis of the materials used in schools can provide insights about what is actually occurring in classrooms.

- Completion of the needs assessment document may be done in several ways. Committee members may complete the tool individually and then work as a group to discuss and explain their ratings. In larger districts, there may be subgroups by grade levels (preschool, elementary, middle school, secondary). Data necessary for completing the needs assessment document can be gathered by facilitators or leaders of the committee. Documents written previously (curriculum guides, literacy plans) can be consulted to obtain information.

- Writing of the needs assessment report may be done by an individual, with members providing input, or by small groups focusing on specific sections.

- The needs assessment should result in a comprehensive plan that contains the following: mission and vision of the district, identification of goals by priority, and an action plan that indicates who will do what and when.

The time it takes to conduct a needs assessment is not wasted time; it can help school personnel make decisions about priorities and answer questions such as the following: What are our immediate needs?; Long-term goals?; At what level should we begin our work?; Who should do what and when? Some districts may have a comprehensive plan based on a needs assessment, and if so, reading specialists and other members of the literacy team may be more involved in the ongoing work of aligning standards with curriculum, instruction, and assessment.

Curriculum
1. Does the school have a vision and mission for its reading program? Has the school established goals and standards (PreK–12)? Has it considered:
- The amount of time for reading instruction at the primary and intermediate levels?
- The relationship between reading and the other language arts?
- The role of content-area teachers at all levels, but especially at the middle school/high school levels in helping students handle the literacy demands of their classroom?
2. Do standards address the need for a developmental continuum that considers the reader at all stages: emergent, beginning, transitional, intermediate, and skilled reading and writing? Do they recognize the needs of learners at the middle school and secondary levels?
3. Are the standards based on what is known about effective reading instruction and assessment, that is, are they evidence based?
4. Do they address the essential elements of effective reading instruction?
5. Have materials, print and nonprint, been selected that enable teachers to address the goals? Do these materials address the needs of all learners (struggling readers, ELL students, etc.)? Do they provide for the varying reading levels of students? Is a variety of materials available (narrative, informational, poetry, etc.)? Do they provide students with opportunities to understand their own backgrounds and that of others?
6. Is there a "written framework" or guide that makes the curriculum visible and usable?

Instruction
1. Has consideration been given to how reading instruction will be organized, including:
Allocation of time to reading at different levels? How the differing needs of students will be met? Grouping options? Materials? Additional time? Additional support of specialized professionals?
2. Is there coordination and coherence among all the reading programs in the school (the core, the programs for struggling readers, ELL students, etc.)?
3. Are teachers given opportunities to gain knowledge and understanding of the current research and literature about effective reading instruction? Is there coherence between the written curriculum of the school and actual classroom practices?

Assessment
1. Is there an assessment system (PreK–12) that is coordinated across the grades? Is there provision for outcome measures? Screening measures? Diagnostic measures? Progress monitoring measures?
2. Is there alignment between the standards of the district and the assessment system, that is, is the assessment system measuring what is being taught?
3. Do the assessment measures address high-level cognitive thinking?

FIGURE 8.2. Developing a comprehensive reading program: Questions to consider. From Bean (2014). Copyright 2014 by Teachers College, Columbia University. Reprinted by permission.

4. Do the classroom assessment measures assist teachers in instructional decision making? Do they assist teachers in identifying the needs of the struggling readers, ELL students, high achievers?

Process for Change
1. Is the committee or group assigned the task of developing the reading comprehensive plan a representative one, that is, it includes constituents at all levels, and so on? To what extent are teachers involved in the curriculum development process? Have they had opportunities to discuss their beliefs and understandings and learn more about how reading can be taught effectively?
2. Is there leadership support for the development of the comprehensive reading plan? Is time provided for meeting and are the necessary resources available to members of the group? Do leaders encourage and support the work of the group members?
3. Have teachers been provided with the professional development they need to implement the program effectively? Does this professional development include opportunity for support and feedback (e.g., literacy coaching)?
4. Does professional development provide teachers with opportunities to learn from each other, to collaborate? In other words, are teachers working together so that change can occur at the school level?
5. Are administrators supportive and involved in the change effort? Do they understand what is required of their teachers so that they can provide the necessary support?

FIGURE 8.2. (*continued*)

Standards as the Basis for Curriculum and Instruction

State and district standards guide the development of specific curricular goals: the selection of instructional practices, materials, resources, and the evaluative measures that determine whether students have met those standards; and if not, what strategies or interventions enable them to do so. Most states across the United States have approved the use of the CCSS (NGA & CCSSO, 2010) that identify outcomes for the English language arts and for literacy in history/social studies, science, and technical subjects. The goals of those responsible for developing the standards were to produce a document that provided for consistency across states in expectations and to increase the rigor of expectations so that graduates would be prepared to function effectively in this ever-shrinking and technologically based world (Wixson & Dutro, 1999). According to developers, the standards identified outcomes but did not mandate or dictate how districts would achieve the goals; in other words, districts were to select or develop their own curriculum, instructional activities, materials, and resources, although as always, they would be guided by state regulations and guidance. Some states have made modifications or adaptations in the CCSS, while maintaining the intent of the standards as critical for graduating students to be college or career ready. Other states have developed their own standards. However, across states, there is recognition of the need for standards with high expectations and the rigor to prepare students who can meet the challenges of living in a complex, global society.

The document developed by the IRA, *Literacy Implementation Guidance for the ELA Common Core State Standards* (2012b), is helpful for educators involved in developing or implementing a school literacy curriculum as it highlights difficult or controversial areas of the CCSS, and provides guidance to districts undertaking the task of familiarizing teachers with the content of the Standards. Issues important for reading specialists and their colleagues to consider are highlighted below.

1. *Use of challenging texts.* Teachers, researchers, and others have raised concerns about the expectation that students read "challenging" texts that may be above their instructional or independent level. As mentioned in the IRA guide, it is not expected that all texts must be challenging. Students can and should read texts at their instructional or independent reading levels as well as those that are more challenging.

2. *Foundational skills.* The basic skills of phonics, phonemic awareness, and so on are not in a place of prominence in the CCSS, but they are there! Developers wanted to emphasize that these skills were a means to an end rather than an end in themselves. Nevertheless, as stated in the IRA document, "Teachers will need to continue to provide high-quality explicit and systematic instruction in these foundational skills if students are to succeed in learning to read" (p. 2).

3. *Vocabulary.* The CCSS call for both teaching of explicit words (in a rich, in-depth manner) and word-solving strategies in all subjects. Vocabulary was placed in the "language" section rather than in the comprehension section.

4. *Writing.* Writing has a strong place in the literacy curriculum and teachers are encouraged to provide meaningful writing activities for students across the curriculum.

5. *The CCSS are best implemented via an integrated curriculum.* The CCSS or other rigorous standards can best be achieved when the curriculum is integrated and focused on themes making learning meaningful. Many current core reading programs are developed around themes (e.g., community workers, learning about the weather). The specific reading, writing, listening, and speaking standards addressed are listed; various types of texts (narrative, informational, digital) are included or identified; and links to the Internet are provided. The core program may

also provide suggestions for a research or inquiry project. But rather than adopting a core program with the expectation that it includes such integration, some school districts have developed their own units, pulling together materials and activities enabling students to meet the standards of their district and state. (See *www.lbschools.net/main_Offices/ Curriculum/Areas/English_Language?Arts/curriculum_docs.cfm* for their integrated framework for literacy and examples of units developed by groups of teachers for the Long Beach School District; see Appendix D for an example of the first few pages of a first-grade unit on animals.)

The comprehensive literacy plan developed by districts, as well as a review of standards, enable them to develop a scope and sequence that illustrates both vertical (grade level to grade level) and horizontal articulation (within grade—what will be taught when).

Guidelines for Curriculum Development: A Process of Change

Curriculum development provides an excellent professional development opportunity for teachers to converse with and learn from each other. In their deliberations about curriculum, instruction, and evaluation they develop a deeper understanding of what they are planning to implement in their classrooms and a commitment to proposed changes. Several guidelines for developing curriculum follow:

• *Begin with standards.* Helping teachers become familiar with the CCSS or the standards adopted by their state and how they impact curriculum and instruction is an important task for reading specialists. I suggest a series of steps below (adapted from McTighe & Wiggins, 2012).

   • Have teachers spend time becoming familiar with the standards by reading the introductory material that explains what the standards are and are not; discuss at grade- or school-level meetings. Talk about how these standards compare with previous ones and discuss the differences (more reading of informational text, close reading).

   • Unpack the standards by doing cross-walks. Review a specific standard across a number of grade levels (e.g., Key Ideas and Details for Literature from K–5) and discuss changes. A grade-level team may review all reading standards for that level initially. In later meetings, other aspects of the language arts may be reviewed. Teachers can discuss again the implications for curriculum.

- Continue the curriculum development process by unpacking the standards, using four categories: *long-term transfer goals* (what we want students to be able to do), *overarching understandings* (what skilled students will need to transfer learning), *overarching essential* questions that engage students in meaning making, and recurring *cornerstone* tasks that are authentic and relevant (McTighe & Wiggins, 2012; see the unit on animals in Appendix D for specific examples).

- Consider how student learning will be assessed. What outcomes are expected and what "cornerstone" tasks can be used to assess those outcomes? Consider various inquiry- or project-based learning opportunities for students.

- *Importance of teacher involvement.* Reading specialists in leadership positions can consider the following as they move forward in the curriculum development process: Will all teachers be involved or a representative few?; If not all are involved, how can others be consulted and informed?; What is the time line for the process?; What are the goals and outcomes of the effort? In developing curriculum, specific teachers can be involved in writing the units or curriculum guide, but they can share on an ongoing basis their work, ask for input, and help all teachers develop an understanding of how the revised curriculum will affect instruction and assessment.

Also, teachers can be involved in curriculum mapping, perhaps at grade-level meetings facilitated by a reading specialist or one of the grade-level teachers. They can be provided with copies of the grade-level standards; in one district, the reading specialist laminated anchor and grade-level standards for each teacher. In another district, the reading specialist placed the mapping form on a white board so that all teachers could see the work that had been done, make comments, changes, or adaptations. Jacobs (1997) described mapping as an activity that "enables teachers to show student work as it actually happens in the classroom and in relation to state or district standards" (p. 8). She lists seven steps in the mapping process. In the first step, teachers actually create a map of the three major elements of their curriculum—(1) content in terms of essential concepts and topics, (2) processes and skills, and (3) products and performances for assessment—using an agreed-upon form approved by the district. Jacobs suggested that teachers use the calendar as a basic guide for compiling the form, recording what they actually do in their classrooms. The remaining steps in her procedure consist of efforts to share what is being taught at the various grade levels and across grade levels, and to make decisions about what needs to be reviewed and revised. Teachers are often surprised by the repetition that occurs across grades or the fact that some things are not taught at all!

• *Base work on current research and theory.* Information from books and journal articles can be shared with teachers; study groups can be formed in which teachers can discuss what they are learning. Also, outside experts may be consulted so that teachers can learn more about current knowledge and theory about reading instruction. Often, districts invite an expert to address all teachers or a representative committee to be followed by opportunities for discussion and debate about the issues presented.

• *Relate teacher beliefs and knowledge about reading instruction to research.* Any curricular effort will involve teachers with different beliefs and perspectives about literacy instruction and assessment. Having a sense of what teachers believe and know about reading instruction is important. Reading specialists can also provide opportunities for teacher reflection and discussion about their beliefs. Teachers bring their own experiences, knowledge, and beliefs to the teaching of reading; they interpret research findings through different lenses. I am reminded of a teacher from a secondary background assigned to teach third grade. Although the work in her graduate courses and experiences in primary classrooms convinced her that students did need to learn phonics, her belief was that such lessons needed to be embedded within a meaningful context, and she experienced much difficulty with the core reading program in which such instruction was not present. She was also frustrated when listening to other teachers talk about their lessons, which seemed to provide little opportunity for students to read and write. Unless the reading specialist was aware of this individual's beliefs and knew how to help her work collaboratively with others and to elaborate on her position, problems could arise when she began to participate in curriculum development meetings.

To develop a common understanding and terminology, teachers may be asked to read current articles about reading instruction that provide a springboard for discussion. These readings can also provide teachers with up-to-date information enabling them to think more deeply about what they do in their classrooms and how it relates to what research indicates is best practice.

THINK ABOUT THIS

Think about the individual teacher, described above, who worked with primary teachers who believed in a strong decoding program. What

problems might arise? How could the beliefs and strengths of this individual be tapped in a way that improves reading instruction? How can
possible misunderstandings be addressed?

• *Organize the curriculum framework so that it is usable.* Too
often, curriculum plans sit on shelves or in teacher's desks, consulted
only infrequently. Those involved in curriculum development can for-
mulate plans that are coherent yet simple to use. Moreover, when plans
provide a sequence of literacy instruction for PreK–12, teachers can gain
a sense of the past (what students have learned), the present, and the
future (what they will learn), providing for better transition and articulation.

• *Plan for dissemination and for implementation.* Too often, it is
the implementation stage that falls short of the goal. Those who have
worked on the development of the plan are committed to it—and perhaps use it. Others, if they do not understand the plan and how it works,
may just ignore it or implement it halfheartedly. If teachers have been
involved during the entire process, they are more likely to accept and use
the plan. Keep all teachers informed and seek their input. Professional
development for faculty is essential if the plan is to become a dynamic,
living document. Professional development can be offered by reading
specialists or coaches over time; initially, general information can be
provided to all teachers and subsequently, reading specialists or coaches
can provide the additional support needed by individual or groups of
teachers.

• *Include evaluation as an integral part of the curriculum framework.* As mentioned above, measurement approaches and tools to be
used to assess student outcomes are an important component of any
curriculum guide. Decisions about assessment instruments, rubrics, and
so forth, should be an integral part of any curriculum development discussion. (This is discussed in depth in Chapter 9.)

Another aspect of evaluation has to do with the curriculum guide
itself. Curriculum development, its implementation and modification,
should be ongoing; it is a recursive process. Thus, a process for obtaining
teacher input about what works and what doesn't work, should be developed. Such input can come from grade-level or subject-area meetings, or
from the work of a curriculum committee. Evaluation can include reactions of teachers, actual observation of what is occurring in classrooms,
and a study of various assessment measures used to document student
learning. At higher levels, especially middle and secondary, input from
students can also inform the evaluation process. Guskey's (2000) five

levels of evaluation, described in Chapter 5, is a useful source for evaluating a school's reading program.

Because reading specialists may have responsibility for leading the development of literacy from the early grades through the middle or secondary levels, below, I discuss in more depth critical issues related to these upper levels of schooling.

The Reading Program for Adolescents

Across the United States, there is an awareness that special attention must be given to secondary schools, especially high schools. Students are not being prepared to meet the requirements for most jobs or for being successful in college. A recent survey conducted by Achieve and Society for Human Resource Management (*www.achieve.org/Achieve-SHRM-Survey*) reported many graduates lacked the skills to advance beyond entry-level positions. Moreover, many positions now require some type of post-high school preparation, either obtained by technical training or an associate's degree, if not college. In the near future, there will be a need for even more highly skilled individuals to compete for available positions. Currently, far too many students, especially those identified as poor, Hispanic, or African American, do not graduate on time (Iriti & Bickel, 2010).

One of the ways in which schools are addressing these disappointing statistics is by aligning their curriculum, instruction, and assessment systems with standards that address college and career success. As indicated by Ippolito and colleagues (2012), there is a "new focus on literacy within the academic disciplines, a more nuanced stance toward comprehension strategy instruction, and an insistence that greater attention needs to be paid to all students reading and writing practices both inside and outside of school" (p. viii). Therefore, at the secondary level, reading specialists may not only have the task of developing or designing programs for students who are having difficulty with reading, but to work closely with content-area teachers to design approaches that help students process content-specific information. In other words, they work with teachers to help students understand the ways in which experts in each academic area communicate, that is, to learn to read and write like historians, scientists, or mathematicians (Moje, 2008; Shanahan & Shanahan, 2012).

A comprehensive literacy program at the secondary levels generally includes several components. There may be a pullout or supplemental program for students experiencing difficulties with reading (e.g., Read 180 [Scholastic, 2002]) taught by a reading teacher or reading specialist).

The program may also include special study skills classes helping students understand effective study strategies, including how to take tests. To meet the needs of all students, however, decisions will need to be made about how teachers in the disciplines can address the thinking, reading, and writing required of adolescents as they grapple with complex texts. Reading specialists can have an important role, working as partners with these teachers; both have something to contribute. Reading specialists provide general knowledge about literacy instruction, and content teachers help identify the literacy skills students need to be successful in specific disciplines. The *Standards for Middle and Secondary School Coaches* (IRA, 2006) can be a useful resource to those working at those levels; in addition to identifying general leadership standards, the document identifies standards for each of four academic disciplines: English, science, social studies, and math.

Other key resources at the secondary level include *Reading Next: A Vision for Action and Research in Middle and High School Literacy* (Biancarosa & Snow, 2004), *Creating a Culture of Literacy: A Guide for Middle and High School Principals* (National Association of Secondary School Principals, 2005), and Adolescent Literacy in the Era of the Common Core (Ippolito, Lawrence, & Zaller, 2013). Elizabeth Moje (2008) raises issues important for those involved in secondary literacy reform: content teachers' knowledge of their own discipline, ways that teachers can encourage students to interact with their content-area texts, role of technology and new media on students' learning, and school structures to facilitate this sort of instruction. She concludes as follows: "The integration of literacy instruction in the secondary schools is a complex change process that will require collaboration, communication, and a commitment to major conceptual, structural, and culture changes" (p. 105).

THINK ABOUT THIS

What are the issues your school, or a school with which you are familiar, needs to consider when developing adolescent literacy programs? What are your thoughts about disciplinary literacy and what it means for reading specialists in secondary schools?

SELECTION OF MATERIALS

Although schools should identify their curricular goals before selecting materials, too often the reverse is true! Materials frequently equal the curriculum. Although materials must reflect the beliefs and goals identified by school personnel, a strict adherence to the identified materials may lead to a narrow program in which there is little adjustment to meet the needs of the students in the school. In other words, the content and quality of materials selected should reflect the needs and interests of students in the school, as well as the forms of diversity that exist in society (i.e., race, ethnicity, gender, cultural, linguistic, economic). Providing such material in schools is important both for increasing student skills and the motivation to read. Although the need for a wide variety of materials in schools exists at all levels, it is especially critical that adolescents be provided with materials to which they can relate. Brozo and Gaskins (2009, pp. 172–180), in a chapter focusing on adolescent boys, present five principles of engagement that are relevant not only for adolescents but for readers of all ages:

1. Create conditions in classrooms that promote self-efficacy, a belief in one's own capacity to achieve;
2. Promote interest in new reading;
3. Connect out-of-school with inside-school literacies;
4. Make sure there is an abundance of interesting texts available;
5. Provide for choice and options.

Teachers frequently make decisions about classroom instruction based on the anthologies or core reading program. And, given that specific materials, once selected, become a driving force for at least 5 or more years, careful attention must be given to selecting materials so they fit with the objectives, goals, and standards formulated by the district. Too often the materials selected become the curriculum guide or plan for the district.

Guidelines for Selecting a Core Program

Once the district has decided it is going to adopt a specific series as a means of providing a core reading program, literacy personnel need to think about both process and content issues.

Process

The process to be used is extremely important because it often involves more than professional issues. Publishers are eager to obtain adoptions; school districts need to abide by the same guidelines or rules for all materials being considered.

- What selection procedure should be used?
- Will all teachers, or a representative group, serve on the committee?

- What are the rules? If publishers are invited to present their "wares," how much time do they get and what can they "give" or provide to teachers?
- Will the district implement a pilot to help with decision making?

A careful consideration of the process reduces the possibility outcomes will be met by accusations of unfairness or bias in selecting materials. Most districts try to select a committee of a representative group of teachers and administrators. All grade levels in which materials will be used should be represented and, if possible, most of the schools. At the same time, parents on the committee provide a unique perspective and help to generate community support. Students may also be included on the committee, especially if the materials to be selected apply to the upper levels.

Content

The following guidelines can be useful in thinking about which basal or anthology to select:

1. *Review the philosophy.* Before proceeding with a review of materials, spend time reviewing or developing the philosophy or goals of the district especially as they relate to the teaching of reading or literacy instruction. In that way, materials selection can be aligned with the goals of the school, thereby reducing the possibility that the scope and sequence of the basal will become the curriculum of the school.

2. *Conduct a needs assessment of teachers in the district.* A short questionnaire or brief talks with all teachers can generate a list of priorities. Often, teachers have specific concerns about current materials and their inability to meet the needs of the children. Time spent obtaining ideas about what the group thinks is important and should lessen any later dissension or conflict.

3. *Plan for a research update.* The committee can be made aware of current research and theory about literacy instruction. An expert can be invited to make a presentation; the group can be given materials to read. Both should be followed by group discussion. A resolution of the IRA board, titled "Buyer Be Wary" (2002a), discusses the need for those involved in selecting materials to be especially cautious in their deliberations. This document encourages program reviewers to look closely at the publishers' claims in relation to program effectiveness.

4. *Decide upon the "ideal."* What should the final material look like? What should it include? By designing a checklist, or modifying an existing one, the group can more efficiently review materials. Dewitz,

Leahy, Jones, and Sullivan, in their book *The Essential Guide to Selecting and Using Core Reading Programs* (2010), provide specific guidance to school districts for considering various programs; their checklists can be downloaded for free from the ILA (formerly IRA) website. Most checklists include suggestions for reviewing content, the teachers' manual, the scope and sequence of skills, the supplemental material (including workbooks), and assessment procedures. Although it might be helpful to start with a published checklist, teachers should review the checklist and modify it so criteria address the vision and goals of the school.

5. *Review materials.* The committee can quickly screen and discard those programs that do not meet the identified criteria. Then an in-depth review must be made of those appearing to be acceptable. The committee can break into smaller groups to review specific texts and present findings to the entire group, or everyone in the group may review all texts. They may consult reviews done by others (e.g., What Works Clearinghouse; *http://ies.ed.gov/ncee/wwc*). The group may decide to track the teaching of a specific strategy or skill through the grades, to determine how the strategy is taught at each level. For example, committee members could focus on how students are taught to summarize from the early grades through grade 8.

Readability of text has always been an important consideration. The CCSS provide a comprehensive framework for assessing text complexity (detailed information is available in the CCSS document, NGA & CCSSO, 2010, Appendix A). The three identified factors provide for a more comprehensive view of readability.

- Qualitative evaluation of the text: levels of meaning, structure language conventionality and clarity, knowledge demands.
- Quantitative evaluation of the text: readability measures and other scores of text complexity.
- Matching reader to text and task: reader variables (motivation, knowledge, and experiences) and task variables (purpose and the complexity generated by the task assigned and questions posed).

6. *Make a final decision.* In addition to using information from in-depth reviews, the committee may talk with teachers in other districts who are using the materials to get their perspectives. They may also consider piloting several programs before making a final decision. Ultimately, the committee should come to a consensus, or if necessary, vote to make a decision about the text to be selected. It is, of course, much better if the group can agree on the core program to be selected, but this is not always possible. If no clear-cut decision emerges, more time may need to be spent in analyzing available materials.

Materials to Help Students Achieve the Goals Established by the School

Although I focus on the core or basal program above, the same criteria apply to the materials used for supplemental or intensive instruction. Schools have the responsibility of teaching all students and providing for them; therefore, consideration must be given about how to meet the needs of gifted students, special education students, ELLs, and so on. Those leading material selection efforts should be able to justify why they are using specific supplemental materials, how they support or enhance the core program, who should use them, and why. Careful attention must be given to how the various materials "fit together."

TECHNOLOGY IN THE READING PROGRAM

We live in a digital world. We can place an order for books, clothes, and toys online, pay our bills electronically, search Google when we have a question (e.g., What is the exact meaning of the word *peripatetic*?). We can also look at the menu for a new restaurant in the city and decide whether we want to eat there—or whether we can afford to eat there! Likewise, children in their homes are accustomed to living with technology: they play with games that have been downloaded on a smartphone or tablet to keep them busy while riding in the car or waiting for a doctor's appointment; they have access to their parents' computers, can interact with their grandparents via FaceTime, and read iBooks that provide for interactivity between reader and text. They use social networking and texting to communicate with their peers, and as coined by Prensky (2001), they are "digital natives." They have grown up with technology, are comfortable with it, and expect it to be part of their lives. In fact, according to a recent large-scale study, almost half of the children in the United States, 8 or younger, have digital devices such as smartphones, electronic book readers, and tablets in their homes (Common Sense Media & Rideout, 2011). And, although there is a gap in access to technology, based on income levels (Common Sense Media & Rideout, 2011), it appears as though, if technology exists in low-income households, children in those homes will have access to it (Gutnick, Robb, Takeuchi, & Kotler, 2011).

The Internet and other forms of information and communication technologies are transforming literacy and learning in the 21st century and redefining the way in which we think about literacy. Technology exists in our daily lives and is rapidly becoming an integral part of the school's literacy program. Teachers in today's schools must be competent users of technology, employing it as a tool to enhance the literacy program in their classrooms. Many teachers are becoming tech savvy. They use technology as an integral part of their repertoire, assigning inquiry projects or group activities, including video projects. Others are using flipped learning (i.e., instructing students online outside the classroom and then having them complete homework in class). According to Wells and Lewis (2006), in 2005, 100% of public schools had access to the Internet, and with the decrease in prices and increase in availability of various mobile devices, access continues to increase. These new literacies "common in the lives of our students include search engines, webpages, e-mail, instant messaging (IM, blogs, podcasts, e-books, wikis, nings, YouTube, video, and many more" (IRA, 2009, p. X).

The CCSS (NGA & CCSSO, 2010) highlight the importance of new literacies, indicating that "to be ready for . . . life in a technological society, students need the ability to gather, comprehend, evaluate, synthesize, and report on information and ideas . . . in media forms old and new"(p. 4). Skills and understandings are embedded throughout the Standards, illustrating specific standards that students are expected to meet (e.g., Anchor Standards for Writing, K–5: Gather relevant information from multiple print and digital sources, assess the credibility and accuracy of each source, and integrate the information while avoiding plagiarism, p. 18).

However, teachers do not always feel prepared or comfortable with using these new approaches to learning. They need many skills to use electronic technology effectively: locating resources about literacy on the Internet; communicating with others using technology; entering, accessing, and interpreting data about students and their accomplishments; becoming knowledgeable about the various software programs that can be used to deliver instruction to students; and integrating technology as part of instructional delivery. Technology requires teachers to assume new and different roles, moving from more teacher- to student-directed instruction (Castek & Gwinn, 2012). Professional learning opportunities, similar to those identified by Coiro (2005), assist teachers in meeting the expectations of these new roles. They include developing learning experiences on a developmental continuum so that teachers can move from novice to expert, differentiating professional learning so it addresses the differing perspectives of teachers about the value of technology, and providing collaborative learning experiences as a means of enhancing learning. Also, teachers must learn how to guide students in using digital resources wisely as a means of supporting learning (Prensky, 2012). These new literacies provide new and more complex learning opportunities for students, and technology in the classroom has become much more than adding a software package to the reading program. At the same time, given the availability of such software, it is important to have criteria for the selection of such programs. McVee and Dickson (2002, p. 639) developed a rubric as a guide for reviewing software for programs designed for use in K–3 classrooms. The rubric identifies the following questions as ones that can be used for reviewing software:

1. What observations can we make about overall media presentation?
2. How easy is the software to navigate?
3. Does the software change over time? With each use? With prolonged interactions? Multiple uses?
4. Which types of assessments are built into the program? How important or useful are these for users and teachers?
5. How closely do activities fit classroom needs? Are they interesting? Educational? Fun?
6. How would we rate the overall value of the software? Would this be a good investment for my classroom?
7. How compatible is this software with an emergent literacy approach that integrates reading, writing, listening, and speaking?

These questions can be adapted for use at the upper grade levels. Also, one resource that can be used by schools to heighten awareness of what is needed in the area of technology is the National Educational Technology Standards for Students (International Society for Technology in Education, 2007), which identifies standards at all levels for both preservice teachers and PreK–12 students.

KNOWLEDGE AND UNDERSTANDING OF STATE AND FEDERAL REQUIREMENTS

Every district, regardless of student demographics, location, or size, is required to comply with state legislation and policy about curriculum, assessment, and instruction (e.g., state standards, state assessment measures). Furthermore, any district eligible for Title I services must apply for funding by writing a proposal addressing requirements (e.g., eligibility, accountability, models for instruction, inclusion of parent involvement programs). Often, reading specialists have responsibility for writing these proposals. In the following sections, the role of reading specialists in relation to various state and federal initiatives is discussed. As part of this discussion, there is a section on No Child Left Behind (NCLB; U.S. Department of Education, 2002b) and Race to the Top.

IMPACT OF FEDERAL OR STATE INITIATIVES ON THE ROLE OF READING SPECIALISTS

Positions of reading specialist, literacy coach, and other specialized literacy professionals are often funded by federal or state legislation with specific requirements or regulations affecting the ways in which these professionals work. Therefore, keeping abreast of what is occurring at both the state and federal levels is an important responsibility of reading specialists. State or federal government agencies send information to school officials and sometimes invite one or more educators from a district to attend informational meetings in which specific initiatives are discussed. Conferences held by the state, local educational support agencies, or professional groups typically offer sessions in which such legislation is described. At the current time, state and federal agencies often sponsor webinars that can be accessed by school personnel at their home site. Information can also be obtained from the state or federal websites on which various legislative actions are described or summarized. The website of the ILA (*www.reading.org*) provides useful information as does the weekly newspaper *Education Week*.

In the previous two editions of this book, I described Reading First, a national large-scale initiative funded by NCLB (U.S. Department of Education, 2002b) because of its enormous impact on reading instruction in schools and on the roles of professionals responsible for literacy instruction. In this edition, I discuss NCLB and some of the adaptations made since its adoption. I also describe briefly some of the outcomes of Reading First, given that some of its elements are still found in many schools today, especially in the ways that RTI is implemented. However, as would be expected, change in federal and state legislation occurs on a regular basis and it is incumbent on school districts and their leadership personnel to keep abreast of these changes.

No Child Left Behind

The NCLB (U.S. Department of Education, 2002b) law (*www.nclb.gov/ next/overview/index.html*) represented the most sweeping changes to the Elementary and Secondary Education Act since it was enacted in 1965. The legislation had an impact on education in grades K–12 and is based on four basic principles: strong accountability, local control and flexibility, an increased role for parents, and scientifically based reading research. Although NCLB is up for reauthorization, Congress has yet to act, and the Obama administration authorized changes that have influenced, in several ways, the requirements of NCLB. These include the American Recovery and Reinvestment Act of 2009, which provided states with the opportunity to apply for competitive funds through its Race to the Top program. The Obama administration also granted awards and waivers to states from meeting the NCLB requirement of 100% of the students reading at proficiency by 2014, if they submitted plans tying teacher performance evaluation to student test scores. Major initiatives of the Obama administration also include improving teacher and principal effectiveness, providing information to families that promote involvement with schools, implementation of college and career readiness standards, and improvement of learning and achievement in the lowest-scoring schools (U.S. Department of Education, 2010). Each of these initiatives affects not only the role of reading specialists in schools but which schools will be awarded funds, and the nature of the educators (preparation, experiences) hired to deliver instruction or support teachers in their instruction of literacy.

THINK ABOUT THIS

What are your thoughts and feelings about any recent adaptations in federal legislation (changes in the Elementary and Secondary Education Act)? How will it affect the school or district in which you work?

At the present time, as part of the accountability effort, each state must develop a set of standards for what children should know and be able to do in various areas, including reading. Then all students must be tested, in grades 3–8, using assessment measures aligned with the standards. The law also requires districts to administer at least one reading and writing measure at grades 9–12. Schools are expected to make adequate yearly progress. Results are disaggregated to determine the growth of various groups, including those that are economically disadvantaged, those from racial- or ethnic-minority groups, those with learning disabilities, and those with limited English proficiency. If progress is inadequate, schools are held accountable—that is, low-scoring schools are penalized. NCLB (U.S. Department of Education, 2002b) affects all public schools in this country, K–12; therefore, reading specialists at all levels need to be familiar with it and the implications it has for students and their teachers.

Reading First Revisited

In the previous editions, I discussed Reading First (U.S. Department of Education, 2002a) and its requirements. Reading First as a funded program no longer exists; however, given its long-term impact on reading instruction in this country, several findings of that national programmatic effort are described. In the national study of Reading First, Gamse, Jacob, Horst, Boulay, and Unlu (2008) found there were differences in classroom reading instruction between Reading First and non-Reading First schools; moreover, teachers in Reading First schools received more professional development than teachers in non-Reading First schools. However, in the national study, no significant differences in reading comprehension achievement between Reading First and non-Reading First schools were found. At the same time, survey results of school personnel (Center for Educational Policy, 2007) and state evaluation reports reported Reading First did make a difference. What is reflected in this story of Reading First is its major influence in many schools across our country, not only in schools receiving funding to implement such programs but in others, which quickly moved to adopt progress monitoring and screening tools, and to implement the scientifically based reading instruction promoted in Reading First legislation. Indeed, much of what is seen in an RTI model is similar to elements found in Reading First. Reading First not only influenced how reading was taught in K–3 in many schools across the country, but it supported the hiring of thousands of literacy coaches, whose responsibilities included providing job-embedded professional development for the teachers in those schools. Reading First provides an example of how legislation and policy decisions influence how reading is taught in schools.

In a follow-up study of the sustainability of Reading First in Pennsylvania and in Utah, Bean and colleagues (2015) found that most elements were maintained 3 years after the termination of Reading First funding. In both states, there was a steady increase during the time of the initiative in students reaching proficiency; in Pennsylvania, that improvement continued, although the pace of increase was less; in Utah, there was a small but steady decrease in percentage of students reaching proficiency. Germane to this discussion is the importance of maintaining the momentum or "keeping the foot on the gas." Reduced funding and less of a focus on improving reading instruction as a priority goal may have affected the results. Nevertheless, in most of the schools surveyed, elements of Reading First were maintained and respondents attributed this sustainability to the buy in of leadership and teachers in the school, the support provided through coaching and provision of resources, and the similarity between some of the elements of Reading First and RTI initiatives in the schools.

One of the aspects of Reading First was its insistence on selecting and using instructional materials and approaches derived from scientifically based reading research, defined as "research that applies rigorous, systematic, and objective procedures to obtain valid knowledge relevant to reading development, reading instruction, and reading difficulties" (No Child Left Behind Act of 2001, Sec. 1208). The IRA's position statement *Evidence-Based Reading Instruction* (2002b) provides a clear definition and a number of resources for those interested in learning more about this topic.

SUMMARY

In this chapter, problems associated with creating change in schools were discussed to provide a backdrop to the issue of developing a school reading program. A discussion about developing a comprehension literacy program includes information about conducting a needs assessment and using standards as a basis for setting goals and curriculum development. Guidelines for developing curriculum were identified, followed by a discussion of selecting materials, emphasizing the need for establishing criteria for analysis. There was also a section about technology and its impact on literacy education in schools. In the final section, information about federal legislation, specifically, NCLB (U.S. Department of Education, 2002b), current modifications and adaptations, was presented.

ADDITIONAL READINGS

Bean, R. M., Dole, J. A., Nelson, K. L., Belcastro, E. L., & Zigmond, N. (2015). The sustainability of a national reading reform initiative in two states. *Reading and Writing Quarterly, 31*(1), 30–55.—In this article, the authors describe a study in two states of the sustainability of Reading First components, as perceived by school leaders. Factors that affected sustainability are discussed.

International Reading Association. (2009). *New literacies and 21st century technologies: A position statement.* Newark, DE: Author.—This updated position statement provides an excellent summary of issues related to the effective use of technologies in schools and the responsibilities of various educators and stakeholders.

Reflections

1. Think about the problems associated with large-scale change described earlier in this chapter as they relate to a school with which you are familiar. Does the school you are thinking about have any of those problems? Others?
2. Meet with several colleagues to talk about your vision of what an excellent reader (at the end of a specific grade) can do. Discuss your views with each other. How similar are they? Different?

Activities

1. If you are a classroom teacher, try to map your reading curriculum for the entire year. Use that map to think about whether the curriculum helps you accomplish the goals that you think are important for your students.
2. Select one of the CCSS for either reading or writing and do a cross-walk across grade levels (e.g., grades 1–5, grades 6–12) to note progression in expectations.

CHAPTER NINE

Assessment of Classroom and School Reading Programs

Not everything that can be counted, counts; and not
everything that counts can be counted.
—CAMERON (1963, p. 13)

Key Questions

- How is assessment defined in this text and how can assessment results be used effectively in schools?
- What are the essential principles underlying effective assessment systems?
- How do limitations of standardized assessment measures affect results and interpretation?

This chapter begins by discussing some of the new directions in assessment, especially large-scale testing. This is followed by sections about purposes of assessment, types of assessment measures, and key principles of assessment. In the final section, I discuss limitations of standardized tests.

Given the current emphasis on testing and more testing (e.g., high-stakes assessment, accountability, teacher performance evaluation), the quotation above, often attributed to Albert Einstein, serves as an important reminder of the limitations of many measures used to make decisions in schools. The term *assessment* generates much emotion in today's schools. There are those who believe the emphasis on assessment is an important means of improving instruction; others believe we put too much emphasis on assessment, narrowing the curriculum and reducing teacher creativity. Some are concerned the type of assessment used in schools measures only one aspect of student learning and puts too much emphasis on the results of standardized testing. There are also concerns about the misuse of assessment (e.g., retention, graduation decisions, teacher performance evaluation). In reality, assessment can be helpful in making decisions about the total school literacy program, and it must be planned and implemented as carefully as the curriculum and instructional plans for the schools. Kapinus (2008) says it well: "The goal of all assessment is to support effective teaching and learning" (p. 145).

Reading specialists may have many experiences in their coursework with assessment, but often the emphasis is on assessment of an individual child or a small group of students. In this chapter, the focus is on assessment directly related to improving reading instruction in a classroom or in a school. In today's schools, the assessment demands of NCLB (U.S. Department of Education, 2002b), the implementation of RTI models in schools, and the current emphasis on rigorous, high-level standards have created the need for reading specialists to be well versed in how to use assessment results to help teachers plan instruction. Furthermore, specialists need to be knowledgeable about how to work with teachers and administrators to interpret and use schoolwide results as a means of improving student learning.

NEW DIRECTIONS IN ASSESSMENT

In 2010, $350 million from Race to the Top monies was awarded to support two consortia, Partnership for Assessing Readiness for College and Careers (PARCC) and Smarter Balanced Assessment Consortium (SBAC), to develop new sets of assessment tools that would assess whether students have achieved the rigorous standards designed to prepare them for college and career, specifically the CCSS. These tests are examples of assessment measures that move away from the multiple-choice, one-size-fits-all assessments used in the past. They are expected to include both summative assessments and formative assessment resources, resources for professional development, and the use of technology. Moreover, in both sets of assessments, students are expected to read multiple texts for information and follow that by writing extended pieces. There is much more emphasis on the integration of various language arts skills as well as the use of technology (Kapinus, 2014). Many states and school districts were involved in pilots of these new assessments in spring 2014, and implementation was scheduled for the 2014–2015 school year, making it the first time that almost one-half of the students in this country were assessed with the same measures. At the same time, these assessments, as well as the CCSS, have generated controversy, which has led to some states withdrawing from participation in the CCSS or from the assessment initiatives. Some states have decided to develop and use their own assessment measures to determine overall student learning.

These new large-scale assessments present new directions in assessment and reflect the need for balance in how we measure student literacy learning. Some issues described by Afflerbach (2014) in which he calls for balance include assessment of skills and how students apply what they learn; basic skills and strategies for higher-order thinking; reading from a single text with reading from many sources, including the Internet; cognitive and affective reading outcomes; and formative and summative assessment. These issues present exciting possibilities as we think about how literacy learning is measured in schools. In the following section, information about assessment, what it is, and types of measures is presented.

WHAT AND WHY?

The terms *assessment* and *tests* are often misunderstood. Assessment is the task of gathering data on which to base evaluative or judgment-oriented decisions. Such data are multidimensional, encompassing more than just standardized tests. Assessment can be *summative* in nature, given infrequently (e.g., end of the year or course) and used to evaluate program effectiveness for groups of students. It can also be *formative*, given at frequent intervals or even during instruction, and the results can be used to make decisions about instruction for students. Assessment measures can range from standardized tests to observations, checklists, and interviews to performance measures such as writing samples in which students retell or respond to a selection they have read. Even as they are teaching lessons, teachers often modify or adapt what they are doing, based on their informal assessment of whether students are "getting it." Think about the many different measures of student learning available in your school or district. They probably include both summative (end-of-year standardized test) and formative measures (teacher-made tests, student portfolios, writing samples).

Assessment measures are necessary for a number of reasons, and they are relevant to many different audiences. Four types of assessment are described below.

Outcome Measures

School administration and the community (including parents and taxpayers) want to know whether their schools are performing satisfactorily.

In this case, assessment measures serve as an *outcome* or accountability tool. These summative tools are generally standardized, norm- or criterion-referenced tests. Performance measures that assess student learning directly (e.g., writing samples or portfolios) may also be used to assess student learning, although their cost, design, scoring, and other measurement issues have diminished their use in schools (Lane, 2010). Outcome measures provide for comparison of students from a specific district or school with others like them; they also provide information about the performance of various subgroups (e.g., English learners, special education students, high-poverty students). Most often these measures are administered to groups of students and use some sort of multiple-choice format. However, test developers are attempting to design tools to better assess high-level, complex thinking skills; they are building assessments that include computer-based task simulations and automated scoring systems, enabling their large-scale use. Likewise, there are attempts to better align curriculum, instruction, and assessment (Lane, 2010).

Information from outcome measures can be helpful to schools in determining in which areas their program is strong (e.g., students do well in reading vocabulary) and in which they might need to improve (e.g., comprehension scores are low). Results are helpful in determining whether specific groups of students (e.g., ELs, special education students) are experiencing difficulty in learning. At times these measures have also been used, with other tools such as teacher observation, to assess teacher performance (i.e., to determine to what degree students have learned while in the classroom of a specific teacher). Such use has its problems, given the many complicated factors that influence student learning.

These measures, however, are not very helpful to teachers for planning daily lessons for the students in their classrooms. They are not diagnostic tools that can be used to inform instruction for individual students. In a study conducted by Buly and Valencia (2002), in which they did additional testing of 108 fifth-grade students who had failed the state reading test given at the end of fourth grade, they found several distinctive and multifaceted patterns of reading abilities that were not discernible in students' performance on the state measure. Their results indicated the state measure was not very useful for making instructional decisions. Yet, these assessments are often known as "high-stakes" measures because they are used to make major decisions; for example, student promotion or retention, availability of school funding, or labeling of schools as successful or failing (Afflerbach, 2004; IRA, 2014). Such measures have also been criticized because, given the focus on accountability, some schools have focused on "teaching to the test" by narrowing their curriculum to emphasize only those skills that appear on the test; too often, these tests are limited in their ability to assess complex and high-level reading tasks. It is important, then, to be cautious about how these measures are used, given their limitations. The position statement developed by the IRA (2014) highlights the importance of using multiple sources of systematic assessments to make high-stakes decisions about students.

Large-scale measures are also used by individual states to assess student performance, and often districts rely on those assessment tools as an important indicator of achievement success. In addition, the National Assessment of Educational Process (NCES, 2015), often called the "nation's report card," provides key information about the status of student learning across the United States.

THINK ABOUT THIS

In what ways are outcome measures used in the schools with which you are familiar? To what extent do the results influence the curriculum in the school—and judgments about the success of the school in educating its students? Do you agree with the concerns raised above about the limitations of these tests?

Screening Instruments

Measures that serve as *screening* tools assist teachers in quickly determining whether students are in need of more assistance or more in-depth assessment. These measures are meant to be administered quickly and they provide a general picture of whether a student may or may not be proficient with a specific reading task. Many commercial reading programs provide their own screening measures that can be used by teachers and reading specialists at the beginning of the year, before various instructional units, to provide baseline information about students and to make initial decisions about which children may need additional support. A screening measure used frequently in schools is DIBELS Next (Kaminski & Good, 2011), which assesses the acquisition of early literacy skills K–6; this set of instruments provides information about students' decoding skills, fluency, and comprehension skills. The authors consider this quick screening to be efficient and compare it to taking a temperature to determine if an individual has a fever. At the secondary level, reading specialists may choose to administer a cloze procedure test as a screening measure to determine the readability of a specific textbook, as well as the abilities of students in a specific content class to read that text. Although these initial screening instruments may be useful, they are "screening" instruments and no more. They are meant to separate those students who need help from those who do not. According to Mesmer, Mesmer, and Jones (2014), they should have four features:

quickly administered, predictive, universal, and objective. In other words, they can be given to all students quickly, they should predict accurately whether students need or do not need help, and administration and results should not vary from screener to screener. Celia (see "Voices from the Field" in Chapter 5) discusses the importance and difficulty of establishing interrater reliability in administering and scoring measurement instruments.

The DIBELS tool (predecessor to DIBELS Next) has had its share of criticism (e.g., Goodman, 2006; Kloo, 2006), although some of this criticism may actually be the result of misinterpretations about what the instrument is really capable of providing. For example, schools that teach the tasks of the DIBELS, instead of using results to guide instruction, are misusing the test. This is an excellent example of the importance of reading specialists being knowledgeable about assessment tools and how to interpret and use the results.

Diagnostic Assessments

Diagnostic assessments assist teachers in making decisions about instruction and in pinpointing possible areas to address if a student is experiencing difficulty. If a child has difficulties on a screening measure, the diagnostic measure can provide in-depth information needed to plan instruction. For example, if a child does poorly on an initial screening of decoding, the teacher or reading specialist may want to administer a more detailed phonics inventory to get a better picture of what the student can and cannot do. Reading specialists often use an informal reading inventory to get an in-depth picture of how well students read materials of different genre at various levels. A diagnostic tool, unlike a screening tool, provides information to help reading specialists and teachers plan the instruction needed by students.

Progress Monitoring

Progress monitoring measures are administered throughout the year to help determine whether students have made improvement and to determine the effectiveness of instruction. Progress monitoring measures might include measures of students' recognition of sight words, fluency checks, or skill learning. Another form of progress monitoring is evidence such as student work samples or checklists completed by the teacher throughout the year to assess whether students are improving in their ability to perform various tasks (see Figure 9.1 for an example of a checklist used when observing the oral reading of primary-grade students). These informal and authentic progress monitoring measures are helpful because they are closely related to the instructional practices at

Key

+ = Exhibits this behavior all of the time
✓ = Need for improvement some of the time
0 = Not evident

	Child's Name								
Reads with appropriate phrasing (not word by word)									
Reads with appropriate expression and intonation									
Reads at appropriate rate									
Uses punctuation as a meaning tool									
Uses decoding to figure out unknown words									
Rereads if meaning is problematic									

FIGURE 9.1. Oral Reading Checklist.

a specific grade level (e.g., teachers assess writing samples of fifth grad-ers three times a year, using a teacher-developed rubric based on their goals). These measures also provide information that can help teach-ers decide whether there is a need for additional support, a change in instructional practice, or a need for a more in-depth diagnostic assess-ment to obtain more information about a child's performance. Reading specialists can help teachers by talking with them about these data to address two important questions: Are students improving as expected, and, if not, what adjustments in instruction need to be made?

One of the ways to assess progress is through the use of formative assessment, or diagnostic teaching. Teachers can make decisions about instruction by listening to students read orally to see how they self-cor-rect when they experience difficulty, and they can ask students to think aloud to get a better sense of their meaning-making skills. Such forma-tive assessments take advantage of the multiple ways in which students experience reading (e.g., the texts they are reading, the level of thinking required). But using such assessments requires a knowledgeable teacher; again, the reading specialist can serve in a leadership capacity by help-ing teachers develop and use these authentic formative assessment tools.

These four types of measures—outcome, initial screening, diag-nostic, and progress monitoring—serve different purposes and require different types of assessment tools. Several key resource books that describe specific measures are *Assessment and Instruction of Reading and Writing Difficulties: An Interactive Approach* (Wixson & Lipson, 2009), *Diagnosis and Correction of Reading Problems* (Morris, 2014), and *Understanding and Using Reading Assessment K–12* (Afflerbach, 2012).

PRINCIPLES OF ASSESSMENT

1. *Facilitate a match between instruction and assessment.* In select-ing assessment measures, especially outcome measures over which the school has control, careful attention must be given to the match between the instruction provided in the school and the measure chosen. Tests selected must align to the curriculum, instruction, and standards of the district. Teachers often bemoan the fact that students are tested on a skill that is not introduced in the curriculum until the following grade level or the month after the test is given! There is strong evidence the closer the overlap between curriculum and test items, the better students will perform; this just makes sense. This is not to say teachers should be teaching to the test, but it is foolish to ignore the demands of a test students will be taking as a measure of their achievement. At times, this

outcome measure is a test developed by the state, based on standards that have been adopted by that state. In that case, it again makes sense for reading specialists and their colleagues to work together to decide how and what the schools are teaching so that students can achieve those standards. Only then will the outcome measure be a fair assessment of students' performance.

Beresik and Bean (2002), in their study of teachers' perceptions about a state assessment test, found that teachers did not feel as though they had received sufficient professional development to help them implement instruction that addressed state standards as measured by that outcome test. This complaint was especially common among teachers who taught at grade levels below the level at which the test was administered.

2. *Develop a systematic approach to assessment (be efficient).* At all levels (i.e., primary, intermediate, middle school, and secondary), reading specialists and their colleagues make decisions about which components of literacy to assess. In the primary grades, assessment measures should focus more on foundational skills as well as comprehension, vocabulary, and writing. In the upper grades, more emphasis should be placed on comprehension, vocabulary, and writing. At all levels, information about students' reading levels is helpful for making instructional decisions. The key is for school personnel to select instruments, reflecting a logical and realistic progression from the early grades through high school and across all components of literacy. School personnel can ask themselves: Are we assessing important dimensions of literacy? Is there redundancy—what can we eliminate? Assessment may be taking too much time away from instruction and adjustments must be made to reduce the time taken from school days for assessment purposes, to eliminate "test overkill." In a recent newspaper article, one school district indicated it was required to give a total of more than 270 tests during the school year across all grade levels, and they were looking for ways to reduce the number of required tests.

3. *Develop a system of literacy assessment reflecting school or district goals.* Too often, there is no agreed-upon system of literacy assessment in the school community. Many different tools are used by school personnel, some of which are disparate with school goals. Other assessment tools may be so complex to administer or score that classroom teachers tend not to use the results, or as stated above, they may take so much time for administration that valuable instructional time is lost. In other cases, assessment tools differ so much from level to level (e.g., elementary to middle school) it is not possible to determine the ongoing literacy learning of students.

4. *Select assessment tools that are reliable, valid, and practical to administer.* Select instruments that are technically valid and reliable;

instruments developed by districts themselves may lack such technical sophistication. For example, if a school decides to assess students' written retelling of a story, careful attention must be given to the rubric used to score this retelling so there is *reliability* or consistency in the scoring of that instrument. Otherwise, little use can be made of the scores. Also, the tools employed must be *valid*—that is, they actually measure what they purport to measure. For example, a spelling test is not a measure of composition skill, although spelling, as part of a conventions rubric, could be used as one indicator of performance in composition.

5. *Teachers need assistance in applying data to instructional decision making.* There is clear evidence that when teachers use data to make instructional decisions, student performance improves. Thus, assessment tools should be usable by the teachers who administer them, whether they are reading specialists or classroom teachers. If teachers see these assessments as a burden, taking time away from the instructional program, and if they are not provided with the training they need to see the value of these measures, there will be little value in administering them. Too often, instruction in the classroom is "activity" or materials based; that is, decisions about instruction are based on the selection that comes next in the book. One of the important roles of the reading specialist is to help teachers make decisions about their instruction, informed by results of assessment data. An example of how a reading specialist worked with one teacher in reviewing assessment data is described below, using data presented in Figure 9.2 that lists scores of students in one third-grade classroom on several literacy assessment measures.

Maria Hernandez, the reading specialist, and Roberta Reed, the third-grade teacher, were reviewing the scores of some of Roberta's students on the initial screening measures given at the beginning of the year. It was obvious to them that students were doing fairly well with basic sight words; almost all students scored 75% or better. Students were not performing as well on the pseudo-word test, with 11 of them getting less than 75% correct. Many students also were experiencing difficulty with fluent oral reading (reading below 80 correct words per minute). The poor scores on the retelling were also of concern, and students had some difficulty responding to questions after reading. Maria and Roberta identified two students (Sally and Henry) about whom they had serious concerns.

After an extended problem-solving discussion, Maria and Roberta made the following decisions.. First, all students in this third-grade class would benefit from activities that emphasized fluency practice, and Maria shared with Roberta various ways to facilitate this (e.g., repeated readings, choral reading). Maria suggested that she come into the classroom 4 days a week to work on decoding with the 11 students who seemed to have the most

Teacher name (last): _____ Grade _3_

Student name	Pseudo word %	Sight word %	Fluency		Comprehension	
			Words read	Words correct	Retell n/55	Question n/8
Frank	60	89	52	44	7	3
Juan	55	93	90	86	6	6
Clyde	85	97	90	87	10	5
Melissa	45	93	102	98	13	5
Cindy	60	95	57	53	13	6
Sally	35	76	25	11	0	4
Bob	90	97	87	83	19	6
Jerome	90	98	143	143	11	8
Ralph	95	82	52	48	14	5
Gail	80	96	102	99	7	8
Celeste	20	95	57	52	11	4
Joseph	25	98	65	61	30	7
Tyrone	25	96	63	59	26	6
Henry	45	67	29	18	15	5
Mark	60	92	81	77	19	6
Julie	40	93	75	71	8	6

FIGURE 9.2. Example of a student data collection sheet, third grade, pretests.

difficulty; she told Roberta that she would emphasize word building using letter tiles to help students apply what they knew about letter–sound matches to identifying new words. All lessons would include opportunities for reading connected text.

Because of the low retelling score, both educators agreed that students did not seem to understand the task of retelling and that the entire group would benefit from lessons that helped them (1) understand the activity of retelling and why it helps them think about a story, and (2) develop strategies to help them with retelling (i.e., story structure or story mapping). They would also be given opportunities to retell orally as well as in writing. Maria and Roberta agreed they needed to develop lessons that gave students opportunities to read more challenging and conceptually difficult text. Therefore, for the entire class, the two educators decided to address one of the third-grade standards that addressed reading of informational text, that is, asking and answering questions to demonstrate understanding and referring to the text as a basis for their answers (CCSS, grade 3). Maria agreed to model a lesson, using the social studies text being used at that grade level.

Maria suggested some additional diagnostic testing of Sally and Henry to get a better idea of their specific problems. She agreed to administer an informal reading inventory to see how they responded to different genres of text at varying levels. She also thought it would be helpful to gather additional data on their decoding and writing skills. She suggested to Roberta it would be a good idea for the two of them to analyze the writing abilities of *all* the students within the next month. (In fact, Maria had asked the third-grade team to bring samples of their student writing to a grade-level meeting to talk about what they could learn about the literacy instruction they were providing and how it might be improved.) Maria and Roberta concluded their meeting by agreeing to meet in 2 weeks to talk about the success of their plans and to make adjustments, as needed.

This example provides a description of how one reading specialist worked collaboratively with a classroom teacher in using test results to make instructional decisions. In Katy's vignette (see "Voices from the Field" in Chapter 4), she discusses her meetings with grade-level teachers and the ways they use their students' writing samples to plan instruction and increase their own understanding of writing instruction and assessment.

At the present time, especially with the RTI initiative, there is an emphasis on using data results to inform instruction. Often, reading specialists, as well as other specialized personnel, meet with teachers at specific grade levels to discuss results across the grade (e.g., to determine the number of students meeting standards or targets, as well as those who are not, and to discuss ways by which the teachers as a group can modify instruction to meet the needs at that grade level). In our work with Reading First, teachers and administrators appreciated the way in which data helped to inform instruction (Zigmond & Bean, 2008). In some classrooms "data walls" were posted, showing results for students and also changes in scores. I have some reservations about such public posting of student scores, and encourage administrators and teachers to recognize some of the problems inherent in such a display (e.g., embarrassment for individual students and teachers; tendency to overemphasize testing;

possibility of negative, public comments about students). Teachers and administrators can discuss the pros and cons of these public displays so they do not have a negative effect on the school and its climate.

In some schools, teachers and reading specialists develop charts, indicating where students are in terms of performance so teachers can visually see the levels at which their students are performing and make some decisions about "next steps." Figure 9.3 shows a summary sheet of the performance of students in three third-grade classrooms at midyear. Two measures—the STAR Reading Test and a fluency measure—were discussed by a team of teachers and reading specialists. The template provides a place where teachers and reading specialists, meeting as a group, can set goals for the next quarter. Specific strategies to be taught or retaught, groupings, or educators responsible for instruction and with whom, can be identified. Reading specialists can develop a form similar to this for use in summarizing the decisions made to inform instructional decisions.

THINK ABOUT THIS

What are the major "take-aways" about assisting teachers in using assessment to inform instruction (Principle 5)? In what ways can Figure 9.3 be useful?

School personnel need opportunities to hold frequent, focused conversations about student learning. Moreover, these discussions about assessments should serve as opportunities for problem solving rather than as ones in which teachers feel as though they are being criticized for the results.

---

6. *Opportunity for student self-assessment and reflection should be built into the program.* Although assessment and accountability are major concerns in schools today, unfortunately, there is less consideration given to the importance of *self*-assessment by the students. Nevertheless, there is strong support for involving students in the process of evaluating their own work (Afflerbach, 2014; Hansen, 1998; Tierney, Johnston, Moore, & Valencia, 2000). Such self-assessment is a hallmark of successful readers, enabling them to make decisions about their own learning. Moreover, involvement in self-assessment, as a means of developing independent learners, is strongly recommended in rigorous, high-level standards, such as the CCSS.

However, students need experiences to develop the ability to self-assess. The use of rubrics in classrooms can promote such self-evaluation. A rubric is a scoring guide, with criteria, for judging the relative quality of

Progress Monitoring Form—Marigold School Grade Level: 3

Date of Meeting: Baseline   1st Quarter   2nd Quarter   3rd Quarter   End of Year

Attending the meeting:

Attendee	Position	Attendee	Position
Darrell	3rd-grade teacher	Thelma	Reading specialist
Ava	3rd-grade teacher	Helena	Reading specialist
Nina	3rd-grade teacher	Franklin	Principal

Performance indicators: Percentage of students at proficient level based on benchmark/standard:

	% At/above benchmark	% On watch (below benchmark)	% Intervention (below benchmark)	% Urgent intervention
STAR Reading	71% (44 students)	18% (11 students)	2% (1 student)	10% (6 students)
Fluency Measure	85% (53 students)		15% (9 students)	

Goals for the next quarter:

STAR Reading	Following eight students will move from on watch (below benchmark) to at/above benchmark: Ben, Brittany, Chad, Sara, Shauntee, Tyler, William, Zack
	Following three students will move from urgent intervention to intervention (below benchmark): Abby, Daniel, Dylan
Fluency	Following five students will move from below benchmark to at/above benchmark: Alosia, Chad, Jacob, Sara, Tyler

Strategies: Reinforce nonfiction text structures and other core reading skills (I/E time); reading buddies (with first graders); comprehension (focus on verifying responses in text; making inferences); vocabulary (synonyms and antonyms).

Groupings: (pullout and in class): Add pullout group of six students (those in urgent intervention) (focus on vocabulary and comprehension).

FIGURE 9.3. Summary sheet of data analysis. Adapted from the form used at Acmetonia Primary School, Allegheny Valley School District, Pennsylvania.

assessment products. Figure 9.4 shows a sample rubric for assessing student fluency developed by the NAEP (Pinnell et al., 1995). Such a rubric can be modified so students can self-assess their own oral reading or that of their peers. Teachers might develop a simple rubric asking students to self-evaluate their oral reading, for example, as follows:

- Do I read at a speed that makes it easy for others to understand me (not too slow and not too fast)?
- Do I know most of the words in the story?
- Do I reread if something doesn't make sense?
- Do I read so that others enjoy listening to me?

A simple 3-point scale can be used by students to self-evaluate each of the elements (e.g., I do a great job, I'm okay most of the time, I need to improve). When students assess their own work, they become knowledgeable about the demands of the task and more comfortable with the notion of self-evaluation.

Portfolio assessment also can be used as a means of promoting ownership of work. Such assessment can begin in the early grades with the collection of student work, writing samples, reading attitude forms, and books read, and progress to more complicated portfolios created at the middle and high school levels.

Level 4	Reads in primarily large, meaningful phrase groups. Although some regressions, repetitions, and deviations from text may be present, these do not appear to detract from the overall structure of the story. Preservation of the author's syntax is consistent. Some or most of the story is read with expressive interpretation.
Level 3	Reads primarily in three- or four-word phrase groups. Some smaller groupings may be present. However, the majority of phrasing seems appropriate and preserves the syntax of the author. Little or no expressive interpretation is present.
Level 2	Reads primarily in two-word phrases with some three- or four-word groupings. Some word-by-word reading may be present. Word groupings may seem awkward and unrelated to larger context of sentence or passage.
Level 1	Reads primarily word-by-word. Occasional two- or three-word phrases may occur, but these are infrequent and/or do not preserve meaningful syntax.

FIGURE 9.4. The National Assessment of Educational Progress's Integrated Reading Performance Record Oral Reading Fluency Scale. From Pinnell et al. (1995).

7. *Assessment systems should include more than testing.* As mentioned, schools should have a well-designed comprehensive assessment system in place and that system should include more than data obtained from tests. A teaching colleague of mine used to say one key measure for assessing the quality of instruction in the classroom is "the number of students with smiles on their faces!" Kapinus (2008) discusses various topics about which data can be collected: attendance, parent involvement and perceptions about the school and its literacy program, safety of students, instructional schedule, and allotment of time for instruction and curriculum (p. 148). Because teachers' views and beliefs affect greatly what they do and how they teach, obtaining perceptual information from them is especially useful. Other important areas are students' motivation to read, the number of books taken out from the library, and the environment that exists in the school as a whole and in classrooms. These data are useful indicators of whether a school is an effective place for learning—and of ways schools can improve their school reading programs. Often, reading specialists are involved in developing questionnaires or surveys that can be completed by parents or by teachers to get a better sense of their views about the school's literacy program. For help in designing questionnaires, consult *Data Analysis for Continuous School Improvement* (Bernhardt, 2013).

THINK ABOUT THIS

How would data such as those described in Principle 7 be collected? What questions could school personnel ask about such topics as instructional schedule? Attitudes of teachers? How can such data be used to improve instruction?

ISSUES IN ASSESSMENT

Who Should Be Involved in Developing the Assessment Plan?

Although assessment plans can be developed by an individual or a small group of administrators, it is best a plan be developed by a team or committee, including teachers, reading specialists, department chairs, principals, and parent representatives. Such a team, led by an administrator knowledgeable about tests and assessments, can make decisions about important issues:

- Which assessments best match the curriculum in our schools, K–12?
- Which assessments are required by the state?

- How can we get the best information with the least amount of disruption to the instructional schedule?
- What staff development is necessary if teachers are to be able to administer, score (if necessary), and use the results?

Too often, decisions about assessment are made in isolation, with changes occurring at one or another level, reducing the possibility of continuity. And too often, districts cannot use their assessment tools to make decisions because they have (1) changed them too frequently, or (2) the measures are not comparable from one level to another.

School personnel should be familiar with the assessment tools being used by the district and able to discuss and communicate the results of such assessments to parents and others in the community interested in the work of the school. The emphasis by the federal government (i.e., in the NCLB [2001] legislation and in Race to the Top) on assessment results and accountability makes it imperative that schools are able to explain not only *what* they are doing but *how well* they are doing!

How Are Assessment Results Reported?

Again, reading specialists may find it necessary to assist in developing ways that schools report assessment results. They themselves may also be responsible for such reporting. Different audiences are interested in these results including teachers, students, district administration, parents, and community members (as well as those on the school board). The school district should have an established means of reporting students' scores to each teacher; such reports may be similar to the one in Figure 9.2. The reading specialist should be available to assist the teacher in interpreting and using the results for instructional decision making. The reading specialist may also assist the teacher in deciding how scores of individual students can best be reported and explained to parents or to students themselves. Building principals may need reports highlighting results for specific populations or areas: class, grade level, literacy component (e.g., reading comprehension, fluency). They may wish to have data disaggregated by ethnic group, socioeconomic or EL status, or special education eligibility. Again, the reading specialist can work with the principal on interpreting the results of the literacy assessment; adjustments in the instruction or curriculum may be indicated. The reading specialist and principal together may make presentations about test results to the entire faculty.

Reporting to parents is certainly a key responsibility of the schools. Reading specialists should, of course, be aware of the ways by which literacy performance is reported and what the specific scores mean: letter grades, effort scores, and grade-level reporting. In addition, they should be able to interpret those results to parents, especially parents of struggling readers. It is probable those parents may want to meet with the reading specialist to discuss their children's scores. Test data should be reported in a simple and clear fashion to parents so they have an understanding of what the scores mean. Although not all reading specialists will have the responsibility for presenting assessment results to the school board or community, including the media, some may. The district should be proactive in sharing assessment results, presenting not only results but recommendations about what the school is doing to improve students' learning.

What Are the Limitations of Standardized Tests?

Reading specialists, because they frequently make use of tests in their work, need to be aware of the limitations of those tests, especially those that are high stakes or have the potential to label or affect students' lives in a detrimental manner. Several limitations are discussed here. First, a test is a *sample* of all questions that can be asked about a subject and, in addition, it is a *sample* of a student's performance at a single point in time. Therefore, although test publishers work to ensure that the items selected constitute a representative sample of important knowledge and skills, the fact remains that some students might have done better if a different sample of equally adequate questions had been used on the test. Furthermore, on any given day, an external factor such as illness or a disagreement with a parent may have affected a particular student's performance.

Second, changes in the schools' scores can be caused by changes in student population. If a school is one whose population demonstrates high mobility or attrition, there can be significant differences in the population from one administration date to another. Some students may not have been in the school for more than 2 or 3 months. In fact, Kane and Staiger in Kober (2002) estimated that more than 70% of the year-to-year variations in average test scores for a given school or grade could be attributed to external factors rather than educational factors.

Third, the ways by which scores are reported affect perceptions in terms of positive or negative outcomes. For example, look at the data in Figure 9.5 illustrating reading achievement proficiency at the third-grade level for two schools over a 3-year period. Which school do you think is doing better?

Pine School has more students reading at proficiency; most likely Pine School met the requirements for "adequate yearly progress" as required by NCLB (2001). However, if we look at change in performance of students, then we see greater growth or change in Oak School where student performance has improved from a low of 20.7% scoring at proficiency to 37.5% at the proficiency level in Year 3. Initially, NCLB considered only status or level of proficiency to determine whether schools were improving satisfactorily. At the present time, some states have been given permission to use evidence of growth or change scores as a means of determining whether schools have improved.

In addition to looking at the results in terms of change or status, those who interpret data can look at trends in a school. For example, in looking at only 2 years of growth for Oak School, we can be misled by the data because in Year 2, 38% of the students were proficient and in Year 3, the proficiency rate was 37.5%; if we use only the previous year's results, we see no improvement, but if we analyze scores from Year 1 to Year 3, we see significant improvement. In other words, we must be careful when analyzing and interpreting assessment results. Results are arbitrary; that is, improvement depends on the approach used for analysis. Reading specialists should be familiar with these limitations. Reading specialists who want to know more about high-stakes testing may wish to read the policy brief written by Peter Afflerbach (2004) at *www.literacyresearchassociation.org/publications/HighStakesTestingandReadingAssessment.pdf* or the position statement on high-stakes assessment (IRA, 2014).

ASSESSMENT AT THE MIDDLE OR HIGH SCHOOL LEVEL

The previous content provides key information for all reading specialists, regardless at which level they work. Assessment is a reality at all levels; currently, the federal government requires that schools conduct an end-of-the-year assessment in grades 3–8 and at least once in high school. However, these tests provide for summative or outcome measures and are not necessarily helpful for making decisions about instruction. So, educators at the secondary level should develop or select formative measures to assist teachers in assessing literacy learning and making decisions to improve instruction for their students. In this section, several key points for those working with adolescent learners are described.

	Year 1	Year 2	Year 3
Oak School	20.7%	38.0%	37.5%
Pine School	56.6%	57.0%	57.5%

FIGURE 9.5. Percentage of third graders scoring at proficiency.

First, given the diversity and range in achievement found among adolescent learners, assessment is an essential tool for learning more about their instructional and literacy needs. In the document "Assessments to Guide Adolescent Literacy Instruction," Torgeson and Miller (2009) discuss the importance of a comprehensive assessment plan for grades 4–12 for achieving the following goals: increase overall levels of proficiency; help students continue to progress so that they can achieve the more difficult, rigorous, standards in the middle and secondary schools; and assist students who are reading below grade level to increase their reading performance (p. 11). A comprehensive plan must show evidence of outcomes, provide for progress monitoring enabling teachers to make instructional decisions, and identify students who need instructional interventions. Again, the importance of self-assessment is emphasized; Torgeson and Miller (2009) recommend providing students with opportunities to reflect on their learning, using rubrics they and their teachers have developed.

One of the challenges at the middle and secondary levels is obtaining information about students' performance in the various content areas or disciplines, and how such information can be used by teachers to make instructional decisions. As indicated in the IRA (2012a) position statement on adolescent literacy, assessment of adolescents should be based on an inquiry framework that explores how learners become independent, collaborative thinkers and problem solvers. The best assessments give students opportunities to "make meaning from an idea in print and then represent their new understandings in a variety of modes (e.g., video, audio, graphical)" (p. 11).

SUMMARY

Assessment is and will continue to be a topic generating much interest and concern in schools. New directions in assessing student growth, however, suggest assessment systems that are multidimensional, focusing on both what students learn and how they apply what they learn. Assessment is an important responsibility of the reading specialist, not only for assessing the strengths and needs of individual students but also for making decisions about the performance of classes, schools, and the district as a whole. Assessment should be closely related to instruction, and there should be a sequential, comprehensive assessment system, PreK–12. In addition, various stakeholders, including teachers and community representatives, must be involved in making decisions about the assessment of literacy. Multiple assessment measures with established technical adequacy should be used. Reading specialists may have responsibility for working with teachers, administrators, and the community interpreting and applying the results of assessment. They should be knowledgeable about the strengths as well as the limitations of all assessment measures, especially those used for high-stakes purposes.

Reflections

What are the strengths and weaknesses of various assessment instruments with which you are familiar?

Activities

1. Interview a reading specialist in a district about his or her role in assessment. Which assessment tools does he or she use? How does the reading specialist work with teachers to use results in planning instruction?

2. Interview a reading specialist or another school leader to discuss a district's plan of assessment, K–12. Does the district have a plan of assessment, K–12, and if so, what measures are used? How does the assessment differ from level to level?

3. Select an assessment tool used by a district with which you are familiar and investigate whether the instrument meets a standard of technical adequacy.

ADDITIONAL READINGS

International Reading Association. (2013). *Formative assessment: A position statement of the International Reading Association.* Newark, DE: Author.—In this brief document, formative assessment is described as an essential component of any assessment plan and questions about formative assessment are answered.

International Reading Association. (2014). *Using high-stakes assessments for grade retention and graduation decisions: A position statement of the International Reading Association.* Newark, DE: Author.—In this position statement, IRA takes the stance that any decisions about grade retention and high school graduation require the use of multiple measures. Retrieved from *www.reading.org.*

Joint Task Force on Assessment of the International Reading Association and the National Council of Teachers of English. (2009). *Standards for reading and writing revised.* Urbana, IL: National Council of Teachers of English.—This document, produced by IRA and NCTE, provides a description of each of 11 standards developed to guide the assessment of literacy in the 21st century.

CHAPTER TEN

School, Community, and Family Partnerships

It takes a village to raise a child.
—AFRICAN PROVERB

Key Questions

- What are the six types of parental involvement as described by Epstein (1995)?
- In what ways can reading specialists work with parents and community to enhance student literacy learning?
- In developing an effective parental involvement program, what essential notions or guidelines need to be considered?

This chapter begins with a discussion of Joyce Epstein's (1995) categorization of how schools can involve parents and community in schools, followed by suggestions as to how reading specialists can develop partnerships with community agencies and institutions. Next, guidelines for working with volunteers and paraprofessionals in the schools are provided. Last, the role of the reading specialist in working with families and addressing issues of parenting, communicating, learning at home, and decision making is explored.

The merit of the often-cited quotation above cannot be disputed. When teachers are asked to identify their greatest problem in working with struggling readers, they often mention the lack of parental involvement in providing additional support or attending to the child's behavioral needs, especially in schools where there are large numbers of students from poor or minority backgrounds. Teachers in the early grades decry that students come to kindergarten without the background knowledge/exposure essential for learning success, and without the literacy and language experiences that support learning to read. Those in the upper grades have complaints about their students who don't complete their homework, are not motivated to learn, or don't come to school!

Parental involvement is critically important and it is positively related to many factors, including test scores, student attendance, and school completion rates (Morrison, Bachman, & Connor, 2005; Sheldon, 2007). Many parents are involved: they come to the initial "meet-the-teacher meetings" at the beginning of the year, talk with their children about school experiences, assist them with their homework, and work as partners with schools to make certain their children are receiving a good education. Their children have extensive experiences that give them a rich language and literacy background; they have rich vocabularies and are familiar with the language of the classroom.

At the same time, in our schools today, there are students whose parents lack linguistic, economic, or social resources, limiting them from participating fully in their children's education (Edwards, Paratore, & Sweeney, 2014). However, too often, schools have not positioned themselves to understand and use the *funds of knowledge* (e.g., knowledge, resources, and competencies) these parents and their children bring to schools (Moll, 2000). In other words, in what ways can educators move from a perception often based on a "deficit" model to one acknowledging the value of students' cultural strengths and experiences?

In the past, some educators believed it was their job to teach and parents to "parent." This viewpoint has changed; the education of the child is one requiring the efforts of both. When there is family involvement and support, students have a much better chance of success in school (Henderson & Berla, 1995; Morrison, Bachman, & Connor, 2005). When families are involved in their children's schooling, children earn higher grades and test scores, and they stay in school longer. The increased pressure on educators to account for levels of student achievement has generated support for even more family involvement. In its NCLB (U.S. Department of Education, 2002b) legislation, the federal government gave parents a range of options to pursue if their children were in unsuccessful schools. Schools were required to provide supplemental programs for children with special needs, and parents had the choice of transferring their children to better-performing public schools, including public charter schools. Whether we agree with this policy or not, all schools and all teachers must think about their involvement in the community in new and different ways.

Epstein (1995; Epstein, Sanders, Sheldon, Simon, & Salinas, 2009), in her research-based framework, describes six types of parental involvement:

1. Parenting: helping families establish home environments that support children's development as students.
2. Communicating: designing and using effective forms of home–school communication about programs and children's growth.
3. Volunteering: recruiting, organizing, and providing opportunities for volunteers to support student learning.
4. Learning at home: involving families in supporting their children's growth (e.g., helping with homework, supporting other school activities).
5. Decision making: including parents in school decisions.
6. Collaborating with the community: coordinating various community resources and services and providing services to the community.

Although these six types of parental involvement help educators think about specific ways to involve parents, an overarching principle is that of acknowledging what children *do* bring to the classroom, rather than focusing only on what they lack. Reading specialists and their colleagues can serve as leaders in helping teachers understand this principle and to implement many different efforts related to each of the six types of parental involvement.

INVOLVEMENT WITH EXTERNAL AGENCIES

There are many different agencies with which reading specialists might work. Involvement with five important entities is discussed here: preschool providers, libraries, community- and faith-based organizations, universities and colleges, and volunteers and paraprofessionals in the schools.

Preschool Providers

The growing understanding that preschool education matters has led to a national initiative led by President Obama to provide universal early childhood education for children in the United States. In 2014, states were invited to apply for development or expansion grants from the federal government through the Preschool Development Grant Initiative (*www2. ed.gov/programs/preschooldevelopmentgrants/index.html*). The focus of the grants is on building, developing, or expanding high-quality preschools for children from low- or moderate-income families. Five-year-olds who enter kindergartens come with a variety of experiences, many of them having attended a day-care center, nursery, or preschool. Some arrive having learned school and learning behaviors, as well as literacy skills, enabling them to move comfortably into the kindergarten setting. Others struggle with literacy tasks and may not have had any preschool experience, or little exposure to literacy in their homes. Research on the cognitive development of young children emphasizes the importance of high-quality early learning experiences. There is evidence of great variability in the quality of preschool experiences children receive, especially in preschool programs serving children from poor families (McGill-Franzen, Lanford, & Adams, 2002; Snow et al., 1998). At the same time, the quality of child-care programs has been identified as an important determinant of language acquisition in the form of preliteracy skills (Barnett, 1995; Barnett, Frede, Mobasher, & Mohr, 1987).

Below I describe three major efforts designed to prepare young children for kindergarten and to improve the preparation they receive in their day-care or preschool setting. First, school districts can work collegially with preschool providers so that there is a clear understanding of what schools expect from entering kindergarteners, and what educational experiences students receive in their preschool settings. Schools also need to know what providers value and why their programs include various activities and experiences. Gathering this information can be accomplished in several ways: (1) schools can share the list of standards or competencies for entering kindergarten; (2) preschool providers can share their curriculum; (3) teachers from the two sites can visit each other's classrooms to get a better understanding of students' experiences; and (4) meetings between the two groups of teachers can bridge the gap that often occurs and eliminate, or at least reduce, the "blame" game. Furthermore, district leadership can acknowledge the importance of such transition activities and provide district-level support and resources.

Second, preschool providers who educate students for a district can be included in available professional development programs. When school districts convene a professional development meeting in which the speaker is addressing an issue relevant to the education of young children, invitations can be extended to preschool providers. It may not be possible for all preschool teachers to attend, but arrangements can be made at the preschools so teachers who attended the session can share the information with their colleagues.

Third, when opportunities for working together arise, seize them! At the present time, the interest in early learning is not only creating such opportunities, it is *demanding* them. Possible proposals for funding can be investigated and written, and community collaboration for such endeavors can be cultivated. Reading specialists can assume an important role in promoting each of these three recommendations and are often the ones who can "create" opportunities for collaborative efforts. They can foster interaction between kindergarten and preschool teachers, especially in the discussion about literacy instruction. They may also be able to provide professional development for the preschool teachers. In Pennsylvania, as part of the Striving Readers grant, in some districts, literacy personnel traveled to specific preschools to provide job-embedded support for preschool teachers who may not have had extensive learning opportunities about literacy and language development. Given this increased focus on early childhood education, new opportunities are available for reading specialists, especially those interested in literacy learning of young children.

Libraries

Reading specialists can work collaboratively with school librarians to develop experiences for students that create excitement and enthusiasm for reading. The reading specialist should be aware of resources available in the school library, and assist the librarian in selecting print and nonprint materials that enhance students' motivation to read and promote learning across curricular areas. The reading specialist may collaborate with the librarian, identifying themes and topics addressed in the academic areas, and selecting books to enrich the curriculum. School librarians can also be involved in supporting the school's literacy program. My colleague and I (Bean & Eichelberger, 2007) evaluated a program in a local school district in which school librarians attended workshops led by district literacy coaches to increase their knowledge and understanding of the strategies and approaches used in the literacy program. These librarians were very positive about this experience, indicating they now had a better understanding of the language of literacy used by teachers and also were able to reinforce in their library classes some of what students were learning in their classrooms.

The community library is also a resource for the school. Most community libraries assign a staff member to interact with personnel from schools who are eager to participate in school–library collaborations. The community librarian may be able to purchase resources that relate to the curriculum emphasized in the school. The reading specialist who takes the time to work with the community librarian is likely to find new ways to enhance student motivation to read. Some of the ways that schools and libraries can work together include the following:

• Librarians can come to school to read books to children and solicit membership in the community library. After reading a book, it can be left in the classroom for follow-up work by the teacher.

• Students can visit the community library on a field trip; the librarian may lead the students through the various sections of the library, explaining the types of resources offered by each, and offer children the opportunity to get a library card.

• School and library personnel can work together to develop a summer program for students. This program can be promoted in the school and recognition given at the school in the fall for those students who complete the program. Research findings indicate that there is a "summer slide" for children of poverty; that is, children from higher socioeconomic groups do not experience the summer learning loss experienced by those in lower socioeconomic groups (Alexander, Entwisle, & Olson, 2001). Summer reading programs can help to decrease this summer slide by providing children with books and opportunities to read.

• Reading specialists can work with community librarians to create programs benefiting both successful and struggling readers. The reading specialist can inform the librarian about special school initiatives (e.g., specific reading programs or efforts that require specific books). Often, the librarian will then make certain that those books are included in the library's collections.

During the past several years, a public library and school district in an urban setting collaborated to develop a special library program designed to promote reading in schools where there were large numbers of struggling readers. This program, funded by a local foundation, was designed to (1) stimulate motivation to read by exposing students to books about children from various cultures, including their own; and (2) enhance reading achievement by introducing and discussing various vocabulary words from those texts. Personnel from the library went to the third-grade classrooms twice a month to read and discuss a book with the children, and then left the book in the classroom. Evaluation of that program indicated students enjoyed listening to the book and often reread the book that had been read to them. Teachers felt the program enhanced students' reading interest, and they (the teachers) enjoyed learning about new trade books they could then use in their classroom work (Genest, 2014; Genest & Bean, 2007).

In another community, the library provides a monthly program for special needs teens enrolled in life skills classes at their high schools. During their 2-hour visit, these students are involved in activities to increase their information literacy and their understanding of the library and its resources. Reference librarians are available to provide technology support. The children's librarian indicated the importance of collaborating with teachers to design programs to reinforce life skills classroom goals (personal communication with children's librarian, Whitehall Public Library, Pittsburgh, Pennsylvania, 2014).

Community- and Faith-Based Organizations

In many communities, churches, community agencies, or organizations provide after-school or summer programs for students. These programs provide a safe place for children whose parents may be working, and they can reinforce school lessons by helping students with homework or providing tutoring and academic support. Recent legislation has deemed faith-based organizations eligible to apply for approval to provide supplemental educational services to low-income students attending underachieving schools. Such services can provide help before or after school, on weekends, or during the summer, in both reading and math.

These organizations, whether faith- or community or service based, can support or extend the work of the school. In order to help them achieve their goals in ways that facilitate the work of the school, reading specialists or other school personnel can get involved in several ways. First, they can help facilitate communication between the school and agencies offering services, so there is better awareness of what additional support students are receiving. Second, reading specialists can volunteer to provide guidance about possible strategies or instruction that best support classroom instruction. For example, if students in a school use a specific literacy program or curriculum, reading specialists might suggest the community-based program use the supplemental books aligned with that program. Or, a check sheet might be devised for classroom teachers to send to the agency, indicating the needs of specific students (e.g., "J needs to practice his new sight words; I'm including them in this packet").

In addition, individuals who work with these organizations can be sources of information and wisdom for schools about a community and its resources. They may advocate for students if the family is not able to participate in more traditional parent involvement programs (Boutte & Johnson, 2014).

Service organizations often have literacy initiatives. Several years ago, Lions Clubs International, the largest service organization in the world, undertook a reading initiative—Reading Action Program—focused on increasing literacy and access to learning resources; service projects and activities were organized to address specific needs within individual communities. In my community, the Lions Club (*www.*

lionsclub.org) sponsored several well-attended events: a Book Walk, Book Bingo, Reading with Stars Night in which local officials read to students, and a community day activity in which children came to the library to read to the dogs! Reading specialists who are proactive can look for ways to work with these organizations. Often, these organizations need the support of local school professionals to obtain access to classrooms or schools and to learn more about local literacy needs. Several organizations devoted to training therapy dogs would also welcome access to schools. As a means of enhancing student motivation to read, reading specialists might want to develop programs in which trained dogs "listen" to students read. If so, the article by Lane and Zavada (2013) describing canine-assisted reading programs, or the website of Therapy Dogs International (*www.tdi-dog.org*), provides useful information.

Universities and Colleges

Many K–12 schools are located close enough to universities to be able to partner with them on projects that bring preservice teachers, volunteers, or faculty into their schools. Faculty involved with preservice education programs look for ways to form partnerships with schools in which there is quality, research-based instruction, and mentor teachers who are excellent role models. Many are eager to cooperate in many different ways: teaching classes on-site and recruiting classroom teachers willing to participate, providing up-to-date resources and information to schools, and holding meetings in which there is in-depth discussion about what preservice students are learning and its congruence with the instruction occurring in the classrooms.

Many faculty at universities and colleges also appreciate opportunities to participate in professional development efforts of schools, or they are interested in conducting research that contributes to the understanding of how students learn to read. Although such partnerships need to be entered into thoughtfully so there is a clear understanding of the benefits for each partner, these ventures can be the catalyst for a win–win situation. In a previous chapter, I described the LEADERS project in which we worked with several school districts on a professional development initiative. The outcome of the project included changes in classroom teacher practices and student achievement; in addition, university faculty learned a great deal about what works in schools, what is difficult to implement, and challenges to consider in efforts to improve the quality of literacy instruction.

Because of the work–study portion of the America Reads Challenge Act of 1997 (*http://eric.ed.gov/?id=ED411504*), which provided funding for college students who were eligible to become volunteer tutors in the schools, many colleges and universities sent their students into schools or community agencies to tutor struggling readers. Much has been written about the results of the America Reads efforts (Fitzgerald, 2001; Morrow & Woo, 2001), and manuals and procedures for implementing tutoring programs have been developed (Bader, 1998; Johnston, Juel, & Invernizzi, 1995). Bean, Turner, and Belski (2002) discussed lessons learned from implementing such a program, identifying issues to be addressed by university and school or community-based personnel. Our results indicated successful volunteer tutoring programs benefited from a well-structured training program that provides a framework for novice tutors. Such a program should include information about literacy instruction and how best to engage students. Furthermore, because tutors are not always familiar or comfortable with the sites to which they were assigned, they need experiences and guidance to help them learn more about the context in which they are going to work. A collaborative program like this requires clear and ongoing communication of expectations and responsibilities between the partners.

For the past 25 years, graduate students in the reading specialist certification program at the University of Pittsburgh, Pennsylvania, have been recruited to serve as reading specialist interns; they are placed in a school site for an entire year to work with students needing reading support and with the teachers of those students; and at the same time these graduate students are enrolled in courses and applying what they are learning in their schools. This partnership has been a win–win for participants. It provides excellent and real experiences for the reading specialist candidates who come to class each week with new issues and ideas. It provides additional support for the struggling readers in these schools, and it provides the classroom teachers and reading specialists in the schools with opportunities to work with teachers new to the profession (see Bean et al., 1999, for a more in-depth description of this initiative). This is only one example of how schools and colleges and universities can work together to promote effective literacy instruction for students. The next section discusses guidelines for working with volunteer tutors and paraprofessionals.

Volunteers and Paraprofessionals in the Schools

Volunteers, of course, can come from many different sources: senior citizens, retired teachers, and parents, as well as college students. They can also come from the business sector or from service organizations. In the past, volunteers often did clerical work—duplicating worksheets, correcting papers—or they assisted in cafeteria or playground duty. Today, there is much more emphasis on using volunteers or paraprofessionals to assist with instruction (e.g., listening to students read orally, reviewing sight words with them, or assisting them as they write). Such volunteer programs can be informal, with parents or tutors following the lead or suggestions of teachers to whom they have been assigned, or much more formal, with volunteers or paraprofessionals serving as tutors for children experiencing difficulties or for those students needing supplemental or Tier 2 instruction in school. In the 2010 Standards for Reading Professionals (2010b), the IRA indicates these education support personnel may assist classroom teachers and reading specialists in delivering reading instruction or working with students in various literacy programs (e.g., after-school or summer programs). They may also prepare instructional materials, assist with assessment, or record keeping (p. 35).

Often, the reading specialist is responsible for recruiting, training, and directing the work of paraprofessionals and volunteers in the school. One reading specialist in a local school was responsible for directing the work of more than 17 tutors who worked with primary children in her building. She had a massive job of coordinating schedules, training these tutors, and then monitoring their work and the progress of students. Lapp, Fisher, Flood, and Frey (2003) described a tutoring program in which reading specialists trained, monitored, and supported aides who provided one-to-one instruction to struggling readers. Both training and monitoring of their work are essential to ensure they are working effectively with students, and especially struggling readers. In one Pennsylvania school, retired teachers were recruited to provide differentiated, supplemental instruction for all students in a lab setting. In this school, volunteers or paraprofessionals who had expertise as teachers were given more instructional responsibilities than less experienced individuals. In other words, although volunteers or paraprofessionals can be helpful, there is justifiable concern about using less qualified personnel to provide instruction for those who need the most help! The following guidelines may be helpful to those interested in initiating such programs in their schools.

1. *Provide adequate training for volunteers or paraprofessionals.* Wasik (1998) reported that in successful tutoring programs, reading specialists (a) trained and provided feedback to volunteer tutors, and (b) wrote and supervised lessons. In other words, tutoring programs may not be successful if careful supervision of tutors is lacking. Indeed, an unsupervised program can result in wasted time and money. On the other hand, Baker, Gersten, and Keating (2000) described a volunteer tutoring program in which community volunteers were given brief training and a broad framework from which to plan. Students in the

experimental group exhibited greater growth on several dimensions of reading, compared with students in the comparison group who received no tutoring. This study suggested that even minimally trained tutors can facilitate progress in struggling readers. The Baker and colleagues study, and a later one by Fitzgerald (2001), indicated there is much we do not know about tutoring by volunteers. The caring relationship that develops between the volunteer and student may be a key element in motivating the child to do better in school. The gains, of course, may have been greater if tutors had received intensive training. However, in instances where fiscal or logistical restrictions limit the amount of training or supervision, leaders can still develop a tutoring program that can have a positive effect on students' attitudes toward reading and their reading performance.

As mentioned earlier, the America Reads tutors who came with little or no experiences with students or with literacy instruction needed assistance in how to motivate and keep children engaged in learning. Furthermore, they benefited from a structured lesson plan to guide them in their work (Bean, Turner, & Belski, 2002). In sum, a successful volunteer tutoring program requires leadership from a knowledgeable educator—often the reading specialist—to provide training, and to monitor and evaluate the program.

THINK ABOUT THIS

What are your thoughts about using minimally trained tutors with struggling readers? As a reading specialist, how would you use paraprofessionals or volunteers in the school in which you work?

2. *Help tutors understand the school culture, school procedures, and regulations.* Many volunteer tutors have little understanding or experience with schools other than the ones they attended, often years ago! Volunteers need to be given specific information about school rules and regulations, appropriate dress, and behavior. They need assistance in understanding how to communicate with classroom teachers and to have a clear understanding of the routines and rules of the classrooms (e.g., what to do if the child is not paying attention and distracting others). Tutors appreciate the time spent on these topics; anxiety and confusion are reduced and there is greater potential for a positive relationship between school personnel and tutors. The more tutors know about their students, the better they will be able to work effectively with them.

3. *Seek input from and provide feedback to classroom teachers.* Classroom teachers can provide useful information about students and

their reading needs. They can also provide information as to whether there are changes in the student's performance as the tutoring progresses. At the same time, the classroom teacher should be informed about the tutoring, its emphasis, and given feedback as to how the student is performing in the tutoring session. Teachers may be more receptive to the tutoring, which may pull students from classroom instruction, if they have input into the tutoring plan. Or if the tutoring takes place in the classroom, the classroom teacher needs to take a leadership role in how the volunteer works with students. Classroom teachers should have occasions to meet and talk with tutors; in fact, the reading specialist may choose to work with the students while the classroom teacher meets for a brief time with tutors. Often, the classroom teachers can provide ideas to tutors about working with specific students.

4. *Monitor and evaluate the program.* The reading specialist responsible for the tutoring program should monitor the work of each tutor and determine whether a student is making progress. If there is little or no progress, changes need to be made. The reading specialist should have a system for evaluating the overall program. If the program is successful, great! But if the program is showing little in the way of results, there must be discussion about how it can be improved.

One of the criticisms of tutoring programs is that they are not aligned with the classroom instruction. This is a legitimate concern that should be addressed by those responsible for the tutoring program. In evaluating the program, the reading specialist can develop and send questionnaires to teachers and parents to determine program effects. Student outcomes can also be investigated by using formal or informal assessment measures.

WORKING WITH FAMILIES

Given the requirements in Title I regulations, many reading specialists have a special role in promoting family involvement. They have to keep parents apprised of the supplemental instruction received by students who have reading difficulties and provide suggestions for how parents can be helpful at home. Specialists may also be responsible for developing comprehensive family literacy programs for parents who may need literacy instruction.

Awareness of the importance of family involvement has generated policies and procedures at all levels of government—federal, state, and local—and has affected school programs and practices. The following sections discuss various ways in which reading specialists can work with parents and families to ensure greater literacy performance for children. First, several important guidelines are discussed:

1. *School personnel must have an understanding of and appreciation for the families whose children they serve.* In today's schools, many teachers do not live in the communities they serve, and for that reason may lack an in-depth understanding of the culture and experiences of their students. Teachers may believe children are not learning because of their backgrounds or the lack of support from home. And although the educational task may be more difficult when children do not arrive at the school door with expected literacy experiences or skills, teachers with an understanding and appreciation of the talents and experiences that children *do* bring can be more effective in working with them. Some schools have asked teachers to conduct home visits; others schedule parent conferences in neighborhood agencies that are close to children's homes (especially necessary when children are bused to schools a far distance from their homes). The reading specialist can serve as a catalyst for helping teachers gain knowledge and an understanding of and appreciation for students, their background, and their culture. As suggested by Boutte and Johnson (2014), helping teachers learn more about the culture of the families of their students provides an important bridge in establishing school–family relationships.

2. *Work with families to help them understand the school's academic and behavioral goals and expectations.* Although schools continue to communicate through written materials, others have begun to develop telephone networks or computer hotlines where parents can find information online. Furthermore, social media has also become a means of communication between schools and parents (Facebook, Twitter, blogs, etc.).

3. *Create an environment that welcomes parents into the schools.* Too many parents, especially those who themselves were not successful in school, are not comfortable going into schools. Perhaps one of the first steps is for schools and parents to plan activities jointly. Ask parents to help develop the agendas for meetings, to make suggestions about the types of activities that might be held. Parents can make presentations to classes about their professions, serve as reader of the day or week, or as supervisors on field trips. In one school, the coordinator of a special reading project developed a program in which parents were responsible for reading a book and then presenting a craft or art activity to the children. The coordinator helped parents select the book and the activity, and the teacher assisted with the lesson and any management problems. Parents were delighted with the teaching experience and the added bonus of seeing their child in the classroom context. Children were excited their mom or dad was going to teach (and other children

often acknowledged, "Billy's mom is teaching today!"). At a celebration breakfast these parents talked about their increased appreciation for the teaching profession—and the teachers of their children! (Teaching is not as easy as they thought.)

In another school, the individual responsible for federal programs held four evening meetings a year to which students brought their families. These meetings were based on a theme: for example, teachers had read *Where the Wild Things Are* by Maurice Sendak (1988), and then each class constructed a large monster drawing to be hung in the school gym. Children and parents arrived at the gym in the early evening to construct masks, to listen to another reading of the book, and to sample light refreshments. The local bookstore sent a "monster" to walk around the gym and decide which of the classes' monsters was the very best. Attendance at these events ranged from 100 to 250 participants and included parents, children and their siblings, grandparents, and interested relatives!

Results of a survey on family and school partnerships (National Center for Education Statistics, 1998) indicated parents are more likely to attend meetings if there is some possibility of interacting with their child's teachers. Parents can also serve on a school advisory team or participate in committees working to improve the school (e.g., a playground or after-school program planning committee).

4. *Parent involvement should extend through the grades.* It is true that parent involvement declines with each grade level, showing the most dramatic decrease at the point of transition into the middle grades (Billig, 2002). Nevertheless, opportunities to build parent involvement in the middle grades are available. Billig (2002) suggests that too often the communication during the middle and high school years tends to be one-way—from the school to the family—and recommends the following five guidelines for schools seeking to form strong partnerships with parents (pp. 43–45):

- Use the challenges of the middle school years to build parent involvement programs. Students will now face more demanding academics and be asked to assume more responsibility.
- Build on the need and value that adolescents place on strong relationships.
- Encourage parent and student participation in decision making. Parents and students can be involved in curriculum decisions (e.g., selection of textbooks).
- Prepare school faculty to work well with parents, how to communicate, how to report student progress, work with volunteers, and become involved with community partnerships.
- Keep families informed about what students are learning.

PRACTICAL IDEAS FOR INCREASING
PARENT INVOLVEMENT IN THE SCHOOLS

This section describes ideas for increasing parent involvement in the schools and resources that may be helpful.

1. *Create a parent involvement program that is an integral part of the school reading program.* Too often, parent involvement efforts are idiosyncratic; that is, they differ from teacher to teacher. Effective programs, however, require procedures for reflecting on what is being done and a systematic effort to involve parents in their children's educational process. This effort includes involving parents in the decision making about the plan itself (i.e., What do parents need and want?) and securing a long-term commitment to the plan on the part of teachers and parents alike. Sometimes it is necessary to educate teachers about how to work effectively with families; often, it means rethinking what parent involvement entails in a specific school or community. In other words, teachers, administrators, and reading specialists should decide as a group what means will be used to communicate with and inform parents. Such a plan may include ideas for formal events such as parent workshops or conferences. It may include ideas for communicating with parents on a regular basis about the accomplishments of their children. The plan may also indicate who is responsible for the various activities (e.g., the reading specialist will plan a meeting that provides suggestions for parents on how they can help their children become better readers, all teachers will send home a "positive" note to parents at least once a semester).

2. *Take every opportunity to communicate with parents, and use many different approaches to communication.* Effective teachers have always reinforced the positive. They send home notes telling parents what their child has done well, reinforce a child's behavior with stickers or a certificate, or even call parents to tell them how "Johnny made my day." In today's world, technology can be used to communicate with parents. One kindergarten teacher created a photograph album of her class, with digital pictures and a caption dictated by the child. At the end of the year, this teacher held a kindergarten graduation at which she showed these photos to the attending parents. Each parent also received a copy of the album. Student success was celebrated! This teacher had no difficulty with parent attendance. She also communicated on a weekly basis with parents, sending a letter that told them what students had learned that week and how parents could reinforce the learning. Other teachers communicate via e-mail messages; some have cell phones, and parents are told that they can call a designated number at a specific time to raise questions or address concerns. Schools are using social media,

such as Facebook and texting, to a much greater extent as a means of reaching families.

In addition to the individual efforts of teachers, there should be a systematic plan for communicating with parents, K–12. Newsletters and bulletins are useful, especially if they include many practical ideas for parents. Some schools send home a calendar over the summer suggesting daily or weekly literacy activities for children.

Reading specialists can develop their own material to send home to parents, or they can select from material that is available. For example, they can provide a handout for parents with tips about reading to their children (specific suggestions can be found on the website of the Keystone State Reading Association (*www.ksra.org*). Encourage families to use the community library to obtain books or suggest book titles their children might enjoy; in the position statement on leisure reading (IRA, 2012–2013), many sources to identify books for children at all ages are listed (e.g., Teachers' Choices Reading List: *www.reading.org/resources/booklists/teacherschoices.aspx*).

In one community, foundations provided support to place large billboards near major highways, displaying a picture of a mother reading to her young child. The goal was to generate awareness of the importance of reading and to motivate families to read to their children.

Reading specialists can develop and hold workshops and meetings, increasing parents' understanding of how important they are to the literacy learning of their children. Ideas about how to help children develop a love of reading and providing an environment that encourages reading can be shared. Parents can be given specific ideas about how to read effectively to their children and how to listen to their children read to them.

3. *Provide training that improves teachers' ability to talk or confer with parents.* Some "do's and don'ts" follow:

- Be prepared. Have examples of student work easily at hand so that parents can be shown what their child can and cannot do. As noted, it is important to talk about what the child *can* do and to emphasize the positive.
- Establish a friendly but professional atmosphere in the conference. It is preferable for the teacher or reading specialist to avoid sitting behind his or her desk; a table is more welcoming and still provides the surface area for various materials and work samples.
- Talk only about the child and what he or she can do. Do not compare the child to other children in the classroom.
- Be a good listener. Educators learn so much more if they listen and seek information from parents about their children (what they enjoy in school, how they feel about school or specific subjects, what might motivate them to read, any health or emotional issues).

Their comments will enhance teachers' understanding of children and parental expectations of them.

• Refrain from using school talk or jargon. Parents may not be familiar with terms such as *phonemic* or *phonological awareness*, *fluency*, or *concepts about print*. It is best to *show* parents what is challenging their child.

SUMMARY

This chapter discussed the rationale for building partnerships with communities and families, and described various ways in which reading specialists can work to build relationships with community agencies including preschool providers, universities, libraries, those who offer supplemental programs for students, and volunteers. In addition, the importance of parents' involvement and ways of enhancing that involvement in their children's education were discussed.

ADDITIONAL READINGS

Funds of Knowledge (*www.youtube.com/watch?v=PO3gmPxnPuc*).—A middle school teacher talks about her students, who they are, and what they bring to the learning environment. A thoughtful video to view and discuss.
International Reading Association. (2012–2013). *Leisure reading: A position statement.* Newark, DE: Author.—Discusses the importance of leisure reading and the positive relationship between such reading and student literacy learning. Makes suggestions about how to increase leisure reading in and out of school. Identifies resources for learning more about materials for leisure reading.

Reflections

1. Why would some parents feel uncomfortable about meeting with a teacher? How could this discomfort be alleviated?
2. What activities and programs does your local library offer that enhance reading performance of students in the school? How could your school partner with the local library?

Activities

1. Develop a friendly newsletter for parents that provides them with ideas about how they can work effectively with their children. The newsletter can be one for

parents of students in a specific age group (i.e., preschool, primary, intermediate, middle school, or secondary).

2. Using the guidelines in this chapter, practice holding a conference with a parent, using one of the scenarios described below. Role-play in threes: one person is the family member, the other is the teacher or reading specialist, and the third is the observer who provides feedback about the conference.

Scenario 1: Sally. Sally's mom is concerned about her daughter's performance in school. She does not understand why Sally is receiving help from the reading specialist. Sally is a fourth grader at an urban elementary school. She is coming to the reading specialist because she is having difficulty in her social studies and science classes. She received all A's in reading and spelling in grades 1, 2, and 3, but this year she seems to be having trouble with her content subjects. She complains to her mom that she can read the words but she does not know what they mean, and that when she gets to the end of a passage or chapter, she cannot remember anything she has read.

Sally, an only child, has always lived with her mother and grandmother, who both work. Finances are limited, and Sally has not had many opportunities that might enrich her literacy background. Although her caregivers have taken her to the museum, the local zoo, and so on, time is limited (given their work schedules). There are few books in the home, and although the mother indicates that she would love to read to Sally, she is tired at the end of the day, and somehow there never seems to be time. Sally has good health; she wears glasses (although she forgets them much of the time). She loves school and her teachers (except for the social studies teacher—who keeps asking her difficult questions). She also loves books—especially storybooks. She hates her content subjects, though, because "everything is just too hard" (or so she tells her mom). She has always received praise from her reading teachers for her excellent reading; she loves to read orally, and with expression. She cannot understand why she is unable to comprehend her new books in fourth grade.

Scenario 2: Henry. Henry's parents have come for a consultation about Henry's poor grades. They are eager to help him. Henry is a ninth-grade student at a suburban high school. He is getting D's and F's in courses such as American literature and history. He does fairly well in algebra and biology. Henry moved to this high school from a small rural school this past year. He had always been an average student in school. He knows that he is a slow reader and often has difficulty figuring out the words. Once he knows the words, he realizes that he does know the meaning. Henry does not read much, but when he does read, he chooses material about dog care (he has a Labrador retriever that he trains) or magazines dealing with the outdoors. He cannot remember reading a book that was not required reading. Henry likes classes where he does not have to read much—and he hates to write. (His handwriting is slow and laborious.) He does love working on the computer, though, and his parents have agreed to get one (he is really excited about that). Math is his favorite subject, and he likes science too (especially biology).

Henry is the oldest boy of four children (he has an older sister and younger twin brothers). All of his siblings are excellent readers, and Henry realizes that he is the one who has the most difficulty in school. His parents try to help him with his schoolwork, but he does not like to bother them because they have lots of things to do with his younger brothers. The family is very supportive of all the children. Henry has decided to go out for the track team, and he knows that his family will attend all of the games.

Henry has good vision and hearing. He had one serious illness in second grade, when he missed a great deal of school and was tutored at home for almost 3 months. Since that time, he has not had any difficulty with his health. He has always had difficulty with reading, especially after his return to school in second grade.

CHAPTER ELEVEN

Writing Proposals

Key Questions

- In what ways can externally funded grants have a positive effect on the school's literacy program?
- What are some general guidelines to consider when writing a proposal or grant application?

In this chapter, general guidelines for writing a proposal are described followed by a discussion of the elements of a good proposal. Suggestions are given for developing each aspect of a proposal. Proposals can be written for many reasons:

- The fifth-grade teachers want to apply for a mini-grant to support a special unit on diversity in which students conduct interviews and write oral histories of local citizens. Teachers want funding to purchase additional books for their classrooms and for digital voice recorders for note taking.
- The superintendent is excited about obtaining additional funds from the state to develop a summer school for struggling readers.
- The Title I proposal is due soon, and a reading specialist has the responsibility for writing it.
- There is an opportunity to obtain funds from a local foundation to upgrade computers in the school, if the proposal includes information about how computers will be integrated into classroom instruction.
- The reading specialist wants to apply for funding from a professional organization to conduct an action research project about the effects of a student book club for adolescent boys on their literacy learning.

There are many different reasons for writing a proposal and many sources of funding. So, even if you have never written a proposal or have some hesitations about your ability to write one, take that first step. Once you receive your first grant award, you'll begin looking for funding sources and grants that may be just right for you and your school district. Grant writing can become contagious! Moreover, grant writing is an opportunity to participate in meaningful professional learning.

In today's world, there are many opportunities for obtaining additional funds to support the efforts of schools. Moreover, with the reduction in funds from local, state, and federal levels resulting in budget cuts for schools, grant monies provide resources to support great ideas for improving literacy instruction. But not many small school districts have a designated grant writer; so, often a faculty member gets that assignment. For example, the reading specialists in schools may be required to write proposals to obtain Title I funds, special state funding, or foundation grants. Reading specialists may also take the initiative and write a proposal because they see the possibility of improving the reading program with additional support. There are many different types of proposals, and requirements differ. For example, some research or governmental proposals often require lengthy submissions; some require a review of literature and research that supports the plan, while others may ask for a comprehensive needs analysis as well as other data supporting the request. On the other hand, some proposal applications for obtaining materials or developing a special program may require only the rationale, the plan for use or implementation, and a budget. In fact, there are times when funding is a result of a positive relationship between you and the grant giver (a colleague of mine tells about receiving initial funding as a result of a conversation with a seatmate on an airplane). Generally, proposals have some characteristics in common, however.

GENERAL GUIDELINES FOR PROPOSAL WRITING

1. *Develop a great idea!* No matter how well written or how elaborate a proposal is, without a great idea, it will probably not generate support from funding agencies. Reviewers look for ideas that address an important issue, are creative, and well developed. For example, if there is concern about the fact that primary students are regressing in their reading performance over the summer, coming up with a creative idea for motivating children and families to read over the summer may be the key to obtaining funds from a local foundation. Or, a secondary reading specialist may want to purchase novels supporting a specific unit being taught in a content field (e.g., study of the Civil War in history class).

Some school districts may want to develop a video to be used in explaining their literacy program to the community as a means of enhancing school–community relationships.

Just as authors recognize the importance of writing about a topic well known to them, so too do great ideas for grants come from immersion in the work being considered for funding. The content or ideas in a proposal should be based on reading specialists' expertise, interests, and knowledge of the field (i.e., what has been done and what has worked). Often these ideas come from discussions with colleagues, attendance at a conference, or from reading an article in a professional journal. At other times, ideas come from an identified need in the school (e.g., more parental involvement, greater number of multicultural books in the school library, a Saturday school for struggling readers, increased numbers of electronic tablets for struggling middle school readers to increase motivation to read and write).

2. *Work with others to develop the idea.* There are times when one individual will provide the impetus for moving forward and writing a grant; however, the best ideas generally come about when several individuals collaborate and talk about the idea and how it can be elaborated upon in a proposal. Moreover, most grants will require implementation at a grade or school level. So, by working collaboratively with others, the grant writer can help to establish group ownership and excitement about the upcoming work. To the extent possible, form a team of individuals who can work with you to think about the idea and what it means. You may do the writing, but including colleagues who are excited about the possibility of a new project is important during the writing process and even more important when the grant is funded. Individuals may not appreciate being told about a specific project at the time of its inception.

3. *Address your needs and locate a good match.* Identifying district or school needs is a critical step (e.g., Should the focus of a grant be elementary? Secondary? Should it address the need to improve literacy instruction in the academic disciplines?). Once the need has been identified, sources for grants can be located. Funds may be available from federal, state, or local agencies; corporate foundations; or private foundations. A reading specialist seeking funds to undertake a specific project must locate funders whose priorities match the proposed activities or initiative. The reading specialist would not, for example, send a proposal for a professional development project to a funding agency that indicates they are seeking proposals for summer programs for children. You would be wasting your time and theirs! The goal is to locate a funding source that addresses the needs your district has identified.

Several useful resources are available for those writing proposals to seek additional funds to support their efforts:

- *Grant Writing for Teachers and Administrators* by Bruce Sliger (2009)
- *Grant Writing for Dummies* by B. A. Browning (2014)
- *www.k12grants.org/tips* (provides tips for writing grants)
- *Grants for K–12 Hotline* (biweekly report published by Quinlan Publishing Group, Boston)
- *www.schoolgrants.org*
- *Grants for Teachers* (*www.grantwrangler.com*)

Often, reading specialists are encouraged by school leadership to write proposals for grants available from the state because the state department of education has monies they can allocate to districts. For example, a state may receive federal funds they can allocate to districts that submit successful applications. Recently, in Pennsylvania, over 50 districts that submitted extensive applications to the State Department of Education received multiple-year funding to participate in a comprehensive literacy initiative, PreK–12 (Striving Readers). Applications were reviewed and decisions made based on district need and capacity to implement project activities. At times, a local foundation may encourage school districts to write a proposal for funding (e.g., support for additional after-school programming for students in a high-poverty school who need additional literacy support). Reading specialists who have grant-writing responsibilities may find the book *Getting the Grant: How Educators Can Write Winning Proposals and Manage Successful Projects* (Gajda & Tulikangas, 2005) a useful resource.

4. *Proposal should be well written.* This is, of course, easy to say but more difficult to do. Funders do not look favorably on proposals that have grammatical errors or are difficult to read (e.g., they are difficult to follow or lack meaningful transitions between parts). The following tips may be helpful in thinking about this guideline:

- Use the terminology and organization suggested in the proposal application. If the application calls for a discussion of *objectives* followed by a plan *of implementation*, use those terms to identify those two sections of the proposal. If the application requires two specific types of evaluation (e.g., formative and summative), write the proposal to address those two dimensions. This is a place where creativity may count against the writer!
- Stay away from buzz words and avoid acronyms. Don't assume that reviewers understand educational language (e.g., CCSS, RTI). Explain what you mean by providing examples.

- Follow the rules and address all questions. The submission should not have more than the required number of pages, it should arrive on or before the designated closing date, display the appropriate font size, and so on. The writer also needs to address the priorities mentioned in the proposal. If the funding is being offered for students who have been identified as living in high-poverty areas, receiving a proposal in which the population of students does not qualify as such will immediately disqualify it from consideration by the funding agency. Answer all questions asked in the application proposal. In a recent application, writers were asked to indicate how their project was aligned with the CCSS. For some proposals, the reviewing is done anonymously; thus, the writer's name and district should not be included in the application being submitted. Also, proposals being submitted will need signatures from the superintendent or another school official.

5. *Talk to funders.* It is appropriate to call and ask questions of those who want to fund proposals. After all, they have put out a call, wanting to give funds to worthy recipients. Generally, they are more than willing to answer questions about the proposal before the closing date. Grant writers should feel free to call or e-mail the funder to discuss their ideas or to raise questions about the proposal application itself. If there is a preproposal meeting scheduled for potential writers, it would be beneficial to attend those sessions. In one instance, I was able to collaborate with two educators from other universities in writing a professional development proposal,because we had all attended the preproposal session and had an opportunity to sit and talk about our ideas.

6. *Solicit feedback.* Writing is a lonely task and, too often, writers think that what they have written is very clear! Soliciting feedback from a colleague is an excellent way to determine whether the content makes sense, whether there is enough detail, and whether there are any technical problems with the writing. The goal is to obtain constructive feedback based on a thoughtful, critical evaluation. Although it is not easy to have one's work criticized, I have found (most of the time) that reviewers can help you see where you have been unclear or where you can make some changes to strengthen the argument you are trying to make. So, be willing to make your work public as a means of writing a strong proposal.

7. *Use effective formatting.* Although a great idea is very important, even it can lose its luster in a poorly formatted presentation. A

well-formatted proposal containing a great idea catches the eye and the mind of reviewers. Providing a table of contents and using section headings that guide the reader are important techniques to use. Likewise, use bold, italic, or underlining to highlight the important ideas. Graphics can help to clarify or embellish points made in the narrative text. Sometimes a figure or table can make your point stand out for the reviewer (e.g., table identifying the numbers of English learners in your school at each of the grade levels and their scores on a literacy assessment measure to illustrate the need for funding for a special program for these learners).

8. *Become familiar with the review criteria.* Proposal guidelines often include the criteria for proposal review (e.g., indicating the number of points designated for each section). A smart proposal writer makes certain that each criterion is addressed and emphasizes the sections that are worth a significant number of points.

ELEMENTS OF A PROPOSAL

Most proposals require each of the elements or parts discussed below. When preparing to write a proposal, read all of the proposal guidelines, and then, after writing various sections, reread the guidelines again to determine whether each of the elements has been clearly addressed. You can find samples of successful proposals at *www.k12grants.org*. At the end of this chapter is a short proposal written by a graduate student for a course assignment (see Figure 11.1). It illustrates many of the elements discussed below, although a few differences exist because the writer followed the guidelines of the funding agency.

Goals and Objectives

Although some other elements may not be required in a specific proposal application, all proposals require statements of goals or objectives for the potential project or program. In some proposals, only broad goals are required (e.g., increase teachers' use of digital tools for teaching reading). In other applications, however, the writer must write objectives that indicate specifically what is going to change and by how much and when:

> By the end of 5 years, we will improve the average comprehension performance of Title I students from 30 normal curve equivalents to 50.

Review of Literature

Not all proposals call for a review of the literature; the funding source, the amount of funding offered, and the type of proposal (e.g., research) are the common determinants of this component. When there is a requirement for such a review, identify the relevant and current literature that (1) supports the need for the project being described, and (2) summarizes what is known to date about the proposed issue or project. For example, if a reading specialist wants to develop a project for working with preschool providers, a review of literature about the importance of early learning for young students and its impact on later reading achievement would be helpful to proposal reviewers. Such literature should include information about the need for additional knowledge in this area. The sample proposal in Figure 11.1 contains no literature review because such a review was not required. However, the writer does use research to introduce her project and highlight its importance, given research evidence about the need for exposing young children to informational text.

Project Activities or Methods

In some proposal applications, this section is referred to as the design of the project. It is here the writer explains what he or she plans to do. The activities or design must relate to the identified objectives or goals, and there must be clear evidence the plan will enable the school to reach those goals. Readers of the proposal should know exactly what will be done, when, and how. Examples are critical—let the readers know, by example, what will occur. Described below is an example of part of a methods section:

> We plan to work with preschool providers in two ways. First, we will invite them to visit our kindergartens and then participate in a 2-hour discussion with the kindergarten teachers. Second, kindergarten teachers will visit the preschool programs and, again, participate in a 2-hour discussion. Our expectation is that participants will have opportunities to address issues such as the following: What are the literacy expectations and standards in kindergarten and in what ways can preschool teachers prepare students for their kindergarten experience?; What experiences and activities are currently occurring in preschool programs, and how do they address the literacy needs of students?

Creating a time line for various activities is helpful not only to readers but also to the writer to identify exactly how and when each project or activity will be implemented. Again, graphics or visuals can aid readers in understanding the plan of operation.

Personnel

Funders want to know who will work on the project and what skills and experiences they have to enable them to accomplish the planned work. So, for example, if the reading specialist writing the proposal cited above has taught in a preschool or has already implemented such a program in another district, this experience should be described. Providing specifics about qualifications helps to assure funders that there is the expertise necessary to undertake the project. Likewise, the application may call for an iteration of the resources or capabilities of the organization or institution with which the writer is affiliated. What computer resources are available to assist in data analysis? Does the institution have a testing department to assess the success of the project? Are there other personnel who might be helpful with the project (e.g., director of curriculum, librarian)?

Evaluation

Almost all proposals call for some form of evaluation indicating how the writer will determine to what extent the goals of the funded grant have been accomplished. Evaluation plans run the gamut from simple to complex. Some proposals require districts to agree to participate in specific evaluation activities, such as classroom observations and administration of specific assessment tests to be given at various times. The two types of evaluation that may be required—formative and summative—are described below.

Formative

Formative evaluation requires ongoing documentation of what occurs. This type of evaluation is often used to make midproject corrections or adjustments; in other words, to learn from what has transpired. In the preschool proposal example described above, formative evaluation might include documentation logs of various meetings (i.e., when they occurred and who attended) and evaluation forms completed by attendees indicating their level of satisfaction with the meeting.

Summative

The summative evaluation provides the results, impact, or outcomes of the project; in this case, the effects of the preschool–kindergarten project on participants (e.g., students, teachers, parents). The evaluation may also call for "deliverables"; a manual or listing of activities developed as a result of the project. Often, with summative evaluation, we think of effects as "changes" that have occurred. For example, a writer might propose the possibility of specific changes in teacher classroom practices. Likewise, various pretests and posttests can be administered to students to determine whether there are differences in reading performance, or attitudes toward reading, after the implementation of the project. Both summative and formative evaluation activities are included in Figure 11.1. In addition to documenting ongoing efforts, teachers and parents are asked to respond to a final questionnaire, and results of reading tests are used to assess the impact of the project.

Budget

All proposals require a budget (i.e., because the writer is applying for funds to do something), which can be simple or complex. For example, a budget submission may be as simple as requesting $200 to purchase books, increasing a schools' collection of literature by and about people of different ethnicities. Or, as in the proposal in Figure 11.1, the budget may be somewhat more complex, given the writer had to identify costs for staff development in addition to hiring substitute teachers to cover classrooms while teachers attended meetings. Large proposals may require budgets including costs for personnel, supplies, materials, travel, and so on. In some instances, the writer must include indirect or overhead costs; that is, the amount the institution will charge for housing the grant. This item covers such necessities as lighting, office space, and computer accessibility. Generally, in a school context, the school district or institution has a specific amount or percentage identified. Sometimes the funding agency supplies a ceiling amount or indicates they do not pay overhead costs at all. Often this is the case with foundations. Finally, always note what the grant will and will not fund with grant monies (e.g., teacher salaries, refreshments).

Dissemination Plan

Some proposals require that writers discuss how they will share the information they learn with others. Writers might indicate that they will present at conferences, write papers, or produce a deliverable to be distributed to various institutions and educators.

Continuation or Sustainability Plans

Although not always a required part of a proposal application, many funding agencies (especially foundations) ask for continuation plans because they are interested in the sustainability of various projects. Can they be assured that if they provide monies for a special project, such as a summer program, that the institution will then find a way to continue such an effort? Will grant activities be integrated into the curriculum or instruction? Often, funders are discouraged that projects are disbanded as soon as the funding is gone. In the Striving Readers grant in Pennsylvania, districts were required to write about the ways in which they would sustain their literacy efforts.

Abstract

The all-important abstract, which is the beginning of the proposal submission, is best written after the writing is complete. Only now is the writer ready to summarize, in a few lucid paragraphs, exactly what the plans are. The abstract must catch the reader's eye (the value of a first impression) and identify the goals and activities of the proposed plan succinctly and clearly. It may also include an overview of the evaluation approaches.

SOURCES FOR FUNDING

Locating the right funding agency is important. Many different sources of funding can be investigated to determine whether various grant possibilities exist. Generally, the education department in the state posts announcements about various state or federal funding possibilities on its website; they may also list grants available from various foundations or corporations for specific issues (e.g., community projects, library work, family literacy). Newsletters and websites of various professional organizations are also excellent sources for obtaining information about support (e.g., Association for Supervision and Curriculum Development, International Literacy Association [formerly the International Reading Association], National Council of Teachers of English). Local and national foundations often have calls for proposals on websites; foundation directories describing goals and purposes of these philanthropic organizations are also available. Some local foundations provide mini-grants opportunities for teachers. These grants generally provide smaller amounts of money ($1,000–$5,000), but they provide opportunities for teachers to generate unique and creative ideas to promote student learning. The Grant Idea Grants, a program of the Consortium for Public Education, for example, has supported mini-grants that take advantage of partnerships with other schools or community groups, increase collaborative learning with interdisciplinary teaching, or use nontraditional techniques or community resources.

One of the best ways to seek funding is to work collaboratively with another institution in the area, such as a local university, library, or community agency. Funding agencies look favorably upon such collaborative efforts because the unique contributions made by each partner strengthen a proposal. For example, a university can assist in the evaluation of a project designed by a school district. Or the school district and library can work together to design a summer reading program for struggling readers.

REJECTION

A chapter on proposal writing should not end on a negative note. However, the reality is that not all proposals are funded. All of us who have written proposals have most likely received one or more rejection notices. Another reality, however, is that the key to getting a project funded is to write *and* submit a proposal! Furthermore, rejection notices can be very helpful. Reviewers' comments can be used to rewrite and resubmit— either in a different funding cycle or to a different funding agency. The second time around can be successful! Moreover, writing the proposal enables the writer to cultivate a relationship with the funding agency, increasing the potential for later success.

SUMMARY

This chapter discussed reasons why the reading specialist may be involved in proposal writing. Guidelines for writing proposals and the various elements of a proposal were then described.

ADDITIONAL READING

Jakob, E., Porter, A., Podos, J., Braun, B., Johnson, N., & Vessey, S. (2010, December). How to fail in grant writing. Retrieved from *http://chronicle. com/article/How-to-Fail-in-Grant-Writing/125620/*—A humorous collection of tips about what not to do when writing grant applications.

Reflections

What opportunities to become involved with proposal writing are available to you in your current position? What grants has your school received, for what, and from what agencies? What have the evaluation requirements in those grants required of your school?

Activities

1. Go to your state's department of education website. Locate available grant possibilities to see what is being funded at the state level. Read one of the request for proposals (RFPs) and compare its elements with those described in this chapter. Be prepared to discuss what you learned with colleagues.

2. Interview someone who writes proposals to get his or her ideas about what it takes to write a successful one. Be prepared to discuss what you learned in class or with your colleagues.

3. Locate several proposals that have been submitted and critique them, using the ideas in this chapter (i.e., elements of a successful proposal).

4. Review the proposal in Figure 11.1 and discuss each of its features with your colleagues or classmates.

READING INFORMATIONAL TEXTS IN PRIMARY CLASSROOMS

Mission Statement:

We believe each person has value and the capability to achieve success. Through the commitment of a quality staff and the partnership with home and community, the mission of the Green Valley School District is to educate all students to ethically meet the challenges of a global society through positive life–role performances (Green Valley School District Strategic Plan, 2000).

Introduction:

According to Duke (2000), "In this Informational Age the importance of being able to read and write informational texts critically and well cannot be overstated. Informational literacy is central to success, and even survival, in schooling, the workplace and the community" (p. 213). Typically in today's classrooms, children are not given the opportunity to explore informational/nonfiction literature until the second- or third-grade year. This omission leaves a lapse of 7 to 8 years during which children are not exposed to this type of literature. Upon entering high school and throughout their lives, most of what these children will be reading and writing is informational text. More often than not, adults read material such as newspapers, magazines, manuals, recipes, menus, directions, and brochures far more frequently than a book of fictional literature. For this reason, children should be given the opportunity to see and read informational literature as another genre available to them before they reach high school age. As a representative of Madison Primary School in the Green Valley School District, I propose to create a program that supplies the classroom libraries of our primary school teachers with informational/nonfiction literature. This literature will be available for children in kindergarten through grade 3 to take home and read independently or with family members and to supplement the content area instruction provided in the classroom.

    I am asking the Literacy Link Foundation to become a part of this project to introduce a new literature genre to our young children by donating funds to purchase books, magazines, and other necessary materials to be placed in every classroom library in Madison Primary School. As a sponsor, the Literacy Link Foundation will assist this district's educators in helping the students become knowledgeable and productive citizens through the introduction of and exposure to informational/ nonfiction text. Through the early introduction of this type of text, our students will be better prepared to comprehend the informational literature they will be expected to read throughout their adult lives.

Goals of Project:

The goals and purpose of this program are to

- Expose primary school children to informational/nonfiction literature in their classrooms.
- Encourage the reading of informational/nonfiction literature by primary school children.
- Support primary classroom teachers in their content area instruction.

FIGURE 11.1. An example of a brief proposal. Reprinted with permission from Marsha Turner, Literacy Coach, Ionia Public Schools, Ionia, Michigan.

The goals of this program correlate directly with the mission of the Literacy Link Foundation by providing quality learning opportunities to children at a time in their lives when this opportunity is not usually given.

The educators responsible for achieving the success of these goals and objectives are part of a district comprised of 95 professionals with an average of 15 years teaching experience. In this group, 33% has received a master's degree, and 1% has received a doctorate degree. At Madison Primary School, 354 students are guided by 18 teachers, two reading specialists, and one principal. Each member of this teaching community feels this program would be an added benefit to those attending school in the Green Valley School District. The mission of the district is met by partnering quality staff with family and community members to give each student the capability to succeed within the challenges of a global society. By exposing children to the genre of literature they will be expected to read and understand in their adult lives, this program will improve their chance of success as they develop into knowledgeable and productive citizens.

Project Activities:

The following activities will support each of the three goals listed above:

- All teachers at Madison Primary School will introduce and read aloud to their classes at least two informational/nonfiction books each month.
  1. The teachers will select two books to be read to their classes each month.
  2. Planning for the reading of the selected books will involve writing them in their weekly lesson plans.
  3. The principal will verify that the books to be read are included in the weekly plans.
  4. Teachers will maintain a list of books read to their classes.
- Each classroom will receive copies of informational/nonfiction literature equal to the number of students in the classroom.
  1. By September 1 of each school year, a box for donated books will be placed in the libraries of the upper elementary and middle schools to be given to the primary classrooms.
  2. With book fair profits (a book fair is held each year in March), each teacher will select $25 worth of informational/nonfiction literature to be placed in his or her classroom libraries (district contribution).
  3. Grant funds received will be used to purchase informational/nonfiction literature for each classroom (purchase to be completed by August 1).
- Each child will be required to read at least two informational/nonfiction books each month.
  1. Beginning the second week of school, the classroom teacher or school reading specialist will place one informational/nonfiction book in each child's "Book-in-a-Bag," to be read every 2 weeks.
  2. A classroom chart is maintained with titles of the books read by each child.
- Each classroom teacher will offer an incentive for each child to meet the above objective.
  1. Incentives for reading two informational/nonfiction books each month will become part of the classroom behavior incentive.

FIGURE 11.1. (*continued*)

2. The classroom teacher will give stickers or awards if the objective is met each month (actual reward is at the discretion of the teacher).

- The reading specialist will offer at least one staff development course to each grade level, to focus on using informational/nonfiction literature in the classroom.
   1. The reading specialist will gather instructional methods/materials to be used by the classroom teachers. (Topics to be discussed the following school year must be submitted to the principal or reading specialist by June 1.)
   2. The reading specialist will present the content area materials at a staff development class to be held in August or September of each year.
- All reading specialists employed at Madison Primary School will assist their assigned classroom teachers with instruction, materials, and resources needed for content area instruction.
   1. The school reading specialists will discuss available materials with their teachers (in progress).
   2. The reading specialists will provide a list of materials and resources that can be used as part of instruction (in progress).
   3. The reading specialist will model at least one whole-class lesson, emphasizing the use of informational/nonfiction literature (the total number of lessons should be decided by teacher and reading specialist).

The success of this program will rely on the following actions and processes:

- All children receiving instruction at Madison Primary School will be exposed to informational/nonfiction literature in two ways: (1) easily accessible books will be placed in the classroom library, and (2) books will be read weekly to the class by the classroom teacher.
- All children receiving instruction at Madison Primary School will be encouraged to read two informational/nonfiction books each month. The "Book-in-a-Bag" program and the monthly incentives given to those who achieve this goal will support this encouragement.
- All Madison Primary School classroom teachers will be supported by the reading staff through regular discussions, staff development courses, and the modeling of effective research-based instruction.

Evaluation:

The project will be evaluated as follows:

1. Teachers and parents will be asked to complete a questionnaire to determine the extent to which they valued this program and why.
2. All staff development meetings will include a written evaluation form in which teachers indicate their response to the activities.
3. Reading specialists will document which reading strategies and materials they have introduced in the classrooms.
4. Students' comprehension scores on the standardized reading test given at the end of the year will be compared to scores of the previous year.

FIGURE 11.1. (*continued*)

Program Budget and Narrative:

Category	Expense	Credit
Supplies	$6,044.46	
Staff Development	1,120.00	
Transportation	200.00	
Total	$7,364.46	
District Contribution		($450.00)
Grant Request Total	$6,914.46	

Supplies: Informational/nonfiction literature, as quoted by *Scholastic* and *Scholastic.com*. Include additional bookcases, as needed, for additional literature.

Staff Development: Four substitute teachers to provide coverage in classrooms while teachers meet for staff development.

Transportation: Transportation costs to collect donated materials from both the upper elementary and middle schools. Transportation costs to collect materials from *Scholastic* warehouse.

MARSHA TURNER
Literacy Coach
State and Federal Programs Teacher
Ionia Public Schools
Ionia, Michigan

FIGURE 11.1. (*continued*)

CHAPTER TWELVE

The Reading Specialist
as Lifelong Learner

Addressing Challenges and Changes

Key Questions

- In what ways can reading specialists continue their professional learning?
- When searching for a position, how can reading specialists prepare for interviews?

This chapter focuses on the reading specialist as learner, on the premise that those who stay abreast of developments in the literacy field and in education, in general, will be able to meet the challenges and changes that are sure to occur. It concludes with a section on becoming a reading specialist, providing potential reading specialists with some ideas of what to expect in reading specialist certification programs, and how they might prepare for interviews for reading specialist positions.

Marshall McLuhan once remarked about the hazards of driving "into the future using only the rearview mirror" (*www.brainyquote. com/quotes/quotes/m/marshallmc130541.html*). This statement also applies to reading specialists who have served students in schools in many different ways throughout the years—as supervisors of reading programs, remedial teachers, resource teachers, interventionists, or literacy coaches. After reading this book, it should be apparent that the roles of reading specialist vary and are greatly influenced by the contexts in which they work. Not only are the roles different but so, too, are the titles: reading specialist, literacy or instructional coach, interventionist, reading consultant, facilitator, and literacy consultant, among others. Yet the underlying goal for reading specialists remains one of promoting reading achievement for *all* students, and especially for struggling readers (IRA, 2000b). Fulfilling this goal can be accomplished in a number of ways, from delivering instruction to students to working with teachers to improve classroom instruction. Also, the role is defined by job descriptions, administrative preferences, school needs, funding, and the reading specialists' own experiences and strengths.

The chapters in this book addressed the many functions of reading specialists and also those they may be asked to accept in the future, as responsibilities and roles change. For example, many reading specialists who worked only with students are currently being asked to serve as reading or literacy coaches in their schools. The greatest challenge for reading specialists is to be prepared for changes that may occur. Indeed, change may be generated or initiated by specialists themselves, who see that they can affect student performance more effectively in new and different ways.

PROFESSIONAL LEARNING FOR READING SPECIALISTS

Professional learning for reading specialists, as for teachers, occurs in many different ways (e.g., reading professional materials, either print or via the Internet; formal participation in classes, both face-to-face and online courses; workshops held by the district or state; conferences and sessions of professional groups; networking with other reading specialists or coaches). When reading specialists spearhead professional development sessions for teachers, they learn a great deal by investigating, studying, and preparing presentations. In many schools, reading specialists may also lead or participate in study groups in which they discuss a specific book pertinent to educational concerns or goals. Participation in groups in which teachers and reading specialists discuss something they have read (e.g., *Teaching with the Common Core Standards for English Language Arts, PreK–2* by Morrow, Shanahan, & Wixson, 2014) generates new ideas and expands knowledge of pertinent topics.

Many reading specialists choose to continue their formal education by taking classes at a university or attending professional meetings. Reading specialists can also join, and become active in, one or more professional organizations; becoming a member of a network of educators involved in an organization promotes ongoing learning and sustained motivation. They may become members of their local and state reading associations as well as the International Literacy Association (formerly the IRA; *www.reading.org*), whose professional journals, website, and other resources are invaluable to practicing reading specialists. Other professional organizations that may be joined, depending on grade level or school responsibilities may include:

- American Library Association (*www.ala.org*)
- Association for Supervision and Curriculum Development (*www. ascd.org*)
- Association of Literacy Educators (*www.aleronline.org*)
- International Society for Technology in Education (*www.iste. org*)
- Learning Forward (*www.learningforward.org*)
- Literacy Research Association (*www.literacyresearchassociation.org*)
- National Association for the Education of Young Children (*www. naeyc.org*)
- National Council of Teachers of English (*www.ncte.org*)
- Association for Middle Level Education (*www.amle.org*)

In addition to attending meetings of professional groups and professional development sessions in schools, reading specialists can read professional journals and books as a means of keeping current, not only about reading instruction and assessment but to understand the political and social climate in which they work. Often, literature in a related area (e.g., leadership, school change) or even from another field (e.g., business, sociology) can provide a new way of thinking or looking at an educational issue. In addition, reports from the U.S. government or other agencies synthesizing research on various aspects of literacy can provide important information about current trends or research emphases. Important sources of information for reading specialists include the What Works Clearinghouse (*www.ies.ed.gov/ncee/wwc*) and the Center on Instruction (*www.centeroninstruction.org*). Other key reports that may be helpful to reading specialists include:

- *Report of the National Reading Panel* (National Institute of Child Health and Human Development, 2000)
- *Reading Next* (Biancarosa & Snow, 2004)
- *Adolescent Literacy* (Ippolito et al., 2012)
- *Developing Early Literacy: Report of the National Early Literacy Panel* (2008) (*www.nifl.gov*)
- *Report of the National Literacy Panel on Language Minority Children and Youth* (August & Shanahan, 2006)

Online resources provide much useful information to specialists for their own professional development. The Literacy Coaching Clearing-house (*www.literacycoachingonline.org*), originally funded by the IRA and National Council of Teachers of English, on its website provides briefs of pertinent articles, a list of published articles on topics related to reading specialists/coaches, and a number of practical tools or protocols for coaching. The websites of each professional organization also makes available position statements, articles, and reference lists useful to reading specialists; in previous chapters, many of the position statements of the IRA were cited as sources of learning about various topics.

Reading specialists and literacy coaches in the recent national study (Bean, Kern, et al., 2015) highlighted the importance of role-alike groups (e.g., network of coaches) as a means of learning. New coaches especially indicated that these networks provided an important source of learning; they were able to identify problems or issues and more experienced peers provided alternatives for next steps. Karen, in the vignette in this chapter, discusses the powerful influence her network of instructional coaches has had on her learning.

The reading specialists whose vignettes appear in "Voices from the Field" are examples of educators who are lifelong learners. All have participated in formal education to obtain advanced degrees, all attend and present at various conferences and workshops, and all are readers who keep abreast of what is occurring in their field. Most of all, they are passionate about their profession and eager to learn all they can to improve instruction for the students in their schools.

LOCAL, STATE, AND FEDERAL GUIDELINES

Educators in today's schools face many challenging and complex political and social issues. Reading specialists can advocate for students, literacy education, and for schools in which they work. To do so, they must keep current about the various school-related legislative actions and policies at local, state, and federal levels. As described in Chapter 9, NCLB (2001) and Race to the Top legislation have had a tremendous impact on schools. They have influenced the assessment tools being used, made accountability a key issue for individual teachers and for schools, and affected curriculum and instruction at all levels. Also, reading specialists can work with their professional groups to bring to the attention of legislators issues that affect literacy instruction and assessment (e.g., importance of support for preschool education, literacy coaching in schools). Moreover, because so many reading specialists are funded with monies from Title I legislation, reading specialists need to be aware of the regulations of that program and how they affect literacy instruction in schools.

Rules and regulations in each state influence literacy curriculum, assessment, and instruction at all levels. The emphasis on standards, either the CCSS, or those approved by the state, creates a need for reading specialists to be familiar with state standards so they can assist teacher colleagues in implementing an instructional program addressing those standards. Most states have websites containing resources and other information useful for developing professional development and for addressing policy initiatives.

As mentioned in Chapter 5, reading specialists should share information with teachers with whom they work. In addition to the professional development opportunities described above, one helpful source that provides an update about many trends in education is the publication *Education Week* (*www.edweek.org*). A school subscription to that resource keeps educators aware of what is happening at the national level in the field of education.

LIFELONG LEARNING: A NECESSITY FOR READING SPECIALISTS

All those who work in schools must be lifelong learners; there is always something new to learn—new materials, new approaches, and even new students! Moreover, given the many variables that affect the position of reading specialist and the changes that may occur from year to year within a school—some prescribed by legislation or school needs, others from recommendations by reading specialists themselves—reading specialists must remain lifelong learners. The ideas below may be helpful in thinking about being a lifelong learner.

Set Learning Goals

Perhaps the specialist wants to involve parents more actively in school programs or to work more closely with teachers of content; others may want to improve their knowledge of a specific topic (use of technology as a tool for improving literacy learning). Whatever the specific goal, the reading specialist can identify activities that facilitate its achievement, and set a deadline for accomplishment. Attending one or more conferences, reading several articles or books about the selected topic, and then meeting and sharing the information with teachers (e.g., possibly forming a study group) are examples of lifelong learning activities. Goals can be *personal* ones: for example, enrolling in a program to obtain literacy coaching endorsement or attending the research conference at the national meeting of the ILA to stay abreast of current research efforts. Goals can also be ones related to school efforts or needs: for example, in one middle school, there may be an effort to enhance literacy instruction across the academic disciplines, or in a primary school, the goal may be to increase teachers' understanding of the best ways to instruct ELs. In these cases, reading specialists may choose to identify professional development activities that enable them to assist teachers and other professionals in the schools to achieve those goals. Summer is often a good time to read a new book about literacy, language, or learning. It's also an excellent time to join a book club to discuss a book with other educators interested in the same topic, perhaps while sitting around the pool or in another relaxed setting.

The beginning of the school year is often a good time to set goals and they may be related to your work in a specific school. Thinking about areas in which you have been successful, where you have failed, or perhaps "new" areas to explore (e.g., digital learning) may help you set goals for the school year. You may want to identify individuals who can help you with your goals and the resources needed to accomplish them. It may be helpful to write these goals in a journal so you can review them at the end of the year.

Be Prepared to Change or Modify Past or Current Behavior

Perspectives and times change and so must we! One of the most difficult steps for all of us is to realize that we may have to give up what we have been doing if we are going to make changes that will make us more effective in our roles. Reading specialists who have always worked in a pullout setting may find it difficult to switch to working in the classroom. They may even grieve a little as they lose what they have always found to be a comfortable and rewarding approach to instruction. Grieving is fine, but it is important to *move on* and experience the rewards of the new and different. Research findings contribute to change, with new information and knowledge about literacy learning and assessment influencing how we organize schools and how we teach. Reading specialists can serve as models for teachers who may also find it necessary to modify classroom practices when confronting notions that are in conflict with their present beliefs about teaching or learning. In an earlier chapter, I wrote about the need to be nimble, that is, able to change behavior or role, given new situations or responsibilities. John F. Kennedy in an address in

Frankfurt, Germany, in 1963, made this statement: "Change is the law of life. And those who look only to the past or the present are certain to miss the future," reminding us of the inevitability of change.

Self-Recognition

All of us appreciate the rewards and recognition that come from others—the principal who commends your work with struggling readers, the parent who thanks you for the positive effect you have had on her child, or the student who leaves a note: "Mrs. Blake, you're the greatest." Similarly, reading specialists need to "pat themselves on the back" for what they have accomplished regarding their own learning. After reading a professional book on assessment approaches for classroom teachers, it may be time to reward yourself for a job well done: a special dinner, a week without any professional reading (just a good mystery), going to the gym, or perhaps buying a new pair of shoes. Whatever works for you!

See Problems as Friends

There will always be demands and problems within the school setting that need the attention of the reading specialist (e.g., working with a teacher who is hesitant to change, improving writing performance, planning a professional development program for middle school content teachers). Viewing these demands or problems as opportunities for generating active thinking, group interaction, and the possibility of new and exciting ventures is a better approach than seeing them as burdens or obstacles. Large-scale efforts involving large numbers of people will produce disagreements and questions, but as indicated by Fullan, Bertani, and Quinn (2004), productive conflict is to be expected! Being receptive and listening to divergent ideas can be helpful in solving problems and moving the school in a positive direction.

Self-Reflection

Chapter 5 discusses the importance of teacher reflection to personal learning. Likewise, reading specialists can take time to reflect on, and think about, what they have been doing, what they have learned, and what this learning means for future behavior. Recently, a teacher who had just completed a professional development experience expressed this thought: "It's more than learning a lot of strategies. It's thinking in a different way." In essence, her statement revealed that she was taking the time to reflect not only on her teaching methods—on what worked and what did not work—but also to consider the ways in which she approached teaching and learning. That reflection provided her with the impetus to seek new solutions to classroom problems. Taking the time for reflection means setting time aside, perhaps at the end of the day or the end of the week, to think about what happened and why, and the impact of that experience on future behavior. Some reading specialists and coaches keep logs as a means of self-reflection; they can then look back and think about how they allocated their time, their responses to various events, and use these written records as a means of making what they consider to be positive changes. Figure 12.1 illustrates a partial log of one elementary reading specialist. For those working as literacy coaches, the tool, Self-Assessment for Elementary Literacy Coaches (*www.literacycoachingonline.org/briefs/tools/self_assessment_for_elem_lit_coaches.pdf*), provides a framework useful for thinking about one's own skills, knowledge, and dispositions.

By being a lifelong learner, the reading specialist models for others in the school the behavior that is necessary for the school as an organization to change in order to become more effective. Leaders within a school provide the impetus for others to become lifelong learners.

BECOMING A READING SPECIALIST

When I ask those who enter the reading specialist certification program at my institution why they have chosen to do so, they often tell me that they have become curious about students in their classrooms who have reading difficulties and wonder how they can better help them to achieve. Some tell me that they feel unprepared to teach reading, given the few courses they received in their teacher preparation programs. Some want to work especially with struggling readers, whereas others are clear that they do not really want to leave the classroom; rather they want to become more proficient at teaching reading and meeting the needs of all students in their classrooms. Others are eager to work with struggling readers but have no desire to work with classroom teachers; they are hesitant to step out of their "comfort zone" to work with other adults.

These are all good reasons for entering a reading specialist preparation program. Most universities have well-developed programs that meet the standards required of their state and of the ILA (IRA, 2010b). Such programs require students to become knowledgeable about the underlying theoretical bases for literacy development and acquisition, literacy assessment and instruction, and issues related to leadership and working

Harry
What I Did Today   **Comments/Reflections**

Morning	
Pullout class of five fourth graders (using expository text; focus on "during text" understandings and inferences).	Group works well together (good discussion and thinking). Science text on reptiles worked well because of their interest; get similar text specific to snakes (they were fascinated).
Met with sixth-grade teachers to discuss results of writing samples from their classes. What can we do to improve students' ability to summarize from their reading? Teachers felt need for some "input" and were very receptive to this.	I need to check my books and do some research, get some material that they can read. What about Beers's SWBS strategy? Check her book (Beers, 2003, p. 147). Others?
Worked in classroom of fifth-grade social studies teacher; how to introduce vocabulary and set a purpose (we actually co-taught this introduction).	Sam is excited about this; he wants me to continue working with him (wonder if he would be willing to do more with small group to get kids engaged). Will discuss with him and get his ideas; what are his goals for students (important!)?
Afternoon	
Planning for workshop on differentiation of instruction for all intermediate teachers.	Yikes! I need to focus on what my goals are. What do I want teachers to know and be able to do? What are they ready to do—next steps?
Meeting with principal to go over test results (which I discussed with sixth-grade teachers this morning).	She is concerned about writing test coming up in several months. Wants me to be sure to work with these sixth-grade teachers. (I need time—and they do too!) Asked her whether the workshop on differentiation should be postponed. Should we focus on writing? Too many directions for teachers. She agreed!

FIGURE 12.1. Partial log of a reading specialist.

with others. They usually require students to participate in practica or clinical experiences in which they demonstrate that they can fulfill the requirements of the position. Most offer many practical experiences as an integral part of their programs, so that reading specialist candidates become proficient in working with struggling readers and with teachers. As completion of the program draws near, candidates begin to think about applying for positions as a reading specialist. They are curious about possible questions that they may be asked and how they can prepare for the interviews that generally are part of the application process. Questions that may be part of an interview are discussed in Appendix E. Candidates for a reading specialist position may wish to think about the questions and how they would answer them. Those in a reading specialist certification program may role-play an interview in class, using some of the questions identified there.

In addition to acquiring the knowledge and understanding needed to become a reading specialist, another important attribute of any candidate for such a position is enthusiasm. School district personnel want to employ individuals who are excited and enthusiastic about becoming a reading specialist and having the opportunity to make a difference for all the students in a school.

Before an interview, candidates for positions may want to reread the notes that they have taken in their coursework. They may also want to read several articles in which roles of reading specialists are described. At the end of each chapter, additional readings are suggested and some of these may be read to provide more in-depth information about the role of reading specialists. Several key articles that may be helpful include Bean, Swan, and Knaub (2003), in which the many roles of the reading specialist in exemplary reading programs are listed, or the Lapp and colleagues (2003) article, describing the dual role of reading specialists in an urban setting. Dole's (2004) and L'Allier and colleagues' (2010) articles, in which they discuss the coaching role of reading specialists, may also be useful. Some of the briefs available on the Literacy Coaching Clearinghouse (*www.literacycoachingonline.org*) provide specific information about aspects of the coaching role. Rereading the vignettes of the reading specialists in this book may also provide candidates with a better idea of what reading specialists might be asked to do. These reading specialists in "Voices from the Field" exhibit passion and enthusiasm for their positions, regardless of challenges or problems.

SUMMARY

This chapter described ways in which reading specialists can continue their learning and become lifelong learners. The importance of familiarity with federal, state, and local legislation was described. What reading specialist candidates might expect in a preparation program and ideas for participating in a job interview for the reading specialist position were also discussed.

ADDITIONAL READINGS

Crow, T. (2014). The pause that refreshes. *Learning Forward, 35*(3), 4.—In this
   brief editorial, Crow suggests applying a 20–20–20 exercise for reducing
   eyestrain to developing a framework to enhance reflective learning.
Dole, J. (2004). The changing role of the reading specialist in school reform.
   The Reading Teacher, 57(5), 462–471.—This article discusses the evolu-
   tion of reading specialists to reading coaches and how these professionals
   can work with teachers to enhance their learning.

Reflections

1. Which type of learning—formal or informal—is most appealing to you, given
   where you are in your professional career? How can you take advantage of the
   opportunities that are available to you?
2. Think about the ideas suggested for those who are lifelong learners. Identify
   something you want to learn, and develop a plan for doing so. Set a goal,
   develop a plan of action, set a deadline—and plan for a reward.

Activities

1. Organize a study group in which you and several others agree to read and discuss a specific article or book that addresses an issue or problem in your school
   or setting.
2. Participate in a role-play of a job interview, using the questions in Appendix E.

Some questions to think about:

What lessons can be learned about the role of the reading specialist in this vignette?

In what ways does Karen serve as a leader?

What questions come to mind after reading this vignette?

KAREN: A LIFELONG LEARNER

I am a mother of four children, and in that role, have been a teacher and coach for 30 years! However, my professional career began with an opportunity to work as a substitute teacher, teaching students in both the PreK and kindergarten classes of a Montessori school. This experience solidified my passion for teaching. After that experience I transitioned back into college and began to formally complete the course work necessary for an elementary education degree and certification. While I was working on my degree, I was offered a position as a half-day kindergarten teacher in an urban public school district. This position supported a program in which struggling students were able to attend full-day kindergarten through a regular morning session and an afternoon session in which they were with a smaller group. In this school, 99% of the students received free lunch and in 3 years only a few of my students spoke English. Throughout this time I continued my status as a full-time student and mother.

After graduating, I began to seek a full-time contracted teaching position, hoping to work in a district which aligned with my education philosophy and could support my professional goals. I was offered a position at the Exeter Township School District. I began teaching in Exeter as a sixth-grade long-term substitute and eventually was given a contract as a second-grade teacher. I taught on this grade level for 7 years. During this time I earned my masters of education degree, specializing in reading.

Three years ago I was approached by our district reading supervisor and asked to consider leaving my classroom for 1 year to assume the role of literacy coach K–6.* I respectfully declined this offer at first. There were too many unknowns! My principal returned with the reading supervisor the next day and they gave me an outline of the position and promised to allow me to return to my classroom at the end of the year. In addition, they were committed in supporting the work of the literacy coach with both administrators and teachers. I decided to push past my comfort zone and accept the position. That summer I purchased several books about coaching and researched content online to develop an understanding of this work. The realization of the enormous multitasking required with this position was evident. However, through raising four children, being a full-time student, and working as a teacher, I knew I was ready for the challenge.

Our reading supervisor clearly defined my position and I was introduced to staff on the first service day of the year. The effective communication to staff and the clarity of my position, outlined and supported by administration, were truly foundational in my future success with establishing relationships with teachers and administrators. However, I didn't know many of the facets of coaching and was thirsty for knowledge and experience from others in this field. In October 2012, during Hurricane Sandy, I traveled 3 hours to Penn State University for the Pennsylvania Institute of Instructional Coaching (PIIC) conference. I was the only attendee from our intermediate unit. However, I was so excited to learn how to begin this craft and began networking with the many professionals in attendance. PIIC was my oxygen! The leaders welcomed me and introduced me to coaches, intermediate unit (IU) mentors, and Penn Literacy Network facilitators who were happy to engage in discussion about instructional coaching. The professional development offered created a foundational understanding of my role and supported me in organizing my time and resources. To date, PIIC is the single most important resource of my work. They provide coaches with many types of resources. There is an updated website (*www.pacoaching.org*) that archives past and present PIIC resources and hosts a blog for ongoing professional dialogue. In addition, they publish and distribute a newsletter. I have been assigned a coach mentor at my local IU, through PIIC, who visits my school, provides me with support, and communicates with administrators about coaching and how it serves as an important learning experience for our teachers. Every time I attend a conference I learn more and am able to get deeper with my understanding of my work and how to best support teachers through implementing research-based literacy practices. I meet with other coaches in my IU throughout the year to engage in professional development and dialogue which supports the work at the district level. Through PIIC there is a partnership with the University of Pennsylvania graduate school, Penn Literacy Network. There is grant money available to promote research-based balanced literacy practices in all content areas. Coaches are able to bring teams of teachers and administrators to attend this course and this academic experience builds teacher capacity throughout a district.

As a coach my duties include creating and leading professional development sessions every month for three primary and one middle school. In addition to the monthly sessions, I am part of a team that creates and leads professional development for both the junior and senior high school teachers during in-service and summer flex days. I have led and worked on a team to create curriculum for English language arts and other content areas. As a coach I work with teachers one-on-one and with grade-level teams, model lessons, co-teach, plan, research, find resources, and clarify balanced literacy practices. Student data are consistently used to develop an understanding of a student's needs so we can differentiate instruction as needed. I have worked with teams to create common formative and summative assessments and how to use the results of these assessments to inform instruction. I work in both general and special education classrooms. I also work with the reading and intervention specialists at each building to plan goals using student data. My work involves multiple levels of communication with teachers and administrators in a nonevaluative manner. The primary nonnegotiable in my job is the understood confidentiality I have with our teachers.

Challenges

One of my biggest challenges is that there is only one of me. My weekly schedule is never the same. I travel between six schools and my office at the administration building. I create my schedule through teacher requests and send them a reminder that is automatically embedded into my calendar. My meetings last between 30 and 40 minutes and I create a written record of every meeting. This record includes the topic of discussion, date, time, and location of the meeting, and who is in attendance. I also record general topics of discussion, any resources requested by the teacher(s) and our next meeting date. After a meeting is complete I save these notes to my computer and immediately e-mail them to all teachers in attendance. I encourage them to file these meeting minutes in their evidence binder which supports their professional development within the teacher effectiveness rubric. This documentation serves several purposes for me. It allows me to create goals with teachers, plan, and look at the trajectory of progress throughout the year. The teacher can produce these minutes to administrators, who may inquire about their professional development with the literacy coach. Confidentiality is imperative in this work. However, there are times when teachers are explicitly told to contact me and the meeting minutes provide evidence that teachers have followed through with the directive. Because I have developed relationships with teachers and honor my promise of confidentiality, teachers feel comfortable contacting me. My weekly schedule is always full and I find little time to do the necessary office tasks to sustain my work. I freely give my cell phone number and encourage teachers to text me if they have an important question or concern. Mostly I communicate via e-mail.

Another challenge I face is to understand that my role is not to "fix" anyone or anything. I am not an educational therapist. My job is to work side by side with teachers, in a supportive, nonevaluative role, so that they can eventually successfully implement the practice independently. When I enter a classroom it is imperative to establish an understanding of goals and plan steps to successfully achieve them. This plan is never one size fits all. It is dependent on several variables that I encounter and it is always important not to overwhelm the teacher. Small steps to get to the big picture can be a challenge when working with so many different grade levels and differentiating for all levels of educators.

Success

I find success, daily, in all that I do to serve the teachers and administrators at Exeter. A positive moment can be discovered within the most challenging experiences. Teachers know I am here to serve them and their students, and my goal is to support student success in balanced literacy. Success for me is when I look at my schedule and view all of the teachers who want to consistently reflect on their practice, find ways to improve, and tirelessly continue the work so that they can guide their students to succeed. This empowers and motivates me to do my best work for them. I am the only coach at Exeter, but I am part of a team of educators who work cohesively to create the best learning opportunities for students.

Lessons Learned

- All teachers want to do their best for their students.

- Coaching success has to involve a BDA (before, during, after) cycle with the teacher. Goal setting and planning are just as important as modeling a lesson. Reflection concludes the cycle and usually ignites the beginning of the next cycle.

- Administrators are willing to listen and want to support their teachers.

- Professional development is the oxygen of successful teaching.

- Cooperative learning, for teachers and students, creates the highest level of learning.

- A coach can be the conduit within a district. He or she can communicate and share, with a teacher's permission, so many great ideas!

- CONFIDENTIALITY is important. There is NO room for judgment.

- A smile generates a feeling of ease. Laughter energizes people and becomes contagious.

- Don't run with your hands in the air and yell "Fire!" When challenges arise, be the calming agent who initiates a problem-solving plan in lieu of sharing complaints and fears.

- Trust yourself, and when in doubt be honest.

- You can't take a step in life by standing still. However, small steps may be necessary to arrive at your destination . . . be patient.

- High-stakes testing is one snapshot of the big picture.
- Encouragement can sustain the motivation of a tired teacher.
- Do not look for the opportunity to be offended.
- Serving others is an awesome way to live your life!
- Coaching involves high-energy multitasking.
- A coach is not an educational therapist.
- Oh yes, 3 years later and I am still a coach!

KAREN DIANNE DeNUNZIO, MEd
Literacy Coach
Exeter Township School District
Reading, Pennsylvania

Appendix A. **The Observation Cycle**

Teacher: _____ Grade: _____ Date: _____

PLANNING

Goals of lesson (What do you expect students to learn?):

Purpose of observation (What does teacher hope to learn? What is the focus?):

What will students be doing? (What should I expect to see? What would you like me to look for?):

_____

ANALYSIS (Key points [related to goals set by teacher])—TO BE USED FOR DISCUSSION

_____

FOLLOW-UP

Teacher:

Coach:

Appendix B. **Observation Protocol for Content-Area Instruction**

Teacher: _____ Grade Level: _____

Date: _____ Time Begin: _____ End: _____

Students Present: _____ Content Area: _____

Lesson Focus: _____

Materials: (Check all that apply)

☐ Textbook Grouping: (Check all that apply)

☐ Board/Chart ☐ Whole Class

☐ Computer ☐ Small Group

☐ Worksheet ☐ Pairs

☐ Student Work ☐ Individual

☐ Other: _____

Protocol to be used as a guide. Scale to be completed after the observation has been completed.

Scale:	Great Extent	Some Extent	Minimal Extent	Not Observed
	(4)	(3)	(2)	(1)
Classroom Environment				
Materials supporting literacy are available *Books, visuals, print and nonprint materials about topic are evident*	☐	☐	☐	☐
Provides for social interaction *Areas for small-group/partner work*	☐	☐	☐	☐
Strategies for learning are displayed *Informative, positive strategies (e.g., why and how of summarizing)*	☐	☐	☐	☐

(cont.)

Scale:	Great Extent	Some Extent	Minimal Extent	Not Observed
	(4)	(3)	(2)	(1)
Instruction				
Before Reading				
Sets purpose, makes connections, development of vocabulary	☐	☐	☐	☐
Small-group discussion	☐	☐	☐	☐
Engages in coaching/scaffolding, teacher models strategies	☐	☐	☐	☐
During Reading				
Think-alouds by teacher, connects to students' experiences, points out text features	☐	☐	☐	☐
Questioning that requires high-level thinking, engages in coaching/scaffolding	☐	☐	☐	☐
After Reading				
Small-group discussion or writing activities that require responding to text	☐	☐	☐	☐
Activities require high-level thinking	☐	☐	☐	☐
Opportunities for differentiation to meet student needs	☐	☐	☐	☐
Teacher monitors and supports student work	☐	☐	☐	☐

Scale:	Great Extent	Some Extent	Minimal Extent	Not Observed
	(4)	(3)	(2)	(1)
Classroom Climate/Engagement of Students				
High level of student participation *Students are actively engaged*	☐	☐	☐	☐
Positive learning environment *Interactions are respectful and supportive, encourages risk taking*	☐	☐	☐	☐
Students use strategies to learn *Evidence of students knowing when, how, and which strategies to use (e.g., note taking, summarizing)*	☐	☐	☐	☐
Students show evidence of being able to think about their own learning *Provide justification for thinking, evidence of being able to organize own learning*	☐	☐	☐	☐

Notes:

Appendix C. **Sample Observation Form**

Teacher's name: _____ Grade Level: _____ Date: _____

Start time: _____ **End time:** _____ **Number of students:** _____

Focus of lesson: _____

Grouping: Whole class _____ **Small group** _____ **Individual** _____

Overall impressions of environment:

Teacher	Students

Appendix D. Aligning Curriculum to the CCSS

Animals

Unit Goals – Stage 1

Unit Description: *Students will expand their understanding of animals.* Students will read multiple informational texts to gain the knowledge needed to identify similarities and differences in the characteristics and needs of animals. Students will continue to write quality sentences through observational comment writing with a focus on informative/explanatory writing.

Approximate Duration: 5 Weeks

Transfer Goals

Students will be increasingly able to independently use their learning to….
- Read closely and analytically to comprehend a range of increasingly complex literary and informational text. (Claim 1)
- Produce effective and well-grounded writing for a range of purposes and audiences. (Claim 2)
- Employ effective speaking and listening skills for a range of purposes and audiences. (Claim 3)
- Engage in research and inquiry to investigate topics, and to analyze, integrate, and present information. (Claim 4)

Making Meaning

CCR Anchor Standards:	UNDERSTANDINGS	ESSENTIAL QUESTIONS
R.CCR.1 Read closely to determine what the text says explicitly and to make logical inferences from it; cite specific textual evidence when writing or speaking to support conclusions drawn from the text.	**Students will understand that…**	**Students will keep considering…**
R.CCR.2 Determine central ideas or theme of a text and analyze their development; summarize the key supporting details and ideas.	• Animals can be classified according to a variety of attributes.	1. How can animals be classified?
R.CCR.3 Analyze how and why individuals, events, and ideas develop and interact over the course of a text.	• Informative/explanatory writing names a topic, supplies facts and provides some sense of closure.	2. How I can gather information from sources to include facts in my writing?
R.CCR.5 Analyze the structure of texts, including how specific sentences, paragraphs, and larger portions of the text relate to each other and the whole.	• Reading more than one text on a particular topic can provide additional information and deepen our understanding.	3. How does the additional information in this text add to my knowledge on this topic?
R.CCR.6 Assess how point of view or purpose shapes the content and style of a text.	• Various text features such as headings, table of contents, bolded words, captions, and photographs can be used to locate key facts and information in nonfiction texts.	4. How can I use various text features to locate information?
R.CCR.7 Integrate and evaluate content presented in diverse media and formats, including visually and quantitatively, as well as in words.	• Knowledge and understanding is built through asking and answering questions about key details in text read aloud or information presented.	5. How can I show I understand what I read, hear and/or see by asking and answering questions?
R.CCR.10 Read and comprehend complex literary and informational texts independently and proficiently.		
W.CCR.2 Write informative/explanatory texts to examine and convey complex ideas and information clearly and accurately through the effective selection, organization, and analysis of content.		
W.CCR.8 Gather relevant information from multiple print and digital sources, assess the credibility and accuracy of each source, and integrate the information while avoiding plagiarism.		
SL.CCR.1 Prepare for and participate effectively in a range of conversations and collaborations with diverse partners, building on others' ideas and expressing their own clearly and persuasively.		
SL.CCR.5 Make strategic use of digital media and visual displays of data to express information and enhance understanding of presentations.		
L.CCR.1 Demonstrate command of the conventions of standard English grammar and usage when writing or speaking.		
L.CCR.2 Demonstrate command of the conventions of standard English capitalization, punctuation, and spelling when writing.		
L.CCR.6 Acquire and use accurately a range of general academic and domain-specific words and phrases sufficient for reading, writing, speaking, and listening at the college and career readiness level; demonstrate independence in gathering vocabulary knowledge when encountering an unknown term important to comprehension or expression.		

Acquisition

Knowledge	Skills
Students will know…	**Students will be skilled at (Do)**
• Vocabulary: survive, shelter, space, energy, protection, classify, group, habitat	• Classifying animals based on specific criteria
• The four basic classifications of animals (mammal, bird, reptile, insect)	• Writing informative/explanatory pieces
• Elements of informative/explanatory writing	• Building knowledge through asking questions about information
• To ask and answer questions to show understanding of information	• Determining if a text is fiction or nonfiction
• Characteristics of nonfiction text	• Identifying nonfiction text features

Partial example from the Long Beach School District. Reprinted with permission from Long Beach Unified School District. Created by Lisa Worsham, Nicole Jackson, Jenny Spicer, Amy Love, and Shayla Brown.

Grade Level Standards – Stage 1

Reading	Writing	Speaking and Listening	Language
Literature	**Text type**	**Comprehension and Collaboration**	**Conventions**
RL.1.1 Ask and answer questions about key details in a text.	W.1.2 Write informative/explanatory texts in which they name a topic, supply some facts about the topic, and provide some sense of closure.	SL.1.1 Participate in collaborative conversations with diverse partners about grade 1 topics and texts with peers and adults in small and larger groups.	L.1.1 Demonstrate command of the conventions of standard English grammar and usage when writing or speaking.
RL.1.5 Explain major differences between books that tell stories and books that give information, drawing on a wide reading of a range of text types.		a. Follow agreed upon rules for discussion.	b. Use common, proper, and possessive nouns.
Informational Text	**Research to Build and Present Knowledge**	b. Build on others' talk in conversations by responding to the comments of others through multiple exchanges.	c. Use singular and plural nouns with matching verbs in basic sentences (e.g., *He hops; We hop*).
RI.1.1 Ask and answer questions about key details in a text.	W.1.7 Participate in shared research and writing projects.		
RI.1.2 Identify the main topic and retell key details of a text.	W.1.8 With guidance and support from adults, recall information from experiences or gather information from provided sources to answer a question.	c. Ask questions to clear up any confusion about the topics and texts under discussion.	d. Use personal (subject, object), possessive, and indefinite pronouns (e.g., *I, me, my; they, them, their; anyone, everything*). CA
RI.1.5 Know and use various text **structures (e.g., sequence) and text features** (e.g., headings, tables of contents, glossaries, electronic menus, icons) to locate key facts or information in a text.		SL.1.2 Ask and answer questions about key details in a text read aloud or information presented orally or though other media.	e. Use verbs to convey a sense of past, present, and future (e.g., *Yesterday I walked home; Today I walk home; Tomorrow I will walk home*).
RI.1.7 Use the illustrations and details in a text to describe its key ideas.		SL.1.3 Ask and answer questions about what a speaker says in order to gather additional information or clarify something that is not understood.	f. Use frequently occurring adjectives.
RI.1.9 Identify basic similarities in and differences between two texts on the same topic (e.g., in illustrations, descriptions, or procedures).			
Foundational			
RF.1.2 Demonstrate understanding of spoken words, syllables, and sounds (phonemes).			
a. Distinguish long from short vowel sounds in spoken single-syllable words.			
b. Orally produce single-syllable words by blending sounds (phonemes), including consonant blends.			
RF.1.3 Know and apply grade-level phonics and word analysis skills in decoding words both in isolation and in text. CA			
b. Decode regularly spelled one-syllable words.			

Evidence of Learning – Stage 2

Evaluative Criteria (LBUSD Achievement Report Evidence)	End of Unit Assessment Evidence
See Scoring guide located on Intranet • Engages in collaborative conversations about grade level topics and texts • Listens and interprets information and ideas • Produces complete sentences when expressing ideas and feelings • Uses grade-appropriate language & vocabulary	*Performance Task* Students will work as zookeepers in small groups to analyze a picture of an animal and respond to a series of questions related to the content knowledge built during this unit. Once groups have answered all of the questions, they will present their ideas to the class.
See CCSS-Aligned Informative/explanatory Writing Rubric • Organizes and maintains focus to support purpose • Uses appropriate details and precise language to develop the topic • Spells simple words using common spelling patterns and more difficult words phonetically • Applies grade level appropriate rules for capitalization and punctuation	*Informative/explanatory Writing Task* Students will write a WtB Level Three Observational Comment piece on horses.

Evaluative Criteria (LBUSD Achievement Report Evidence)	Other Evidence – may also be used formatively
• Asks and answers questions about key details in a text • Uses key details to identify main topics and retell stories • Identifies common types of texts and text features • Listens and interprets information and ideas • Uses grade-appropriate language & vocabulary	*Participation during Read-Alouds*
• Organizes and maintains focus to support purpose • Makes connections between texts • Applies grade level appropriate rules for capitalization and punctuation • Spells simple words using common spelling patterns and more difficult words phonetically • Uses grade-appropriate language & vocabulary	*Listening and Learning Logs*
See CCSS-Aligned Collaborative Discussion Rubric • Engages in collaborative conversations about grade level topics & texts • Listens and interprets information and ideas • Produces complete sentences when expressing ideas and feelings • Uses grade-appropriate language & vocabulary	*Large and Small Group Collaborative Discussions*
• Organizes and maintains focus to support purpose • Uses appropriate details and precise language to develop the topic • Spells simple words using common spelling patterns and more difficult words phonetically • Applies grade level appropriate rules for capitalization and punctuation	*Journal Writing*
• Demonstrates an understanding of spoken word, syllables and sounds • Reads grade level text with accuracy and fluency	*Foundational Reading Skills Assessment*
• Demonstrates an understanding of spoken word, syllables and sounds • Asks and answers questions about key details in a text • Reads grade level text with accuracy and fluency	*Small Group Instruction*

Learning Plan – Stage 3

Instructional Sequence Overview

Days	Reading and Responding to Text and Vocabulary Acquisition	Language Conventions and Observational Comment Writing- Informative/Explanatory Writing	Foundational Reading Skills
1	*Giraffes* (Science, Chapter 2, p. 62-63)	Observational Comment **Day 1 of WftB Level 2**-Giraffes • Nouns: common • Pronouns, possessive pronouns	
2-5	*Animals Everywhere* (Science, Chapter 2, Lesson 1)	Observational Comment **Days 2-3 of WftB Level 2**-Giraffes • Mini lessons and Journal Writing • Nouns: common • Pronouns	
6-10	*What Do Animals Need?* (Content Connections-Big Book)	Observational Comment **Days 1, 2, 3 of WftB Level 2**-hawks • Mini lessons and Journal Writing • Nouns: Singular and Plural Nouns: common, proper, possessive, singular, plural • Possessive pronouns	**Do the following daily:** • OCR Green Section • Small Group Instruction • Workshop
11-15	*How Animals Get Food* (Science, Chapter 2, Lesson 3)	Observational Comment **Day 1, 2, 3 of WftB Level 3**- tigers • Mini lessons and Journal Writing • Pronouns • Possessive pronouns • Adjectives	
16-18	*Munch Crunch*: The Food Animals Eat (OCR, Unit 2)	Observational Comment **Day 1, 2, 3 of WftB Level 3** • Pronouns • Possessive pronouns • Adjectives	
19-21	*Hermit Crab (OCR, Unit 2)*	• Mini lessons and Journal Writing • Observational Comment **Day 1, WftB Level 3**- • possessive pronouns • Adjectives • Verbs nouns match tense	
22-23	*My Animals Book (Science, Chapter 2, p. 90-95)*	• Observational Comment **Day 2, 3 of WftB Level 3**-	
24-25	**Performance Task**	**Observational Comment Writing Task-Informative/Explanatory**	**FRSA**

| Other Available Resources | • OCR Unit 2: Leveled Classroom Library
• Animals Big Bok
• Classroom Library Read Alouds related to theme | • **WftB Narrative Binder pgs. 37-76**
• **WftB Setting the Stage**
• Language Arts Big Book | • FRS Teacher Guide (located on intranet) |

Giraffes
Day 1

Vocabulary
knobby, velvet

Theme Connections
This text provides students an opportunity to learn about animals through poetry.

Reader and Task Considerations
Having just completed a unit on poetry, students are likely to have a lot of knowledge about poems that they will want to share. It may be beneficial to have students "Turn and Talk". Have students turn "knee to knee" to their shoulder partner and have each take a turn sharing something they know about poems.

Focus of Instruction: Reading and Responding to Text and Vocabulary Acquisition

Learning Targets	

Reading for Comprehension

- Tell students that poems often use adjectives or describing words to tell how things look, feel, smell, or taste.
- Prior to reading, review the features of poetry Circle Map with students. Add that poets often use adjectives to describe things.
- Tell students that there are major differences between books that tell stories and books that are nonfiction and give information.
- Explain that you are beginning a unit on animals and will be reading many nonfiction books to gain information about animals. Some poems, as with the one today, include factual information.

Text Dependent Questions

- What was the author's purpose for writing this poem?
- Is this poem fiction or nonfiction? What evidence do you have?
- What does the author tell us about a giraffe's necks? Is that a fact?
- What does the poet like about giraffes?
- What parts of the giraffe does the poet describe?
- What words did the poet use to describe the giraffe?
- What facts can be learned from this poem?

Activities

- Prior to reading, ask students what words they would use to describe the giraffe in the picture.
- Record these words on a Bubble Map.
- After reading, return to the Bubble Map.
- Did the poet use any of the same words to describe the giraffe?

Vocabulary Acquisition

- The words *knobby* and *velvet* are adjectives used to describe the giraffe. These are words that can quickly be explained to students using examples.
- Have students "Turn and Talk" and give each partner a chance to use each word in a sentence.
- Consider making a Unit Vocabulary chart with two columns: "Words Related to Theme", and "Other Words". Encourage students to use the new vocabulary in conversations throughout the week. At the bottom of the chart, have a place to record a tally mark every time you hear a student use a newly acquired word in their conversations with you or with others.

- I can use adjectives to describe things. **(L.1.1f)**

- I can explain differences between text that tells a story and text that gives information. **(RL.1.5)**

- I can listen closely to a poem and answer questions about key details. **(RL.1.1)**

Appendix E. **Preparation for Job Interviews**

Candidates for positions as reading specialists often raise questions about how to prepare for job interviews. The questions identified below are some that may be asked by school personnel. Often, interviewers ask basic questions to get a sense of the experiences and education of candidates. In addition, they ask questions that elicit candidates' beliefs and perspectives regarding students, literacy teaching, and learning. These questions tend to be more difficult to answer because the interviewer probably has his or her own beliefs and values regarding each area. Be as honest and tactful as possible. The interviewer needs to know whether the reading specialist is a "match" for the district. At the same time, the reading specialist needs to determine whether the district is a place in which he or she will enjoy working.

BASIC QUESTIONS

1. Tell us about your past teaching experiences, especially those that prepare you for this position.
2. What certifications do you have? Where did you receive your reading specialist certification? What were the strengths of the program?

QUESTIONS ELICITING KNOWLEDGE, BELIEFS, AND UNDERSTANDINGS

1. What are your beliefs about reading instruction? Specifically, what are your beliefs about beginning reading instruction? Phonics instruction (primary position)? What are your beliefs about intermediate reading instruction? Secondary reading instruction?
2. How familiar are you with the standards in this state (CCSS or state standards)? What experiences have you had in learning about them, developing curriculum based on standards, and so on?
3. What assessment instruments have you had experience administering and interpreting? Talk about them and their possible uses.
4. What do you think about the advantages of pullout and in-class reading programs? Is one better than the other? Why?
5. What do you think is important in working effectively with teachers whose students you will be teaching? Why? Describe ways you might collaborate with them.
6. In addition to teaching struggling readers, what other kinds of contributions can you make to the reading program?

301

7. Have you had any experience in conducting professional development? If so, what?
8. What strengths (qualifications) do you think you would bring to this position? Why do you want this position?

QUESTIONS THE READING SPECIALIST SHOULD ASK

The interview should also provide an opportunity for the reading specialist to obtain information about the position. Interviewers often ask if the interviewee has any questions, so the reading specialist should go into the interview with several questions important to him or her. Broad categories of topics follow:

1. *Duties required:* What are the expectations of the position regarding teaching, assessment, and so on?
2. *Resources:* What materials and resources are available for teaching reading?
3. *Opportunities for collaboration:* In what ways can I collaborate with teachers, parents, and community entities such as libraries, and so on?
4. *Professional opportunities:* Does the district encourage continuing education and provide opportunities for teachers to attend conferences?

The following guidelines might also be helpful in an interview:

1. *Listen carefully before answering any question.* Be certain you know what is being asked.
2. *Answer questions honestly.* If you do not know a specific answer, it is best to say so (or qualify your answer by saying that you are not certain, but to the best of your ability, you think . . .).
3. *Show enthusiasm and interest in the position.* Indicate why you want to work in that school or district, and why you believe you would be an excellent candidate for the job.

Appendix F. **Ideas for Course or Workshop Instructors**

In this section are additional ideas for activities that can be used by those using this book with a class or leading professional development sessions. Although I suggest activities immediately after each chapter, these additional ideas are ones that may be useful to those wishing to expand on the chapter activities.

CHAPTER 1

1. Have participants work in small groups to brainstorm current issues faced by educators, especially those involved with literacy instruction. Begin by talking briefly with them about issues that you believe are important ones: for example, literacy across the curriculum, or issues about how to assess student learning in literacy. After participants identify the issues, share across groups to look for commonalities and differences. (This list can be used for further group work later in the term, if desired.)

2. Ask participants to read the latest issue of the survey conducted by Cassidy and others. "What's Hot, What's Not" generally found in *Reading Today*, a publication of the ILA, and discuss whether they agree with experts in the field who have identified specific reading topics as "hot" or "not hot."

3. Ask participants to download and read the most recent position statement on the roles of the reading specialist from the website of the ILA (*www.reading.org*). Assign various sections to small groups of participants to read and identify important ideas. Discuss with the whole group. Compare that document with Figure 1.1 in Chapter 1, in which the various roles of reading specialists are described.

4. Read and discuss one or both of the following articles:

> Dole, J. A. (2004). The changing role of the reading specialist in school reform. *The Reading Teacher, 57*(5) 462–471.
> Quatroche, D. J., & Wepner, S. B. (2008). Developing reading specialists as leaders: New directions for program development. *Literacy Research and Instruction, 47*, 99–115.

CHAPTER 2

1. Read and discuss the following article discussed in this chapter:

> Foorman, B. R., & Torgeson, J. (2001). Critical elements of classroom and small-group instruction promote reading success in all children. *Learning Disabilities Research and Practice, 16*(4), 203–212.

2. Ask participants to conduct a survey at a school in which they work or a school with which they are familiar to determine whether the school is attempting to implement an RTI approach to instruction, and if so, how the school addresses the following:

- Is there a core reading program for Tier 1 students, and if so, what is it?
- What additional support do Tier 2 students get (e.g., Who teaches them?)? What materials are used? How is Tier 2 time scheduled?
- What additional support do Tier 3 students get (e.g., Who teaches them?)? What materials are used? When do students receive Tier 3 instruction?
- What problems does the school have in accomplishing its RTI objectives?

3. Participants who are working at a middle or high school level can conduct a survey to determine whether their school is attempting to implement an RTI framework and how students who are experiencing difficulties with literacy are being supported. What problems does this school face in accomplishing its RTI objectives? Participants should be prepared to discuss their findings in a class session, comparing results from the various schools.

CHAPTER 3

1. Divide the class into three groups (primary, elementary/middle school, and secondary). Have each group read and discuss one of the sample cases of reading specialists in this chapter, using the questions in the "Think about This" sections. Have each group share the results of their discussion with the entire group.

CHAPTER 4

1. Ask participants to write a paper describing themselves as leaders: What do they see as their strengths, limitations, and how might they change? What experiences have they had in their homes or education that have prepared them for a leadership role? Participants can save their papers until the conclusion of the course or workshops and reflect on what they had written.

2. Have participants work on a T-chart in which they list attributes of an effective meeting and an ineffective meeting. This can be done individually or in small groups and then shared with the entire group.

3. Divide the group into two smaller groups. Do a fishbowl activity in which those in one group role-play being a member of a group. The outer group (sitting in a circle around the inner group) serves as observers, watching the other group as it goes through the role-playing experience. They then provide

feedback to the group, responding to the following: What are some examples of active listening? Effective group behaviors (task behaviors, relationship behaviors)? Feedback from observers should be positive and encouraging. Here are examples of some possible role-playing scenarios:

Scenario 1: A group of teachers has to decide how to reward students who achieve the goal of reading 25 books per year. They must decide what the reward will be and who will handle responsibility for deciding that students have met the goal. They must also decide what they will do with students who haven't met the goal. There are issues that they must address in terms of whether they should provide an extrinsic reward for students who have met this goal.

Scenario 2: A group of fourth-grade teachers has reviewed their assessment data and found that students' vocabulary scores are low. The principal has asked them to address two questions: What are the reasons for the low scores? How do they think they can improve student vocabulary learning? (Some of the teachers think that the students come from such poor backgrounds that vocabulary will always be low; others think that perhaps the textbooks don't provide enough rich vocabulary teaching.)

CHAPTER 5

1. Assign this article to participants to read and then discuss in class:

Walpole, S., & Beauchat, K. A. (2008, June). *Facilitating teacher study groups.* Denver, CO: Literacy Coaching Clearinghouse. Retrieved from *www.literacycoachingonline.org/briefs/StudyGroupsBrief. pdf.*

2. Ask participants to use Figure 5.2 to assess the culture of the school in which they work or with which they are familiar. Have participants discuss the results of their assessment with others.

3. Ask participants to think about presentations that they have heard and thought to be effective. Ask them to describe the ways in which the presenter kept them interested. Some ideas for discussion: How did the speaker begin the presentation? End the presentation? Was the audience involved and if so, how? In what ways did the presenter help the audience connect with the topic? Ask participants to generate a list of guidelines for making effective presentations.

CHAPTER 6

1. Form triads to discuss the activities in Figure 6.3. Have triads group the activities into one of three categories: low risk, medium risk, or high risk—in

terms of what would be difficult for them to do—and then discuss what might be perceived as more "threatening" to teachers and more difficult for coaches to do. Discuss commonalities and differences in a large group.

2. Using interview questions developed by the group (see Chapter 6), ask each participant to meet with and interview a literacy coach. Group members should be encouraged to locate literacy coaches working at the preschool, elementary, or secondary levels. Share responses to these interviews. The group can also arrange for a conference call and interview a literacy coach by telephone.

3. Discuss this scenario in small groups and then share across groups:

- Your superintendent has told you that as a coach you are to spend your time with teachers who have low achievement scores and shouldn't spend any time with other teachers whose kids are doing well. You don't think this is the way to establish a relationship with teachers, believing that teachers will not want to work with you. They will realize that "only those having problems" work with the coach! What are some ways of addressing this? What actions can you take?

CHAPTER 7

1. Below are some coaching scenarios that can be used for discussion. Each addresses situations at different grade levels. Meet in small groups to discuss. In the discussion, consider the following:

- What are some ideas for working with the teacher?
- What roadblocks might arise and how could you address them?

Scenario 1. The kindergarten teacher asked the coach to observe her classroom. Although she has taught before (fourth grade), she has never taught kindergarten. She told the coach that she is having difficulties with classroom management. The coach observes and sees "chaos." The teacher is teaching a small group, but has to stop frequently to reprimand students for their behavior: "J, get back in your seat," "S, stop hitting H," and so on. The students are not working in their centers (as they were told), but are wandering around the room. The coach and the teacher are now going to meet for a feedback session. How does the coach begin? What are some important points that need to be made?

Scenario 2. Although the students in this ninth-grade English classroom have "high" test scores, the teacher lectures most of the time and is not attempting to use the classroom discussion approaches that are part of the new literacy framework for use in content-area classrooms. She has indicated to other teachers and to the coach that she sees no need to do this because her students are "doing well." As the coach, you have been charged with helping teachers implement these new discussion techniques. What should and could you do?

Scenario 3. Josh, an experienced eighth-grade social studies teacher, was transferred to the elementary school where he was assigned to a third-grade classroom. He says, "I have never taught reading. All I know is that there are a number of students in my classroom who can't read the materials we use in reading class. I've been trying to use strategy instruction but the kids are having trouble summarizing information." He has asked to meet with the coach to discuss this problem. The coach wants to get some idea of what Josh knows and believes about "teaching reading," and how he is actually facilitating the work of the students.

THINK ABOUT THIS

- What types of questioning might you use?
- What strategies might be helpful?
- What roadblocks might arise and how could you address them?

---

2. Assume that you have just been hired as a literacy coach for a school (you decide on the level). Write a letter you could send to teachers about you and your role. Share the letter with other participants. Compare similarities and differences across letters.

CHAPTER 8

1. Ask participants to meet in small groups to discuss factors that positively or negatively affect change in their own schools. Have them think about the six factors described in this chapter on pages 192–195 (Fullan & Hargreaves, 1996). Are any of these factors present in their schools? Others? Is the culture of their school one in which teachers would be receptive to change and why?

2. Ask participants to interview an administrator or school leader at a local school to discuss the reading program (K–12). Questions that might be asked include:

- What is the process for decision making in curriculum development?
- What materials or documents are available to explain the program?
- What materials are used in the program to meet the needs of students of differing abilities and needs?
- What professional development is provided for teachers to help them implement the program?

3. Use the Internet to locate needs assessment documents and copies of comprehensive literacy plans from various states (if possible, from the state in which you are from). After reading Chapter 8 in this book, discuss the documents with peers and compare their content to the recommendations in this

book. Discuss the question: How helpful would completing a needs assessment be for your school?

CHAPTER 9

1. Ask participants to identify and discuss specific assessment measures used at various levels. You may choose to group participants by level (e.g., primary, intermediate/middle school, high school). Share results of discussion with the entire group. Ask them to indicate purposes of the instruments: initial screening, diagnostic, progress monitoring, and outcomes. You can provide participants with a chart similar to the following:

	Primary	Intermediate	Middle School	High School
Initial Screening				
Diagnostic				
Progress Monitoring				
Outcomes				

2. Divide students into two groups. Ask one group to read the IRA (2013) position statement on formative assessment and the other group, the IRA (2014) position statement on high-stakes assessment. Ask each group to summarize what they learned and to discuss the difference in the perspectives of the two documents. Ask students to relate what they learned to the "reality" of their schools.

3. Ask students to read the various vignettes in the "Voices from the Field" sections throughout the book, and then discuss what assessments are used by these reading specialists and how they use these results in their work with teachers.

CHAPTER 10

1. Form small groups and then ask participants to discuss one of the following scenarios. Have them share with the entire group.

Scenario 1. The parents of Natalie, a kindergarten child, ask for an appointment with the reading specialist to talk about their child. They tell the reading specialist that the child is reading chapter books, similar to those that a second- or third grader would read. She is now getting "homework" in kindergarten, which consists of activities such as the following:

cut out pictures of things that start with the letter *B* and glue to a large sheet of paper; practice writing two new letters (*A* and *I*); and practice writing your name (which Natalie has been doing since she was age 3). Her parents indicate that this homework has not been "very exciting" and it's hard to get her interested. She would rather spend time reading independently or working on the computer, playing with video games requiring reading. Her parents are concerned Natalie will find school boring. Should they be considering options (e.g., a private school, skipping a grade)? They are seeking help from a reading specialist.

Scenario 2. The reading specialists in one district recognize their student population is changing and they now have a large number of students from many different countries in their schools. They would like to take advantage of this cultural diversity; in addition, they would like to help all parents understand the value of "culturally responsive" instruction. They are meeting to discuss whether they should pull together some material that would be "parent friendly" to address this topic, hold some workshops, have an ethnic fair, and so on. How should teachers be involved? Is this something that should be done only at the elementary level, or at higher levels?

2. Ask participants to interview the school librarian to determine in what ways she or he collaborates with teachers in the schools. Providing related materials? Coordinating instruction with the content teachers? How aware is the librarian about the literacy program in the school? Are there opportunities to collaborate with teachers? What does the librarian think should be done to improve the ways in which he or she works with teachers to improve instruction?

CHAPTER 11

Have students write a proposal that addresses the following mini-grant opportunity. This could be an individual assignment, or could be done in small groups. Opportunity to share the finished product can be provided.

A local foundation is willing to provide $500 to classroom teachers who wish to implement a creative project for their classroom to enhance the reading performance of their students. The proposal should include the following elements: goals and objectives, plan of activities, time line, personnel, evaluation, and budget (describe the funds you will need and how they will be used).

CHAPTER 12

1. Use a fishbowl activity to role-play a candidate applying for a reading specialist position. Two participants should volunteer to be in the fishbowl: one who is the candidate for a reading specialist or literacy coach position;

and the other, the interviewer (perhaps a principal or curriculum director). The outer group (sitting in a circle around the two participants who have agreed to role-play an interview situation) observes and then provides feedback about the interview to the participants.

2. Ask participants to keep a reflection log for several days in which they describe their activities and also write a reflective statement about those activities. After keeping the log for several days, have them discuss in a small-group setting the benefits of such a self-reflective process, and any limitations or challenges to keeping such a log.

3. Ask participants to go to a website of a professional organization (e.g., *www.reading.org*, *www.ncte.org*) or to the Literacy Coaching Clearinghouse website (*www.literacycoachingonline.org*). Have them identify and share with others the possible opportunities for professional learning that are available on that site.

4. Assign one of the six vignettes to a small group of class members. Ask them to read the vignette carefully, thinking about how the writer exemplifies lifelong learning. Discuss similarities and differences in how each functions in the schools and the challenges they face. Ask each group to share with the entire class what they learned about the role of the reading specialist from the vignette. Ask each group to write and present in one sentence what they learned from their reading.

References

Afflerbach, P. (2004). *National Reading Conference policy brief: High stakes testing and reading assessment.* Oak Creek, WI: National Reading Conference. Retrieved January 10, 2009, from *www.nrconline.org/publications/HighStakesTestingandReadingAssessment.pdf.*

Afflerbach, P. (2012). *Understanding and using reading assessment K–12* (2nd ed.). Newark, DE: International Reading Association.

Afflerbach, P. (2014, May). *What's new in literacy teaching?: Assessment.* Paper presented at the annual meeting of the International Reading Association, New Orleans, LA.

Alexander, K. L., Entwisle, D. R., & Olson, L. S. (2001). Schools, achievement, and inequality: A seasonal perspective. *Educational Evaluation and Policy Analysis, 23*(2), 171–191.

Alexander, S. H. (1990). *Mom can't see me.* New York: Macmillan.

Allington, R. L. (1986). Policy constraints and effective compensatory reading instruction: A review. In J. Hoffman (Ed.), *Effective teaching of reading and research and practice* (pp. 261–289). Newark, DE: International Reading Association.

Allington, R. L. (2006). *What really matters for struggling readers: Designing research-based programs.* New York: Pearson.

Allington, R. L. (2013). The six traits of effective elementary literacy instruction. Retrieved from *www.readingrockets.org/article/six-ts-effective-elementary-literacy-instruction.*

Allington, R. L., & McGill-Franzen, A. (1989). School response to reading failure: Instruction for Chapter 1 and special education students in grades 2, 4, and 8. *Elementary School Journal, 89,* 529–542.

Allington, R. L., & Shake, M. C. (1986). Remedial reading: Achieving curricular congruence in classroom and clinic. *The Reading Teacher, 39*(7), 648–654.

American Recovery and Reinvestment Act of 2009. (2009, February 19). Public Law No. 111-5, 123 Stat. 115, 516.

Anders, P. L., & Clift, R. T. (2012). Adolescent language, literacy and learning: Implications for a schoolwide literacy program. In R. M. Bean & A. Swan Dagen (Eds.), *Best practices of literacy leaders: Keys to school improvement* (pp. 162–183). New York: Guilford Press.

Anonymous. (1986). Where have all the children gone? *Scanner, Shaler Area Education Association, 13*(2), 3.

August D., & Shanahan, T. (2006). *Report of the National Literacy Panel on Language Minority Children and Youth.* Philadelphia: Erlbaum.

Ayers, W. (2004). *Teaching toward freedom: Moral commitment and ethical action in the classroom.* Boston: Beacon Press.

Bader, L. A. (1998). *Read to succeed: Literacy tutor's manual.* Upper Saddle River, NJ: Prentice-Hall.

Baker, S., Gersten, R., & Keating, T. (2000). When less may be more: A 2-year longitudinal evaluation of a volunteer tutoring program requiring minimal training. *Reading Research Quarterly, 35*(4), 494–519.

Barnett, W. S. (1995). Long-term effects of early childhood programs on cognitive and school outcomes. *The Future of Children, 5*(3), 25–50.

Barnett, W. S., Frede, E. C., Mobasher, H., & Mohr, P. (1987). The efficacy of public preschool programs and the relationship of program quality to efficacy. *Educational Evaluation and Policy Analysis, 10*(1), 37–49.

Barth, R. S. (2013, October). The time is ripe (again). *Educational Leadership, 72*(2), 10–16.

Bean, R. M. (2001). Classroom teachers and reading specialists working together to improve student achievement. In V. Risko & K. Bromley (Eds.), *Collaboration for diverse learners: Viewpoints and practices* (pp. 348–368). Newark, DE: International Reading Association.

Bean, R. M. (2004). Promoting effective literacy instruction: The challenge for literacy coaches. *The California Reader, 37*(3), 58–63.

Bean, R. M. (2008). Developing an effective reading program. In S. B. Wepner & D. S. Strickland (Eds.), *The administration and supervision of reading programs* (4th ed., pp. 11–29). New York: Teachers College Press.

Bean, R. M. (2009). *The reading specialist: Leadership for the classroom, school, and community* (2nd ed.). New York: Guilford Press.

Bean, R. M. (2011). The reading coach: Professional development and literacy leadership in the school. In T. Rasinski (Ed.), *Rebuilding the foundation: Effective reading instruction for 21st century literacy* (pp. 315–336). Bloomington, IN: Solution Tree Press.

Bean, R. M. (2014). Developing a comprehensive reading plan (pre-K–Grade 12). In S. B. Wepner, D. S. Strickland, & D. Quatroche (Eds.), *The administration and supervision of reading programs* (5th ed., pp. 11–29). New York: Teachers College Press.

Bean, R. M., Belcastro, B., Jackson, V., Vandermolen, J., & Zigmond, N. (2008, December). *Literacy coaching in reading: The blind men and the elephant.* Paper presented at the National Reading Conference, Orlando, FL.

Bean, R. M., Cassidy, J., Grumet, J. V., Shelton, D., & Wallis, S. R. (2002). What do reading specialists do?: Results from a national survey. *The Reading Teacher, 55*(8), 2–10.

Bean, R. M., Cooley, W., Eichelberger, R. T., Lazar, M., & Zigmond, N. (1991). In-class or pullout: Effects of setting on the remedial reading program. *Journal of Reading Behavior, 23*(4), 445–464.

Bean, R. M., & DeFord, D. (n.d.). *Do's and don'ts for literacy coaches: Advice from the field.* Denver, CO: Literacy Coaching Clearinghouse. Retrieved March 29, 2009, from *www.literacycoachingonline.org/briefs.html.*

Bean, R. M., Dole, J. A., Nelson, K. L., Belcastro, E., & Zigmond, N. (2015). The sustainability of a national reading reform initiative in two states. *Reading and Writing Quarterly: Overcoming Learning Difficulties, 31*(1), 30–55.

Bean, R. M., & Eichelberger, R. T. (2007). *Evaluation of improving literacy through school libraries grant.* Unpublished technical report.

Bean, R. M., Eichelberger, R. T., Turner, G., & Tellez, F. (2002). *Evaluation of four parochial elementary schools.* Pittsburgh, PA: Extra Mile Foundation.

Bean, R. M., & Eisenberg, E. (2009). Literacy coaching in middle and high schools. In K. D. Wood & W. E. Blanton (Eds.), *Literacy instruction for adolescents: Research-based practice* (pp. 107–124). New York: Guilford Press.

Bean, R. M., Fulmer, D., & Zigmond, N. (2009). *Reading First Observation Checklist and Rating Scale.* Unpublished instrument, University of Pittsburgh, Pittsburgh, PA.

Bean, R. M., Grumet, J. V., & Bulazo, J. (1999). Learning from each other: Collaboration between classroom teachers and reading specialist interns. *Reading Research and Instruction, 38*(4), 273–287.

Bean, R. M., Kern, D., Goatley, V., Ortlieb, E., Shettel, J., Calo, K., et al. (2015). Specialized literacy professionals as literacy leaders: Results of a national survey. *Literacy Research and Instruction, 54*(2), 83–114.

Bean, R. M., & Lillenstein, J. (2012). Response to intervention and the changing roles of schoolwide personnel. *The Reading Teacher, 65*(7), 491–501.

Bean, R. M., & Morewood, A. (2007). Best practices in professional development for improving literacy instruction. In L. B. Gambrell, L. M. Morrow, & M. C. Pressley (Eds.), *Best practices in literacy instruction* (3rd ed., pp. 373–394). New York: Guilford Press.

Bean, R. M., Swan, A. L., & Knaub, R. (2003). Reading specialists in schools with exemplary reading programs: Functional, versatile, and prepared. *The Reading Teacher, 56*(5), 446–455.

Bean, R. M., & Swan Dagen, A. (2012). Schools as places of learning: The powerful role of literacy leaders. In R. M. Bean & A. Swan Dagen (Eds.), *Best practices of literacy leaders: Keys to school improvement* (pp. 355–378). New York: Guilford Press.

Bean, R. M., Trovato, C. A., & Hamilton, R. (1995). Focus on Chapter 1 reading programs: Views of reading specialists, classroom teachers, and principals. *Reading Research and Instruction, 34*(3), 204–221.

Bean, R. M., Turner, G. H., & Belski, K. (2002). Implementing a successful America Reads Challenge tutoring program: Lessons learned. In P. E. Linder, M. B. Sampson, J. Dugan, & B. Brancato (Eds.), *24th yearbook of the College Reading Association* (pp. 169–187). Easton, PA: College Reading Association.

Bean, R. M., & Wilson, R. M. (1981). *Effecting change in school reading programs: The resource role.* Newark, DE: International Reading Association.

Beck, I. W., & McKeown, M. G. (2001). Text-talk: Capturing the benefits of read-aloud experiences for young children. *The Reading Teacher, 55*, 10–20.

Beers, K. (2003). *When kids can't read: What teachers can do (a guide for teachers 6–12).* Portsmouth, NH: Heinemann.

Beresik, D. L., & Bean, R. M. (2002). Teacher practices and the Pennsylvania system of school assessment. *Pennsylvania Reads: Journal of the Keystone State Reading Association, III*(II), 16–29.

Bernhardt, V. L. (2013). *Data analysis for continuous school improvement* (3rd ed.). New York: Routledge.

Berger, J. G. (2012). *Changing on the job: Developing leaders for a complex world.* Redwood City, CA: Stanford University Press.

Biancarosa, G., & Snow, C. E. (2004). *Reading next: A vision for action and research in middle and high school literacy: A report to Carnegie Corporation of New York.* Washington, DC: Alliance for Excellent Education. Retrieved from *http:// carnegie.org/fileadmin/Media/Publications/PDF/ReadingNext.pdf.*

Billig, S. H. (2002). Involving middle-graders' parents. *Education Digest, 67*(7), 42–45.

Blachowicz, C. L. Z., Buhle, R., Ogle, D., Frost, S., Correa, A., & Kinner, J. D. (2010). Hit the ground running: Ten ideas for preparing and supporting urban literacy coaches. *The Reading Teacher, 63*(5), 348–359.

Blanchard, K., Bowles, S., Carew, D., & Parise-Carew, E. (2001). *High five: The magic of working together.* New York: HarperCollins.

Borman, G. D. (2002–2003). How can Title 1 improve achievement? *Educational Leadership, 60*(4), 49–53.

Borman, G. D., & D'Agostine, J. V. (2001). Title 1 and student achievement: A quantitative synthesis. In G. D. Borman, S. C. Stringfield, & R. E. Slavin (Eds.), *Title I compensatory education at the crossroads* (pp. 25–58). Mahwah, NJ: Erlbaum.

Boutte, G. S., & Johnson, G. J. (2014). Community and family involvement in urban schools. In H. R. Milner & K. Lomotey (Eds.), *Handbook of urban education* (pp. 167–187). New York: Routledge.

Briggs, D. A., & Coulter, F. C. (1977). The reading specialist. In W. Otto, N. A. Peters, & C. W. Peters (Eds.), *Reading problems: A multidisciplinary perspective* (pp. 215–236). Reading, MA: Addison-Wesley.

Browning, B. (2014). *Grant writing for dummies* (5th ed.). Hoboken, NJ: Wiley.

Brozo, W. G., & Gaskins, C. (2009). Engaging texts and literacy practices for adolescent boys. In K. D. Wood & W. E. Blanton (Eds.), *Literacy instruction for adolescents: Research-based practice* (pp. 170–186). New York: Guilford Press.

Bryk, A. S., Sebring, P. B., Allensworth, F. E., Luppescu, S., & Easton, J. Q. (2010). *Organizing schools for improvement: Lessons from Chicago.* Chicago: University of Chicago Press.

Buehl, D. (2011). *Developing readers in the academic disciplines.* Newark, DE: International Reading Association.

Buly, M., & Valencia, S. (2002). Below the bar: Profiles of students who fail state reading assessments. *Educational Evaluation and Policy Analysis, 24*(3), 219–239.

Burkins, J. M. (2007). *Coaching for balance: How to meet the challenges of literacy coaching.* Newark, DE: International Reading Association.

Camburn, E., Rowan, B., & Taylor, J. (2003). Distributed leadership in schools: The case of elementary schools adopting comprehensive school reform models. *Educational Evaluation and Policy Analysis, 25*(4), 347–373.

Canady, R. L., & Rettig, M. (1995). The power of innovative scheduling. *Educational Leadership, 53*(3), 4–10.

Canady, R. L., & Rettig, M. (2008). *Elementary school scheduling: Enhancing instruction for student achievement.* Larchmont, NY: Eye on Education.

Cameron, W. B. (1963). *Informal sociology: A causal introduction to sociological thinking.* New York: Random House.

Carroll, K. (2007). *Conversations with coaches: Their roles in Pennsylvania Reading First schools.* Unpublished doctoral dissertation, University of Pittsburgh.

Cassidy, J., & Cassidy, D. (2009, February/March). What's hot for 2009: National Reading Panel influence wanes in 13th annual survey. *Reading Today, 26*(4), 1, 8, 9.

Castek, J., & Gwinn, C. B. (2012). Technology in the literacy program. In R. M. Bean & A. Swan Dagen (Eds.), *Best practices of literacy leaders: Keys to school improvement* (pp. 295–316). New York: Guilford Press.

Center for American Progress and the Education Trust. (2011). *Essential elements of teacher policy in ESEA: Effectiveness, fairness, and evaluation.* Washington, DC: Author.

Center for Education Policy. (2007). *Moving beyond identification: Assisting schools in improvement.* Washington, DC: Author.

Clay, M. (1985). *The early detection of reading difficulties* (3rd ed.). Portsmouth, NH: Heinemann.

Coburn, C. E. & Woulfin, S. L. (2012). Reading coaches and the relationship between policy and practice. *Reading Research Quarterly, 47*(1), 5–30.

Coiro, J. (2005). Every teacher a Miss Rumphius: Empowering teachers with effective professional development. In R. Karchmer, M. Mallette, J. Kara-Soteriou, & D. J. Leu, Jr. (Eds.), *New literacies for new times: Innovative models of literacy education using the internet.* Newark, DE: International Reading Association.

Collins, J. (2001). *Good to great.* New York: HarperCollins.

Common Core State Standards Initiative. (2010). Common core state standards for English language arts and literacy in history, social studies, science and technical subjects. Available at *www.corestandards.org/the-standards.*

Common Sense Media & Rideout, V. (2011). *Zero to eight: Children's media use in America.* San Francisco: Common Sense Media.

Cook, L., & Friend, M. (1995). Co-teaching: Guidelines for creating effective practices. *Exceptional Children, 28*(3), 1–16.

Costa, A. L., & Garmston, R. J. (2002). *Cognitive coaching: A foundation for Renaissance schools* (2nd ed.). Norwood, MA: Christopher-Gordon.

Covey, S. R. (1989). *The 7 habits of highly effective people.* New York: Simon & Schuster.

Covey, S. R. (2004). *The 8th habit: From effectiveness to greatness.* New York: Free Press.

Cunningham, P. M., & Hall, D. P. (1994). *Making words.* Torrance, CA: Good Apple.

Dagen, A. S., & Bean, R. M. (2014). High-quality research-based professional development: An essential for enhancing high-quality teaching. In L. E. Martin, S. Kragler, D. J. Quatroche, & K. L. Bauserman.(Eds.), *Handbook of professional development in education: Successful models and practices, PreK–12* (pp. 42–64). New York: Guilford Press.

Darling-Hammond, L., Wei, R. C., Andree, A., Richardson, N., & Orphanos, S. (2009). *Professional learning in the learning profession: A status report on teacher development in the United States and abroad.* Oxford, OH: National Staff Development Council.

DePree, M. (1992). *Leadership jazz*. New York: Dell.

Desimone, L. M., Porter, A. C., Garet, M. S., Yoon, K. S., & Birman, B. F. (2002). Effects of professional development on teachers' instruction: Results from a three-year longitudinal study. *Educational Evaluation and Policy Analysis, 24*(2), 81–112.

Dewitz, P., Leahy, S. B., Jones, J., & Sullivan, P. M. (2010). *The essential guide to selecting and using core reading programs*. Newark, DE: International Reading Association.

Diller, D. (2005). *Practice with purpose: Literacy work stations for grades 3–6*. Portland, ME: Stenhouse.

Dole, J. A. (2004). The changing role of the reading specialist in school reform. *The Reading Teacher, 57*(5), 462–471.

Draper, R. J. (Ed.). (2010). *(Re)Imagining content-area literacy instruction*. New York: Teachers College Press.

Duffy, G. G. (2014). *Explaining reading: A resource for explicit teaching of the Common Core Standards*. (3rd ed.). New York: Guilford Press.

Duffy, H. (2009). *Meeting the needs of significantly struggling learners in high school: A look at approaches to tiered intervention*. Washington, DC: National High School Center. Retrieved from *www.betterhighschools.org/docs/NHSC_RTIBrief_08-02-07.pdf*.

Edwards, P. A., Paratore, J. R., & Sweeney, J. S. (2014). Working with parents and the community. In S. B. Wepner, D. S. Strickland, & D. J. Quatroche (Eds.), *The administration and supervision of reading programs* (5th ed., pp. 214–222). New York: Teachers College Press.

Elbaum, B., Vaughn, S., Hughes, M. T., & Moody, S. W. (2000). How effective are one-to-one tutoring programs in reading for elementary students at risk for reading failure?: A meta-analysis of the intervention research. *Journal of Educational Psychology, 92*(4), 605–619.

Elementary and Secondary Education Act of 1965. (1965). Public Law No. 89-10, 29 Stat. 27.

Elish-Piper, L., & L'Allier, S. K. (2014). *The common core coaching book: Strategies to help teachers address the K–5 ELA standards*. New York: Guilford Press.

Epstein, J. (1995). School/family community partnerships: Caring for the children we share. *Phi Delta Kappan, 76*(9), 701–712.

Epstein, J., Sanders, M. G., Sheldon, S., Simon, B. S., & Salinas, K. C. A. (2009). *School, family, and community partnerships: Your handbook for action* (3rd ed.). Thousand Oaks, CA: Corwin Press.

Erdmann, A., & Metzger, M. (2014). Discussion in practice: Sharing our learning curve. In J. Ippolito, J. F. Lawrence, & C. Zaller (Eds.), *Adolescent literacy in the era of the common core* (pp. 103–115). Cambridge, MA: Harvard Education Press.

Fitzgerald, J. (2001). Can minimally trained college student volunteers help young at-risk children to read better? *Reading Research Quarterly, 36*(1), 28–47.

Fixsen, D. L., Naoom, S. F., Blasé, K. A., Friedman, R. M., & Wallace, F. (2006). Implementation research: A synthesis of the literature (FMHI Publication No. 231). Tampa: University of South Florida Louis de al Parte Florida Mental Health Institute. National Implementation Research Network.

Foorman, B. R., & Torgeson, J. (2001). Critical elements of classroom and small-group instruction promote reading success in all children. *Learning Disabilities Research and Practice, 16*(4), 203–212.

Frost, S., & Bean, R. M. (2006, September 27). *Qualifications for literacy coaches: Achieving the gold standard.* Denver, CO: Literacy Coaching Clearinghouse. Retrieved from *www.literacycoachingonline.org.*

Fullan, M. (1991). *The new meaning of educational change.* New York: Teachers College Press.

Fullan, M. (2001a). *Leading in a culture of change.* San Francisco: Jossey-Bass.

Fullan, M. (2001b). *The new meaning of educational change* (3rd ed.). New York: Teachers College Press.

Fullan, M., Bertani, A., & Quinn, J. (2004). New lessons for districtwide reform. *Educational Leadership, 61*(7), 42–46.

Fullan, M., & Hargreaves, A. (1996). *What's worth fighting for in your school?* New York: Teachers College Press.

Gajda, R., & Tulikangas, R. (2005). *Getting the grant: How educators can write winning proposals and manage successful projects.* Alexandria, VA: Association for Supervision and Curriculum Development.

Galloway, E. P., & Lesaux, N. K. (2014, April). Leader, teacher, diagnostician, colleague, and change agent: A synthesis of the research on the role of the reading specialist in this era of RTI-based literacy reform. *The Reading Teacher, 67*(7), 517–526.

Gamse, B. C., Jacob, R. T., Horst, M., Boulay, B., & Unlu, F. (2008, November). *Reading First Impact Study: Final report* (NCEE No. 2009-4038). Washington, DC: U.S. Department of Education, National Center for Educational Evaluation and Regional Assistance, Institute of Education Science.

Genest, M., & Bean, R. M. (2007). *Bringing libraries and schools together (BLAST): A collaborative program between Carnegie library of Pittsburgh and the Pittsburgh Public School District (year 5).* Unpublished technical report.

Genest, M. T. (2014). Reading is a BLAST!: Inside an innovative literacy collaboration between public schools and the public library. *Reading Horizons, 53*(1), 4. Available at *http://scholarworks.wmich.edu/reading_horizons/vol53/iss1/4.*

Glickman, C. D. (1990). *Supervision of instruction: A developmental approach.* Boston: Allyn & Bacon.

Goodman, K. (Ed.). (2006). *The truth about DIBELS: What it is; what it does.* Portsmouth, NH: Heinemann.

Green, J. F. (1996). *Language!: A literacy intervention curriculum* (2nd ed.). Longmont, CO: Sopris West.

Grierson, A. (2011, April). *Walking the talk: Supporting teachers' growth with different professional learning.* Paper presented at the annual conference of the American Educational Research Association, New Orleans, LA.

Guskey, T. R. (1986). Staff development and the process of teacher change. *Educational Researcher, 15*(5), 5–12.

Guskey, T. R. (2000). *Evaluating professional development.* Thousand Oaks, CA: Corwin Press.

Gutnick, A. L., Robb, M., Takeuchi, L., & Kotlr, J. (2011). *Always connected: The new digital media habits of children.* New York: Joan Ganz Coonery Center at Sesame Workshop. Retrieved from *www.joanganzcooneycenter.org/wp-content/uploads/2011/03/jgcc_alwaysconnected.pdf.*

Hall, B. (2004, Fall). Literacy coaches: An evolving role. *Carnegie Reporter, 3*(1), 10–19.

Hansen, J. (1998). *When learners evaluate.* Portsmouth, NH: Heinemann.

Hanushek, E. A. (1992). The trade-off between child quantity and quality. *Journal of Political Economy, 100*(91), 84–117.

Harari, O. (2002). *The leadership secrets of Colin Powell.* New York: McGraw-Hill.

Hasbrouck, J., & Denton, C. (2005). *The reading coach: A how-to manual for success.* Boston: Sopris West Educational Services.

Henwood, G. F. (1999–2000). A new role for the reading specialist: Contributing toward a high school's collaborative educational culture. *Journal of Adolescent and Adult Literacy, 43*(4), 316–325.

Hersey, P., & Blanchard, K. (1977). *Management of organizational behavior: Utilizing human resources* (3rd ed.). Englewood Cliffs, NJ: Prentice-Hall.

Hoffman, A. R., & Jenkins, J. (2002). Exploring reading specialists' collaborative interactions with school psychologists: Problems and possibilities. *Education, 122*(4), 751–758.

Hord, S. M. (2004). *Learning together: Leading together.* New York: Teachers College Press.

Individuals with Disabilities Education Improvement Act of 2004. (2004). Public Law No. 108-446, 118 Stat. 2647.

International Reading Association. (1968). *Guidelines for reading specialists.* Newark, DE: Author.

International Reading Association. (1999). *Adolescent literacy: A position statement.* Newark, DE: Author.

International Reading Association. (2000a). *Making a difference means making it different: A position statement.* Newark, DE: Author.

International Reading Association. (2000b). *Teaching all children to read: The roles of the reading specialist.* Newark, DE: Author.

International Reading Association. (2002a). *Buyer be wary: A resolution of IRA board* [Online]. Newark, DE: Author. Available at *www.reading.org/Libraries/resources/On_Buyer_Be_Wary_1.pdf.*

International Reading Association. (2002b). *Evidenced-based reading instruction: Putting the National Reading Panel report into practice.* Newark, DE: Author.

International Reading Association. (2004). *The role and qualifications of the reading coach in the United States.* Newark, DE: Author.

International Reading Association. (2006). *Standards for middle and high school literacy coaches.* Newark, DE: Author.

International Reading Association. (2009). *New literacies and 21st century technologies: A position statement.* Newark, DE: Author.

International Reading Association. (2010a). *Response to intervention: A position statement.* Newark, DE: Author.

International Reading Association. (2010b). *Standards for reading professionals—Revised.* Newark, DE: Author.

International Reading Association. (2012a). *Adolescent literacy: A position statement of the International Reading Association.* Newark, DE: Author.

International Reading Association. (2012b). *Literacy implementation guidance for the ELA common core state standards.* Available at *www.reading.org.*

International Reading Association. (2012–2013). *Leisure reading: A position statement.* Newark, DE: Author.

International Reading Association. (2013). *Formative assessment: A position statement of the International Reading Association*. Newark, DE: Author.

International Reading Association. (2014). *Using high stakes assessment for grade retention and graduation decisions*. Newark, DE: Author.

International Society for Technology in Education. (2007). *ISTE's educational technology standards for students*. Washington, DC: Author. Retrieved from *www.iste.org/docs/pdfs/20-14_ISTE_Standards-s_PDF.pdf*.

Ippolito, J. (2010). Three ways that literacy coaches balance responsive and directive relationships with teachers. *Elementary School Journal, 111*(1), 164–190.

Ippolito, J., Lawrence, J. F., & Zaller, C. (Eds.). (2013). *Adolescent literacy in the era of the common core: From research into practice*. Cambridge, MA: Harvard Education Press.

Ippolito, J., & Lieberman, J. (2012). Reading specialists and literacy coaches in secondary schools. In R. M. Bean & A. Swan Dagen (Eds.), *Best practices of literacy leaders: Keys to school improvement* (pp. 63–85). New York: Guilford Press.

Ippolito, J., Steele, J. L., & Samson, J. F. (2012). *Adolescent literacy*. Cambridge, MA: Harvard Education Review.

Iriti, J. E., & Bickel, W. E. (2010). *Secondary education in the United States*. Briefing report prepared for the Heinz Endowments' Education Program for strategic planning. Pittsburgh, PA: Evaluation for Learning Group at the Learning Research and Development Center, University of Pittsburgh.

Jacobs, H. H. (1997). *Mapping the big picture integrating curriculum and assessment K–12*. Washington, DC: Association for Supervision and Curriculum Development.

Jaquith, A., Mindich, D., Wei, R. C., & Darling-Hammond, L. (2010). *Teacher professional learning in the U.S.: Case studies of state policies and strategies*. Dallas, TX: National Staff Development Council.

Johnson, D. W., & Johnson, F. P. (2003). *Joining together: Group theory and group skills* (8th ed.). Boston: Allyn & Bacon.

Johnson, D. W., & Johnson, F. P. (2013). *Joining together: Group theory and group skills* (11th ed.). Boston: Pearson Education.

Johnston, F., Juel, C., & Invernizzi, M. (1995). *Guidelines for volunteer tutors of emergent and early readers*. Charlottesville: University of Virginia.

Jolles, R. L. (2001). *How to run seminars and workshops* (2nd ed.). New York: Wiley.

Joyce, B., & Showers, B. (1995). *Student achievement through staff development: Fundamentals of school renewal*. White Plains, NY: Longman.

Joyce, B., & Showers, B. (2002). *Student achievement through staff development* (3rd ed.). Alexandria, VA: Association for Supervision and Curriculum Development.

Kaminski, R., & Good, R. (2011). DIBELS Next. Retrieved from *www.soprislearning.com*.

Kaner, S., Lind, L., Toldi, C., Fisk, S., & Berger, D. (1996). *Facilitator's guide to participatory deicsion-making*. Gabriola Island, BC, Canada: New Society.

Kapinus, B. A. (2008). Assessment of reading programs. In S. A. Wepner & D. Strickland (Eds.), *The administration and supervision of reading programs* (4th ed., pp. 144–156). New York: Teachers College Press.

Kapinus, B. A. (2014). Assessing students' reading achievement. In S. A. Wepner, D.

Strickland, & D. J. Quatroche (Eds.), *The administration and supervision of reading programs* (5th ed., pp. 125–144). New York: Teachers College Press.

Kindler, A. L. (2002). *Survey of the states' limited English proficient students and available educational programs and services: 2001–2002 summary report.* Washington, DC: National Clearinghouse for English Language Acquisition.

Kise, J. A. (2006). *Differentiated coaching: A framework for helping teachers change.* Thousand Oaks, CA: Corwin Press.

Kloo, A. (2006). *The decision-making utility and predictive power of DIBELS for students' reading achievement in Pennsylvania's Reading First schools.* Unpublished doctoral dissertation, University of Pittsburgh, Pittsburgh, PA.

Knaub, R. (2002). *The nature and impact of collaboration between reading specialists and classroom teachers in pullout and in-class reading programs.* Unpublished doctoral dissertation, University of Pittsburgh, Pittsburgh, PA.

Knight, J. (2007). *Instructional coaching: A partnership approach to improving instruction.* Thousand Oaks, CA: Corwin Press.

Kober, N. (2002, November). What tests can and cannot tell us. *The Forum*, pp. 1–2, 11–16.

L'Allier, S., Elish-Piper, L., & Bean, R. M. (2010). What matters for elementary literacy coaching: Guiding principles for instructional improvement and student achievement. *The Reading Teacher, 63*(7), 544–554.

Lambert, L. (1998). *Building leadership capacity in schools.* Alexandria, VA: Association for Supervision and Curriculum Development.

Lane, H., & Zavada, S. W. (2013, October). When reading gets ruff: Canine-assisted reading programs. *The Reading Teacher, 7*(2), 87–95.

Lane, S. (2010). *Performance assessment: The state of the art* (SCOPE Student Performance Assessment Series). Stanford, CA: Stanford University, Stanford Center for Opportunity Policy in Education.

Lapp, D., Fisher, D., Flood, J., & Frey, N. (2003). Dual role of the urban reading specialist. *Journal of Staff Development, 24*(2), 33–36.

Leana, C. R., & Pil, F. K. (2006). Social capital and organizational performance: Evidence from urban public schools. *Organization Science, 17*(3), 353–366.

Learning Forward. (2011). *Standards for professional learning.* Oxford, OH: Author.

Lieberman, A., & Miller, L. (2008). *Teachers in professional communities: Improving teaching and learning.* New York: Teachers College Press.

Lieberman, A., & Miller, L. (2014). Teachers as professionals: Evolving definitions of staff development. In L.E. Martin, S. Kragler, D. J. Quatroche, & K. L. Bauserman (Eds.), *Handbook of professional development in education: Successful models and practices, PreK–12* (pp. 3–21). New York: Guilford Press.

Little, J. W. (1993). Teachers' professional development in a climate of education reform. *Educational Evaluation and Policy Analysis, 15*, 129–151.

Lyons, C. A., & Pinnell, G. S. (2001). *Systems for change in literacy education: A guide to professional development.* Portsmouth, NH: Heinemann.

Manset-Williamson G., & Nelson, J. M. (2005). Balanced strategic reading instruction for upper-elementary and middle school students with reading disabilities: A comparative study of two approaches. *Learning Disability Quarterly, 28*(1), 59–74.

Mason, P. M., & Ippolito, J. (2009). What is the role of the reading specialist in promoting adolescent literacy? In J. Lewis (Ed.), *Essential questions in adolescent literacy: Teachers and researchers describe what works in classrooms* (pp. 312–336). New York: Guilford Press.

Matsumura, L. C. (2006). *Creating high-quality classroom assignments*. Lanham, MD: Scarecrow Education.

Matsumura, L. C., Sartoris, M., DiPrima Bickel, D., & Garnier, H. E. (2009). Leadership for literacy coaching: The principal's role in launching a new coaching program. *Educational Administration Quarterly, 45A*(5), 655–693.

McGill-Franzen, A., Lanford, C., & Adams, E. (2002). Learning to be literate: A comparison of five urban early childhood programs. *Journal of Educational Psychology, 94*(3), 443–464.

McKenna, M. C., & Walpole, S. (2008*). The literacy coaching challenge: Models and methods for grades K–8*. New York: Guilford Press.

McTighe, J., & Wiggins, G. (2012). From common core standards to curriculum: Five big ideas. Retrieved from *http://grantwiggins.files.wordpress.com/2012/09/mctighe_wiggins_final_common_core_standards.pdf.*

McVee, M. B., & Dickson, B. A. (2002). Creating a rubric to examine literacy software for the primary grades. *The Reading Teacher, 55*(7), 635–639.

Mesmer, E. M., & Mesmer, H. E. (2009). Response to intervention (RTI): What teachers of reading need to know. *The Reading Teacher, 62*(4), 280–290.

Mesmer, H. A. E., Mesmer, E., & Jones, J. (2014). *Reading intervention in the primary grades: A common-sense guide to RTI*. New York: Guilford Press.

Messina, L. (2013). Disciplinary literacy in practice: The disciplinary literacy network as a vehicle for strengthening instruction across content areas. In J. Ippolito, J. F. Lawrence, & C. Zaller (Eds.), *Adolescent literacy in the era of the common core: From research into practice* (pp. 37–60). Cambridge, MA: Harvard Education Press.

Miller S., & Miller, P. A. (1997). *Core communication: Skills and processes*. Evergreen, CO: Interpersonal Communications Programs.

Moats, L. (1999). *Teaching reading is rocket science: What expert teachers of reading should know and be able to do* [Online]. Washington, DC: American Federation of Teachers. Retrieved May 5, 2004, from *www.aftacts.org/tools-for-teachers/professional-resources/37-teaching-reading-is-rocket-science.*

Moje, E. B. (2008). Foregrounding the disciplines in secondary literacy teaching and learning: A call for change. *Journal of Adolescent and Adult Literacy, 52*(2), 96–107.

Moll, L. (2000). The diversity of schooling: A cultural–historical approach. In M. Reyes & J. Halcon (Eds.), *The best for our children: Critical perspectives on literacy for Latino students* (pp. 29–47). New York: Teachers College Press.

Morris, D. (2014). *Diagnosis and correction of reading problems* (2nd ed.). New York: Guilford Press.

Morrison, F. J., Bachman, H. J., & Connor, C. M. (2005). *Improving literacy in America: Guidelines from research*. New Haven, CT: Yale University Press.

Morrow, L. M., Shanahan, T., & Wixson, K. K. (2013). *Teaching with the common core standards for English language arts PreK–2*. New York: Guilford Press.

Morrow, L. M., & Woo, D. G. (Eds.). (2001). *Tutoring programs for. struggling readers: The America reads challenge*. New York: Guilford Press.

Nater, S., & Gallimore, R. (2006). *You haven't taught until they have learned: John Wooden's teaching principles and practices*. Morgantown, WV: Fitness Information Technology.

National Association of Secondary School Principals. (2005). *Creating a culture of literacy: A guide for middle and high school principals*. Reston, VA: Author.

National Center for Education Statistics. (1998). *Parent involvement in children's education: Efforts by public elementary schools*. Washington, DC: Author.

National Center for Education Statistics. (2015). The national report card. Available at *http://nces.ed.gov/nationsreportcard/about/*.

National Center on Time and Learning. (2014). *Leveraging expanded time to strengthen instruction and empower teachers*. Boston: Author.

National Governors Association Center for Best Practices & Council of Chief State School Officers. (2010). *Common Core State Standards*. Washington, DC: Authors.

National Institute of Child Health and Human Development. (2000). *Report of the National Reading Panel. Teaching children to read: An evidence-based assessment of the scientific research literature on reading and its implications for reading instruction* (NIH Publication No. 00-4769). Washington, DC: U.S. Government Printing Office. Available at *www.nichd.nih.gov/publications/pubs/nrp/Pages/smallbook.aspx*. (This document can be downloaded or ordered from the National Institute for Literacy at ED Pubs, 800-228-8813.)

National Staff Development Council. (2001). *Standards for staff development* [Online]. Oxford, OH: Author.

Newmann, F. M., & Wehlage, G. G. (1995). *Successful school restructuring: A report to the public and educators*. Madison: Center on Organization and Restructuring of Schools, Wisconsin Center for Education Research, University of Wisconsin.

No Child Left Behind Act of 2001. (2001). Public Law No. 107-110, 1-1076, 115 Stat. 1425-2094.

O'Connor, R. E., Bell, K. M., Harty, K., Larkin, K. R., Sackor, S. M., & Zigmond, N. (2002). Teaching reading to poor readers in the intermediate grades: A comparison of text difficulty. *Journal of Educational Psychology, 94*, 474–485.

Ogle, D. (1986). K-W-L: A teaching model that develops active reading of expository text. *The Reading Teacher, 39*, 564–572.

Ogle, D., & Fogelberg, E. (2001). Expanding collaborative roles of reading specialists: Developing an intermediate reading support team. In V. Risko & K. Bromley (Eds.), *Collaboration for diverse learners: Viewpoints and practices* (pp. 152–167). Newark, DE: International Reading Association.

Parker, S. (2012). *Lead simply: How to create that special team of people*. Richmond, VA: Give More Media.

Parrott, L., III. (1996). *High-maintenance relationships: How to handle impossible people*. Carol Stream, IL: Tyndale House.

Pikulski, J. (1994). Preventing reading failure: A review of five effective programs. *The Reading Teacher, 48*, 30–39.

Pinnell, G. S., Pikulski, J. J., Wixson, K. K., Campbell, J. R., Gough, P. B., & Beatty, A. S. (1995). *Listening to children read aloud*. Washington, DC: U.S. Department of Education, Office of Educational Research and improvement.

Prensky, M. (2001). Digital natives, digital immigrants. *On the Horizon, 9*(5), 1–2.

Prensky, M. (2012). *From digital natives to digital wisdom: Hopeful essays for 21st century learning*. Thousand Oaks: CA: Corwin Press.

Quatroche, D. J., Bean, R. M., & Hamilton, R. L. (2001). The role of the reading specialist: A review of research. *The Reading Teacher, 55*(3), 282–294.

Rasinski, T. V. (2000, October). Speed does matter in reading. *The Reading Teacher*, *54*, 146–151.

Ravitch, D. (2010). *The death and life of the great American school system: How testing and choice are undermining education.* New York: Basic Books.

Reed, D. K., Wexler, J., & Vaughn, S. (2012). *RTI for reading at the secondary level: Recommendations for literacy practices and remaining questions.* New York: Guilford Press.

Rettig, M. D., & Canady, M. L. (2013). *Scheduling strategies for middle schools.* New York: Routledge.

Rivkin, S. G., Hanushek, E. A., & Kain, J. F. (2005). Teachers, schools and academic achievement. *Econometrica*, *3*(2), 417–458.

Robbins, P. (1991). *How to implement a peer coaching program.* Washington, DC: Association for Supervision and Curriculum Development.

Rohlwing, R. L., & Spelman, M. (2014). Characteristics of adult learning: Implications for the design and implementation of professional development programs. In L. E. Martin, S. Kragler, D. J. Quatroche, & K. L. Bauserman (Eds.), *Handbook of professional development in education: Successful models and practices, PreK–12* (pp. 231–245). New York: Guilford Press.

Sackor, S. (2001). *Three-to-one tutoring: Strategies to enhance the reading comprehension of poor intermediate readers.* Unpublished doctoral dissertation, University of Pittsburgh, Pittsburgh, PA.

Salinger, T., Zmach Tanenbaum, C., Thomsen, K., & Lefsky, E. (2008, December). *Examining the impact of adolescent literacy interventions.* Paper presented at the National Reading Conference, Orlando, FL.

Samuels, C. A. (2009). High schools try out RTI. *Education Week*, *28*(19), 20–22.

Sandberg, S. (2013). *Lean in.* New York: Knopf.

Saunders, W. M., Goldenberg, C. N., & Gallimore, R. (2009). Classroom learning: A prospective, quasi-experimental study of Title I schools. *American Education Research Journal*, *46*(4), 1006–1033.

Scholastic. (2002). *Scholastic's READ 180: A heritage of research.* New York: Author. Retrieved January 11, 2003, from *http://read180.scholastic.com/pdf/research/read180_Heritage_of_Research_.pdf.*

Sendak, M. (1988). *Where the wild things are.* New York: Harper & Row.

Shanahan, T. (2008). Implications of RTI for the reading teacher. In D. Fuchs, L. S. Fuchs, & S. Vaughn (Eds.), *Response to intervention: A framework for reading educators* (pp. 105–122). Newark, DE: International Reading Association.

Shanahan, T., & Shanahan, C. (2008). Teaching disciplinary literacy to adolescents: Rethinking content-area literacy. *Harvard Educational Review*, *78*(1), 40–59.

Sheldon, S. B. (2007). Improving student attendance with school, family, and community partnerships. *Journal of Educational Research*, *100*(5), 267–275.

Slavin, R. E. (1987). Making Chapter 1 make a difference. *Phi Delta Kappan*, *69*(2), 110–119.

Slavin, R. E., Madden, N. A., Dolan, L. J., & Wasik, B. A. (1996). *Every child, every school success for all.* Thousand Oaks, CA: Corwin Press.

Sliger, B. (2009). *Grant writing for teachers and administrators.* Durham, CT: Strategic Book Group.

Snow, C., Burns, M. S., & Griffin, P. (Eds.). (1998). *Preventing reading difficulties in young children.* Washington, DC: National Research Council.

Sparks, D., & Loucks-Horsley, S. (1990). Models of self-development. In R. Houston (Ed.), *Handbook of research on teacher education* (pp. 234–250). New York: Macmillan.

Spillane, J. P. (2005). Distributed leadership. *Educational Forum, 69,* 143–150.

Spillane, J. P., Halverson, R., & Diamond, J. B. (2001). Investigating school leadership practice: A distributed perspective. *Educational Researcher, 30*(23), 23–28.

Stauffer, R. G. (1967). Change, BUT—. *The Reading Teacher, 20,* 474–499.

Steinbacher-Reed, C., & Powers, E. (2011/2012). Coaching without a coach. *Educational Leadership, 69*(4), 68–72.

Stigler, J. W., & Hiebert, J. (1999). *The teaching gap: Best ideas from the world's teachers for improving education in the classroom.* New York: Free Press.

Supovitz, J., Sirinides, P., & May, H. (2010). How principals and peers influence teaching and learning. *Educational Administration Quarterly, 46*(1), 31–56.

Swan Dagen, A., & Bean, R. M. (2007). Providing professional development to improve literacy achievement: Tinkering or transforming? *Pennsylvania Reads, 8*(1), 27–40.

Swan Dagen, A., & Bean, R. M. (2014). High-quality, research-based professional development: An essential for enhancing high-quality teaching. In L. E. Martin, S. Kragler, D. J. Quatroche, D., & K. L. Bauserman (Ed.), *Handbook of professional development in education: Successful models and practices, preK–12* (pp. 42–63). New York: Guilford Press.

Taylor, B. M., & Pearson, P. D. (2002). *The CIERA school change classroom observation scheme.* Minneapolis: University of Minnesota.

Taylor, B. M., Pearson, P. D., & Rodriguez, M. C. (2005). The CIERA school change framework: An evidence-based approach to professional development and school reading improvement. *Reading Research Quarterly, 40*(1), 40–69.

Taylor, B. M., Pressley, M., & Pearson, P. D. (2002). Research-supported characteristics of teachers and schools that promote reading achievement. In B. M. Taylor & M. Pearson (Eds.), *Teaching reading: Effective schools, accomplished teachers* (pp. 361–374). Mahwah, NJ: Erlbaum.

Thibodeau, G. M. (2008). A content literacy collaborative study group: High school teachers take charge of their professional learning. *Journal of Adolescent and Adult Literacy, 52*(1), 54–84.

Tierney, R. J., Johnston, P., Moore, D. W., & Valencia, S. W. (2000). Snippets: How will literacy be assessed in the next millennium? *Reading Research Quarterly, 35*(4), 244–250.

Toll, C. (2004). Separating coaching from supervising. *English Leadership Quarterly, 27*(2), 5–7.

Toll, C. (2006). *Lenses on literacy coaching: Conceptualizations, functions, and outcomes.* Norwood, MA: Christopher-Gordon.

Toll, C. A. (2005). *The literacy coach's survival guide. Essential questions and practical answers.* Newark, DE: International Reading Association.

Torgeson, J. K., & Miller, D. H. (2009). *Assessments to guide adolescent literacy instruction.* Portsmouth, NH: RMC Research Corporation, Center on Instruction.

United States Agency for International Development (2014, February). *The power of coaching: Improving early grade reading instruction in developing countries.* Washington, DC: Author. Retrieved at *http://pdf.usaid.gov/pdf_docs/pa00jv67.pdf.*

U.S. Department of Education. (2002a, April). *Guidance for the Reading First program*. Washington, DC: Office of Elementary and Secondary Education. Available at *www.ed.gov/programs/readingfirst/guidance.pdf.*

U.S. Department of Education. (2002b). *No child left behind: A desktop reference.* Washington, DC: Office of Elementary and Secondary Education. Available at *www.ed.gov/admins/lead/account/nclbreference/page_pg5.html#i-b1.*

U.S. Department of Education. (2010). A blueprint for reform. The reauthorization of the elementary and secondary education act. Available at *http://www2. ed.gov/policy/elsec/leg/blueprint/.*

U.S. Department of Education. (2014). Preschool development grant initiative. Available at *www2.ed.gov/programs/preschooldevelopmentgrants/index.html.*

University of Texas at Austin. (2003). Introduction to the 3 tier reading model. Retrieved from *http://resources.buildingrti.utexas.org/PDF/Intro3TierModel _4ed.pdf.*

Vescio, V., Ross, D., & Adams, A. (2008). A review of research on the impact of professional earning communities on teaching practice and student learning. *Teaching and Teacher Education, 24,* 80–91.

Walp, T. P., & Walmsley, S. A. (1989). Instructional and philosophical congruence: Neglected aspects of coordination. *The Reading Teacher, 42*(6), 364–368.

Walpole, S., & Beauchat, K. A. (2008, June 2). *Facilitating teacher study groups.* Denver, CO: Literacy Coaching Clearinghouse. Retrieved from *www.literacy-coachingonline.org/briefs/StudyGroupsBrief.pdf.*

Walpole, S., & McKenna, M. C. (2008). *Differentiated reading instruction: Strategies for the primary grades.* New York: Guilford Press.

Wanless, S. B., Patton, C. S., Rimm-Kaufman, S. E., & Deutsch, N. L. (2013). Setting-level influences on implementation of the responsive classroom approach. *Prevention Science, 14*(1), 40–51.

Wasik, B. A. (1998). Volunteer tutoring programs in reading: A review. *Reading Research Quarterly, 33,* 266–292.

Wasik, B. A., & Slavin, R. E. (1993). Preventing early reading failure with one-to-one tutoring: A review of five programs. *Reading Research Quarterly, 28*(2), 178–200.

Wei, R. C., Darling-Hammond, L., Andree, A., Richardson, N., & Orphanos, S. (2009). *Professional learning in the learning profession: A status report on teacher development in the United States and abroad.* Dallas, TX: National Staff Development Council.

Wei, R. C., Darling-Hammond, L., & Adamson, F. (2010*). Professional development in the United States: Trends and challenges.* Dallas, TX: National Staff Development Council.

Wells, J., & Lewis, L. (2006). Internet access in U.S. public schools and classrooms: 1994–2005 (NCES No. 2007-020). Washington, DC: U.S. Department of Education, National Center for Education Statistics.

Wilson, B. A. (1996). *Wilson reading system.* Millbury, MA: Wilson Language Training Corporation.

Wixson, K., & Lipson, M. (2009). *Assessment and instruction of reading and writing difficulties: An interactive approach* (4th ed.). New York: Allyn & Bacon.

Wixson, K. K., & Dutro, E. (1999). Standards for primary-grade reading: An analysis of state frameworks. *Elementary School Journal, 100*(2), 89–110.

Wood, D. (2007). Teachers' learning communities: Catalyst for change or a new infrastructure for the status quo? *Teachers College Record, 109*(3), 699–739.

Zigmond, N., & Bean, R. M. (2008). *External evaluation of Reading First in Pennsylvania.* Annual report, University of Pittsburgh, Pittsburgh, PA.

Zygouris-Coe, V., Yao, Y., Tao, Y., Hahs-Vaugh, D., & Baumbach, D. (2004). *Qualitative evaluation of facilitator's contributions to online professional development.* (ERIC Document Reproduction Service No. ED485072)

Index

Page numbers followed by *f* indicate figure, *t* indicate table

327

importance of, 59–60
scheduling and, 62–66
School librarians, 101, 245
School literacy programs
assessment of. *See* Assessment
barriers to changing, 192–195
conducting needs assessments, 197–201
essential supports for changing, 195–196
guidelines for curriculum development, 203–208
impact of federal and state initiatives on reading specialists, 214–218
parental involvement programs and, 255
selecting materials for, 208–212
standards as basis for, 201–203
technology in, 212–214
School psychologists, 101–102
Screening instruments, 224–225
Scripting, 173, 176
Secondary schools
assessment and, 238–239
case vignette, 158–161
coaching and, 8, 17, 153–154
focus on meeting specific needs, 37
school literacy programs and, 207–208
See also High schools; Middle schools
Second-language learners, 16
Self-assessment, students and, 232, 234, 239
Self-recognition, 282
Self-reflection
in professional development, 127
reading specialists and, 282–283
teachers and, 184
Service organizations, 247–248
7 Habits of Highly Effective People, The (Covey), 86
"Skill-and-drill" methods, 6
Smarter Balanced Assessment Consortium (SBAC), 221–222
Social capital, 148
Software, questions for reviewing, 214
Special educators, 101

Specialized professionals, 100–102
Special needs students, 101
Standardized tests, 6, 237–238. *See also* Assessment
Standards
as basis for curriculum development, 203–204
as basis for school literacy programs, 201–203
keeping current on, 280
National Educational Technology Standards for Students, 214
See also Common Core State Standards
STAR assessments, 79
Station teaching, 32–33
Striving Readers program, 2
Struggling readers, instruction for, 21
Student–adult reading, 98*f*
Students
analyzing work of, 107, 125
classroom success of, 35–36
fostering discussion among, 69
meeting specific needs of, 35, 36–37
Response to Intervention and, 37–41
self-assessment and, 232, 234
Study groups, 124–125, 277
Summative assessment, 78–79, 222. *See also* Outcome measures
Summative evaluation, for proposals, 267–268
Summer reading programs, 246
"Summer slide," 246
Supplemental materials, selecting, 212
Sustainability plans, for proposals, 268–269

T

Targeted teaching, 33–34
Teach and monitor approach, 34–35
"Teacher as learner" model of coaching, 145
Teachers
collaboration with. *See* Collaboration
conferring with, 179–182
evaluating performance of, 12
getting feedback from, 73, 74*f*